MW01406132

ONE SIGNAL
PUBLISHERS

ATRIA

BARBIE LAND

THE UNAUTHORIZED HISTORY

TARPLEY HITT

ONE SIGNAL
PUBLISHERS

ATRIA

New York   Amsterdam/Antwerp   London
Toronto   Sydney/Melbourne   New Delhi

**ONE SIGNAL
PUBLISHERS**

ATRIA

An Imprint of Simon & Schuster, LLC
1230 Avenue of the Americas
New York, NY 10020

For more than 100 years, Simon & Schuster has championed authors and the stories they create. By respecting the copyright of an author's intellectual property, you enable Simon & Schuster and the author to continue publishing exceptional books for years to come. We thank you for supporting the author's copyright by purchasing an authorized edition of this book.

No amount of this book may be reproduced or stored in any format, nor may it be uploaded to any website, database, language-learning model, or other repository, retrieval, or artificial intelligence system without express permission. All rights reserved. Inquiries may be directed to Simon & Schuster, 1230 Avenue of the Americas, New York, NY 10020 or permissions@simonandschuster.com.

Copyright © 2025 by Tarpley Hitt

All rights reserved, including the right to reproduce this book or portions thereof in any form whatsoever. For information, address Atria Books Subsidiary Rights Department, 1230 Avenue of the Americas, New York, NY 10020.

First One Signal Publishers/Atria Books hardcover edition December 2025

ONE SIGNAL PUBLISHERS/ATRIA BOOKS and colophon are trademarks of Simon & Schuster, LLC

Simon & Schuster strongly believes in freedom of expression and stands against censorship in all its forms. For more information, visit BooksBelong.com.

For information about special discounts for bulk purchases, please contact Simon & Schuster Special Sales at 1-866-506-1949 or business@simonandschuster.com.

The Simon & Schuster Speakers Bureau can bring authors to your live event. For more information or to book an event, contact the Simon & Schuster Speakers Bureau at 1-866-248-3049 or visit our website at www.simonspeakers.com.

Interior design by Davina Mock-Maniscalco

Manufactured in the United States of America

1 3 5 7 9 10 8 6 4 2

Library of Congress Cataloging-in-Publication Data has been applied for.

ISBN 978-1-6680-3182-7
ISBN 978-1-6682-1370-4 (int exp)
ISBN 978-1-6680-3184-1 (ebook)

CONTENTS

PART I

INTRO		3
CHAPTER 1	The Gambler	7
CHAPTER 2	The King	15
CHAPTER 3	Lilli	23
CHAPTER 4	The Receipts	36
CHAPTER 5	Mr. Mass Motivation	45
CHAPTER 6	Christmas in July	56
CHAPTER 7	Barbie v. Barbie	62

PART II

INTRO		73
CHAPTER 8	The Playboy	77
CHAPTER 9	The Babysitter	87
CHAPTER 10	Francie	97
CHAPTER 11	Operation Bootstrap	103
CHAPTER 12	The Suits	110
CHAPTER 13	The Leaks	120
CHAPTER 14	The Strike	131

PART III

INTRO		145
CHAPTER 15	Hostile Takeovers	150
CHAPTER 16	The Collectors	162
CHAPTER 17	The *Buddenbrooks* Cycle	177
CHAPTER 18	President Barbie	186
CHAPTER 19	Sex, Death, and Lawsuits	197
CHAPTER 20	Master of Your Domain	207

PART IV

INTRO		219
CHAPTER 21	House on Fire	222
CHAPTER 22	Two Big Kahunas	235
CHAPTER 23	The Bratz Brief	248
CHAPTER 24	The Midnight Ride	259
EPILOGUE	The Last Resort	269
ACKNOWLEDGMENTS		279
NOTES		281
INDEX		331

"Am I to become profligate as if I were a blonde?"
—Frank O'Hara, *Meditations in an Emergency*

PART I

INTRO

Barbie's real home, the corporate office of Mattel, Inc., sits in a nondescript business park in El Segundo, California, a place that got its name more than a century ago when Standard Oil moved in to open its second refinery. El Segundo means "the second." The refinery, now run by Chevron, comes first in other things, like water pollution. From time to time, it catches on fire. It takes up almost a third of the town.

Mattel's campus sits two miles from the refinery and looks about as inviting. The on-site Starbucks is private. Only the lobby and a ground-level toy store are open to the public. Security personnel roam the grounds to ensure visitors don't stray. The neighborhood has the air of a military base, which makes sense. The Los Angeles Air Force Base is three blocks away. Barbie's home is surrounded on three sides by defense contractors—Boeing to the north, Raytheon to the south, Northrop Grumman and Lockheed Martin to the east. El Segundo calls itself the "Aerospace Capital of the World," and the capital is only getting more concentrated. Investors like tech industrialist Peter Thiel have made "the Gundo," as they're trying to call it, a mecca for start-ups with sci-fi ambitions, like producing pharmaceuticals in space. This town was the childhood home of Chris McCandless, the nomadic adventurer whose fatal experiment in going off-grid inspired the book *Into the Wild*. His parents both worked in aerospace. Walking around, it's not hard to understand why he wanted to leave.

I drove there on a dry day in April, passing the first Mattel building on a broad avenue called East Mariposa. The architecture here is concrete and low-slung. It looks riot-proofed, and maybe it is; a guard told me the "Mattel Inc. Handler Team Center" is among the highest-security buildings, being the home of research and development. One street over, I drove by the main office, its fifteen stories dwarfing the nearby warehouses. My destination was a third building one road farther, a flat construction with mirrored windows at the end of an unmarked driveway. I parked beside a handful of sedans and minivans and one bright pink Corvette. The Barbie movie was slated to come out in three months, and the marketing campaign had been underway for a full year. The Corvette sat roped off under a cardboard proscenium, where a 2D Margot Robbie smiled down from a pink step-and-repeat. The other cars likely belonged to people who'd been officially invited for the day's event. I had not been.

A guard in a crisp white shirt manned the door. I told him my name was Ann, which wasn't untrue. It is one of my many legal names, a side effect of having southern Episcopal parents, who favor long strings of appellations handed down from grandmothers and great-aunts. The idea, they liked to say, was to give me some "normal backups" in case the other name which everyone called me proved too unusual. In this case, I thought maybe it had. I'd made several attempts to contact Mattel before my visit. Each had been coolly rebuffed. *Please note we aren't able to participate in titles that are not licensed*, a spokeswoman had told me. *Without a license, any use of Mattel intellectual property, including but not limited to trademarks and logos are* [sic] *prohibited and it would need to be clear that this item is not in partnership or authorized by Mattel.* Even ex-employees, people who had left the company decades ago, seemed reluctant to talk. Most of my calls and emails and LinkedIn messages had been fired off into the void, the recipients too anxious or indifferent to respond. Many of those who did reply did so only under the guise of anonymity, citing binding exit packages or the specter of retaliation. The company's pervasive secrecy had started to make me paranoid. I imagined they had my too-unusual name on a blacklist somewhere, or signs with my face on it crossed out in red Sharpie, like bodega printouts of shoplifters caught on CCTV. My delusions of grandeur proved somewhat overwrought. The guard led me into the lightly air-conditioned atrium and left me waiting by a hostess stand. The scene was less CIA than walking into an exclusive restaurant without a reservation.

At the same time, my concerns weren't entirely made-up. Mattel's proximity to national security's toy makers was not just some accident of real estate, but the natural by-product of a corporation that has always invited comparisons to the defense industry. ("The M-16 rifle is based on something Mattel did," a Pentagon spokesman once told the *Times*.) The company's founders, Ruth and Elliot Handler, sold one of their first products to Douglas Aircraft; they designed their fifties facilities with defense work in mind. The toy world, like the Pentagon, is highly secretive, obsessed with the threat of espionage and the potential theft of secrets. At trade shows, many toy makers silo their upcoming lines in private showrooms, limiting entry to a select few, assuring silence with embargoes or NDAs or posters worded in stern legalese. Mattel takes a particularly aggressive approach. The company has operated with a private showroom for decades and highly restricts attendees. It has brought hundreds, maybe thousands, of lawsuits and legal actions against alleged Barbie infringers, from Nicki Minaj's "Barbie-Que" potato chips to a latex and leatherwear store in Calgary, Canada, called "Barbie's Shop." (The owner's name was Barbara.)

But even those precautions don't always safeguard against theft. The company's intense oversight of Barbie rivals would culminate in a two-decade-long lawsuit, beginning in the 2000s, in which Mattel would accuse a rival of stealing a billion-dollar doll—Barbie's greatest threat in decades—straight from its El Segundo office. The rival, meanwhile, would unearth evidence that Mattel had maintained a long-running corporate espionage operation from within the same facility. For at least fourteen years, the lawsuit alleged, Mattel had sent members of its "Market Intelligence" team into competitors' showrooms to steal trade secrets, posing under fake names as buyers for fake companies, collecting intel on unreleased products. "She used a fake business card for a store that didn't exist," Mattel's own lawyer admitted of one spy at trial. So I didn't feel too bad about doing the same thing.

"Are you on the list?" the hostess asked. I said I thought so, which was a lie, and that I worked for a magazine, which was true. She took a note and paged someone. The atrium was lined with bags and folders, the detritus of various guests, a couple loose lanyards. It led into a larger hall that was blocked off by black room dividers. I had an idea of what was behind it. This building held Mattel's private gallery, and in it, the upcoming season's still-secret toys. For years, the company had been reducing its presence at the major trade fairs; among the major toy brands, the invite-only showrooms of New York and Nuremberg and Hong Kong seemed to have become too risky. Mattel had opted instead for its own presentations, whose grandness seemed to grow even when they withdrew from public expos. This year, the company wouldn't even bother coming to New York's Toy Fair at all. They were having their private show now, in that gallery, behind those dividers.

As I waited at the check-in, executives strolled in unimpeded. The hostess and the guard looked at me with a familiar face, the steely tight-lip of an unimpressed bouncer. A hand on my elbow steered me toward the exit. It seemed so goofy, all this secrecy. And yet it was in line with what I'd come to expect from Mattel, which once had a lawsuit dismissed partly for "not having a sense of humor." The company made many of its billions on Barbie, whose tidy image is half of her appeal. Her life is frictionless, her house pristine. There is no clutter in the Barbie box—every accessory has its proper place—and there's still less outside it. Barbie now has no parents, no in-laws, no continuous lore—at least as far as Mattel is concerned, having long since ditched any biographical detail, down to all but a last name. The billion-dollar-doll is less a character than a template, a set of signifiers attached to an essential blank.

CHAPTER 1

THE GAMBLER

Ruth Handler, born Mosko, short for Moskowicz, had, on many occasions before this one, gambled and lost. Risk was a matter of pain tolerance, and Ruth's threshold was so high it seemed hereditary. Her father, after all, had died at a card table, just slumped in his seat one night, over Hold'em or Razz or Seven Card Stud, and stayed there. Now, in the near-spring of 1959, Ruth Handler had no parents, but two children—and something like a third on the way, a new doll which was about as big a bet as Ruth had ever wagered. At forty-two, Ruth was compact and tidy, everything cinched and curled. A strand of pearls sat at her throat, as if the nacre had been secreted right there from her own neck. She was rarely far from a cigarette, depending when you asked (some weeks she'd quit smoking; others she'd quit quitting), and on the morning of March 9, she had enlisted several cigarettes in her siege on pain.

Ruth was in Manhattan for the city's fifty-sixth annual Toy Fair, where she and her husband, Elliot Handler, were preparing to unveil their latest designs. It was not the Handlers' first rodeo; their rodeo-related products had sold quite well in Toy Fairs past. But in fact, it was a first in other ways: the Handlers' first attempt to enter the market for young girls and Ruth's first stab at a doll of her own devising, a figurine barely longer than a forearm that almost everyone had dismissed as a sure loser.

The way Ruth told it, she had come up with the idea more than a decade earlier. In 1945, the year after her father died, she and Elliot had started their own company, Mattel Creations. Ruth had given birth to their first child, a daughter, in 1941. They called her Barbara. Their son followed in 1944. His name was Kenneth. Motherhood didn't suit Ruth, who liked her children but loathed staying home. She was a bad cook—her fallback was French toast drowned in canned peas, canned tuna, and canned cream of mushroom soup. But in the toy economy, motherhood could be a kind of market research. Barbara—they called her Babs, sometimes Babsie—rarely played with baby dolls. In that, Ruth could relate. "I was a tomboy," she said. "I hated dolls."

But Babs liked some dolls, the paper kind. She liked folding tabs of two-dimensional gowns over their two-dimensional shoulders, playing games about the kinds of grown-up errands performed by grown-up women, the type of independent woman Ruth was and Babs would one day become. Ruth would say that it dawned on her then that young girls were hemmed in by societal expectations, even in the toy aisle. Three-dimensional dolls, the non-paper ones you could squeeze or carry around or bring to tea parties without sogging up, were all babies. Where were the women? (There were, Ruth told a friend, some supposedly teenage dolls on the market. But they had "big bellies" and "these ugly clothes." They were built "like fat, ugly, six-year-olds.") The demand was there, she thought, for a doll that resembled a woman, not a baby—which meant, in the symbolic vernacular of figurines, a doll that had breasts.

A stacked doll initially struck the Mattel men as market napalm, a perversity that would never sell. But Ruth pressed on. She spent three years developing her model. She dispatched staff to far-flung places to find workers willing to toil for the lowest possible price. She set up shop in Japan in an era when "offshoring" sounded more like a boat vacation than anything involving labor. She studied plastics and odd polymers and obscure tooling techniques to find fake flesh that a kid could really grab onto. She wooed a woman from Los Angeles's Chouinard Art Institute, a fashion designer named Charlotte Johnson, to design tiny outfits with tinier buttons that looked plucked from the runways of Paris. She hired a Hollywood makeup artist who'd painted faces for so many major motion pictures that *Man of a Thousand Faces*, the 1957 film whose makeup he also did, may as well have been about him. She deployed her top deputy, Jack Ryan, a former Raytheon missile designer and a sexual libertine whom you might call an autodidact in female anatomy, to perfect the doll's appendages. He patented her hips. When demos arrived with delineated nipples, he filed off her areolas by hand.

The result was a slender hunk of polyvinyl chloride, chiseled into a triangular torso, elliptical hips, and two pin gams. The doll looked out sideways, under arched eyebrows, above a surgically small nose. Her synthetic hair was rooted, not glued, directly into her skull, pulled taut into a blonde ponytail with tight coiled bangs. Her arms extended into articulated fingers, topped with tiny red nails. The legs sloped into pee-wee feet permanently arched for stilettos—so slanted they could not support her body. Her soles came pre-stabbed so she could be speared onto a stand. As for her breasts, twin sources of so much agita, they sat just below her collarbones, perfect hemispheres unmoved by gravity.

There were already toy Barbaras and Babses on the market, so Ruth settled for an alias that had not yet been copyrighted. She would let reporters believe that it had been one of her daughter's other epithets. But that was not quite true. It was because of the doll, not the girl, that, at age eighteen, Barbara Handler came by a new nickname. I think it's fair to say we all know what it was.

Ruth and her husband had not started their toy firm in New York, the domestic axis of the toy economy, but in Los Angeles, city of movie sets and sanatoriums. The American toy world was something of an adolescent—all but nonexistent before the twentieth century, it had swollen in six decades and secured itself firmly to the States' right coast. Its home base was stationed at 200 Fifth Avenue, catty-corner from the Flatiron. A former circus theater called Franconi's Hippodrome, the address had once been frequented by "gamblers, rowdies," a "dancing horse named Johnston," and later, Mark Twain. But in the intervening years, the square complex had become so overrun by toy makers and doodad hustlers that the city nicknamed it something simpler: Toy Center.

The Handlers were not from New York. They did business in Los Angeles, but they weren't from there either. Both Ruth and Elliot had grown up in Colorado, on the landlocked Front Range. Ruth's father had fled there from Warsaw during the pogroms in 1907, building wagons until he saved enough to send for his wife and six kids. The family lived in a home under a bridge in Denver, and there the Moskos had four more children. Ruth, born in 1916, was the last. By then, her mother was too sick to care for another toddler. Ruth was raised by her eldest sister, Sarah, and her husband, who ran a drugstore and soda counter.

Ruth met Elliot in the thirties, at age sixteen, in a scene straight out of *West Side Story*. "We lived at opposite ends of the wrong side of the tracks," she said. Elliot was from the Jewish West Side; Ruth and her older sister lived in the more mixed East. He went by "Izzy" then, short for Isadore. Elliot was his middle name. Once, Ruth drove by him in her Ford Deuce Coupe, eyeing his "oversize head with these exquisite, gorgeous black ringlets." She honked; he recognized her from a picture at her brother's house, where he'd played craps. Elliot was in a gang called the "Gigolos," though the most dangerous thing they seemed to do was dance. Two weeks after the drive-by, he spotted Ruth at a carnival and asked her to join him. Each dance cost a nickel and Elliot only had one. He crowdsourced change from the Gigolos to keep going.

Elliot's family, also Jewish immigrants but from Ukraine, was less upwardly mobile than the Moskos. And Elliot's dream of becoming a cartoonist did not inspire confidence in his future fortune. Her sister worried Ruth would "starve to death in some garrett." Ruth tried to stay away. She started school at the University of Denver and considered becoming a lawyer. She hitched a ride to Los Angeles to visit her sister's friend Evelyn, whose job at Paramount sent her on regular run-ins with celebrities. Ruth pestered Paramount until they hired her as a stenographer. In 1936, Elliot followed her out West. He had come for art school, he told her. The Denver Art Institute was mediocre, he said, and Chicago's was too cold. *Sure*, Ruth thought. They married two years later, Ruth in a satin gown with a lace hat, Elliot in a rented tux.

Ruth's stenography job, she later recalled, was "terribly exciting"—the mad dash of typing up scripts and running them through the mimeograph, knitting during downtime, taking messages for Lucille Ball. But she was also "appalled at the waste of money and poor management." She liked celebrities but found the workers lazy. Once, she snuck Elliot onto the set of *Thanks for the Memory*, a comedy about a wife who goes to work while her husband stays at home, failing to pursue a life of the arts.

In school, Elliot gave up on illustration for industrial design. He took odd jobs, moonlighting at a lamp factory. He became obsessed with plastics, the new synthetic polymers that could be molded into any shape, modeled after anything. He fiddled around with Lucite and Plexiglas, fashioning them in his downtime into furniture and other knickknacks—coffee tables, candelabras, picture frames, small boxes for Ruth's cigarettes. He was cripplingly shy. "He was the kind of guy that if we walked into a restaurant," Ruth said, "he was embarrassed to place an order." Ruth was his opposite: brash where he was quiet, driven where he was laid-back. She was cutthroat and pragmatic. It was her idea for Elliot to drop his nickname, "Izzy." It sounded so Jewish, she said. It was her idea too, to start selling his designs. One landlord let them use an old laundry on Olympic Boulevard—$50 for six months. Elliot quit school and Ruth became his best salesman, toting a suitcase full of plastic samples everywhere from upscale shops to military contractors. Elliot made Plexiglas clocks for Douglas Aircraft that were built into model DC-3 planes.

The Handlers were not inventive with names. They called their first venture "Elzac"—a blend of Elliot and his partner, Zachary Zemby. In 1945, Elliot started another, with Harold Matson, a tree-sized Swede he'd met at Elzac. ("A kinda stupid guy," Ruth said. "Very stupid in many ways.") They named their new company another portmanteau, this time of Elliot and Matson—Mattel.

Mattel's first product was practical: plastic picture frames. It made a certain sense in the motion picture capital. Synthetic products for an acetate city. The Handlers turned to toys almost by accident. Ruth was in her car when she heard the bad news: all plastic would be restricted to military use. World War II had become, effectively, America's only industry. "There will be no other use permitted," the radio seemed to sneer, "not even from plastic scrap."

Instead, they made their frames from wood. When scrap did reappear, it was just enough to whittle into miniature furniture—tables so tiny they would only fit a doll. The Handlers had good timing. Many toy makers had been enlisted in the war effort. Elliot himself was not exempt. He was drafted in the spring of 1945, but stationed close enough to come home on weekends. While many major competitors were churning out bombs and bullets, Ruth managed to sell their doll furniture to a chain of clothing stores. But the fact remained that with no New York connection, the Handlers still had no idea how the business worked.

***

I must have walked past the New Yorker Hotel hundreds of times before I found out it was the place where Barbie was born. Across the street from Penn Station, diagonal from Madison Square Garden, it's hard to avoid, and yet still easy to miss: a faded Art Deco façade, forty-three-stories of limestone and brick. These days, fewer than half of its shabby rooms are available to the public. The rest are reserved for members of the Unification Church, better known as the "Moonies." The hotel is the U.S. headquarters for the cultish religious movement founded by Korean anti-communist Sun Myung Moon, whose crusade to save humanity from sin involved marrying thousands of couples in mass weddings called "Blessings." Not that you'd know that from the street; the hotel is operated as a franchise of Wyndham Resorts.

But the building, opened in 1930, once represented the height of New York glamour: the "hotel of the future," outfitted with its own gilded bank vault, a secret tunnel to the subway, and a retractable ice rink. By the time the Handlers booked a room there in March of 1959, each suite had its own four-channel radio and a "Protecto-Ray"-ed bathroom, whose combo of high-intensity U.V.-light and cellophane sealing promised the cleanest in cutting-edge toilets.

Ruth spent that March morning chain-smoking. There were some two dozen Barbies stationed in little dioramas, one designed for each outfit. Barbie was as much a New Yorker as anyone, in that she came from somewhere else. But the mood of Ruth's room was more stereotypically Californian, crowded as it was with impossibly small plastic women sporting barely there outfits, most of which seemed, even on a rather warm March day, better suited for summer. The "Original" wore a zebra-striped bathing suit, while another covered up in a sheer "Nighty Negligee." Her "Barbie-Q" ensemble paired an apron with a pink sleeveless dress. The "Gay Parisienne" scene found Barbie in a bubbled taffeta gown and a pearl necklace similar to Ruth's regular strand. Barbie embraced diversity only in hair color. Even still, Ruth's biographer observed, "blondes outnumbered brunettes two to one." Because Barbie traveled from so far abroad,

Ruth had ordered ambitiously: sixty thousand dolls were to be delivered each week from Japan for more than six months, and those were just the bodies. Ruth figured they could sell three or four outfits along with every doll. They had an enormous amount of stock to unload.

Outside, the hallways of Toy Fair seemed warm with collective relief. The "heavy volume of orders," one paper observed, proved a welcome change from "last year's caution," when the country had been plagued by recession. The recession was more than over; it had been steamrolled by the boom in births, the babies now kids of five or six or seven, old enough to tug on shirts and ask for toys. This new generation seemed smarter, more worldly than their squalling predecessors, inoculated with the tech savvy of the space age. The toys showed it—to-scale replicas of a subsurface missile launcher and a nuclear reactor, as if toddlers were being drafted into the Cold War. (Per one headline, they were: "Toy Makers Are Helping Uncle Sam in Science Race with Reds.") Even those less keen on science offered a certain moral instruction—as with one vendor's "foot-high model of the Crucifixion."

But the reception in the Handlers' hotel room did not measure up to Ruth's imagination. "For the most part, the doll was hated," one sales rep said. Another fashion doll had debuted the year prior, and she had languished on store shelves. Now the buyers weren't biting. "They saw these large inventories left over from this other doll and said fashion dolls are passé," Ruth remembered. The bigger complaint concerned parents. Barbie promised no strategic advantage in science; she would be useless against the Russians. Nor did she offer any educational value. If anything, she seemed to imply the opposite, an unmarried tart with too many shoes. "The American mother," the wholesalers said, "will never accept this doll."

Not even half the browsers ordered Barbies that day. The representative for Sears, the "Mr. God of the toy industry," as Ruth later put it, wouldn't even take a sample. The press ignored her outright; no major papers mentioned the doll in their roundups. Ruth immediately contacted the Japanese supplier and slashed Barbie orders almost in half. That night, Ruth sat in her suite and sobbed. "She was very upset," Elliot recalled. "She did not cry often, but she cried."

The doll she had spent so much time designing did not seem destined for the record books. At most, Barbie might be a footnote in some fringe business history. Her best bet was to kill the line. But the toy maker, even close friends would concede, struggled to admit any tactical error, preferring to bulwark herself in fortresses of self-justification. It was among her greatest strengths, or her greatest shortcoming, depending on whom you asked. Ruth had a way of willing things into existence, wrangling an idea until she made it real. She shared that with her cardsharp father: she had a problem with walking away.

CHAPTER 2

THE KING

If the Handlers wanted to break into New York's toy empire, it was obvious who they'd have to dethrone. At the time, "there was only really one big name in the U.S. toy business," wrote trade historian Sarah Monks, "and that was Louis Marx and Company." Louis Marx was a short man with a large bald head. The "Henry Ford of the toy industry" specialized in small tin play sets and toy soldiers. He made novelty figures of famous and infamous men: Dwight Eisenhower, Douglas MacArthur, Robert E. Lee, himself. He made several of himself, actually. In one of those mini self-sculpts, Marx looked like the wry butler at a British manor—rotund and squat in a gray suit, extending a cigar. In another, he was dressed like Napoleon. In a third, as Genghis Khan.

Even at five-foot-four, Marx could make himself seem much larger. "Louis Marx was not very tall, but very imposing," one friend recalled. "When you were with him you felt, you know, vibrations." Which is perhaps to say he yelled a lot. Born to a German tailor and Austrian homemaker in New York, he spoke with an accent long after he forgot his first language, the sound an erratic mix of Teutonic consonants and Brooklyn vowels which emerged most audibly during his regular soliloquys.

Magazines dubbed Marx "America's Toy King," and he played the part. He lived in a Georgian mansion in Scarsdale—a white-pillared estate equipped with nine fireplaces, fourteen baths, sixteen dogs, a four-car garage, both a tennis and a paddle court, and a caretaker's cottage, itself large enough for a family of five. In the fall, Marx would drain his full-sized swimming pool, fill it with lawn furniture, and host meetings from his Adirondack in the deep end.

16 BARBIELAND

Marx worked from dawn until well past dusk, when he would pace for hours enunciating multipage pseudo-philosophical memos into his handheld Dictaphone. He maintained a "mink-lined foxhole" at the Waldorf Astoria in Manhattan, where he'd sleep after late nights in his office at Toy Center or the 21 Club, the Prohibition-era speakeasy-turned-starlet hot spot. His bodyguard was a painter and martial artist who'd taught jujitsu to the FBI. A fanatical jogger, he built his own track on the roof of Toy Center, where he could often be found running in circles as he read vocabulary terms from his black journal, an obsessive habit he developed to make up for missing college.

Marx had what you might call a pragmatic approach to the concept of property. His childhood sports were "baseball, basketball, ice-skating, and shoplifting." Once, Marx and a friend snuck into a department store and walked off with a full-sized canoe—heaving it over their heads and slipping out the delivery entrance unnoticed. He left high school early after allegations of cheating, which he would continue to deny long after anyone cared. His first job in the toy industry was itself an apprenticeship in mimicry: he worked for Ferdinand Strauss, a densely browed Bavarian who'd pioneered some of America's first mass-produced mechanical toys—including a climbing monkey called "Trixo" and an unsubtly offensive minstrel named "Jazzbo Jim." Under Strauss's tutelage, Marx learned that success in the toy world stemmed less from original inventions than from a capacity to reproduce others' at scale. Soon, Marx took old Strauss ideas and updated them, adding a bell or whistle or brighter paint and passing it off as the next big hit. "There is no such thing as a new toy," Marx liked to say, "only old toys with new twists."

Strauss had another advantage. He was from Germany, which, for decades, had been the epicenter of global toy production. Commercial toy-making had existed there for at least five hundred years, and it had heavily industrialized over the last century. An industry of guilds and master craftsmen had given way to massive operations staffed largely by low-paid "outworkers"—women who worked at home. Those women regularly worked seventeen-hour shifts. Their children, some as young as six, often put in another eight or ten hours on top of school. But then, as now, labor horror stories did little to assuage the desire for cheap goods. In 1903, the German Empire exported nearly thirty-five thousand tons of toys, per *Scientific American*. "Toys constitute one of the more important branches of German manufacture," the magazine reported. "There is hardly any country in the world to which German toys are not exported."

The American toy business, meanwhile, was what one trade group called "late to the party." Craft dolls were among the earliest American immigrants: settlers brought a wooden doll to Roanoke in 1585, as a "gift" for the Native tribes. And for three hundred years, they mostly stayed that way: imported, at least among the rich, mostly from Germany. Everyone else made their own or bought the occasional figurine. Even as the growing middle class gave children more time to play, Americans largely gave up "trying to compete with the Germans." Instead, they numbered among Germany's biggest customers, second only to the Brits.

But when World War I stranded toy soldiers at German ports, the U.S. market flooded with toymen on the make. In Connecticut, a doctor and part-time magician named Alfred Carlton Gilbert debuted a construction-themed kit called the Erector Set. In 1915, a political cartoonist named Johnny Gruelle secured a patent for a simple doll named Raggedy Ann. The next year, the architect Frank Lloyd Wright's son, John, started selling toy sets to construct wood cabins using interlocking "Lincoln Logs." The new class of American toymen organized quickly to stamp out any competition from overseas. In 1916, they formed a trade group, the Toy Manufacturers of the USA, to combat German imports. Fearing peace would also bring an excess of unshipped product from the "German menace," the new allies launched an ad blitz to make Raggedy Anns and Lincoln Logs a matter of national interest. A poem ran in papers across the country: "*The pennies spent on little toys / For Uncle Sam's own girls and boys / In turn, of course, go back again / To our own loyal working men.*" The group's first logo featured a cornucopia of toys bursting from Uncle Sam's hat (and a perhaps ill-conceived abbreviation: "TOY M'F'RS USA"). "The word *toys*," Gilbert said in 1919, "does not mean 'made in Germany.'"

When the trade group founded a "Toy Industry Hall of Fame," Louis Marx numbered among its first inductees. By the time the Handlers arrived on the scene, Marx was entering his third decade as Toy King. He represented not only the nation's emergence into the global play sector, but also the first wave, and soon the old guard, of American curios. His innovation was pumping out playthings at the lowest possible cost. He hunted for newer, cheaper materials. Like Elliot Handler, he'd been quick to dabble in an emerging medium called plastic. He mastered mass production, automating machine lines long before his peers. He obsessed over cutting labor costs. Early to offshore his operations in the thirties, Marx set up the first American toy outpost in Japan. By mid-century, he had plants in seven countries, and the first American subsidiary in Hong Kong, the Elm Tool and Machinery Co. ("Elm" stood for his initials, but also, people said, the "Excellent Louis Marx.")

To any up-and-coming toy maker, Louis Marx would be the blueprint, or at least someone to steal from, though that was one of his trademark moves too. "When they copy you, it's piracy," Marx told *Time* magazine. "When you copy them, it's competition." There was a joke in the industry, years later, that Marx's research and development team was "a Xerox machine and two patent attorneys."

The Handlers were not yet fluent in the toy world's vernacular of theft. But they picked it up quickly. In 1946, they found their first hit in Arthur Godfrey, a boyish broadcaster who played the ukulele with the skill of "a hunt-and-peck typist." His biggest hit was a "comedy" single called "Too Fat Polka (She's Too Fat for Me)." The lyrics were about as delicate as you might expect. But the instrument suited Godfrey, the so-called "Huck Finn of radio."

No toy maker had yet tapped into the growing demand for Godfrey's signature accessory. Elliot mocked up a model from plastic, a blue-and-coral ukulele kids could use to plunk out simple songs. In January of 1947, Ruth rushed thousands of ukes into production, with a plan to sell them for $1.49 a pop. But the new saleswoman had made a mistake. New York's Toy Fair, already the biggest event for toy buyers, was not until March. When Elliot showed up to advertise what Mattel was calling their new "Uke-A-Doodle," the toy had been on the market for nearly two months, and without a patent. In the meantime, a rival company, Knickerbocker Plastics, had nicked the idea. "They had the gall to buff off the Mattel name and were using our Uke-A-Doodle as a sample to pre-sell their *own* ukelele [sic]," Ruth later wrote, "which would be an exact copy of ours." The toys were identical, only Knickerbocker's cost thirty cents less.

The two companies entered a price war and a race to the bottom—an incident so rattling that Harold Matson, who had invested his life's savings in the start-up, cashed out of the company. The battle was so disturbing to Ruth, so formative in shaping her business philosophy, that she would refer to it, with less irony than anger, as the Ukulele War of 1947. "We won that war," she fumed five decades later. "We held our own, and we beat Knickerbocker down."

As the company grew, the Handlers made originality a righteous cause. In interviews, they cited four important lessons for aspiring toy makers—and two concerned copying. "Products have to be unique, original, and different in appearance and operation," went Lesson One. "You cannot succeed by copying or by making products too easy for others to copy," added Lesson Two. (The third was something about children; the fourth about avoiding "disastrous price competition.") Mattel began to treat toy concepts as state secrets. As Ruth put it, "stealing designs was a common practice in the deceptively bright, cheery, and innocent world of toymaking." The entire industry, one reporter agreed, was "wrapped in super-security, anti-social for real fears of espionage." No one spoke in the Toy Center elevators, one exec said: If you [mentioned] your new product line on the sixteenth, it would be knocked off before you got to the ground floor. It was as tough to get a toy maker to divulge their inventions, another wrote, as "to get Russia military blueprints from the chief of staff of the Soviet Army."

The Handlers' security borrowed heavily from the military. They plucked their most infamous designer, Jack Ryan, straight from Point Magu Naval Air Missile Test Center, where he was designing the Hawk and Sparrow missile systems for arms manufacturer Raytheon. They outfitted their factories like fortresses and circulated a book of their design specs among prospective military clients. ("In addition to doing toys," Ruth said, "we felt that we could do defense work.") The company "constantly checks its plant for bugging," the *Los Angeles Times* reported, "to be sure some unplayful competitor is not listening."

Memos were shredded; models were destroyed after use. The Research and Development Department was limited to only its employees, each outfitted with numbered badges to check in at designated turnstiles. Some areas were restricted to only top personnel, with select guests accompanied by escort. Armed guards surveilled the section 24/7. Aerospace companies visited Mattel just to study their security. "We were literally locked up," one designer reported. "We were sworn to secrecy. We weren't even supposed to talk to our families about what we were working on." The Handlers had been stolen from before, they had made a moral virtue of not doing it themselves, and they would be aggressive in ensuring it did not happen again.

Marx had one particularity: he had never believed in advertising. In 1955, while his company was grossing more than $50 million, Marx boasted that he had spent just $312 on ads. "He didn't believe in trying to manipulate a child's desires," one vice president said. "If a toy couldn't make it on its own, he got rid of it." So far, it hadn't hurt him. Of all the toys sold in the U.S. each year, some 10 percent were his.

But the Handlers, headquartered in the movie capital, sensed that the country was entering a different kind of visual age. In 1954, they hired Carson/Roberts, a Los Angeles public relations firm well suited for children's media. Their logo was a smiley face. The year Marx bragged that his ad budget cost less than a used car, Carson/Roberts proposed another tack. Disney was developing a new children's show at ABC, an hour-long program that would air at five p.m., five days a week. The Disney cartoon library had never been aired on television, and the network was cocky: "ABC promised it would reach almost every child in America on a daily basis." They were calling it *The Mickey Mouse Club*.

The expense was gargantuan, and Disney needed sponsors to front the capital for fifteen minutes of airtime each week, corporations that could easily commit to year-round, noncancelable contracts. Mattel was not yet that kind of place. The sponsorships cost $500,000—then Mattel's entire net worth.

But the Handlers were interested. Elliot was "convinced that no one could reach children as well." This too was a borrowed idea: two years earlier, a product called Mr. Potato Head had become the first toy advertised on television. But no toy company had ever sponsored an entire show, advertising year-round to their primary customers, kids. Ruth called in their comptroller, Yasuo Yoshida, an accountant who had become Ruth's right hand. She was blunt: "If we spend $500,000 for fifty-two weeks on television, but the program doesn't produce the extra sales we need, will we be broke?" Yoshida shook his head. "Not broke," he said. "But badly bent."

Ruth gambled. They splurged on the sponsorship. At Toy Fair that spring, Mattel screened its first commercial for the "Burp Gun," a replica of a machine gun used by paratroopers, which could "rapidly fire fifty shots on one pull of the trigger." When *The Mickey Mouse Club* hit the airwaves in the fall of 1955, kids across the country watched a boy stalking elephants with what resembled a plastic Kalashnikov. By Christmas Eve, "there wasn't a Burp Gun to be found anywhere at Mattel," Ruth said, save for two that had been deemed defective. Even those were quickly claimed—one to a sick boy in San Francisco, the other to the White House, "so as not to disappoint a young grandson named David Eisenhower."

Marx reacted as he knew best, by copying. The Toy King began pushing his own products on shows like *Howdy Doody* and *Captain Kangaroo*. He announced a "saturation campaign" blanketing all three major networks with six Marx-sponsored programs, and a suite of ads on local stations. "Some people say it's the biggest thing ever done on TV," Marx told the press.

In response, the Handlers sponsored another series, *Matty's Funday Funnies*, a cartoon variety show hosted by a boy named "Matty Mattel," who intermittently played with Mattel products. They called him, coyly, "the King of Toys."

Marx still had more in his arsenal, not least a mascot of his own ("Magic Marxie"). He also had an army. The toyman liked to collect five-star military generals as friends. During the Depression, he'd helped a future cofounder of the RAND Corporation find an obscure toy part. He'd repaired a model train for a young Dwight Eisenhower. By the fifties, "all his friends were great Generals and Air Force people," a Marx executive recalled. He went fishing with the director of the CIA. He sent toys to J. Edgar Hoover. He bet on boxing with the namesake of the Marshall Plan. These were more than casual acquaintances: four of Marx's six sons were named for famous generals, including Eisenhower, who doubled as his namesake's godfather.*

These connections, cultivated over years, helped Marx find his real edge against Mattel. A decade before the advertising feud, over the spring of 1945, Eisenhower had enlisted Marx to conduct a five-week tour of German toy makers, or at least the ones that remained. Officially, Marx had spent this tour as a "consultant to the Allies," advising his friend "on how toy manufacturing could aid reconstruction efforts." At the same time, Marx, who'd lent his own factories to the war effort, reconfiguring production lines to pump out "carloads of ammunition," was inspecting nearly two hundred facilities to ensure the Germans weren't still doing the same. But Marx was also, one biographer wrote, evaluating the plants "for his own purposes, of course," acquainting himself with German toy sculptors and painters, some of whom he later hired. It was likely there that Marx encountered a German toy maker known as O&M Hausser, the firm that would become his strongest ally against Mattel. Their shared weapon would be a doll that bore a striking resemblance to Barbie.

---

*At least one of the toymaker's children inherited his interest in the military, though not in the ways Marx may have hoped. His daughter Patricia, an anti-war activist, would marry RAND Corporation analyst Daniel Ellsberg, not long before he leaked the Pentagon Papers, a trove of classified documents revealing the Lyndon Johnson administration's deceptions about the scale of the Vietnam War. It was reportedly as a favor to Marx that J. Edgar Hoover declined to probe Ellsberg's psychological records during his trial. Marx, however, considered the leak treason and slashed his daughter's inheritance. He never spoke to his son-in-law again.

CHAPTER 3

LILLI

Almost exactly sixty-four years after Barbie's first Toy Fair, I flew to Berlin. It was March 4, 2023. I was staying in the second bedroom of an old fourth-floor walkup with a former DJ in her thirties, who now ran a seasonal arepa stand. The apartment was sandwiched between a street named for Karl Marx and one whose namesake discovered an inflammatory disorder that can cause rectal bleeding.

I had just read a trend report, predicting the year would be marked by what it called "franchise fatigue," the collective exhaustion brought on by the "constant and inevitable churn" of spin-offs and reboots. The movies and TV shows of the past decade had been dominated by sequels, remakes, and familiar storylines repackaged from video games, bestsellers, and tweets. One site had declared 2022 "The Year of the Reboot," and the new year showed no signs of slowing down. Just three of 2023's forty "most anticipated" releases, per one list, would be based on new material; the others broke down into "17 sequels, eight reboots and remakes, and four spin-offs." If anything, the adaptations seemed to be getting more brazen. That spring alone was slated to bring three movies about inanimate objects (the BlackBerry, Air Jordans, Cheetos), and two about games (D&D, Tetris). Fatigue seemed inevitable. It was "entertainment's law of diminishing returns," the trend report observed; the sequel was always worse. And yet in the midst of all this, Hollywood was reviving another familiar media property, this one certain to make a fortune. A Barbie movie was coming out that summer and opening with it a fire hose of merchandise. The trailer alone had already started a craze.

To some extent, it was obvious why Barbie was about to make a lot of money. Any adult can reel off the fad toys of their childhood that did not make it past their puberty. But kids continue to buy Barbie, year after year. At one point, by Mattel's count, two Barbies were selling every second. She spent decades as not only the top-selling doll in the country, but the top-selling toy in the world. She had become not just a child's accessory but a symbol, as synonymous with American consumerism as the Golden Arches and French fries. She was "forever," like diamonds or microplastics. (Given that she is made from a cocktail of at least five fossil fuel–based polymers that secrete nanoplastics easy to inhale and ingest, it's plausible that someone, as one friend put it, "has Barbie in their balls.") She was everywhere, unavoidable, and yet kept coming back.

The trailer depicted Barbie as not merely an icon but as an origin story—an alien construction whose descent to Earth, like the monolith in *2001: A Space Odyssey*, catalyzed a new era in human civilization. In Stanley Kubrick's version, the monkeys who stumble upon the monolith learn to use weapons, thus bringing about, per the title card, the "dawn of man." The trailer's homage to that scene, a nearly shot-for-shot re-creation, posits Barbie as instead the genesis of modern girlhood. "Since the beginning of time, since the first little girl ever existed, there have been dolls," the voice-over explains. "But the dolls were always and forever babydolls, until . . . "—until, that is, Barbie.

If the tone was tongue-in-cheek, the assessment of Barbie's impact was blunt and sincere: Barbie, the first adult doll, had molded American girldom, a modern Prometheus making children from clay.

But Barbie's cultural dominance was somewhat mysterious to me for the fact that she was not—as the trailer claimed and as Mattel has maintained—the first adult doll brought into toy stores. She was not an original invention, or even the original Barbie really, but a knockoff, copied from another doll, in another country, and not subtly either. The two dolls were virtually identical. Nor had the original been some relatively unknown quantity, rebranded before anyone got a clue. This other doll had been distributed all over Europe, sold not just to children and women, but to grown adult men. She'd had a department store aisle of accessories; she had been made in marzipan; she had been photographed with Errol Flynn. This doll too had been made into a movie, a film to which an entire nation paid attention, whose promotional campaign had wormed its way into everyday consciousness. All that had happened in Germany, which was not America's favorite place in the 1950s, if it was thought about at all. But this doll was popular enough that she had been covered by American newspapers. She had, in fact, been shipped across the Atlantic, distributed at stores, and displayed at Toy Fair a full three years before Barbie's debut.

But she had mostly been forgotten. Barbie had somehow beaten out one of the most famous dolls in the global toy capitol and kept it hidden for decades, disappearing her predecessor into a marketing parable about Mattel's supposedly novel adult doll.

Perhaps most curious of all was the fact that this proto-Barbie had not originated with some small craftsman or mom-and-pop, but from the operations of the most powerful newsman on the continent, an executive whose control over the information ecosystem of postwar Europe drew more comparisons to monarchs than publishers. "No other man in Germany, before Hitler or since Hitler, has accumulated so much power," one of his rivals said, "with the exception of Bismarck and the two kaisers." This man was, in other words, not the type to get stolen from and move on. His middle name was Caesar, and he acted like it. He often answered the phone, sans irony: "This is the king himself speaking." I was in Berlin to visit his court.

I was commuting each day to an unusual office building—a black glass cube, with horizontal wedges cut out at the corners and lined with white columns as thin as baleen. The German president had declared the new construction a "symbol of the radical transformation" of a "company in perpetual motion." But from the street, the façade looked like a sinister Pac-Man with teeth.

The building was the headquarters of Axel Springer, a media empire that had been based on that street, called Axel-Springer-Straße, since the fifties. The founder, also named Axel Springer, had built his headquarters just twelve meters from the border between East and West Germany—a portent of their eventual reunification, but also of his publishing ambitions. He wanted a national monopoly. After the Second World War, with little competition remaining, Springer assembled a stable of German papers, covering news morning, evening, night, on every topic, but especially those dearest to him. As he saw it, the liberal papers of earlier years had failed to stop fascism, and then the war had wiped them out, along with most of bourgeois life. The stage was set for a new kind of journalism, a lighter mode of addressing the public: emotional, spiritual, conservative, if not yet openly so.

Springer had always been careful about exposing himself to allegations of agenda-pushing. During the war, he had not been a Nazi, albeit though on a technicality, having secured a medical exemption from military duty. Instead in 1934, Springer, age twenty-one, had joined the National Socialist Motor Corps—ostensibly, he said later, to make him "a Nazi-uniformed buffer for the family." The organization, he alleged, "made no great ideological claim," but merely "combined politics with the motor sport that I loved so much"—though one prerequisite for admission was an "inner willingness to fight," and the group had been founded to actualize Hitler's belief that mobile operations were essential for disseminating "National Socialist ideology and election propaganda." But his father, a publisher in Altona, near Hamburg, kept printing well into the regime. The family's careful avoidance of anything political kept the Springers' newspaper alive until 1941, and their book press open for years after.

After the war, Springer's attitude toward national affairs was unambiguously right-wing; the pro-austerity capitalist and German nationalist would become, as *Tablet* put it, "the closest thing the Germans had to a Rupert Murdoch." But in print, he masked overt politics behind an unrelenting cheeriness—blending human interest, celebrity gossip, animal-centric stories ("Cat Adopts Blind Dog"), and the horoscopes that Springer himself, who had a private astrologer on his payroll, followed obsessively. "It was clear to me since the end of the war that one thing the German reader didn't want was to think deeply," Springer told an interviewer. "And that's what I set up my newspapers for."*

---

*Springer had a strong instinct for marketing, promoting his papers with "happiness" campaigns of surprise publicity stunts, like the time he ordered 120,000 bouquets and passed them out to women on the street. He held an annual national contest to find the "ideal German woman," a maybe tone-deaf exercise in postwar nationalism that

I'd come to look at the archives of maybe his most influential outlet, a daily paper called *Bild Zeitung*. Founded seven years pre-Barbie, in 1952, *Bild* was a knockoff in its own way—a German version of an English tabloid Springer had seen on a trip, called, aptly, the *Daily Mirror*. Picture-heavy, offering shorter stories and bolder headlines, the coverage was so sensational that in 1949, a judge sent the top editor to jail for three months over potentially prejudicing a murder trial. But it spoke to what Springer called the "simple people"—in the fifties, it was the best-selling paper in the U.K.

The *Mirror* was also, notably, sexy. The paper's comic, Jane, was a pinup whose wardrobe malfunctions seemed to take the term comic strip literally. Originally titled *Jane's Journal, Or the Diary of a Bright Young Thing*, the cartoon followed a "curvaceous blonde secret agent," who "tangled with Nazi spies, tumbled down cliffs and became caught in tree branches in episodes that invariably concluded with her stripped down to her underclothes." The series, launched in 1932, was Britain's precursor to American pinups: the drawings of illustrators like George Brown Petty, whose sketches of half-naked women started appearing, just months later, in a new men's magazine called *Esquire*. As American soldiers ogled the so-called "Petty Girls," it was Jane who appeared pasted above the beds of Brits. "One admiral told me," the cartoon's model once said, "that there wasn't anybody on the ships, from the lowest rating to the highest in the fleet, who didn't have a drawing of Jane in his pocket or on his bunk."

The *Mirror* struck Springer "as the printed answer to the electronic age," a visual medium primed to contend with a burgeoning competitor called television. In 1952, Springer set out to replicate its success with a tabloid for Germany. He wasn't inventive in names either. *Bild Zeitung* translates to "picture newspaper."

---

nevertheless attracted thousands of applicants. He understood, in particular, the power of a mascot. Springer gave his radio paper, *Hör zu!* (Listen!), a Mickey Mouse–like hedgehog named Mecki, hiring a small person to dress as a porcupine and tour the country in a small propeller plane.

Bild was an instant hit, the German equivalent of the *Daily Mail* or *New York Post*, known, as one reporter put it, for serving up "tripe, trash, tits and, almost as an afterthought, a healthy dose of hard news." The paper reached some four million readers within its first decade. When politics appeared in its pages, it was synonymous with the publisher's brand of postwar conservatism. Springer's foremost enemy was Communism, which he saw as the obstacle to both a united Germany and a united news market. (Rumors, ones Springer fiercely denied, circulated that the paper had gotten funding from the CIA.*) "When we hit five million subscribers," Springer once wrote to a friend, "then we will order the people to walk on their hands and they will do it."

But over the summer of 1952, the tabloid Springer would call his "dog on a chain" was barely a puppy. On the morning of June 24, the day Springer's astrologer promised would be most favorable, the publisher laid out articles on his office floor and glued together the mock-up himself. The four-page broadsheet was almost ready, but at the presses, he noticed a problem. There was a blank on page two. Amid the pasting of pictures and inverted pyramids, he had ignored a narrow chasm, too small for a photo, too large to leave empty. A comic could fit, or some simple drawing.

Springer summoned a friend, a hulking blond giant of a man named Reinhard Beuthien. Beuthien, an illustrator at another Springer paper, was as cartoonishly macho as Barbie would be feminine. When Hitler had banned comics, he'd worked as a boxing trainer, then as a sailor. Years later,

---

*Springer's early financing has drawn much speculation, not least because he claimed to have been "completely penniless" after the war. In 1982, national security writer Murray Waas reported in *The Nation* that the CIA had "secretly funneled some $7 million to West German press baron Axel Springer in the early 1950s" to help "serve American geopolitical interests." The company "emphatically" denied the claim, but Waas stood by his reporting, citing four informants and written documentation. At minimum, Springer would have been a "suitable recipient for American secret service help," German historian Gudrun Kruip concluded, and had secured some Marshall Plan funding. (He was also likely wealthier than he let on, she argued, thanks to Nazi compensation for shuttering his father's paper.) Certainly, the publisher's virulent anti-communism earned him many American fans, including Charles Z. Wick, director of the propaganda arm of the United States Information Agency. Springer "has been a strong supporter of the United States," Wick wrote to then–CIA head William Casey in 1982, "and this is reflected in the editorial policies of his widely read newspapers."

he would still send friends messages in Morse code. He chain-smoked cigarillos and spent his free time hunting; his home was lined with antlers. He signed his drawings with his nickname: BEUTH.

The paper was already printing when an editor ran to Beuthien's office, shoved a copy under his nose, and pointed to the void: "I need something immediately to fill in this blank." Beuthien sketched a pretty cherub with plump cheeks. But the editor was not interested in cartoon babies; he wanted the kind of silhouette that would keep readers coming back. "In the greatest silence, I erased the plump cheeks and drew a thinner face," Beuthien recalled. "The colleague was still not satisfied; I drew the face even thinner, and the colleague continued to rage." Beuthien swapped its newborn frame for a starlet's body, its Winston Churchill scalp for a blonde ponytail, its nappy for a pencil skirt. The editor snatched the sketch and ran. The next morning the paper debuted on newsstands with a comic one critic called the "ultimate woman-child fantasy." Her name was Lilli.

This new character seemed as much an imitation as the paper itself, an answer to the *Daily Mirror*'s Jane. Like Jane, Lilli was an archetypal blonde with an affinity for flouting dress codes and pursuing rich men. (In the first edition, Lilli visits a psychic, as Springer often did. The caption read: "Do you know the name and address of a tall, beautiful, rich man?") Men apparently liked her back; the comic attracted a following nearly overnight. The paper kept her on, paying Beuthien 100 marks for each cartoon (about $283 in today's dollars). She became a hit, the rare drawn character in Germany to get her own fan mail. "Readers look for 'What Lilli said today,'" Beuthien told a friend, "then throw away the newspaper." Lilli would appear in *Bild* for the next nine years.

Lilli was the physical embodiment of the paper, the two syllables of her name plucked from the center of its own. ("Five narrow letters that sound very bright," former editor Hans Bluhm wrote, "just like the name of the newspaper, *Bild*.") Soon, she was omnipresent on merchandise—from postcards to champagne bottles to novelty perfume. Life-sized Lilli cutouts adorned street kiosks, guiding readers toward the paper like a cardboard Vanna White. The cartoon seemed to promise such longevity that Springer gave Beuthien a contract for twenty-five years. But Beuthien wanted something more solid for his ambassador, an effigy that everyone would instantly associate with the paper. Around *Bild*'s third birthday, Lilli gained a dimension and became a doll.

⟿

Beuthien liked to call Lilli his "daughter," and in the months before she was reborn in plastic, he played the part of the overprotective parent. A dozen different toy firms from across Germany drew up prototypes; the artist nixed them all. The model must immediately conjure the Lilli of the comic, he insisted. She must be pretty, but insolent; sultry, but cherubic. The trick in crafting the perfect Lilli cartoon was setting a scene that would seem innocent to any child, sufficiently chaste to *Bild*'s most conservative readers, but imbued with insinuation and "double meaning." He needed a perfect replica, a doll that could imply all that even without a caption.

Only a few years earlier, Beuthien would have been well positioned to find the best sculptor for the job. But during the war, half of Nuremberg's toy factories had been "completely destroyed," and many of their workers killed. As the industry rebuilt, the Germans faced new competition from the Americans and Japanese. When some production resumed in occupied Nuremberg, the toys were sent off marked, "U.S. Zone, Germany."

It was against that backdrop that Beuthien encountered the firm O&M Hausser, founded in 1904 by brothers Otto and Max, which specialized in highly detailed figurines, formed first from a sawdust and glue concoction, then from plastic. After Max died in World War I, Otto had left the company with his two sons, Rolf and Kurt. Their particular molding method proved so effective that its trademarked name—Elastolin—became a generic word in German for toy soldiers. The Haussers' line ranged from miners to angels to every kind of soldier from "Americans to Zouaves," the North African unit of the French Army. One mostly forgotten catch: the company's catalog also included a wide variety of Nazis.

Their surviving catalogs from the time are so detailed one might mistake them for war photos, if not for the occasionally visible stroke of paint. Kids could collect soldiers from every unit of the armed forces, as well as Hitler's street enforcers, his personal guard, the Reich Labor Service, Hitler Youth, its sister division the League of German Girls, and Springer's old mates, the National Socialist Motor Corps. Parents could buy "personality figures" of Nazi leaders like Hermann Göring, like-minded dictators like Benito Mussolini or Francisco Franco, and at least seven different versions of Hitler himself—one in a motorcar, another in a raincoat.

When Hitler came to power, the Nazis had relocated the Haussers' factory from its hometown of Ludwigsburg to a hamlet in northern Bavaria, once the axis of German toy production. A party-appointed executive had evicted a Jewish business, the Rosenthal Porcelain Company, from its domineering brick complex, and installed the Haussers in their stead. The Nazis ostensibly orchestrated the move to solve the region's unemployment problem, but many of the Haussers' employees came from somewhere else—forced laborers from Eastern Europe imported by the party. The town was also home to a concentration camp. For a time, in addition to toys, the Haussers produced wooden shoes for the Nazis' slave labor.

After the war, Rolf and Kurt maintained they'd had no choice but to join the National Socialist Party. Their father, they noted, had been arrested for being a Freemason. "I had to take the greatest caution," Kurt said at his denazification trial. Though, evidently, the brothers did not feel much guilt for evicting the Rosenthals. "They were lucky they weren't killed," Rolf told a reporter. The brothers were certainly under pressure. The regime restricted many avenues of cultural production, even comics. The Haussers could not produce figures of opposition parties or dissidents. But there was no legal inducement to manufacture specifically Nazi toys, or quite as many as they did. Failure to do so would have merely, one chronicler observed, brought about "a loss of sales." The Haussers were, in other words, just complying with the exigencies of the market. Years later, Kurt would chalk up their Nazi soldiers to business. "We were a commercial company trying to do business during the sixty most cataclysmic years the world has ever known," he explained. "What a period, unlike no other in modern history." Their toys were simply sideshows, he seemed to say, ensemble characters in the pageantry of the past.

By 1955, the Haussers had put the war behind them; the brothers were now experimenting with dolls, opening a subsidiary called Greiner &

Hausser. Rolf Hausser introduced Beuthien to his best sculptor, Max Weissbrodt, who submitted a Lilli model closer than anything the illustrator had seen. "You are the first to convince me that Lilli can be shaped in this way as I would like her to be," Beuthien wrote. The silhouette was perfect. The only issue was her "ordinary" face. "You couldn't say this doll has a certain something," Beuthien complained. "This rather banal young woman is found everywhere." Weissbrodt went back to the lab.

The doll that debuted in August of 1955 looked like a plastic Marlene Dietrich—impossibly thin, synthetically perky, eyebrows angled over a sidelong gaze, already bored by her beholder. Like Barbie, her painted-on stilettos were too pointed to provide support; Lilli's feet had holes so she could be nailed to a stand. Rolf Hausser's mother-in-law, Martha Maar, made her clothes, designing a wardrobe of a hundred-odd costumes, from flight attendant to nurse to something called, simply, the "Hungarian." The dolls came in two sizes: a smaller 7.5-inch model, which retailed for around 10 marks, and a larger 11.5-inch version, which sold for twice that (about $35 and $65 in today's dollars). Each came with a tiny copy of *Bild*.

The miniature papers featured miniature articles, each about Lilli, each seeming to heed Beuthien's insistence on "double meaning," which is to say they were subtly horny. "'I've been waiting for you for a long time,' says Lilli," read one headline. "Today, since you have me, you will never be alone," another said. The doll's implicit audience was not children, but adults. She was too expensive, initially, for most kids. Lilli was sold at newsstands and tobacco shops, an advertising gimmick that became a raunchy gift for girlfriends or bachelor parties. A car ornament model proved especially popular with men. "She was an irresistible gag," one buyer said. "Imagine, a doll with big tits and long legs! Nothing like her existed before, and she was such a clever joke. We'd have such laughs over this gadget, especially on Saturday nights when we'd all drive around cruising for girls and having beers at local pubs."

But Lilli was not, as many have claimed, an "escort" or "call girl" or, per one outlet, "a fictional prostitute" who would "do anything with sweaty clients, provided the money was right." She was not even a "sex doll," at least not in the modern sense. She was an adult doll, and sex was always her subtext. "The prudery of the Nazi era was still rife in Germany in those years," *Bild* editor Hans Bluhm recalled. "Lilli was a sex ingredient of a saucy but harmless kind." Rolf Hausser agreed. The doll was "not intended for men more than for women," he insisted. "This is most important: no one could say she wasn't a virgin." She was about as pornographic as Betty Boop or the *Daily Mirror*'s Jane. *Bild* took precautions to ensure she never became anything more. The doll's patented legs were fixed to move in parallel. "In other words," an announcement read, "Lilli keeps her legs together when she sits."

Eventually, children became her customers too, as Lilli moved to airport lobbies, then toy stores. "Product for all, from child to grandpa," one ad read. The Haussers saw Lilli "as something that everyone would immediately associate with the *Bild* newspaper, a systematic identification that of course would make a nice gift—in a word, something pleasant to look at."

Above all things, Lilli was a marketing strategy, an extension of the Springer brand and its most effective ad. When Springer hired models to dress as the doll for a cross-country press tour, Germans lined up for autographs and the occasional kiss. Lilli was more than *Bild*'s public face, she was a symbol of the consumer society the publisher had endeavored to bring about. (As Springer ramped up his support for reunification, an internal memo noted that a commercial about Lilli would be used for "propagandistic activity" across West Germany.)

Lilli's fame reached its apex in 1958, when *Bild* produced a feature-length film and held a national contest to find its star. The director didn't want a well-known face; he wanted an everywoman, so long as she was blonde, thin, and under twenty-five. Springer orchestrated an ad blitz across all his papers. One grocer spotted a slim blonde in his store, a twenty-one-year-old Dane named Ann Smyrner, and insisted she apply. When Smyrner won not long after, the story made international news. German outlets fumed over the foreign selection; American ones simply gawked at the new blonde. Her headshot ran everywhere from the *Fort-Worth Star-Telegram*, to the *Daily Oklahoman*, to the *Reporter Dispatch* in White Plains.

In the film, Smyrner plays a reporter at a major newspaper. She hunts down stories with a mix of combat skills—she is trained in jujitsu—and the suggestion of sexual prowess. Her boss sends her to a missionary conference in Sicily, but on the boat ride there, she stumbles upon a murder. She befriends a man who, unbeknownst to her, is an undercover agent, and together they unravel the mystery. By the climax, they have found themselves mixed up in an international syndicate of highly skilled counterfeiters.

※

I had thought, maybe foolishly, that Axel Springer would have the complete Lilli archive, or at least a decent chunk of it. The company kept a records library, which collected everything from advertising materials to building construction history to documents "from all departments and units" of Axel Springer dating back to its founding. The library had a robust online presence, including an illustrated history of the doll.

But when I reached the firm's archives, where I was to spend the next few days, I realized my mistake. The archivist's name was Lars Broder-Keil, a man in his forties with glasses, gray hair, and the careful demeanor of someone who reminds a lot of visitors to please put on gloves before touching anything. He had laid out on a small table everything he could find on Lilli: a few Springer biographies, one history on German publishing, and a couple original Lilli dolls in their signature plastic tube. He'd dug out old issues of *Bild*—oversized broadsheets bound together by year, in equally oversized books. There was one self-published Lilli history, one teddy bear from the German toy maker Steiff (who had produced Lilli's pet poodle), and one thick binder of seemingly every email the archive had gotten that mentioned the doll's name.

But little of it came from the fifties. There were no memos from Springer about design specs or breakdowns about rollout. There were no *Bild* Lilli sales stats or fan letters or staff notes. Of course, it's possible that Axel Springer had simply elected not to share its internal records. As a private company, Axel Springer wasn't obliged to disclose trade secrets to the press. But Lars himself seemed confused about the other missing files; the archivists had spent years looking for Lilli material, he told me. His predecessor had taken out newspaper ads and posted on forums, looking for any surviving accounts of how exactly she came to be. (Most of the emails he had, in fact, were just replies to those posts.)

Lars suggested I look through municipal archives to see if I could turn up the Haussers' corporate records. I did, along with basically every state archive, library, or Barbie collector I could find in northern Bavaria and several more outside it. (For all its supposed efficiency, German record-keeping is even more convoluted and labyrinthine than its equivalent in the U.S.) I looked on Facebook and eBay and fringe collector forums. Eventually, I found some records in the city archives of Ludwigsburg, a small town near Stuttgart where the Haussers had first started the firm. The archivist did have birth, death, and marriage records for its founders, as well as "construction files for the factory buildings, tax books and business files," like the Haussers' custom stationery.

But there too the search for Lilli came up empty. "Unfortunately," the city archivist wrote, "we do not have any detailed documents on the Hausser toy factory." Nor did Rolf Hausser's living daughter, a veterinarian and accomplished violinist, whom I texted on WhatsApp. Or Silke Knaak, the German collector who wrote the self-published history on Lilli. Or Peggy Gerling, a Barbie collector who investigated Lilli for trade magazines in the nineties. The Haussers appeared to have thrown their papers out, or misplaced them, or sold them, or somehow let them vanish. "I absolutely didn't want to believe that Lilli's documents had disappeared," Italian economist Marina Nicoli, who herself went on a Lilli deep dive earlier that year, told me. But she'd heard as much from Dieter Warnecke, a German Barbie historian who'd corresponded with Rolf Hausser for years. He "kept insisting that I needed to accept reality."

Lilli, apparently, remained something of a blank. But that seemed somewhat intentional. Mattel had spent years obscuring Barbie's backstory, avoiding any mention of *Bild* Lilli and sending legal threats to those who happened to bring her up. Mattel had sued collectors and magazines and self-published authors and smothered more with cease-and-desists. The campaign stretched well past the fifties, into the twenty-first century. But it had started years earlier, with Louis Marx, with the Haussers, and above all with Ruth.

CHAPTER 4

THE RECEIPTS

About a month after I returned from Berlin, I flew to what was, for a time, its outpost in the States. In the mid-century, Los Angeles became a haven for German expats, exiles, and refugees. I was staying with a friend on the west side, not far from where many of Germany's cultural giants had waited out the Second World War. The surrounding neighborhoods had once housed playwright Bertolt Brecht and novelist Thomas Mann. Theodor Adorno had been living six streets east when he wrote *Dialectic of Enlightenment*; his coauthor, Max Horkheimer, had opted for a bungalow a few blocks further west. Heinrich Mann, Thomas's brother, had moved around, but spent his last two years on a quiet street just across the Santa Monica border.

Germans love toys, not just making them. The doll in particular has taken up a non-miniature space in the regional imagination. Critic Walter Benjamin, himself a toy collector, saw in playthings a perfect snapshot of the "hideous features of commodity capital," while Rainer Maria Rilke mused on how dolls seemed to both tease and frustrate the possibility of their own interior life. "The more Romantic the writer," Evelyn Juers wrote in her family history of my sort-of neighbor Heinrich Mann, "the greater the conviction that the marionette replicates not life but its essence, its signature, that within their wooden core the dolls carry a spark of soul."

Many of these doll stories ended in madness. In E. T. A. Hoffmann's *The Sandman*, the protagonist jilts his fiancée for a "pretty doll" of a girl, whose beauty and apparent sentience obscure other red flags: a weirdly low body temperature; a stiff gait, seemingly wound by clockwork; and the fact that she can't talk. ("She was, indeed," Hoffman wrote, "a lifeless doll.") In the end, the man becomes delusional and dives off a cliff. This is a recurring theme: a year after dramatist Heinrich von Kleist wrote his own doll story, he shot his lover, then himself, in the head.

That month at least, I got where they were coming from. I was hoping that proximity to Ruth Handler's home might solve some of the mysteries of Barbie's origins. The various accounts of who invented this billion-dollar doll—and when and where—were laced with inconsistencies, which maybe stemmed from faulty memory or slight exaggeration, or perhaps from intentional obfuscation. One question I couldn't figure out was how Ruth Handler first found Lilli. The official story, initially, was that she hadn't. For years, she never mentioned the German doll, leaving the presumption, for a long time, that Barbie was an original. Ruth had tried to pitch an adult doll a decade earlier, she would say, inspired by her daughter's affinity for paper ones. She'd become convinced that young girls deserved a post-pubescent figurine, even if the retailers themselves weren't ready. The media filled with stories about the doll's runaway success; the entrepreneurial couple who had started their company in an old laundry and generated millions; the savvy mother who had divined, almost mystically, what young women really want. Among the hundreds of articles I read from that time, only one mentioned Lilli by name. "Barbie's own debut was clouded because she had the same neck joint as a German look-alike named Lili [sic]," *The Wall Street Journal* noted in 1964. "Mattel says this was inadvertent."

When the truth finally emerged, nearly three decades after the fact, that Barbie had a German cousin, a near-clone who predated her by several seasons, and whose uncanny resemblance to her more famous successor was not an accident but very much by design, Ruth changed her story. She said she had, in fact, seen Lilli. She had stumbled upon the doll while on vacation in Europe. Over the summer of 1956, almost a year after Lilli became a doll, all four Handlers had hopped onto a transatlantic superliner called the *Queen Mary* and set sail for England. They'd spent two weeks touring London, Paris, and Zurich before arriving in Switzerland, driving by private car to the alpine town of Lucerne. It was there that the family had wandered up to a store called Franz Carl Weber, an old-school toy shop founded, naturally, by a German from greater Nuremberg. Ruth became "absolutely transfixed" by a scene in the window: six notably adult-looking Lillis, each wearing a different ski ensemble. One sat on a swing.

Ruth had seen the dolls, her story went, not as something to steal, but as proof-of concept—evidence that she could manifest the idea she had already been harboring well before then. She was not a thief, in other words, she was ahead of her time. "I didn't then know who Lilli was or even that its name was Lilli," Ruth claimed. "I only saw an adult-shape body that I had been trying to describe for years, and our guys said couldn't be done."

Perhaps Ruth was still telling the truth, that she had thought of Barbie even before then. Who can parse how the half-formed phrases of early inspiration first take shape in our heads? But thirty years is enough time to edit, and some details had definitely been tweaked. In lawsuits, for example, Mattel dated Ruth's lightbulb moment—the second she first dreamed up an adult-looking doll—to "as early as 1946," six years before Lilli was even a sketch. But Mattel's own press releases from the time cited a later date, the year after her trip. "In 1957, she noticed that her daughter, Barbara, had outgrown 'baby' dolls," one read just months after Barbie's debut. (Barbara, notably, would have then been sixteen.) And the Handlers did not keep records of that moment in the forties or even of Ruth's efforts to realize it after. Perhaps they'd been lost. But the Handlers were pack rats, the kind of people who kept a carbon of seemingly every thank-you note they wrote. They held on to fistfuls of receipts from their train stubs to a letter to a Denmark cutlery store complaining that their dining ware order arrived short eight knives. They kept their customs reentry form, dated that September of 1956, on which they declared $2,465.26 worth of souvenirs, including fifteen dolls.

Ruth's receipts show, for example, that she bought two Lillis on the spot that day in Lucerne, along with some accessories: a pennant, a scarf, three caps, and the swing. They must have stayed on her mind, because nineteen days later, now in Vienna, she bought a third. Ruth would claim that she had been unable to buy any of Lilli's separate outfits. If true, it would distinguish Lilli from Barbie, who served primarily as a vehicle for the future sale of countless individually packaged accessories. But Lilli had dozens of ensembles available for single purchase, and Ruth must have known as much. Her receipts show that she personally bought nine of them.

Maybe Ruth had really never heard of *Bild* Lilli before her trip to Lucerne, but it would have taken some effort. By mid-1956, Lilli was all over Europe. She was a standard gift for American visitors; she'd posed with famous actors and executives. If anyone in the Mattel extended universe had, that February of '56, happened to swing by the Nuremberg Toy Fair, —where America remained the biggest buyer— it would have been hard to miss the Haussers' display carousel of rotating *Bild* Lillis. But the Haussers would claim that Ruth didn't even need to go to Germany to see her. In February, five months before the Handlers' Eurotrip, they said, Lilli had been on display at Toy Fair in New York, where Mattel had been presenting for at least two days.

German doll collector Silke Knaak, who self-published the first *Bild Lilli* book, suspects that the Handlers had known about the doll before their vacation. "From my personal opinion, the story that Ruth Handler told—she was walking through Switzerland and saw this doll in a shop window—I don't think [it was] so," Knaak told me. "I'd guess they came to the Nuremberg Toy Fair and saw Lilli there. So they had to tell some kind of story."

For months, that's what I thought too, though it struck me as more likely the Handlers would have seen her in New York. But then I picked up one of the books I'd brought to L.A.: an out-of-print tome from adman Cy Schneider of Carson/Roberts, the exec who pitched Mattel on *The Mickey Mouse Club*. It's a half memoir, half business history from 1987, which bills itself as "the first positive book" about children's television. The text is riddled with typos, digressions, and casual errors, the kind of history that is probably more faithful to Schneider's memory than the particulars of any given event. But some of his memories about Barbie are illuminating:

> I have yet to see anything in print which has reported the story accurately. The Barbie doll did not spring from the mind of a Mattel inventor. Nor did the idea of an 11½ inch doll with breasts come from Ruth Handler's imagination as some stories have told it. Barbie had a progenitor and her name was Lili [*sic*].

Schneider was, actually, not the only person to point this out; the club kid and Andy Warhol muse Billyboy* wrote about Lilli in his book the same year (though he framed her connection to Barbie as a theory, and their similarities as "debatable"). But more interesting was what Schneider disclosed a few sentences down:

> The doll was hardly known in the United States and Paul Guggenheim, a Swiss who originally distributed Lili [sic] in the United States, remembers he was only able to sell a few of the dolls to Uncle Bernie's, an expensive toy import shop in Beverly Hills.

This was the first I'd heard of a "Paul Guggenheim," though I knew of "Uncle Bernie's Toy Menagerie," the ultra-upscale toy emporium once located on shopping mecca Rodeo Drive. The so-called "Tiffany's of toy stores" was famous for its decor—a blend of Willy Wonka's factory and Saks Fifth Avenue. Outside, the front door was guarded by two gargantuan candy-cane columns of inlaid marble. It was a hot spot for Hollywood stars, a favorite of Jack Benny, Lana Turner, and Barbara Stanwyck. Over the holidays, a news agency said, it attracted "more celebrities than at a premiere." If *Bild* Lilli had been at Bernie's, Ruth Handler would have known about it. Uncle Bernie's was, per *The New York Times*, "the best known toy store on the West Coast." It was also an eight-minute drive from her house.

On one of my last days in L.A., I drove to Uncle Bernie's old building to make the trek myself. The candy columns had been razed, paved over for a building with so much glass it looked like one big window. I continued south along Rodeo, past a golf course and onto the semicircular street where the Handlers had lived. Their old home had also been demolished, replaced by what a Zillow search revealed to be an $8 million mansion with appropriately corporate decor. The private basketball court had been Astroturfed with the Air Jordan logo. The couches had yellow pillows shaped like emoji. I'd spent much of the past week in dreary Los Angeles basements, dredging up old lawsuits and corporate filings, looking for some snapshot of Ruth on the record. At least under oath, I'd figured, she couldn't lie. But most of her depositions had gone the way of Uncle Bernie's; thrown out to make room for something else. This short drive was maybe the only thing that hadn't changed.

THE RECEIPTS   41

A few months after I returned from L.A., Marina Nicoli, the Italian economist also obsessed with *Bild* Lilli, sent me a post on LinkedIn. Back in 2023, Mattel had shared a *Bloomberg* article about the *Barbie* movie, and directly below, one user had left a comment, using the handle "Guggenheim Philippe."

> @ Mattel; the story on Bloomerg [sic] relates really the true story of the Barbie doll? Ruth Handler went to Switzerland? Does the name of Paul Guggenheim recalls anything? I really wish to read you and would appreciate your answer. Many thanks

Philippe Guggenheim, it turned out, is Paul's son. His father, a Swiss salesman, ran an import-export business called Calcon Importing Co. He had seen *Bild* Lilli at the Nuremberg Toy Fair in 1956, and he had sold several to Uncle Bernie's. Philippe says it was there that Ruth Handler first saw them. "This guy displayed the dolls in the window, and one day Ruth Handler walks by," he recalled. "She sees the doll. She pops in. What is this doll? Where does it come from? *Blah blah blah*." As Philippe tells it, Uncle Bernie's put Ruth in touch with his father, who in turn had told her about the doll that was taking over Europe. It was his father's tip, Philippe said, that sent Ruth to Switzerland over the summer of 1956.

Ruth Handler never mentioned Paul Guggenheim in her history of Barbie. In the canon of Barbie-related books, of which there are enough to fill a modest library, I have never seen his name come up outside Cy Schneider's memoir. Of course, family histories are as prone to bias as business narratives. But Philippe's timeline checked out. His father, I later found, had told the same story to a small Berlin paper in 1987, a few months before Schneider released his book. (Ruth, Paul confirmed, "came regularly" to Uncle Bernie's to see the latest imports.) And their account made a certain sense to me—how much more likely that Ruth would have stumbled upon the doll just blocks from her house, rather than in some city nearly six thousand miles away.

At the very least, Ruth certainly knew Paul Guggenheim: she'd hired him. The Swiss toyman got a job setting up Mattel International, doing for Barbie exactly what he'd done for Lilli—selling the dolls abroad. The Handlers had offered him the role not long after Barbie launched, Paul said. The doll had barely hit the market before she was competing with knockoffs, enough for Mattel to file suit. Paul had been called as a witness, testifying before the court about the "business with Lilli." Perhaps Ruth could imagine him telling the story elsewhere. Because after the trial in 1961, Mattel bought his company—and with it, he suggested, years later, himself.

⁂

If we buy Ruth's story, she had picked up the Lillis almost in passing—she only had three, after all. And perhaps for someone who wanted them only as inspiration, three might have been enough. But it evidently wasn't for Ruth, because two months after she returned to the U.S., she placed five more orders for Lillis, buying another twelve from the Lucerne shop and another six from a store in Munich.

Ruth needed more supplies, because, at that moment, Mattel was looking for a manufacturer that could reproduce the Lilli doll, but at a cost lower than one could find in the American market. Jack Ryan, the former Raytheon designer, was already planning a research trip to Japan—which had rapidly taken Germany's place as America's top toy rival. "Just as I was leaving," he recalled, "Ruth stuck this doll into my attaché case." Ruth claimed she told him to "find someone who could make a doll of this approximate size." Ryan remembered her phrasing differently: "See if you can get this copied."

It's not hard to imagine why Ruth would have first looked to Japan. As the twentieth century wore on, a certain narrative had emerged about the nation's toys: "The Japanese are adept imitators," read one item. "Japanese manufacturers are noted for their skill in copying foreign goods," went another. An urban legend circulated that one toy maker, in a small, then-unincorporated town in southern Japan, had cashed in on his village's name: Usa. By supposedly stamping his toys "Made in USA," one article claimed, "he made big money selling the 'foreign' toys to his own people, while Americans bought them under the impression they were patronizing home labor!" Was it true? The stories, which trickled out over decades, never singled out any particular company, and exports were conventionally marked by countries of origin, not unincorporated villages. But the anecdote captured the American paranoia over foreign copycats. Since the Industrial Revolution, the toy industry had essentially operated like a Matryoshka doll of intellectual property; almost every new idea could be split open to find its distinctly similar progenitor. But somehow Japanese goods gained a reputation for a kind of existential mimicry, a font of knockoffs fundamentally faker than anything found in the domestic market. Perhaps that appealed to Ruth. "We were hearing that Japanese imports were a threat to our toy industry," she said in an interview. "Since we felt we couldn't fight 'em, we decided to join 'em."

There was also another reason to go abroad. "Wages as low as 10 cents a day are paid to the Japanese toy workers—many of whom are children—and the majority of the assembly work is done at home," the Toy Manufacturers of the USA director cautioned. "They work from 12 to 17 hours a day." The Handlers wanted to make a "three-dollar doll," a figurine less expensive than the *Bild* Lilli, so middle-class parents wouldn't mind tacking on a few accessories. An American-made doll would cost at least seven or eight dollars. "We couldn't make it in the United States," Elliot said in an interview; they'd have to pay American wages. Like Marx, the Handlers looked abroad. "Labor costs were high," Ruth recalled. "You had to go to the Orient in order to get your costs down."

Ruth wanted a softer doll, something more malleable that would feel as real as it looked. *Bild* Lilli had been made in a hard plastic, a brittle synthetic resin called polystyrene that was melted down, then squished into hollow casts of her form through a process called "injection molding." But the soft vinyls Ruth wanted would not fill the small corners of a *Bild* Lilli's dainty casts. Ruth's designers found an alternative: polyvinyl chloride, or PVC, an unusual polymer derived primarily from chlorine, which nature writer Elizabeth Royte called "Satan's resin." PVC was extremely versatile. It was very hard to destroy. And it called for a new technique: a rotational process where the injected molds were slowly turned like a spit pig, to push the hot plastic into the tiniest crevices. To develop it, Mattel teamed up with Kokusai Boeki Kaisha, a former rubber ball manufacturer in Tokyo that had grown into a vast constellation of contractors and subcontractors and women working from their homes.

The Handlers not only had new allies in Japan, they also had a common enemy: "Louis Marx is hated here because he did things the N. York way," Elliot wrote in a letter. "So even The King can make mistakes. They published a very nasty article in [the] newspaper about Louis Marx last week—will bring it home."

But Mattel too, in this intercontinental exchange, had some cultural confusion. "A lot fell through in translation," said Carol Spencer, a Barbie fashion designer who worked at Mattel for thirty-five years. The American participants, like the media before them, framed the Japanese in tellingly racial terms. The Japanese "are very obedient," Ryan said. "They'll always do what you tell them." The homeworkers who stitched Barbie's clothes for cents per piece were "ideally suited" for Barbie-sized tailoring, Ruth wrote, because of "their smaller hands and traditionally more nimble fingers."

Bild Lilli had been conceived to fill a literal blank, and Ruth wanted Barbie to seem similarly empty. The face should have, she said, a "blank" expression, "so that little girls could project their fantasies into the doll." But even blankness could be biased in the eyes of the beholder. "The first shipment of Barbie dolls—a small one—to arrive in America from Japan had Oriental eyes!" Ruth wrote. "While this may seem like a comical problem now, back then it was a real crisis." In retrospect, that "crisis" seemed easier to fix than what Ruth faced months later, at Toy Fair, in the New Yorker Hotel, the night Barbie bombed.

CHAPTER 5

MR. MASS MOTIVATION

Maybe Ruth had sensed that Barbie would flop, that to push Barbie into the playrooms of the American public, she needed a smarter sales pitch, something to make this adult doll seem marketable to children weaned on Raggedy Anns. Certainly, it couldn't hurt to explore alternative advertising options. After the success of *The Mickey Mouse Club*, Mattel now prided itself as a pioneer in the art of the ad. Which perhaps explains why, three months before Barbie failed, Ruth reached out to a man who was himself something of a pioneer—the public face of a marketing strategy Mattel had not yet tried.

The field was called "motivational research," or M.R.—a relatively new flavor of advertising that borrowed its approach from one Sigmund Freud. The Austrian analyst, whose psychological principles had been imported and watered down over the decades prior, had reconfigured middle-class conceptions of the human mind. He had popularized the notion of "the unconscious," a cryptic terrain of people's psychic landscapes that could be plumbed for forgotten childhood traumas, hidden sexual agendas, and desires unmentionable within the bounds of civil society. By the 1950s, psychoanalysis was more than mainstream; it was "one of the hottest intellectual vogues of the decade." Every subject, every industry was suddenly ripe for Freudian exegesis, from "the mystery behind Marilyn Monroe's sex appeal" to premature balding.

No field was keener to uncover the unseen forces guiding human motivation than advertising. Wartime industrial advancements had, as historian Lawrence R. Samuel has observed, allowed manufacturers to easily copy their competitors' successes, yielding store aisles of "increasingly look-a-like, act-a-like products." Brands sought new ways to make their mops or coffee makers stand out among sameness. And "motivation research" seemed like an answer. The still-novel area of study purported to explain why customers purchased specific products, what moved them to choose Ivory Soap over Camay or the Chevrolet Bel Air over the Cadillac Coupe deVille.

The field had ballooned so quickly that it had already prompted backlash. If boosters characterized M.R. as a blend of psychoanalysis and market research, critics called it mass manipulation. In 1957, the writer Vance Packard had published *The Hidden Persuaders*, a landmark investigation into how merchandisers mined the public's "secret miseries and self-doubts" to hawk their wares. His ominous survey featured an array of ad men and Madison Avenue gadflies sounding off on the slyest means of subtle messaging. But there was one researcher he cited more than most, a man so enmeshed in the American advertising complex that he seemed to star as the book's quasi-protagonist: an Austrian psychologist named Ernest Dichter.

The doctor cut an unthreatening profile. "Dr. Dichter," as Packard summed him up, "is exuberant, balding." Dichter exuded a certain professorial mien—staring out from horn-rimmed glasses, toking from a long wooden pipe, whose smoke he believed doubled as a "form of masculine perfume." He was also a former psychoanalyst. Many proselytizers of motivational research traced some lineage to Sigmund Freud, but Dichter's ties were more direct than most. He had studied at Freud's alma mater in Austria and had been trained by several of Freud's protégés. He once ran his practice on the very Vienna street where Sigmund himself lived. By the late fifties, the so-called "Freud of Madison Avenue" had earned a reputation as "as someone who used Freudian and sexual references in dramatic ways."

The Hidden Persuaders had been pitched as an exposé, not an advertisement. But its account of how marketers were attempting, as *The New Yorker* put it, "to turn the American mind into a kind of catatonic dough that will buy, give, or vote at their command" merely made Dichter more popular. By April of 1958, Packard's book had spent forty-six weeks on the best-seller list. By December, the analyst had landed himself a new client: Mattel.

Dichter's father, whom the doctor saw as a loser, had been a "spectacularly unsuccessful salesman." In Vienna, the family subsisted off such little money that, as a child, Dichter frequently snuck off to the countryside, illicitly selling family heirlooms in exchange for food. Dichter's sole tie to relative wealth was his uncle, who ran a small department store in the city and hired his nephew as a salesclerk. Dichter worked at the store for four years, dressing window displays while learning much about seducing the consumer and the "difficulty of selling an idea."

Dichter's time at the store also offered him some less licit instruction. "Some of my female companions and teachers were partners and objects of my sexual training course," he wrote. Because these exploits "had to be carried out somewhat hurriedly," Dichter and his tutors would stand "behind dolls and electric trains waiting to be given a place in the visible shelves at the front of the store." He offered a hypothetical title for his ad-hoc seminar: "How to make love in a stock room."

Dichter's own motivations did not need much analysis to uncover. As a young man, he was deeply insecure—scrawny, pink-faced, with a halo of red hair. He resented his father's failure and craved female attention, experimenting with a bohemian intellectual vibe when he enrolled at the Sorbonne to study literature. He even bought a beret. But he fell for a psychology student and soon switched his major to match hers. "As is often the case," Dichter wrote, "I wanted to find solutions for my own problems and I wanted to please my girlfriend at the same time."

Later, back in Vienna, he studied under analysts like August Aichhorn, who specialized in psychoanalytic child development, and Wilhelm Stekel, a frenemy of Freud's whose works spanned from sadomasochism to the "sexual root of kleptomania" to a study of masturbation titled *Auto-Erotism: A Psychiatric Study of Onanism and Neurosis*. Their work inspired Dichter to focus on a "more immediate application" of Freud's principles—mostly involving sales. He wrote pop science articles about consumer motivation. He taught an adult education course on advertising. And he took a position at the Psychoeconomic Institute, studying the "milk-drinking habits of the Viennese."

As a subject of research, milk might have seemed innocuous enough, but in 1936, Austrian authorities detained him without explanation. Dichter, who was Jewish, had rarely experienced overt ethnic discrimination (though he hated his hair, it had, he said, shielded him from being "considered by strangers to be Jewish"). Now suddenly he was in jail being grilled about milk. "What was the secret meaning of all these questionnaires?" his interrogators asked. "What was the real meaning of the obvious code-word 'milk'?" Dichter was held for weeks with little explanation. The Nazi newspaper *Völkischer Beobachter* later reported him as a suspected "subversive" alongside Albert Einstein, Karl Marx, and Friedrich Engels—somewhat odd bedfellows for a man who later identified as a "scheming capitalist."

Dichter decided it was time to return to France, and from there, make a run for the United States. At the U.S. embassy in Paris, he secured his visa, he said, by making "the best sales pitch of my whole life." Dichter lambasted an official there about American hypocrisy: "All you're interested in is having people come to the U.S. who have rich relatives or clergymen or some other occupation that is of immediate interest." He promised that he would bring motivational research to the States, and use "depth psychology" to root out the ills of "criminality, productivity, strikes, vandalism." By 1938, Dichter and his wife, a concert pianist, were in New York.

Dichter did not, it turned out, spend his first years eradicating crime with his arsenal of Freudian jargon. As it happened, he was studying milk again. He had phoned up the first market research firm he could find, and they'd stuck him on the beverage beat. But Dichter did well enough that he started looking to strike out on his own. In 1939, he sent letters to prospective companies, offering his services to outfits from Ivory Soap to *Esquire* magazine. The struggling men's monthly signed on as Dichter's first client, sending him off to investigate its appeal among men.

Dichter presented himself as a "scientist," but he scorned the quantitative approach of the so-called nose-counters. Like many Freudians before him, he determined that people rarely answered direct questions honestly, and instead had to be examined as unreliable narrators whose true desires lay only in their unconscious mind. This approach could yield somewhat obvious results: after talking "at great length to a number of men," Dichter concluded that *Esquire*'s draw on the American male stemmed primarily from its "photographs of naked girls."

Between articles, the magazine featured nude pictures and pinups, the so-called Petty Girls drawn in the mold of the *Daily Mirror*'s Jane. Dichter told *Esquire* to tout them as an asset, as a feature of the brand's overall image or *gestalt* (Dichter claimed, dubiously, that he "developed" the former term). He came up with a scientific-sounding justification. "When men look at pictures of nudes, they are visually oriented," he wrote. "Their pupils are opened more widely, they are more attentive to visual stimuli." This visual orientation was key, he concluded, because they "pay more attention to advertisements."*

In 1946, Dichter started his own firm, the Institute for Mass Motivational Research (he later dropped the "Mass," he said, because it sounded too "People's Republic"). He soon bought a twenty-six-room mansion upstate in Croton-on-Hudson, a baronial stone manor equipped with an "honest-to-goodness pipe organ." His sixty-odd-person staff commuted to his "castle on the Hudson," some working out of the eleven bathrooms that Dichter converted into offices. Country life, the analyst found, proved equally rife with unconscious urges and sexual symbolism. When his chickens fell victim to disease, forcing Dichter to execute them en masse, he concluded:

> Once again, Freud was proven right: we all have a killer instinct and killing is very close to sexual excitement. To my shock and surprise, I discovered that after I had gotten the knack of chopping off the heads of the chickens, I had an erection.

One critic described Dichter as "the most prominent retailer of Freud going today," and he certainly sold it, lacing his work with Freudian

---

*That may have been the case, but the pinups still got *Esquire* in trouble. Three years later, the Postal Service yanked the magazine's mail permit, prompting an obscenity trial that went all the way to the Supreme Court. The court's ruling in its favor both granted the pinup the imprimatur of social acceptability and ushered in a wave of adult magazines, like *Playboy*, over the next decade.

buzzwords like *reality principle, repression, neurosis, libido,* and *subconscious.* But as historian Daniel Horowitz noted, Dichter's analysis overlooked some of Freud's darker theories about sexual trauma and parental conflict: "His work reminds us of how American interpreters of Freud turned a pessimistic vision that concentrated on the darker implications of sexuality into an optimistic ideology that equated sexuality with liberation."

Dichter's vision of liberation consisted mainly of the freedom to buy more stuff. This made him quite popular in corporate America. By the 1950s, Dichter had been hired by companies up and down the S&P 500 and racked up a litany of nicknames: motivational research's "dean," "patron saint," or "unquestionably the high priest." To some, he was simply: "Mr. Mass Motivation Himself."

⁓

It was not uncommon for Dichter's deep dives to uncover a hidden sexual agenda governing product preference. While studying car-buying habits at Chrysler, he deduced that men saw cars as surrogates for sexual fantasies—the "mistress" convertible versus the "wife" sedan.

For Ivory Soap, he argued that soap invoked the erotic undertones of bathing—"one of the few occasions when the puritanical American was allowed to caress himself." In studies on smoking, he claimed that a malfunctioning lighter "frustrates a deep-seated desire for mastery and control," while a working one "becomes a kind of symbol of the flame which must be lit in consummating sexual union." Holding a cigarette in your mouth was, naturally, "comparable to sucking at the nipples of a gigantic world breast."

Ruth, who saw herself as "very gutsy" in marketing, sought Dr. Dichter's advice in the winter of 1958. At that point, Dichter's institute offered a full suite of services that seemed to draw more from performance art than science, among them, as one paper described, "Motivational Theater (a sort of role-playing game)," and a variation of it called "psychodrama." Dichter's key innovation was coining the term "focus group." He had installed in the castle what he called his "Living Laboratory," a staged living room, where he would conduct "depth interviews" with a range of families from the neighboring area. The families would watch TV or play or talk, while being observed by hidden cameras. This was the kind of research Mattel commissioned that winter, paying him $12,000 to study four categories of controversial toys: guns, holsters, water-rockets, and dolls.

Perhaps it seemed out of character for a man who only three years earlier had published an article called "Put the Libido Back into Advertising" to take on products directed at children. But Dichter was clearly interested in the subject. Despite his large staff, he took the Mattel case on himself. The analyst had strayed into children's merchandising before, having studied the Davy Crockett craze, on which American parents had spent some $300 million in 1955. In the aftermath, merchandisers agonized over the root of the fad. To the uninitiated, as Packard wrote, this kind of national obsession could seem little more than a "cute bit of froth on the surface of American life." But in a report that Mattel must have found appealing, Dichter had concluded that such fads could, in fact, be orchestrated—if, as Packard paraphrased, its promoters targeted "an unsatisfied need of youngsters."

Toys proved as rife with sexual symbolism as anything else. Dichter's survey of 425 participants—68 parents, 166 boys, and 191 girls—found no shortage of "unsatisfied needs" that Mattel products could address. His report alluded to boys' preference for longer guns, which could be "explained in terms of the gratification of the need for power," he wrote. "The longer his gun, the bigger and stronger the child feels." And Barbie's sexiness, it turned out, was part of her appeal. Most of the girls thought she was beautiful and elegant (though one preferred a Barbie competitor because they were "real pretty like this one only bigger and fatter"). Only one child seemed truly put off by Barbie; Dichter dismissed her as a tomboy outlier:

(RUTH ANN WAS LESS ABLE TO ENGAGE IN ACTIVE PLAY WITH THE DOLL. SHE HELD HER IN HER HAND AT SOME DISTANCE AND SAID QUIETLY:) "The eyes look strange [sic] forbidding. I don't think I like a doll with so much eye shadow."
    (SHE QUICKLY HANDED THE DOLL TO ANOTHER GIRL TO PLAY WITH AND DIVERTED HERSELF TO THE SELECTION OF A WARDROBE FROM THE CATALOGUE. SHE CHOSE MAINLY SPORT CLOTHES.)

In general, Dichter concluded that the girls wanted "someone sexy looking, someone that they wanted to grow up to be like," as his wife later put it. "Long legs, big breasts, glamorous."

Parents were another question. In the section on parental attitudes, the first bullet point read: "The Doll Is Too 'Sexy.'" The parent participants "reacted immediately to the 'sexy' appearance of the doll," Dichter wrote. "There was some embarrassment, some laughter and giggles." One upper-middle-class mother seemed "very much embarrassed" by the doll, so much so that she "stared at the doll for a long time," and appeared to be "actually blushing." Another scoffed:

> I know little girls want dolls with high heels but I object to that sexy costume (POINTING TO SHEER PINK NEGLIGEE). I wouldn't walk around the house in an outfit like that.... Actually, I'd call them 'daddy dolls'—they are so sexy. They could be a cute decoration for a man's bar.

Even without Lilli's branding, in other words, Barbie seemed like a men's toy. Dichter's task was to create a new narrative, a sales pitch that would articulate what the mute doll could not. In this regard, Dichter had a breakthrough. The sexiness was not in itself a deal-breaker, especially when paired with Barbie's elaborate wardrobe. "The mothers admired the Barbie clothes just as much as the children did," he wrote. One mother, who had dismissed Barbie as "too sexy," changed her mind upon hearing her daughter squeal that the doll was "so nicely groomed." She determined that the doll might "encourage good habits of self-grooming in her child." As another header put it: "The Clothes Sell the Doll."

The key to cornering the parent market, Dichter determined, was not to shy away from the doll's semi-preposterous silhouette, but to double-down on her stylishness. Playing and pretending with these glamorous models would initiate the child into the rites of womanhood, Dichter observed. It would awaken "in the child a concern with proper appearance"—an important skill for the conformist fifties. The era's ideal woman, a college-aged Sylvia Plath cracked, was "a painted doll who shouldn't have a thought in her pretty head other than cooking a steak dinner." If young girls modeled themselves on Barbie, the doctor wrote, she could convert even the most tangled, sticky tomboy "into a feminine, poised little lady." Tell parents that buying Barbies is pragmatic, Dichter advised, a convertible with the perks of a sedan.

⟜⟝

Dichter's study was not yet finished when Ruth brought Barbie to Toy Fair. The doctor, with all his "depth interviewing" and "Motivational Theater," took half a year to complete his report. He submitted the final draft in June of 1959, three months after the fair. Just weeks later, Barbie, suddenly and somewhat mysteriously, emerged from her sales slump. By mid-summer, Ruth later recalled, Mattel cranked the production schedule back up, not just to their original ballpark of sixty thousand a week, but double or triple that, "as much as we could get."

Did Dichter make the difference? His study benefited from coinciding with school break. But he gave Mattel something to say, and his advice seemed to stick with them. In the early sixties, Mattel produced a twelve-minute movie called *Pigtails to Ponytails*. The film, which they toured to women's groups around the country, instructed mothers on how Barbie could teach girls self-grooming. Around the same time, Ruth gave a speech to the New York Society of Security Analysts. While rehearsing the Q&A portion, her publicists predicted that someone might ask about Barbie's distinct "grown-up look." If they did, Ruth had a scripted response:

> I guess that you mean the *sexy look*. That was one of the first questions raised when we introduced the Barbie doll. I think all girls expect to look like this toy doll when they grow up. They all admire this appearance and look forward to the day when they expect to look like that, too.

But if Ruth was now willing to speak openly of Barbie's "sexy look," she was less forthcoming about who had advised her to do so. In 1967, Mattel was contacted by a reporter working on a feature for none other than *Esquire*. Years had passed since *Esquire*'s obscenity problems. Now it was the mid-sixties, and in the pages where the Petty Girls once trembled, the magazine was taking a more puritanical tack, mounting a pearl-clutching investigation into why the new generation of children seemed more sexually precocious. This American nymphet population seemed to be "maturing earlier and learning all there is to know about sex," the reporter observed. "They are not embarrassed because it doesn't mean the same thing to them. Sex is a legitimate element of the environment itself, fire, water, and land—life as information and life as sensory apparatus."

The writer wanted to know, among other things, how Mattel had deployed sexuality and child psychology in their product design and marketing. More emphasis, after all, had been placed on "dolls as recognizable sexual objects," he wrote. Had they slipped anything sinister or subliminal, maybe vaguely sexual, into their regularly scheduled programming? Had they been influenced at all by the writings of Sigmund Freud? In a written statement, Mattel dismissed the question outright.

> Although our testing has for a number of years included professional child psychologists, our goal is to evaluate play value and *we do not seek out, or try to instill, any Freudian aspects in this testing* [emphasis mine]. And one of the principal reasons we do not is that we have found, over many years of experience, that children in our basic age group—from toddlers to 12—are not normally concerned with this sort of subject matter.... But beyond that I'm afraid we cannot at this point in time be more specific.

The answer may have been correct in some respects; maybe toddlers were not especially concerned with the kind of "tactile confrontations" or latent Freudian impulses *Esquire* was investigating. But the response was also a lie. Mattel had indeed sought to "instill" some "Freudian aspects" in their testing; they had hired the Freud of Madison Avenue to do it. His insights had helped shape the public presentation of what had by then become their best performing product.

Just three months after the doctor turned in his Barbie report, he drafted a new proposal for Ruth, laying out the terms of yet another study. This one would be "broader and deeper" in scope, pulling on "entirely different techniques." He planned to perform a three-sixty analysis of Mattel's "brand image"—its general reputation among the public and what the Handlers could do to nurture their perception as "the 'Ideal' Toy Company." Foremost among Dichter's many concerns was the question of how calculated the company should appear. "Should you create the impression of being delightfully and charmingly absorbed in the sheer fun of making toys and spreading cheer?" Dichter asked Ruth. Or "is it 'all right,' in the emotional sense, for a toy company to seem mainly interested in making money?"

If the second study was conducted, I found no record of it. But it's not hard to imagine what Dichter might have discovered. As far as Ruth was concerned, the second question's answer was no.

CHAPTER 6

CHRISTMAS IN JULY

It's one thing to pitch a product, to convincingly identify a need that only a certain screwdriver or stain remover or Electrolux Automatic F-series vacuum cleaner can solve. It's another to keep selling them. At a certain point, there are only so many vacuum cleaners a suburban family can buy, at which time the door-to-door notions peddler will find himself sinking into what the novelist Helen DeWitt has called the "festering swamp of market saturation."

Over a century ago, a shaving company devised one route out of the swamp. The idea began with an idiosyncratic tycoon named King Camp Gillette, who founded the eponymous razor brand in 1901. But the decade prior, when his name was just unusual and not yet a bathroom staple, Gillette was a cork salesman and congenital tinkerer, always inventing some knickknack. Toward the end of the century, he had been working on something he hoped would be more permanent—an earnest, prescient, and intermittently hilarious tome of utopian social reform called *The Human Drift*.

The manifesto took aim at the gross inequality of the Gilded Age and laid out a plan that might "dam the golden flood which flows incessantly into the hands of the nonproducers, the interest-takers, the schemers, and the manipulators." Gillette loathed market competition. The eternal fight for material wealth at the expense of everyone and everything else was, in his view, an "insane idea," an "element of chaos" that could only lead to one end: "the final control of the commercial field by a few mammoth corporations." (At one point in the book, he wrote an extended verse monologue in which Satan describes inventing capitalism to keep "alight the fires of hell.") Gillette wanted to ensure the equitable distribution of goods and resources. But—and perhaps this is where he lost some readers—his solution was to replace all production with one unified stock corporation, run, along with the rest of society, from a gargantuan, perfectly rectangular, ceramic-tiled mega-city to be constructed near and powered by Niagara Falls.

And yet shortly after the book came out, Gillette was struck with another idea: a razor with disposable blades. "It was almost as if Karl Marx had paused between *The Communist Manifesto* and *Das Kapital* to develop a dissolving toothbrush," Gillette's biographer remarked. A decade later, after years of honing the manufacturing protocol, Gillette was awarded the first patent for a mass-produced disposable razor.

In the process, he inspired a business model perhaps as influential as the device itself. His company realized they could sell the razor at a loss—luring in customers with a low-cost product—and profit instead from the marked-up blades they inevitably came back to buy. Gillette continued his writing career, self-publishing a pamphlet on a plan for universal employment and elaborating on his public corporation in two more books, one cowritten with Upton Sinclair. But in the end, Gillette became better known for his shorter writing. As his possibly apocryphal line went: "Give 'em the razor, sell 'em the blades."

Gillette's "razor blade model" spawned many copycats. Consumers still encounter it now, when suspiciously affordable printers beget years of extortion for ink. But the technique did not translate neatly into the world of toys. Toy manufacturers are beholden to seasonality. Men need razors year-round; offices can run out of toner cartridges any old month. But while parents may buy the odd game or doll or gun for birthday parties or the occasional treat, mass toy-buying is concentrated around the holidays. Many toy companies will spend most of the year in the red, only to enter the black in the final quarter. It was a perpetual worry for American toy makers. As early as 1916, one trade association had tried to float the idea of turning Independence Day into the toy-buying equivalent of a Christmas in July. It didn't take off.

Seasonality remained an issue when Mattel entered the toy business, and by the time Barbie debuted, it had become a subject of great concern. If Mattel went public, as the company planned to the following year, the Handlers would face Wall Street pressure to deliver profits, not just annually or in the months before Christmas, but every quarter. Sponsoring *The Mickey Mouse Club* had been an early major attempt to solve the problem. Mattel had become the first, and for a time, the only toy advertiser "to use network television 52 weeks a year."

But Mattel's investment in year-round advertising had attracted "many imitators," and not just from toy makers. "Suddenly programming which used to be a TV toyland," a Mattel memo read, was selling "candy, cookies, toothpaste, cereal, soft drinks, gym shoes, et cetera." The Handlers worked hard to maintain their lead. But even with TV show tie-ins for every season, Mattel noted, "the majority of buying was still concentrated in the last quarter."

But Dichter had pointed out that, when it came to Barbie, the "clothes sell the doll." His idea was to not just pitch kids on buying one or two dolls, but to bill Barbie as a talisman to what Ruth called "the World of Barbie"—not a terminal product that ends with the first sale, but something to collect, nurture, and feed with a constant supply of costumes and accessories, or risk missing the latest small shoe or bitty bag and finding their figurine comically out of date. If this "'collection' type sequence is promoted," Dichter wrote, "continued purchases could be encouraged."

The Handlers embraced Gillette's razor blade technique—but Mattel did it even better. Barbie wasn't free, or even, in the grand scheme of toy price points, especially cheap (a $3 doll, adjusted for inflation, would now run about $32). And yet she had the same effect. In lieu of the dead-ends of toy companies past, Mattel continued creating new stars in the Barbie cosmos, offering a collection kids could never complete. Internally, staff would call her: "Our Lady of the Perpetual Income."

By Barbie's first birthday, Mattel had already sold some 351,000 Barbies, and "several hundred thousand" outfits, prompting such an order backlog that they ran out of their first edition—the coveted model collectors call the "No. 1 Ponytail"—and started putting out No. 2 (which featured a lighter, plastic stand), then No. 3 (which sported a softened brow). By

1961, when No. 5 came out (featuring a hollower, and thus cheaper, body), Barbie's wardrobe included three dozen costumes. Her hair came in blonde, brown-black, and "Titian red," styled with curly bangs or in a Jackie Kennedy–inspired "Bubble Cut." Barbie had become so popular that she started to get fan mail, as Lilli once had. Soon, Ruth gave Barbie a plus-one. As a press release announced in August: "Mattel Creates Ken, Boyfriend for Barbie."

Ken followed the Barbie format, debuting with his own collectible accoutrements, selling so successfully that other companies copied the idea. In 1964, three years after Ken's debut, the rival toy maker Hasbro introduced its own boy doll, whose accessories included a literal long rifle, G.I. Joe. He was billed, not as a doll, but as "an action figure."

Ken was just the beginning. Over the sixties, Barbie's social network grew to include her friend Midge, who came in four hair colors; Ken's friend Allan, whose sole selling point was that he fit in Ken's clothes (slogan: "All of Ken's Clothes Fit Him"); a younger sister, Skipper, who introduced junior versions of Barbie's outfits; Skipper's two friends, Skooter and Ricky; and a cousin named Francie, the first Mattel doll to come as both white and black. Soon, Barbie acquired two new twin siblings, Tutti and Todd; Tutti's friend Chris; four more friends, Casey, Stacey, Twiggy—based on the distinctly unbusty model of the era—and Christie, the second black doll in the Barbie canon, but the first to be given her own name.

As Barbie's social scene grew, so did her résumé, adding gigs as a fashion designer, singer, flight attendant, ballerina, and nurse. She became a "career girl" in 1963, and a "drum majorette" the year after. Her professional ascent endowed her with new marketable skills. "Miss Barbie" introduced bendable legs. "Color Magic Barbie" could use a special solution to dye her hair. And "Talking Barbie" gave the doll, suffering in silence for nine years, her first words. (Among them: "I love being a fashion model.") Ken evolved in his own way too. The first iteration, which had three-dimensional hair, turned out to suffer from male pattern baldness when washed. Mattel secured his successor's hairline by coloring it onto his scalp.

Barbie and friends had a range of transit to choose from, including a Ken's red hot rod, Barbie's lilac convertible, a lime-green speedboat, and a blue "sports plane." At night, they could curl up in the first Barbie Dreamhouse, initially a cardboard single-story home, in a ranch style with red plaid drapes and "mid-century wood grains." Barbie enthusiasts could join the "Official National Barbie Fan Club," read Barbie short stories in the official *Barbie* magazine, or dive into longer Barbie novels via several Random House Barbie books. Barbie herself was a reader. One doll came with three knuckle-sized manuals: *How to Travel*, *How to Get a Raise*, and *How to Lose Weight*. The last one advised: "Don't eat!"

Barbie's success was contagious. "She was a merchandiser's dream," an *Esquire* article noted, "a mixture of precocious sex and instant affluence." Mattel licensed the Barbie name liberally, and devised their own products too. The market flooded with Barbie-adjacent goods: Barbie bubble baths, Barbie suitcases, Barbie bedspreads, Barbie diaries, Barbie record players, Barbie records, Barbie beds, Barbie cars, Barbie friendship rings, Barbie lockets, Barbie makeup, Barbie books, Barbie comic books, Barbie puzzles, Barbie greeting cards, Barbie thermoses, Barbie lockets, Barbie pencil cases, Barbie lunch boxes, Barbie tea sets, Barbie clothing patterns, Barbie umbrellas, and, to bring it full circle, Barbie paper dolls. In a speech on merchandising, Ruth announced: "The name Barbie is magic."

As Barbie expanded, so did Mattel. The company went public in 1960, the year after her debut, with a small offering of over-the-counter stocks—shares that were "quickly spoken for." By early 1962, Mattel was raking in nearly $50 million in annual sales, a record they were "well ahead of" before Christmas. The next August, Mattel debuted on the New York Stock Exchange. The Handlers flew east to watch as the ticker tape read off the first trades. "Oh boy, what a big gala affair that was—boy, was that a big event!" Ruth recalled. "Our stock went up to the sky, immediately, and kept going and going and going and split and resplit." In 1964, Mattel opened new factories in Los Angeles, Canada, and New Jersey. They set up a sales office in Geneva, Switzerland, and a new headquarters building in Hawthorne, California. "Business is not only good," Elliot told shareholders at an annual meeting, "in fact, it is very good."

The company was growing fast and unchecked, but each new spurt seemed to only multiply sales. "We were gutsy people," Ruth said. "We were young and full of fire and cocky and everything worked." Mattel had hit on a formula, *The Wall Street Journal* drooled: "once a toy craze has been created, ride it for all it's worth with an endless proliferation of new items tied to the original product." Mattel expanded its product line by some 50 percent in 1965—then "the biggest increase in the company's history." That year, sales topped $100 million. They were making so much money, they seemed to barely know what to do with it. At one point, just to keep their retailers in good spirits, the company spent two years and "well into six figures" producing an all-male original musical called *Mattelzapoppin'*—then toured it to some eight thousand toy buyers across twenty-seven different cities. One Christmas, the R&D Department splurged on thousands of frozen turkeys—one for every employee. When the staff got a little buzzed at the office party, they began "clobbering each other with the rock-hard birds."

The mood at Mattel was one of "near euphoria," a reporter observed, "a feeling that Mattel had the Midas touch." It seemed the Handlers could do no wrong. "Mattel is energetic, deep-thinking, and far and away above the field in product development," a Chicago toy buyer told the *Journal*. "I simply can't see its downfall."

CHAPTER 7

BARBIE V. BARBIE

It was easy for Louis Marx to picture Barbie's downfall. He'd orchestrated many a toy's obsolescence. How many times had he seen a solid product, remade it in cheaper plastic, using cheaper labor, and sold his own for less? "He was the big bully on the block," Hot Wheels designer Fred Adickes once said. "He'd go to a toy fair, see what was there, and he'd knock it off quickly." There was a reason all his friends were generals and baseball players and not designers or inventors. "He made very few friends in the toy industry," a British toy executive remembered. "He always believed that if he got friendly with his competitors he couldn't knock off their products."

Barbie was a particular sore spot for Marx. He had been making tens of millions before Mattel even launched their first toy. He had been on the cover of *Time* magazine only a few years before, in 1955. It was, by Ruth Handler's own admission, "unthinkable" that Mattel would ever catch up. But something had changed. "We were on our way up into the hundreds of millions, and he was standing still or doing less," Ruth said. The Handlers had gotten "the taste of growth, success," she confessed. "We felt we could do no wrong."

Now Marx was the one who felt ripped off. He told colleagues that he—not Reinhard Beuthien or Rolf Hausser or Ruth Handler—was the one who first thought up Barbie. In the 1950s, the story went, he had run into the Handlers on the *Queen Mary*, the same ocean liner they took to Europe. One night after dinner, Marx found himself chatting with the couple, talking over the Nuremberg Toy Fair, where all three were headed. Marx's reputation preceded him, the toy maker would say, and the Handlers wanted advice on how to pick a "red hot hit," as he'd done so many times. Marx supposedly mulled, crunching the numbers, running down trends. "A doll," he offered. "The world is ready for a pretty girl doll."

If Marx believed the world was ready for an adult-looking doll, he hadn't yet bothered to make one himself. But over in Germany, the Haussers certainly had. When Barbie debuted on the American market in March of 1959, Lilli had been circulating Europe for nearly four years. The Haussers had been planning to bring her to America: they'd applied for a U.S. patent a year after she launched. But unbeknownst to the Germans, their international plan had been usurped. The machinations of American bureaucracy were too slow to keep up. As the Haussers' patent inched along toward approval, the Handlers had forged ahead without one. By the time the Haussers got their patent in February of 1960, Mattel had sold nearly $1.5 million worth of Barbies her first year alone.

The Haussers had not yet heard of Barbie. They found out their doll had been copied soon after—from Louis Marx. The toy king saw that the patent gave the Haussers an opening, albeit an imperfect one. It did not cover the full *Bild* Lilli design; just the mechanism that allowed her legs to move forward and backward, "simulating human walking movements." But Marx suggested he could use it to challenge Mattel's right to make Barbie. The Haussers listened. In May of 1960, their lawyers reached out to Mattel about the twin dolls. But the Handlers were in no rush to respond. They had since filed for their own patent, signed by Jack Ryan, though it wouldn't be approved for more than a year. Why pay for this foreign doll—foreign hip joint really—when they were already making millions without it?

The Haussers were more pressed for time. Convincing Barbie knockoffs, and by extension *Bild* Lilli knockoffs, were already being made in Hong Kong. That June, Marx and his wife met the Haussers in Germany, laying out a contract to last for ten years. Marx would get the exclusive rights to sell *Bild* Lilli in America, Britain, Canada, and Hong Kong. He could call her something more American, or at least less German. In exchange, he would pay the Haussers $3,000 and a licensing fee for each doll sold.

After the deal was finalized on July 4, Marx owned Lilli's likeness in the United States, and by extension, arguably, Barbie's. The partners implied as much to Mattel's American contacts, warning wholesalers and distributors that Marx owned the *Bild* Lilli license and suggesting that this new hit doll was not the Handlers' invention, but was stolen from abroad. The Hausser firm "is now conducting a campaign of harassment and intimidation," the Handlers in turn complained, pestering their clients about something so inconsequential as a patent. One buyer forwarded Marx's letter to Mattel. "I would guess that the enclosed letter was sent to hundreds of accounts in the United States," the buyer wrote. "I don't know all the facts in this case, but I would assume that some action must be considered to stop the importation and sale of the Barbie doll."

Suddenly, the Handlers seemed much more interested in *Bild* Lilli's patent. That September, one of Mattel's German associates contacted the Haussers about making a deal. But now it was Marx who owned the exclusive rights; Mattel would have to go through him. It's not hard to imagine how this news hit the Handlers: their longtime rival coming into a legal claim on their most popular product. Ruth must have understood Marx's not-so-veiled threat: "It would seem advantageous to settle the matter promptly," the lawyers wrote, "in view of the many unauthorized imitations already started in Hong Kong and elsewhere, and which may soon flood this country in great quantity if the Hausser patent is not respected."

Ruth would have guessed the subtext: that not all of those "imitations" were "unauthorized" because it was Marx who was making them. And he was planning to make more.

Marx delivered on the promise: he started selling Lillis that fall. He didn't stop with the original. He flooded the market with Lilli dupes, made for cheap in Hong Kong. "Bonnie" was a Lilli clone with Barbie's proportions; she could borrow her clothes. "Miss Marlene" resembled Barbie but in the smaller Lilli's size, sporting a similar blonde hairstyle, with a pointed widow's peak. And then there was "Miss Seventeen," a beauty queen who came with a crown and red cape. At around fifteen inches, she towered over the other dolls even in flat feet.

The savvy collector could easily distinguish these dolls from Barbie: Miss Seventeen was taller, Miss Marlene was shorter. Their faces were painted by different hands. Some had thinner eyes, or wider noses, or varying amounts of makeup. The hostile circumstances in which Marx made his imitations led some to see his dolls as symbols of depravity. ("If Barbie was tawdry, Miss Seventeen was downright mangy," M. G. Lord wrote in her history *Forever Barbie*, "as slutty as Lilli, but not nearly so healthy"—her skin "jaundiced," her eyes unfocused, "as if bleary from drugs.") But the similarities overwhelmed the minor variations. To the untrained eye, Barbie, Lilli, Bonnie, whatever—they were essentially the same girl.

Marx wasn't the only toy maker who tried to replicate Barbie's success. Ideal Toy Company's Mitzi turned into Tammy, who spawned Misty, Pepper, and Samantha. Eegee's Babette became Miss Babette, who begat Annette. Larami Corp. put out Janie, while Elite Creations Inc. threw in Bonnie and Wendy. At least three Hong Kong firms put out Lilli clones, and another four made more in Japan. And yet Marx remained Mattel's toughest competition—"not because she was captivating," Lord argued, "but because she didn't fight fair."

Was Marx's approach any less fair than Mattel's? The Handlers hadn't bothered with the Haussers' rights at all. Marx had gone through the legal channels. He had a license, good for ten years. It's true that Marx had no delusions that customers would care, that they would gravitate toward the legal owner on principle. His deal with the Haussers had planned for contingencies. In addition to Lilli's likeness, the contract also granted Marx the right to defend it from copycats. The partners clearly had one offender in mind. "It is known that the patent infringements have been committed by Matell Inc. [*sic*]," the agreement read. "If a lawsuit should become necessary," Marx and the Haussers would split the proceeds in half.

A lawsuit soon became necessary. Or rather, multiple lawsuits. In early 1961, the quasi-identical dolls went to court. Mattel and Marx seemed to have decided on legal action at precisely the same time. On March 23, Marx got served at his office in Toy Center; Mattel was suing him in New York. The next day, Marx and the Haussers filed their own suit in Los Angeles. The cases got complicated quickly: Marx countersued Mattel in New York, while Mattel countersued in Los Angeles, alleging that Marx had not only ripped off Barbie, but that he had ripped off their Burp Gun too. Claims and counterclaims and various legal motions piled up on both coasts, but the core dispute remained, more or less, constant.

As Marx saw it, Barbie was obviously a "direct take-off" of Lilli—the "design, posture, facial expression," and the "overall attractive and distinctive appearance" made Barbie, beyond a shadow of a doubt, a flagrant "copy." Mattel had "willfully, knowingly and deliberately" infringed upon Lilli's patent and falsely advertised the doll as their own. In so doing, Marx alleged, Mattel had committed a "fraud and a hoax upon the public."

The Barbie defenders disagreed. The Haussers' patent wasn't even valid, Mattel argued, because it "failed" to describe "anything which was not already within the public domain." The doll construction described in the patent was, apparently, not original at all. Contra Ruth's story about the radical novelty of Barbie's adult body, this silhouette was actually widespread, "common knowledge" already described in no fewer than nineteen other patents, so widely disseminated that it made one wonder what Barbie's innovation really was. As they told it, Barbie had not even been inspired by her German doppelganger. Ruth's real muse had been a book on wooden dolls from nineteenth-century Vermont.

If anything, Mattel claimed, it was their opponents who were playing dirty. It was Marx and the Haussers who were "aiding and abetting one another," who had lied their way into legal ownership. (The "lie," Mattel later claimed, was based on an unsubstantiated tip that Rolf Hausser had known about a similar patent before getting his own, "but concealed it from the Patent Office.") It was the Lilli camp who had intimidated their customers and threatened them with lawsuits; who had "conspired" to market an "inferior doll" of "confusingly similar appearance" and leech off Barbie's big name. Marx and the Haussers had "subtly manipulated and contrived to compete unfairly," the Handlers' lawyers wrote. They had tried "to confuse and mislead" the public by hawking "imitations" and passing them off as Barbie.

The war dragged on for nearly two years, neither side ceding ground.

But in the early months of 1963, both sides unceremoniously surrendered. The cases were dismissed on all claims, with prejudice. "This was legal jargon for 'A pox on both your houses,'" Lord wrote. Though in truth, Marx and Mattel had quietly reached an out of court settlement. Mattel had agreed to sublicense the *Bild* Lilli patent for just $2,000 a year—a fraction of what Barbie made in a month.

Marx had been, on a basic level, outgunned. Patent law, in the American mid-century, was less sympathetic to inventors than it would one day become. And Mattel understood that Barbie was bigger than any one part, that legal ownership was almost immaterial to the conversation. Americans now associated those same shapes and curves with a single commercial source. When Barbie debuted, Mattel had plastered ABC, an ad partner with commercials from coast to coast. They had spent almost as much on TV advertising that year as they'd made in Barbie sales. More than any other children's product before or since, Mattel's own ad agent wrote, "the Barbie doll is testimony to the influence of television advertising on children."

The following winter, Rolf Hausser got a call from an associate of Mattel. The company was now, apparently, interested in acquiring the worldwide rights to the Lilli doll. While Rolf chatted through the terms, he probably didn't recognize the man on the other end of the line. But they'd done business before, if through a subsidiary. The Mattel man arranging the deal was Paul Guggenheim, the Swiss dealer who'd sold *Bild* Lillis in the States.

In February of 1964, four Mattel employees arrived at the Haussers' office in Germany. One of them was Guggenheim. Another was Mattel's general counsel, R. Kenton Musgrave, a former lawyer for Lockheed Aircraft. Over the course of a week, they negotiated a contract that would grant Mattel the rights to the doll—her patents, trademarks, copyright, and the Lilli brand itself in all but four countries granted to Marx. Once the contract was signed, the Haussers would be barred from ever producing the doll again. They would also surrender any claim to her name. For all this, the Haussers would walk away with four lump-sum payments totaling 100,000 deutsche marks, 15,000 of which went to Axel Springer, and another 15,000 of which wouldn't arrive until Marx's license expired in 1970. The Haussers would take home about $21,600. Basically pennies for Mattel, which just weeks earlier, had announced sales of more than $85 million over the prior nine months. But Rolf, he admitted later, had only a loose grasp of Mattel's profitability.

He finished negotiating the deal at the Frankfurt airport and signed it that Valentine's Day, officially waiving any claim to Barbie. The contract was the beginning of the end of the Hausser empire; the company filed for bankruptcy in 1983, and for years after the fact, Rolf Hausser would regret the day he ever signed it. He would spend the last years of his life writing Ruth long, single-spaced letters, wavering between morose pleas for recognition and bitter rants against the "evil role Mattel played" in stealing "millions of dollars" by copying *Bild* Lilli. In one letter, he compared Mattel to Serbian authoritarian and war criminal Slobodan Milošević.

In the end, Rolf's only victory was his story. He had wondered many times whether his version of events would ever reach the press. And by the nineties, it had. The critic M. G. Lord dug into Lilli in her book, *Forever Barbie*, which came out in 1994. And Ruth Handler told her own version of the story in her own memoir, *Dream Doll*, which she released, in an expert maneuver of narrative control, the very same year as Lord's. But few books or outlets have investigated very deeply into *Bild* Lilli's backstory, aside from her then-known link to Barbie. And perhaps for a reason. Owning the rights to the German doll gave Mattel multiple advantages. It protected their ability to reproduce Lilli unimpeded. It also gave them the power to ensure few else did.

Even after Lord's book came out, investigations into Lilli had a habit of disappearing from the public record. A four-part series on the doll in *Barbie Bazaar* was abruptly cut short over what one coauthor described to me as "bad blood between Hausser and Mattel." The final installation, though written in full, never ran. Stefanie Deutsche's collector guide, *Barbie: The First 30 Years*, included a chapter on Lilli when it came out in 1996; by the second edition, the chapter had been removed. Around the same time, *Miller's*, a homespun Barbie fan magazine run by a married couple in Washington published an interview with Rolf Hausser in what it promised to be a two-part series. The second part never came out either. Mattel sued the spouses for trademark infringement in federal court and won.

The German doll collector Silke Knaak encountered something similar only a few years later. In 2003, she wrote what was to be the most comprehensive history of the doll. She named the book something simple: *Bild-Lilli*. The editors didn't think it would cause any problem. They would, of course, have to pay Mattel a small fee to use the trademarked name. "We have been successful in doing this on all our Barbie projects, which Mattel also owns rights to," the American publisher wrote. "This is why [we] did not foresee any trouble with obtaining a license agreement to do your book."

But when the publisher tried to get permission, Mattel refused. "I spoke with Mattel's legal department today and they simply will not grant us permission," the imprint told Knaak. "Without their permission, we are not willing to publish this book." Knaak sat on the manuscript for over a decade, before releasing a different version herself, with a lighter focus on Lilli. She gave it a new, more anodyne, name: *German Fashion Dolls of the Fifties and Sixties*.

Marx, for his part, got somehow still less than the Haussers. Mattel continued to pay his licensing fee. He still had the American rights to *Bild Lilli* until 1970, and despite Mattel's effort to persuade him to part with it, he would hold it until the day it expired. But the toy king had been deposed. The Louis Marx Company was sold to Quaker Oats just two years later and filed for bankruptcy shortly before the Haussers. Barbie, meanwhile, was ascendant. Not long after the settlement, an internal memo warned Ruth: "Talk from the Marx camp is that Louis Marx has declared war on Ruth Handler!" But it didn't matter. He had already lost.

PART II

INTRO

One morning, amid the euphoria of Barbie's first year, the Handlers held a kind of debate. They brought in the toy marketing team. And the ad guys, Cy Schneider and his cohort from Carson/Roberts, though they were mostly there to listen. The real presence was the exuberant doctor with a shrinking halo of red hair. Ernest Dichter was visiting from New York. On this particular day, as Schneider later remembered, the Handlers called him in to discuss a controversy that had been tearing the office apart, dividing old allies and forging unlikely alliances, and which so far seemed to have little prayer for resolution. The hope was that the Freud of Madison Avenue could bring some much-needed clarity to the question of Ken's penis.

The company had gone public in April of 1960, and almost on cue, the Handlers found themselves contending with the public more directly than ever before. It wasn't just their shareholders, it was the fact that they were big enough to have shareholders, that Mattel had transitioned from a West Coast start-up to a national entity with millions of customers, millions of fans, and millions of opinions on what they should do. In a way, Mattel's problem was its own popularity. The early Barbies had come with a pamphlet, encouraging girls to write to their new doll at her very own address. But few could have predicted how many kids followed through. Letters arrived in such volume that Mattel hired a secretary just to handle the doll's mail. The outpouring was so intense, it seemed to steer Ruth's decision-making. The pamphlet had promised periodic responses, so Mattel began issuing a newsletter, which only compounded the problem—the reaction was "enormous."

The newsletter evolved into a magazine, then a club. "We formed a Barbie Fan Club almost from the pressure," she said. It became the second largest girl's organization in the world, after the Girl Scouts. These avid Barbie fans were cacophonous, but some cries were louder than others. As Ruth remembered: "There were a tremendous amount of requests for a boy doll."

The phrase "boy doll" was, at that point, almost an oxymoron. Toymen had long sold tin soldiers and masculine figurines, but to attempt a "doll," the consensus went, was to appeal to a market made up of girls. As toy execs saw it, girls did not want boy dolls. The brave few toy makers who had tried, had failed. Mattel had considered it, of course, though they saw it as a risky experiment better left for a more stable future. "We were scared to death of boy dolls," Ruth said, "and so was the rest of the toy trade." But the public demanded a boyfriend for Barbie, so the company acquiesced. On that, Ruth was unambiguous: "Our consumers pushed us into the Ken doll early."

The sculptors had to consider what a boy Barbie might mean. Ken was to be the first new character in the Barbie universe, and so his design raised questions about the norms of that world. Would they build his persona from scratch, or would they try to follow the same formal rules as the original doll? One of Barbie's distinguishing features, like Lilli's, was her anatomy. She was not the first "adult" doll, but she was blunter about her age. Any kid could pull down her shirt to find two tremendous emblems of adulthood. Ruth figured Ken should have some too. He needed some suggestion of "the male organs," she said. "I was ahead of my time in that respect. I did want them."

The fight started out innocently enough. Ruth asked Mattel's sculptors for a slope of sorts, "nothing outstanding," not even especially realistic. ("None of us wanted a doll with a penis showing," she said). The sculptors responded with blank stares. The Research and Development Department found Ruth's suggestion ludicrous. In fairness, maybe it was. Barbie's breasts had been plenty controversial, and she didn't even have nipples. The doll's claims to anatomical realism ended with the plastic strip between her legs. For Ken to hit the scene with anything more articulated was an invitation for outrage.

The Ken question became so controversial it sucked in staff from across the company—sculptors, costumers, market researchers, advertisers, high-ranking executives. Ruth found an ally in fashion designer Charlotte Johnson; both felt strongly about the doll's penis, though they could barely speak of it. Ruth called it a "bulge." Johnson called it a "bump." When the sculptors pulled up their first mold, all but identical to Barbie below the waist, the women voted it down. The designers came back with a Three Bears assortment of possible Ken crotches. "One was—you couldn't even see it," Johnson recalled. The second was "a little bit rounded," and the third "really *was*." She and Ruth picked the Goldilocks option, the middle one "that was nice-looking."

The men were "terribly embarrassed." The vice presidents, whom Ruth called the "guys who made the decisions in all these things," wanted a "permanent swimsuit"—painted on, to avoid the suggestion of something below. But paint, Johnson countered, would merely whitewash the problem: "Do you know what every little girl in this country is going to do?" she asked. "They are going to sit there and scratch that paint off to see what's under it." She had a point. If Barbie was America's doll, then her boyfriend's bulge or bump or whatever they called it amounted to some blunt symbol of America's virility. There was bound to be some curiosity about just how big it was.

This discussion had reached something like a standstill when Dichter arrived. The doctor was, if nothing else, a strategic choice of consultant. This was a man who got an erection from killing chickens, who called on his colleagues to "put the libido back in advertising." He saw the world as a series of encrypted symbols, and these symbols seemed to always translate as sex. So it was no surprise when Dichter sided with the pro-bulge faction. His own Barbie study had found that kids valued the act of "dressing and undressing" and came to expect a degree of realism as they aged. "Interest in detail is high," he wrote, and thus the child is "quick to look down upon the 'imitation.'"

It was enough to bring the committee to a compromise: Ken would wear a "permanent set of jockey shorts," and keep a subtle lump. The size had to be adjusted once Johnson noticed that pants only exaggerated his proportions ("I realized when we were putting zippers in the fly—and the zipper on top of that bump—it got bigger and bigger.").

But none of it mattered. Once the molds went off to Japan for manufacturing, an engineering supervisor found the shorts too time-consuming and the lump too expensive. The adjustments added "about a cent and a half worth of plastic to the product," Schneider wrote. "He arbitrarily eliminated both." After all that, it turned out, the real arbiter was money.

The Ken that debuted at Toy Fair in March of 1961 was smooth and commando. (Ken was "just like Barbie," one ad seemed to wink, "down to the smallest detail.") Ruth's anger stayed with her for a while. The doll had "almost no bulge," she complained years later. "It was very unrealistic. I never forgave those people."

But it was a feeling she'd get used to. The battle of the bulge distilled the exact kind of clashes Ruth would spend the sixties and seventies fighting, inside Mattel and out. Ken had been the first Barbie character designed in dialogue with the public. But the public would continue weighing in, and Ruth would not always like what they were saying. As the brand grew, so did the company, bringing with it more people, more oversight, more Brutuses scheming for control. In Barbie, Mattel had orchestrated what Dichter called a "craze," and with visibility came scrutiny. And while Ruth wanted Barbie to reflect the world around her, there was rarely consensus on what that world should be.

CHAPTER 8

THE PLAYBOY

The horse trailer smelled faintly of dung. It was a Halloween night in the mid-sixties, and Gwen Florea was standing inside the dim barn-on-wheels, staring at a naked young woman, holding a knot of ankle-length hair. Florea worked at the Mattel Acoustics Lab—the audio-engineering arm responsible for producing the short sound bites, each no longer than 3.24 seconds, that issued from the mouths of Mattel's talking toys. (When Talking Barbie first spoke in 1968, it was Florea's voice that came out.) Tonight, she was technically off the clock. But the party was work-related; one of her bosses, Jack Ryan, was its host.

Ryan was a titan at mid-century Mattel. Overseeing the expensive and secretive Research and Development Department, he had authored some thousand patents over his career, including several for Barbie. But Ryan was also famous for his parties: crowded, star-studded, frequently drug-fueled, and often orgiastic—the kind of affairs frequented by "fortune-tellers, jugglers, handwriting analysts, calypso musicians, go-go dancers, minstrels, and harpsichordists," as his second wife, the actress Zsa Zsa Gabor, recalled.

Ryan had summoned his subordinate to deal with a crisis. He was still legally married to, and lived with, his first wife. But he tended to collect girlfriends, often blondes who bore a striking resemblance to Barbie. At the time, he was seeing a girl named Kimberli, who had planned to attend the party dressed as Lady Godiva. Ryan liked to make an entrance, and for this one he had rented a "live white horse with a liveried handler." Kimberli would ride in bareback, with nothing on but an ankle-length, blonde wig, custom designed by Mattel's in-house hairstylist and glued where necessary to cover the key bits.

But on the evening of the party, as the would-be Godiva tried to assemble her hairshirt, she'd dropped it in the lightless trailer. The fumbling that ensued refashioned the weave into a knotted mass. Whatever glue the stylist had used became unstuck. Strands that, minutes before, had been combed into careful locks, now formed new alliances with faraway tufts. Ryan asked Florea, a former hairstylist, to see what could be salvaged. So in the darkness, she wrapped the girl with a nearby blanket. Using a "makeshift wig stand from a pitchfork," Florea set about chopping, cutting off the sections too tangled to repair, trimming the edges, trying to hide the more obvious holes. The result was uneven, too short in parts and untethered in the "crucial areas." But it seemed presentable enough. When Kimberli emerged, a handler dressed in "medieval regalia" helped her onto the bareback horse. The wrangler held the reins, while Ryan, who had come dressed as a knight in custom-built armor, steered the trio toward the party.

The Halloween party was for a group called the Thespian Club, which had a playhouse across the street—one that handily featured "horse-sized doors." Ryan had planned for Godiva to ride in accompanied by the wrangler, three liveried trumpeters, and himself, in all his armor, at which point the pair would toast before the applauding crowd. Each of Ryan's stunts, Florea said, was meticulous, plotted "like a missile launch." And at first, everything seemed to go as scheduled: the baroque trumpet soundtrack, the grand entrance, the drinks proffered via silver tray by another medievally dressed server. The animal was a "veteran stunt horse and a movie experienced actor," the wrangler had said. He would behave. But after the toast, both Lady Godiva and her steed started to squirm. A quick, whispered conference with Ryan and some rapid arm gestures signaled to the wrangler to help the lady dismount. Kimberli tried to swing her pantsless leg over the horse. But the animal lurched sideways. The girl locked her legs around its middle only to slide left, falling off its back and directly between its feet.

What remained of the wig did not provide much cover. For his part, the so-called veteran stunt horse was not holding it together either. "He knocked over a drink table and sent ice, glasses and bottles across the floor," Florea recalled. "People screamed." Florea threw a black velvet curtain over the crying Kimberli and escorted her out. The next morning, Florea heard a rumor that Ryan and his date had wound up in the emergency room. As Florea put it: "Apparently, bare horsehair and bare bottoms don't mix."

⸺

All told, cantering livestock and shrieking naked women were not unusual appearances at a Jack Ryan affair. He hosted some 150 parties a year, attended by a who's who of mid-century America. Many of the people at Mattel in those years, before everything became so serious, called the company a "family." Jack Ryan was some cross between its free-spirited aunt and its alcoholic uncle.

The former missile designer was a living symbol of the company's success, in a fairly literal sense. When Mattel hired Ryan, they could not yet match his missile engineer salary. But they offered him something else. He came on not as a full-time employee, but as an independent contractor. For every patent he got approved, he received a percentage of that product's gross sales. As Mattel's revenue skyrocketed, so did Ryan's royalties. He was the rare inventor who made millions, and he spent them living like a prince. He outfitted his own 1935 Reo fire engine with "operative pumps and a stereo tape deck" and drove it around Los Angeles like a party bus.

Ryan's eccentricity seemed, at times, to rub off on Barbie, perhaps a side effect of his unusual compensation scheme. In the sixties, Barbie began amassing new features, many of which Ryan patented as his own inventions—removable wigs for 1963's "Fashion Queen Barbie"; bendable legs for "Miss Barbie" the next year; and reversible hair dye thanks to 1965's "Color 'n Curl Hair Set." She finally learned how to dance in 1967, when "Twist 'n Turn Barbie" gave the doll a patented rotating waist.

Barbie's house became more elaborate too. Her modest cardboard ranch home from 1962 evolved into a grander construction in 1965, with a range of add-ons—a pink heart-speckled "Dream Room," a fully stocked "Kitchen-Dinette," and a "Barbie Doll and Ken Little Theatre," which came with changeable sets for six possible "productions." For

King Arthur, Ken dressed as a medieval knight with a full suit of armor. Barbie played Guinevere, another noblewoman of legend; this one came with clothes.

⁂

Jack Ryan knew something about dream houses. He had grown up in Westchester County just north of New York City, the scion of a celebrity contractor father, who designed homes for every A-lister from Katharine Hepburn to the Hearsts. Ryan's taste for upscale shelter followed him into adulthood; while Mattel was developing Barbie's Dreamhouse, the engineer was working on his own, though his was a bit bigger, in that it was a castle and regularly compared to a theme park.

The same year Barbie bought her first house, Ryan scooped up the second-oldest home in the affluent enclave of Bel-Air. It was the former residence of actor Warner Baxter, who'd installed a labyrinth of secret passageways hidden behind wooden panels. The sprawling lot had been subdivided and sold off when Baxter passed (he got an elective lobotomy in 1951, then died from pneumonia three weeks later). But Ryan bought the two adjoining parcels and recombined them into a nearly five-acre estate, complete with a 16,000-square-foot Tudor mansion, which had, not two or three, but seven kitchens, and so many other rooms and chambers that he siloed five of them—including Baxter's original hidey-hole, with its secret stairwell—into his own private quarters. He could access the rest of the house, which he called the "family" area, via a special door that only opened from one side.

Ryan was obsessed with the sacral excess of medieval architecture and the perpetual connectivity promised by technological progress. His home combined elements of both. Visitors passed through the iron gates and across an actual moat, before arriving at a wooden drawbridge and towers outfitted with battlements. An Edenic assortment of pets roamed the grounds: cats, dogs, hamsters, rabbits, fish, birds, ducks, chickens, at least one pony. (He talked about installing animatronic alligators in his moat, which would snap on command.) The front door was taken from a fifteenth-century Spanish castle. A "real Italian royal crest" was involved. The whole place was connected by an elaborate intercom system with some one hundred phones, built from the repurposed parts of a navy destroyer.

At one point, Ryan spent a fortune on oakwood paneling from fellow castle-owner William Randolph Hearst's own estate, though like many of Ryan's ambitious projects, the panels were forgotten when he moved on to his next idea, and so they moldered on the property, uninstalled. "Everything around the house had been bulldozed, jack-hammered, looking something like post–World War II Dresden," his daughter recalled, "because of these constant changes." There was no fun in finishing something, Ryan would say. Then you'd have to stop playing with it.

Reporters flocked to the Ryan compound several times a year. Some profiled his gang of a dozen UCLA frat guys, the so-called "Ryan's Boys" who tended to groundskeeping and party security—wearing custom police costumes with Spanish capes and crests that read "RYAN." Others covered the semiregular dinners where attendees ate meat exclusively with their hands, as Ryan watched from an actual throne, former property of the Prince of Parma. (He'd originally bought it for one of his dozen-odd bathrooms, only to find the hulking gold cathedra didn't fit). The estate was so sprawling and complex he kept a guidebook to track it all. The manual was called *It's a Party*.

Ryan wasn't exactly a Ken. His head was massive, but his eyes were so bulbous they seemed to run out of space—one magazine called them "baggy, cold, saucer-like." Elliot Handler once said he looked like Peter Lorre. But the designer had no problem finding dates. He met Zsa Zsa Gabor after she complained his parties were too loud. (After they wed, he joked: "I had to marry Zsa Zsa to shut her up." After they divorced: "That marriage cost me $400,000 a bang.") The road to divorce began on their honeymoon in Japan, when Gabor discovered her sixth husband was "a full-blown seventies-style swinger." The tip-off allegedly came on the second day, Gabor wrote in her memoir, when Ryan disappeared and hired a local gigolo to take his place in bed. Back on domestic soil, Gabor encountered Ryan's sex "dungeon," which she described as a "torture chamber," lined with black fox fur. The nuptials ended after seven months, when the actress realized Ryan neither planned to give up his castle nor stop sleeping with his "ex-wife and two mistresses, who all lived there with him."

Ryan remarried three more times. His next wife was one of his mistresses, a former secretary whom Ryan had employed since she was sixteen. When she discovered Ryan was, again, having an affair, possibly multiple affairs, she took to drinking. When she gained weight, Ryan divorced her. In the aftermath, as one Ryan biographer wrote, she "stopped eating altogether, even stopped drinking water, became fatally anorexic, and died watching TV in her bed of an apparent heart attack. She was in her thirties."

It wouldn't take a Dichter "depth interview" to understand why Ryan lived the way he did. His childhood had been isolated. His socialite mother refused to let him spend time with other children on the grounds that "they weren't good enough to play with him." Being alone reminded him of his boyhood manor, an ex-girlfriend said, which was "always empty when he was coming home after school."

In adulthood, Ryan seemed to muse on loneliness in every interview he gave. For a time, he considered founding a grant at UCLA for a "scientific study of loneliness." His "life was the laboratory," he told one reporter. "My friends, other scientists, lonely people who live solitary lives." Human feelings were important to him, he was more attuned to latent sorrows than most, and while he "wouldn't say that" *he* was "lonely," he was saying that he had "that need, and a lot of people may have that need and may or may not realize it." That's why he once threw a party and invited his waiters, who give parties but "never get invited" to them. "Some of the loneliest people in the world sit in nightclubs," he explained, "and some of the loneliest people serve them."

(Perhaps it's no surprise that, while Ryan was building his castle, Barbie started to make more friends; she needed to fill her Dreamhouse too.)

※

In the end, really, the thing that mattered to Ryan was "to be, accepted, liked, respected." And for a time, at Mattel, the inventor very much was. Despite all his extracurriculars, Ryan worked as zealously as he drank. During office hours, he played the consummate professional to the point of seeming austere. One designer described him as "very controlled," even "stern." He kept track of everything happening in the building, a quality she attributed to his dyslexia. "In the beginning, I was almost frightened of him," she told me. But she realized he'd acquired certain mannerisms "to overcome his disability." Then at night, he seemed to switch. He breathed exuberance into parties. "The charm, the seduction," another staffer said. "He was a magician."

Ryan was also, in the mind of some, a headache in the realm of public relations. Mattel had spent years trying to desexualize Barbie. But the man who had all but signed her birth certificate had not deployed the same strategy in his well-publicized personal life. The result was a growing division between Ryan and others at Mattel. Charlotte Johnson, who oversaw the fashion design team, would bring her staff to Ryan's parties. She knew the blowouts often "ended up sort of orgies with pot, you name it," Carol Spencer, who worked under her, told me. At an early hour, before any nonsense got underway, Johnson would summon her "girls"—there were few male fashion designers at Mattel in those days—and escort them all home. "She would make sure we got out of there before things got too inappropriate," Spencer said. "She wanted her girls to be above board."

Few colleagues tired of Ryan's schtick as much as the Handlers, and especially Ruth. The Handlers initially tolerated Ryan's extravagance; it attracted publicity, and the growing company needed it. "Any article about Jack usually mentioned he worked at Mattel and he named the Mattel toys," a former secretary said. It's not as if the Handlers were slumming it themselves. They had long since moved out of their cramped apartment into a $400,000 Bel-Air estate (over $4 million in today's money). Elliot had taken up sports cars; at various points, he "owned nearly every make made." But when the lore around Ryan started to attract more attention than any of his inventions, the Handlers began to distance themselves from his lifestyle. "We are very simple people living a very simple personal life," Ruth told one reporter. "Our travel and entertaining is related to business: we're just not swingers."

There was also the matter of credit. "Jack wanted all the credit," Spencer said. Ryan's royalty agreement became more elaborate as Mattel grew—evolving into something so "extraordinarily complex" that only three people understood the contract (Mattel's comptroller, Ryan, and Ryan's lawyer). But because of Ryan's payment scheme, he often insisted that his name appear as the "originator" on new patent applications, even if he was not the primary inventor. "The real originator would be kind of secondary on it," Spencer recalled. As a result, his name appeared on nearly every Mattel patent of the era.

Ryan's tendency toward self-mythology did not endear him to the Handlers, either. The couple was, *The New York Times* reported in 1968, "reluctant to credit any single person with the invention of new toy principles." The tension also partially concerned his fees, which by that point had already grown to some $500,000 a year. More irritating to Ruth, he also liked to style himself as the force behind Barbie. Though the source of Barbie's inspiration was a secret among even high-ranking Mattel staff, Ryan would admit that Barbie was borrowed from a German doll. (When a Mattel archivist came across Lilli and asked about the similarities, Ryan allegedly answered: "Plagiarize, plagiarize, that's how God made your eyes. Now put it back, and I don't ever want to hear you mention that doll again.") But Ryan shared Ruth and Marx's obsession with Barbie's origin story. And in his version, he was its protagonist.

At conferences, he claimed *he* had first noticed Barbara Handler playing with paper dolls. He'd been reminded of his childhood obsession with the pinups in *Esquire* magazine, the very *Jane*-esque cartoons that Ernest Dichter once studied. Ryan had told Ruth about his idea for a doll with a sexy figure, and it was this, he implied, that had primed her to see the potential in Lilli. The proof was in the patent, after all, which he had signed. Not to mention her name, which Ryan insisted had come from his first wife, Barbara.

Ryan's story made some sense—the idea that Barbie's impossible proportions might have been dreamed up by a man. His interest in her body was obvious from his Research and Development Department, where staff staged black-stockinged Barbies in various sexual poses. But it did not sit well with Ruth, who dismissed his influence at every opportunity. Ryan was a brilliant engineer, she would say, but he "couldn't think of anything original."

⁓

The quiet rift between Ryan and Ruth occasionally crept into the public eye. In 1968, *The New York Times* reported that "earlier publicity around Mattel"—which had attributed a range of their top hits to Ryan, including

Barbie—had "caused a top-level chasm that has yet to be bridged." What began as a PR concern evolved into a PR war when, around that time, Ryan hired his own publicist, Russell Birdwell, the celebrity comms maven who had single-handedly managed the media campaign for the movie *Gone with the Wind*. It was Birdwell who booked Ryan on *The Merv Griffin Show* and scored him a photo spread in *Esquire*. The nine-page exposé opened with a photo of Ryan in bed, holding one of his many phones, in nothing but a robe. It included quotes like: "Somebody slept in the guest room. I don't even know who it was."

The article did not disguise its indifference to Mattel's founders. It referred to the Handlers as "The Couple." Tensions between Ruth and Ryan had been rising precipitously during the sixties, erupting over issues both miniature and macro. Ryan, for example, hosted fundraisers for the progressive Jerry Brown and Vietnam war critic George McGovern. When Jane Fonda was ostracized for her early opposition to the war, Ryan kept her on his invite list. Ruth, meanwhile, was more moderate. The Handlers were Democrats on paper but harbored certain conservative aversions to regulation and taxes. Initially opposed to Richard Nixon, Ruth came to like him, serving on not one but two of his national committees and befriending his vice president's wife, Betty Ford.

To many, it seemed the Handlers were trying to wrench their company away from Ryan's influence. "At the end of one of his contracts, they did not renew it," Spencer told me. "And then they worked hard on Barbie to break his patents"—adjusting the designs to avoid parts that Ryan technically owned. Ryan noticed that his "royalty checks were significantly less than they had been in the past," his daughter Ann Ryan recalled. In the early seventies, Ryan sued the company for $24 million, accusing the Handlers of "shortchanging him." A Mattel accountant named Paul Ashcraft confirmed that the company had "falsely computed" Ryan's royalties. But Mattel denied underpaying him: "The simple fact is that Ashcraft does not know what he was talking about."

Ryan's daughter claimed Mattel tried to drag the case out "for as long as possible, hoping that my father would run out of money." If so, the strategy worked. For nearly a decade, Ryan said, nearly all his income was tied up in lawsuits. He had to sell his Dreamhouse, swapping the castle for a rental in a less elite corner of Los Angeles. He fell into a deep depression. His drug abuse escalated. He started cycling through wives and girlfriends faster.* Ryan told friends he believed the Handlers were trying to erase him from Barbie history. And soon, their version became harder to rebut. In 1989, Ryan suffered a severe stroke that left him partially paralyzed. "Little by little, his speech faltered," his former staffer Annie Constantineco recalled. "It was very difficult for him to communicate."

One weekend in August of 1991, he visited Constantineco for lunch. As they sat on her patio, Ryan seemed tired. She offered to help him lie down, escorting him into the guest room. She asked if he was okay. He shook his head, trying to say something. He held a finger gun to his temple and mimed pulling the trigger. At the time, she understood this as a joke. But two days later, at the age of sixty-four, he took his own life with a bullet to the head.

Ryan's death did not soften Ruth's crusade for sole credit as Barbie's inventor. The publicity battle over Barbie lasted well after his death, even as Ruth approached her eighties. In 1994, *The New York Times* wrote a minor news item, a 112-word entry that was less an article than an aside. It referred to Ryan as "Barbie's creator." Ruth wrote in with a correction almost as long as the piece:

> Your Sunday feature "Billion-Dollar Barbie" (March 27) contained an inaccuracy. The late Jack Ryan was not Barbie's creator. My husband, Elliot, and I were the founders of Mattel Toys, and I was the creator of the Barbie doll. Jack Ryan, in his role as head of the research-and-development department, managed some of the design work relating to the doll and her accessories. RUTH HANDLER Los Angeles.

---

*Among them: the actress Robyn Hilton, then known as the "very buxom redhead" Mel Brooks motorboats in *Blazing Saddles*, who had adopted what Ryan's daughter called "a clothing-optional lifestyle." But Hilton perhaps understood Ryan's sadness, having grown up on a three-thousand-acre farm in Idaho, "where out of loneliness," she told the *Spokesman-Review*, "I wrote and acted in plays for the cows."

CHAPTER 9

THE BABYSITTER

Through some act of cosmic sadism, the remnants of Ruth Handler's life are immortalized at the Schlesinger Library, a women's archive in Cambridge, Massachusetts, which also houses the papers of several ideological foes—from the National Organization for Women, to the consumer advocate Esther Peterson (once called "the most pernicious threat to advertising today"), to the children's TV crusader Peggy Charren (whom Ruth thought "was nuts"). Visitors to the bright, angular reading room can sift through the folios of bold-name feminists like Betty Friedan, Angela Davis, and Susan B. Anthony, and many less bold ones too. In the catalog, I saw a listing for Yeastie Girlz, a Berkeley-bred eighties band who describe their music as "live vagina-core acapella rap."

In general, Ruth Handler did not associate with many other women. She especially did not associate with the kinds of women whose papers are now stored in the same climatized basement aisles as her own. She never identified as a feminist and openly scorned those who did. "Women had always bored me," she told one interviewer. She had never liked girls as a child; she "thought 'girl talk' was stupid." She did not have female friends. But as symbolic storage facilities go, there are worse places to wind up. Ruth was the human face behind what had become one of the most recognizable, most reproduced women, or womanlike entities, in the world. And Barbie rose to these heights of femininity at a moment when the country was entering a tense reconsideration of what exactly that category entailed.

In 1960, exactly fourteen months after Barbie launched at Toy Fair, the FDA approved the birth control pill—the first commercial version of the contraceptive developed by Margaret Sanger—and with it hastened the decoupling of sex from one of its most expensive side effects. At the same time, the trope of the "trapped" woman "burst like a boil through the image of the happy American housewife." Mainstream papers and magazines filled with reports of the nation's depressed wives, women who, like Ruth, had not found motherhood to be the life-fulfilling telos they'd been led to expect. The problem was so widespread that pundits began to prescribe drastic measures. One *Harper's* dispatch proposed a national draft to conscript bored women as social workers and baby-sitters.

Something was changing in the public imagination of the second sex, and that change was tied up with commerce. It was also in 1960 that Helen Gurley Brown began writing *Sex and the Single Girl*, a breezy sexual manual for unmarried women whose tips ranged from how to "balance a checkbook" to how "not to have a baby." (The publisher cut the latter chapter as "a commercial consideration.") Brown, a proto-Peggy Olson-cum-Carrie Bradshaw, had worked her way through eighteen secretarial jobs before becoming a copywriter for companies like Max Factor and Lockheed. When her book became a bestseller, she sold the movie rights, wrote several sequels, and took over as editor of *Cosmopolitan* magazine. Brown's vision of femininity both ignored the patriarchal standards of the sexual marketplace and harnessed them; a dogma of self-improvement that sanctioned women to pursue sex as aggressively as men did, while offering her mostly working-class audience a means of social advancement through consumption, transforming the female body into a competitive product that could transcend the strictures of class. "I'm a materialist," Brown told *Time* magazine, "and it is a materialistic world." Not long after *Sex and the Single Girl* hit the market, Sylvia Plath went on the BBC to read "The Applicant," a new poem written like one of Brown's old slick ads. The aggressive salesman of a speaker pitches a hapless bachelor, Plath told the listeners, on a new "marvelous product."

> *A living doll, everywhere you look.*
> *It can sew, it can cook,*
> *It can talk, talk, talk.*

It works, there is nothing wrong with it.
You have a hole, it's a poultice.
You have an eye, it's an image.
My boy, it's your last resort.
Will you marry it, marry it, marry it.

Perhaps no one articulated the role of advertising in the construction of American womanhood more famously than Betty Friedan, Ruth's roommate at the Schlesinger. *The Feminine Mystique* took aim at "the problem that has no name"—a "schizophrenic split" plaguing American women as they struggled to reconcile the reality of their inane lives, she wrote, with "the image to which we were trying to conform." Friedan, a former leftist and labor reporter who had traded her career for a husband and three children, spoke from experience. Potty-training and housekeeping and buying various appliances left her empty. Her marriage was cratering. Her husband called her "that bitch."

Housewife existence seemed a cheap knockoff of the "pretty picture of femininity" that society had promised. Friedan, like Ruth, had paid a visit to the Institute of Dr. Ernest Dichter. She had interviewed "Mr. Mass Motivation Himself" in person and devoted an entire chapter to him in her book, referring to him only as "the manipulator." Dichter and his peers, Friedan argued, had helped subdue the anxieties of domesticated American housewives by redirecting their creative energies away from careers and toward the accumulation of stuff.* As she paraphrased his philosophy: "Properly manipulated ('if you are not afraid of that word,' he said), American housewives can be given the sense of identity, purpose, creativity, the self-realization, even the sexual joy they lack— by the buying of things."

This process of subtle seduction began well before women became wives. "The real crime," Friedan argued, "is the callous and growing

---

*One of Dichter's famed innovations was advising Bisquick to remove powdered egg from its mixes so as to, in Packard's paraphrase, "always leave the housewife something to do." Friedan asked Dichter if he couldn't instead boost the powered egg product by telling women to "use the time saved to be an astronomer." In order to buy more pie mix, "the woman has to want to stay in the kitchen," Dichter replied. "If we tell her to be an astronomer, she might go too far from the kitchen."

acceptance of the manipulator's advice 'to get them young,'" promoting ads "deliberately designed to turn teenage girls into housewife buyers of things before they grow up to be women."

When *The Feminine Mystique* came out in February of 1963, Ruth Handler was thinking about motherhood and marketing herself. Since the introduction of Ken two years prior, customers had begun to agitate for what was still understood to be a natural next step for a young couple, plastic or otherwise: a baby. It was Ruth's intention to keep Barbie as blank as possible, alienating no one. Perhaps Ruth had read that *Harper's* dispatch, because one month after Friedan's book hit stores, Mattel unveiled a strategic compromise. Their new addition to the Barbie universe was not a mother, but a maternal figure, with all the requisite accessories— a bottle, a bassinet, and a small plastic baby. The box included an illustrated booklet called *Barbie the Babysitter*.

"We dared not give Barbie and Ken a baby of their own," Ruth said. "Barbie can babysit. What the child does with the baby is up to her."

Ruth saw the Friedans of the world, at worst, as self-righteous harpies, and at best, as an easy joke. The year *The Feminine Mystique* came out, Ruth gave a speech at UCLA advising undergrads on how to succeed as women in the workplace. "Frankly, with me, the best way I've found is to sleep with the boss," she told the eighteen-year-olds. "I've been doing it for 25 years!" In interviews, she was more direct. The softer sex couldn't handle corporate jobs, she told one outlet. "They just don't want success badly enough. It's a man's world. Things are as they should be."

But if Ruth could separate herself from the nascent women's movement, it became harder to insulate Barbie. The doll's omnipresence made her a perfect figurehead for the national discourse on womanhood; and her blankness, her focus-grouped ambivalence toward not only marriage and motherhood but also women's rights made her the perfect canvas on which any side could project its rage. "Barbie— the Hex Symbol of Modern Woman," read a headline in 1965. The feminist children's writer Eve Merriam slammed Barbie as a "post-Lolita figure," a consumerist idol reducing America into "one interminable stretch of spiritual slum." A year later, Friedan scribbled the acronym

"NOW" on a napkin, then authored the National Organization for Women's first statement of purpose, writing in one section: "we will protest, and endeavor to change, the false image of women now prevalent in the mass media." The group protested outside Toy Fair, slamming the stereotypes in conventional dolls. Plying girls with mini household appliances and practice babies, they argued, reduced their nascent image of women to that of "either homemakers or sex objects." The group reserved its "greatest wrath," one article noted, for the industry's idol to vanity, Barbie.

Not all of Barbie's critics were feminists. In the press, one father described his "almost pathological hatred" for the doll he called "that bitch." She was craven, pornographic, "lascivious," as another parent told *The Wall Street Journal*, "the archetype of everything that's wrong with American culture." In a sense, Mattel had sold Barbie too well. They had pitched this doll as a good influence on girls. Now she was established and influential, and customers were wondering how good her influence was. "Just what is the character that Mattel and its affiliated corporations are molding? Do they want a nation of power-mad girls bent on establishing an all-female government?" asked *Ramparts*, the New Left magazine whose countercultural bona fides had evidently not matured in the arena of gender politics. To anyone with a basic grasp on financial incentives, it was obvious that Barbie's claims to influence were in service of her sales, but some started to assume the inverse. "Mattel is less interested in making money," *Ramparts* wrote, "than in shaping the coming generation."

Mattel was certainly interested in making money; the question was how. A splintering society turned out to be harder to synthesize in 11.5-inch outfits. But the Handlers certainly tried. Mattel's sixties catalogs seemed calibrated to their loudest critiques. The same year Barbie began babysitting, Mattel released "Midge," a blander "best friend" with a less femme-fatale face. Her body was identical to Barbie's so she could share her wardrobe, which grew to include garb for either outlook on women's lib—a "Graduation" outfit, but also a "Bride's Dream" gown; a "Career Girl" pantsuit, but also a domestic ensemble called "Apron and Utensils." Barbie finally moved past pink-collar careers in 1965 by going to space as "Miss Astronaut," but soon after came her "Togetherness" look—a matching set named for the then-ubiquitous campaign from *McCall's* magazine, which emphasized women's obligations to the family and home.

If these outfits offered slightly different takes on traditional gender roles, they shared an aversion to anything "too controversial." (Barbie and Midge are always portrayed "as well-dressed young ladies," a Mattel advertising manager wrote in a letter. "At no time do we show them in 'beatnick' or 'sloppy' outfits which would 'horrify' adults.") In any case, customers did not buy Barbie's less-sexualized friend. After disappointing sales, Mattel executives instructed contractors to eliminate Midge "from your thinking."

Some Barbie historians have upheld one stylistic choice as a turning point. For her first decade, Barbie's face had been frozen in a sidelong glance inherited from *Bild* Lilli. Ken debuted staring the customer straight-on, but the women looked out, unfocused, into some hazy middle distance. But in the late sixties, Mattel began to experiment with a more direct gaze. By the time Malibu Barbie hit the market in 1971, the doll's eyes bored straight into her viewer's. Some hailed this transition as a rupture as radical as Manet's *Olympia*, an observable transition from submissive passivity to dominant agency, though this subtext may have been lost on the average five-year-old. At minimum, it's hard to read much into any change that gave Mattel something else to copyright, as they had Malibu Barbie's head three years prior.

Certainly, whenever Mattel released anything that could be construed as progressive, they seemed to counter it with something more staid. "The toy industry has spoken," Mattel executive Walter Ross said in a speech. "If you are zealous about women's lib—so are we; if you think it's foolish—we sympathize with that view; if you couldn't care less—we won't insist."

Perhaps the feminist movement's most iconic protest took place outside the 1968 Miss America pageant in Atlantic City. A group called New York Radical Women had set up a "huge Freedom Trash Can" and invited activists and women of every persuasion for a cathartic binning of all the accessories of commercial femininity. Participants were encouraged to bring their own "woman-garbage," a category that read like a list of Barbie accessories: "bras, girdles, curlers, false eyelashes, wigs," issues of Gurley Brown's *Cosmo*, and other "instruments of female torture." The event became a national news story—a sign of the movement's ascension into public consciousness, if not yet the mainstream. "A word to ardent feminists and women's liberation members," one newspaper sneered the following year. "This Christmas season is relatively unchanged in terms of traditionally oriented toy buying."

But Mattel responded in its own way. A year after Malibu Barbie hit the market, customers became acquainted with the "Miss America" dolls—a pair of beauty pageant Barbies. One could strut down a runway; the other could curl her hair. The dolls were sponsored by Laurel Lea Schaefer, the reigning Miss America of 1972.

Barbie may have figured out eye contact, in other words, but she was far from throwing her hot iron in the Freedom Can. In interviews, Ruth tamped down any expectation that Barbie would be bra burning in the immediate future. As one headline put it: "No Liberation for Barbie."

It wasn't that Ruth didn't know what the libbers were talking about. She would recall one time when she was scheduled to address some stock analysts. She and Elliot arrived at the office of the hosting firm to find two men waiting outside. The men walked them indoors to the elevator bank, pressed the right button, and led them off to the same floor. But as the doors glided shut, the first stockbroker steered Elliot in one direction; the second guided Ruth in another. While Elliot headed straight to the private room reserved for their meeting, Ruth was led on a labyrinthine trek, through the bowels of the building, past the kitchen and garbage room, before finally arriving at the same room where Elliot had already gone and where some twenty other men were waiting for Ruth. "There were no women in the financial community," she explained. Much of the building, it turned out, was limited to men.

Ruth had been here before. Not this building, but this situation. There was the time she was scheduled to speak in Chicago, only for the venue to change at the last minute because "women were not allowed." Or the time she'd shown up for a special event with the chairman of the Federal Reserve and wondered why the audience had been crammed into a "very strangely shaped" multipurpose hall far too small for the crowd of several hundred. Her tablemate told her: "Because of you."

(Ruth was the first, and then only, woman board member of a Federal Reserve bank.) Maybe the most insulting was when she became the first woman vice president of the Toy Association's board. The news came with a caveat. The association had arranged, for the first time ever, to appoint a second, male vice president, lest a woman be in line for the presidency. "It was not a glass ceiling in those days," Ruth said. "It was concrete."

By the mid-sixties, Ruth had already served as Mattel's executive vice president for more than two decades. When *Fortune* surveyed the 6,500 executives at America's top companies, Ruth was one of only eleven women. But Ruth did not see herself as evidence that women could cut it in business; she saw herself as an exception, a "freak," who had more in common with men. She swore constantly. She had a crass sense of humor. She was a brutal boss; colleagues called her Ruthless, or on occasion, "that bitch."* Once she met with an East Coast buyer who remarked that she was "not at all what I expected." They were sitting in her office at Mattel's Hawthorne headquarters. Ruth wasn't sure what he meant. "Well, from what I'd heard," he explained, "I thought you'd have your feet up on the desk and you'd be barking orders and have a cigar sticking out of the side of your mouth."

If Ruth had wanted more women in her rooms, she was well positioned to invite them in. But her C-suite remained nearly all-male. She also had the opportunity to influence federal policy. In 1972, the year Miss America Barbie came out, Ruth was appointed to several oversight committees in the Nixon administration, including the "Advisory Committee on the Economic Role of Women." The group was tasked with drafting a set of guidelines for corporations on how best to establish equality in the workforce—and at a crucial moment. That summer, Congress had passed the Equal Opportunity Act, an amendment to the Civil Rights Act that strengthened Title VII's protections against employment discrimination. Among other things, it authorized the Equal Employment Opportunity Commission to haul non-compliant

---

*One former Mattel employee remembered sitting in the office of vice president Cliff Jacobs, when Ruth rang. "Over his phone speaker, I heard her say: 'Cliff, get your ass up here,'" he said. "As soon as Cliff put the phone down and rushed out, he was saying: 'That bitch gave me one heart attack, and she isn't going to give me another one.'"

companies into court. As part of her role, Ruth helped draft recommendations for the private sector on how to adopt policies, from affirmative action to maternity leave.

Ruth, of course, understood the appeal of maternity leave. After her own pregnancies, she'd been desperate to return to work, and she'd been able to do so on her own terms. But few other women had that option. Companies in the fifties and sixties rarely offered maternity leave; many corporations at that time required pregnant women to resign. Only in 1972 did the EEOC determine that pregnancy (as well as childbirth, miscarriage, and abortion) should be covered by benefits and granted appropriate leave—a recommendation that was instantly contested by lawsuits. Opponents complained that it would be too expensive, too onerous. But initially, the Nixon committee intended to advise companies to follow it.

In the original draft, the committee members called on companies to treat maternity leave "the same as any other temporary disability"—offering the same health insurance, job retention guarantees, and pay. But Ruth deleted that section by hand—literally crossing it out in red pen, citing "significant cost increases for employers." Ruth wrote: "Since there is great controversy regarding this subject and it is being disputed in the courts, I feel we should await such resolution." She told the committee, in other words, not to put its thumb on the scale, but to wait until a court struck the provision down—as the Supreme Court did, four years later.

Ruth also deleted provisions for both paternity leave and health benefits for part-time workers, an accommodation for mothers who could not work full-time. ("This treads too heavily on the economic decision making power of companies," she wrote of the clause on part-time benefits.) She eliminated the draft's few references to race, replacing the phrase "women and minorities, including minority women," with just "women and men"—on the grounds that the former seemed "to discourage men." And perhaps most notably, she took aim at a page on sexist portrayals of women in the media. As one paragraph read:

> The subcommittee urges the media to examine voluntarily their output and carefully purge them of unnecessary sexist content.

Particular attention should be given to TV commercials directed to young children and to advertising that seeks to make the using of a product important for maintaining one's sexual identity or for maintaining successful inter-personal relationships with members of the opposite sex.

The committee might as well have come out and ordered Mattel to rethink Barbie's entire branding strategy. The subtext was not lost on Ruth. "I would recommend that all of the 'media' section starting on page 18 be deleted," she wrote to the committee chair. "I feel that it is too far removed from the main topic and that the issue is controversial and deserves more discussion."

Barbie was supposed to reflect the world, but she couldn't "reflect every facet of life," Ruth explained, "only some—the better facets." It was a telling comment. Because for years, neither Ruth nor her feminist critics seemed to notice that Mattel had chosen one particular facet to reflect in Barbie's design—that their rendering of the all-American everywoman, the "blank" doll onto which kids could supposedly project themselves, was, by default, white.

CHAPTER 10

FRANCIE

Eight days after Barbie bombed at Toy Fair New York in 1959, a new film debuted in Chicago. *Imitation of Life* was the final feature of Douglas Sirk, another German immigrant and a director of fifties melodramas, often dismissed by contemporaries as "lady's pictures." His latest focused on a black mother, a white mother, and their two daughters. The white mother is a professional imitator, a middling actress too busy to look after the blonde and oblivious Susie (a "Barbie-doll child," a critic said). The black mother moves in to care for Susie, bringing her own daughter, Sarah Jane, who is white-passing, and old enough to notice that Susie moves through life with the edges sanded off. Sarah Jane's frustration becomes obvious when the two girls play with dolls. "Here Sarah Jane, you can have Nancy," Susie says, offering up her black doll. "I don't want the black one," Sarah Jane answers, grabbing the white version. Her mother puts the black doll back in her arms. But Sarah Jane lets it fall to the floor.

Imitation was an imitation itself: a remake of a 1934 film, which was itself an adaptation of a Fannie Hurst novel by the same name. And the movie toyed endlessly with its own premise, blurring the ersatz and the "authentic," the fiction and the "fact." "*Imitation of Life* imitated life," one critic noted, by casting Lana Turner, "an actress estranged from her daughter," as the white mother, "an actress estranged from her daughter." (In the movie, Susie tries to seduce her mother's boyfriend; in real life, a year earlier, Turner's daughter had stabbed hers.) The doll scene offered another rhyme with the real. Sirk's choice of dolls as symbols of racial consciousness also invoked, intentionally or otherwise, a landmark psychology study conducted the decade prior by a married couple known as the Clarks.

Mamie and Kenneth Clark were partners, academic collaborators, and respectively, the first black woman and man to receive psychology doctorates from Columbia. At Howard University, Mamie focused her master's degree on the question of when racial identity emerged in children. Observing a local preschool, she wondered how these small children, some as young as three, were taking in their surroundings, Hoovering up the detritus of the world, assimilating scraps of data into the fragile scaffolding of inner being. Her thesis, a study of 150 preschoolers, found that black children seemed to become conscious of their race as early as the age of three. This confused her. "I didn't have any self-hatred," Mamie said, "and I couldn't figure out why, when all these children that we were looking at seemed not to like themselves." (She was singular, Kenneth would say, being "something of a heckler in class" who "never wanted to imitate anyone.")

Kenneth, disturbed by his wife's results, joined in on her research. In 1947, they conducted another study, this time using dolls. At a New York dime store, they bought four dolls for fifty cents a pop. The toys were nude, save the diapers, and nearly identical: one pair was black, the other white. The Clarks directed children to select a doll based on instructions: Which was the "nice doll"? Which was the "doll that looks bad"? Which doll was a "nice color"? Some two-thirds said they liked the white doll "best." Fifty-nine percent thought the black doll looked "bad." The black children, on the whole, not only preferred the white dolls, but thought they looked nicer, prettier, and cleaner.

The first of a series later dubbed the "Doll Tests," the Clarks' study was about as close to a blockbuster as one could find in academic psychology. *Ebony* profiled the couple in 1947. In 1950, the White House asked Kenneth to draft a report on the impacts of prejudice—which wound up in the hands of Thurgood Marshall. The future Supreme Court justice was working on *Briggs v. Elliot*, a civil rights case challenging school segregation in South Carolina. He needed to show the court that Jim Crow inflicted measurable damage on children, and the Doll Tests, so simple and straightforward, seemed to illuminate in miniature the country's moral crisis.

Marshall brought on Kenneth as an expert witness. The Clarks went on to testify for two similar trials in Delaware and Virginia—later consolidated into the 1954 Supreme Court case *Brown v. Board of Education of Topeka, Kansas*. Chief Justice Earl Warren cited Kenneth in his opinion. Later studies would fail to reproduce the Clarks' results, leading some to speculate that the findings varied with cultural understandings of race. But the Doll Tests became a potent national symbol: an agent of legal change and a synecdoche for fifties racial discourse in digestible doll-size.

The toy industry, though, did not seem to be paying attention. "All the toys one commonly sees are essentially a microcosm of the adult world," Roland Barthes wrote three years after *Brown v. Board of Education*. But for most of the mid-century, "blonde-haired, blue-eyed dolls," as one article put it, were "in the overwhelming majority"—so homogenous that even a white doll with brown eyes was greeted as a win for representation. Black doll makers had made many alternatives, but they struggled to find wide distribution. Even civil rights activist Sara Lee Creech, who mounted what one magazine called "the most laborious toy project in history," failed to gain much traction. Creech's proposal for four black dolls was backed by former first lady Eleanor Roosevelt, boosted by David Rockefeller and Jackie Robinson, and organized in collaboration with Creech's friend, the writer Zora Neale Hurston (who, as it happened, had her own ties to *Imitation of Life*, having worked for Fannie Hurst while she was writing the novel). Ideal Toy Company released one of the so-called Sara Lee dolls in 1951, but "ultimately sabotaged" Creech's effort to expand the line. The first was discontinued after just two years.

The Handlers introduced a black doll earlier than most toy companies, with 1962's "Colored Chatty Cathy," a version of Mattel's popular pull-string talking doll from 1959. And unlike other concerns—which, if they had black offerings at all, rarely promoted them—Mattel promoted the doll beside their white products. Mattel's experiment in diversity, however, did not include Barbie. Mattel found no reason to consider adding a black doll to the Barbie line until after August of 1965, when something happened near their headquarters that they tried, but failed, to ignore.

That month, a white highway patrolman pulled over a black

twenty-one-year-old named Marquette Frye. The cop was driving in Watts, a small neighborhood in one of South Central L.A.'s seven nearly all-black census tracts—a geography of what historian Mike Davis called "suburban apartheid," cut off from transit and, by extension, jobs. The cop claimed Frye was drunk driving; Frye, his mother, and many eyewitnesses claimed the cop beat him. As word spread, a crowd formed, fights broke out, the city erupted into protests. For six days, more than a hundred thousand Angelenos took to the streets, overflowing from Watts across South Central, eventually claiming a territory larger than Manhattan. The capital deployed some sixteen thousand officers, including the National Guard. Thirty-four people died, more than a thousand were injured, and four thousand arrested. California's attempt to crush the "mad dogs," as future governor Ronald Reagan would put it, effectively rendered Los Angeles a war zone. The chant of the moment was "Burn, Baby, Burn."

Mattel's headquarters in Hawthorne, California, were situated only nine miles west of Watts, but they might as well have been nine hundred. The six-square-mile hamlet sold itself as "the most beautiful suburban town." "To you who are planning to move to Hawthorne—now or in the future," the Chamber of Commerce wrote in a 1950s ad, "we say HOWDY and WELCOME!" The greeting was a misnomer. Like many L.A. suburbs, Hawthorne was a sundown town. Some residents still remembered when the city limit was marked with a sign: "N***er, Don't Let The Sun Set On YOU In Hawthorne."

This was Barbie's adopted home. Hawthorne's most famous inanimate resident was not just white, but blonde-haired, blue-eyed, and as distinctly Aryan as her German predecessor, though few knew it at the time. If the Handlers, both Jewish, had qualms about rendering Barbie as a textbook shiksa, they did not talk about it publicly. But perhaps because of their own experience with discrimination, they made a point of embracing progressive race relations, at least as employers. Mattel's mostly female workforce had always been integrated. "If you look at our production lines, you'll see that the women are white, black, Latino, Oriental," Ruth boasted. "We were proud to have the rainbow coalition." As the Los Angeles Conference on Community Relations wrote in a letter to Ruth: "A tour of your plant is like walking through the United Nations."

But in the aftermath of Watts, Vice President Hubert Humphrey called on Los Angeles's top business leaders to do something "imaginative and constructive" to employ more black workers. Only one company listened and it was the missile manufacturer Aerojet General—not Mattel. For the moment, Barbieland had other priorities. In a retrospective on the doll's first three decades, *Barbie* magazine skipped over 1965 entirely. The spread summed up the year after with a picture of a Tupperware party. "Mom and Dad and the leaders they elected tried to keep a lid on things in the turbulent mid-sixties," read the caption. "Our inner cities burned, but the pot roast couldn't."

⁂

Mattel was instead working on developing Barbie's cousin, Francie Fairchild. The first Francie, a white doll that debuted in 1966, was in some ways the company's attempt to listen to its critics. Most of Barbie's friends were built with identical bodies, so they could be dressed interchangeably in her extensive wardrobe. But Francie did not have the same cartoonish measurements. She was pitched as Barbie's British cousin: a "MODern" gal with a less elliptical silhouette. She had smaller breasts. She was "less endowed and less curvaceous," Ruth said. The toy trend that year was for more "realistic" dolls, and Francie rose to the challenge on "lifelike bendable legs," looking out from beneath humanlike eyelashes. For her slighter frame, customers could buy outfits with vaguely WASPish names like "Gad Abouts" and "Clam Diggers."

Francie would have been already in the works when Los Angeles went into lockdown. But in 1967, Mattel followed up with "Colored Francie," a version of the British mod and the first black doll within the Barbie line. But much had changed in the five years since "Colored Chatty Cathy," not least the word "colored." The label was dated when Mattel used it the first time. Black organizations had "virtually abandoned" the descriptor by the thirties in favor of "negro," which, by the sixties, was itself becoming passé. In 1967, "colored" was "outmoded, even racist," theorist Ann duCille observed. Deploying the term "in the midst of civil rights and black power activism," she cracked, "suggested that while Francie might be 'MOD'ern,' Mattel was still in the dark(y) ages."

That year, toy makers were still touting their products as more realistic than ever before. Mattel itself said its space toys were scaled with actual NASA size data and that its assault rifle sounded just like the real thing. But the black Francie had evidently not demanded the same attention to detail. She was almost identical to the white version, save her skin. Some have suggested that the black Francie's lack of distinction was merely a matter of timing. Amid the post-Watts urgency to "unite the community in the healing process," historian Kitturah Westenhouser offered, Mattel was "up against the deadline" of the next Toy Fair. They didn't have time to design a new doll from scratch, she argued. Like Lilli, Francie was chosen to "fill the void." It was a generous reading, though duCille gave a blunter one: "Mattel saw a marketing opportunity and rushed into the fray with an all-deliberate speed that integration otherwise lacked."

Within a few months, it became clear that the black Francie wasn't selling. The white Francie had performed well enough, but her counterpart had not attracted white buyers—to whom the implied relation of black and white dolls perhaps evoked, as Barbie Hall of Fame founder Evelyn Burkhalter suggested, not just integration, but miscegenation. Nor did she seem to appeal to black buyers. "Mattel says a 'small but vocal minority' criticizes the use of Caucasian features on Francie, Barbie's Negro cousin," *The Wall Street Journal* reported that fall. Buyer trepidation was not new for Mattel. Barbie, after all, had received a similarly cool reception. But while Ruth had gone lengths to improve the original doll's prospects, Francie did not enjoy the same efforts. Mattel released a second model the next year, with brown hair and slightly darker skin. But she was shelved just months later, her remaining stock relegated to the warehouse floor.

In the meantime, the Johnson administration kept up the pressure, asking Mattel to participate in a new program to train South L.A. workers and hire them in permanent roles. The Handlers were suspicious of government oversight. Mattel "preferred to act entirely on its own instead of participating in job training," a report on the program noted, "as it had been asked to." The Handlers needed to find some other gesture of civic responsibility, which led them to a project called Operation Bootstrap.

CHAPTER 11

OPERATION BOOTSTRAP

When it was first coined in the late eighteenth century, the expression "pull yourself up by your bootstraps" meant something absurd, something that couldn't be done. Physically speaking, when you think through the motions, it is impossible. That the phrase is now beloved by libertarians, "fiscal conservatives," and grumpy tax-thrifts amounts to some rich self-revelation. When Operation Bootstrap first lifted itself up in the wake of Watts, the fact of its name attracted attention from the right. Conservative TV host George Putnam (who would later launch the career of fedora-enthusiast Matt Drudge) was the first to cover the project. Ronald Reagan himself reached out to pitch an idea. "Even the ultra-right-wing John Birch Society," one historian wrote, "dispatched volunteers to help paint OB's new office space."

Bootstrap's conservative flirtations were something of a wink on the part of its founders, Robert Hall and Lou Smith. The two men were not themselves right-wingers, but civil rights activists, both of whom had been affiliated with the Congress of Racial Equality, or CORE. Smith, an East Coast transplant, had been dispatched to build out the organization's wallowing Los Angeles chapter. Hall, an out-of-work salesman, had once numbered among CORE's most active L.A. members, but chafed against the leadership's passivity and fears of "communist infiltration," and left to start his own group.

Smith had been inspired by Leon Sullivan, a Baptist minister who'd taken over an abandoned jailhouse in Philadelphia and opened a job training program of his own. Sullivan had urged a practice of "self-help" which resonated with Smith and Hall. The pair felt that politicians, not least President Lyndon Johnson, had missed the moment to take up the cause of civil rights, that if anyone was going to do something for South Central, activists needed to do it themselves. Hall and Smith envisioned Operation Bootstrap as a kind of multipurpose organizational hub combining adult education classes, political action, black empowerment, job training, and a series of private ventures whose profits would feed back into the neighborhood. The ultimate goal was to construct what Smith called "Freedom City," a community-run, self-policed haven, using profit from its own businesses to provide residents with specialized schooling "from preschool up to a University of Watts."

Though they named the project "Operation Bootstrap," Smith and Hall had no intention of going it alone. But they wanted donations without strings attached, and Watts had eroded their trust in bureaucrats who "seek to control." Public money, by their logic, seemed to cede authority. As an early Bootstrap statement announced: "We do not solicit government funding." They hoped to show that business did not "have to be a greedy, gimme kind of thing." But the duo's receptivity to corporate capital divided black power groups enough that Smith had to defend the decision in an open letter. ("We must use the system's weapon against it," he wrote.) As *Black Enterprise* put it, Hall and Smith "were out on the streets, telling the Brothers to forget about welfare and government subsidies and pull themselves up by their own bootstraps with private capital."

This was exactly the kind of thing the Handlers liked to hear. Elliot Handler met with Smith and Hall in March of 1968, after the group had converted an abandoned auto parts building into a homegrown academy, repurposing the old Watts chant into a new motto: "Learn, Baby, Learn!" The school offered a suite of classes in everything from nurses' aide training to computer programming to black history, and had graduated some 400 students free of charge. Bootstrap had launched multiple businesses: a fashion brand specializing in African fabrics and motifs, two boutiques, a body shop, and a publishing arm for black media. The group's theater troupe, the Bootstrap Players, had written and performed an original play, *A Glass House Shattered*.

Over the course of two meetings, Elliot, Hall, and Smith sketched out another company to add to the roster: a toy business. Smith was aware of the Clarks' tests. "It was frightening," he said of the study. "It was also ridiculous." A doll company—with its educational possibilities and the prospect of influencing young minds, as Barbie had done—seemed a fitting addition to Freedom City. They called the company Shindana, from the Swahili word for "competitor."

The conditions of the arrangement suited both sides. Lou Smith and Robert Hall would serve as Shindana's president and general manager. Mattel, in turn, would provide about $150,000 up front as well as advisory support—making their manufacturing manager, sales specialist, and PR firm available as on-call counsel. One vice president led a marketing seminar. Otherwise, Mattel stayed out of the way. "One of the major stipulations of the agreement," a 1969 *Ebony* article noted, "was that Mattel's help must be offered with no strings attached."

On Bootstrap's third anniversary in October of 1968, Shindana cut the ribbon on cavernous yellow plant in South Central. The widely publicized event was attended by then-mayor Sam Yorty. "It is the first instance," the *L.A. Times* wrote, "of a major corporation in Los Angeles setting up a complete plant, training the staff, and handing over full ownership and management to a Negro community organization."

The firm already had a mock-up of their first toy. The founders did not want their toys to be merely nominally "black"—the kind they characterized as, basically, white dolls "dipped in chocolate." They wanted "to create a doll with our features—features we are known for having," a Shindana executive told *The Atlanta Journal*, "like heavy lips, short noses. Our cheek bones are different." The notion of the "ethnically correct" doll was perhaps a fraught category, as later critics noted, the implication of distilling an "authentic" phenotype redolent of racial essentialism. "How does black look? How does woman look?" Ann duCille wrote. "What would make a doll look authentically African American or realistically Nigerian or genuinely Jamaican?"

Shindana's answer was to draw on local children for inspiration. They surveyed nearby students, soliciting drawings of their ideal doll. The first mold's features were modeled on a real girl from Los Angeles. The result was Baby Nancy, a vinyl doll with a pink dress and a detachable bottle; when fed, she could wet the bed. She debuted at Toy Fair the following

February, in an exhibition space lent by Mattel. In its first year, Shindana produced 130,000 dolls—distributed around the States, as well as in Australia, Japan, and New Zealand. The company grew from twenty to seventy-five employees, churning out some thousand dolls a week. They released a second version of Baby Nancy with natural hair—a head of short Saran curls so unprecedented that it had called for a new production technique. Shindana's line workers had to sew the plastic hairs onto the doll's head, one designer said, "then stick it into the oven and it would crinkle up."

Two seasons later, Shindana had paid off their debt and turned a quarter-million-dollar profit. The company had a direct answer to Barbie: Wanda Career Girl, a bendable fashion doll whose jobs ranged from doctor to zoologist, each accompanied by a booklet highlighting a real black woman who worked in that role. By the mid-seventies, the catalog grew to include six games and thirty-two dolls. Among them: Malaika, whose locally made outfits borrowed from West African prints, Talking Tamu, named for the Swahili word for "sweet," and Slade the Super-Agent, a "tough secret agent out to stop corruption," modeled on the leather-clad P.I. from *Shaft*. When their Flip Wilson toy—a two-sided plushie that "flipped" between the popular comedian and his drag alter ego Geraldine—became their first "million-dollar hit," Shindana used the proceeds to open a preschool providing workers daycare. They spurned war toys in favor of more wholesome male models, partnering with NBA player Julius Winfield Erving II for a "Dr. J" doll and a pre-murder* O. J. Simpson, whose first wife happened to be their head designer's cousin.

But Shindana struggled to find major customers. Initially, distributors were reluctant to buy black toys. "Nobody took them on as a real product that they could make money on," designer James Edwards said. "You'd go in there and they'd say, 'What do you jungle bunnies want? We gave last year.'" When Shindana's sales proved the demand for black dolls, other more established companies simply released their own, often at lower cost. The company had to contend with a much more saturated toy market, and without their rivals' resources. As the Watts riots receded into hindsight, Bootstrap's support network started to lose interest. "Volunteer

---

*Alleged.

teachers and donations fell away," one paper wrote, "leaving silence in the place of many day and night classes."

By the time Mattel wound down their involvement in 1969, Shindana had secured a $200,000 loan from Chase Manhattan Bank, which touted its support in magazine ads. ("A good motive for change is the profit motive.") But as overhead rose, the company struggled to pair their social ambitions with the pressures of growth. "There is a conflict," Mattel executive Art Spear had told them, "between sociological objectives and economic objectives." At one point, Smith's wife Marva said, the workers "in the factory itself were ninety percent community people." They had intended to make every part in Watts too, but doing so would have hindered their ability to compete. So Shindana followed the path of nearly every other toy company. They moved their manufacturing offshore.

༄

Historians have tended to frame Mattel's involvement in Shindana as an act of corporate benevolence. It's true that before Hall and Smith met with Elliot Handler, the post-Watts enthusiasm that sustained Bootstrap's donations had "dried up to practically nothing," Smith said. "Then Mattel Toy Co. came in." When Shindana later began supporting a Native-run toy brand called White Buffalo, Smith saw it as a way to pay the gesture forward: "We want to do for them what Mattel did for us."

But Mattel was, curiously, not forthcoming about its role in the venture. Though articles about Shindana mentioned the two firms' financial relationship, Mattel did not broadcast it—and certainly did not boast about it, as Chase Manhattan Bank had. The company was instead, as one *Chicago Daily News* article put it, "bashful about its consulting role to Shindana Toys." The Handlers played coy about the project. In her notes, Ruth wrote little about Shindana beyond the occasional aside ("Shindana is the company of black ghetto people that we helped form," she scrawled on one memo, "after the Watts riots"). Nor did she mention it much in public. The subject never came up in her memoir. "I once suggested that the whole world should know about it," former Mattel employee John Birdsall said in an interview. "Ruth was adamant and said: 'No, and I don't want you talking about it either.'"

The cost to Mattel may have been minimal, but that did not mean they stood nothing to gain. When Elliot first met with Bootstrap in 1968, Mattel had just, weeks earlier, released their second black doll, "Christie." Most collectors recognize Christie as the Barbie line's first black character—the first to have her own features and her own name. But Mattel still had much to learn about black dolls, both in the craft of making them and in selling them. Shindana had invested significant time and resources into manufacturing techniques that would solve problems that befell other black dolls—from reproducing natural hairstyles to avoiding white-made models' tendency to fade into a dull gray. Shindana had developed a dye that was mixed into the plastic, so the hue would last even after paint chipped. Their motto was: "the more they peel, the blacker they get." Even the purest-hearted executive could hardly fail to notice that financing Shindana doubled as an exercise in market research. Mattel's own catalogs suggested as much. The company's later black dolls, from Christie onward, theorist Aria Halliday wrote in *Buy Black*, "were directly impacted by Shindana's designs, marketing schemes, and failures."

Both sides understood that if Shindana succeeded, the relationship would become less congenial—that at their core, they were rivals. Shindana was up front about it. "Today, Smith says, Shindana's immediate goal is to overtake Mattel," the *Los Angeles Times* reported. Smith told the *Chicago Daily News*: "I won't be happy until we can say 'Mattel—a subsidiary of Shindana Toys.'"

The Handlers laughed off that possibility. "They claim that someday Mattel will be a division of their company," Ruth said at a seminar on corporate responsibility. "And that's what you call real 'venture spirit.'" It was an uncharacteristically lax reaction from a company that by then had brought dozens of lawsuits against alleged copycats.

But internally, Mattel's executives made clear that they did not intend for Shindana to grow any further. In 1970, Elliot Handler received a letter from a merchandiser who pointed out that, though Shindana's sales had already exceeded expectations, their advertising budget still lagged behind those of bigger toy firms. Buyers wouldn't order much inventory without some assurance it might compete with familiar brand names, he wrote. And Mattel was in the perfect position to boost Shindana's visibility. Why not give them the last ten seconds of a few Mattel commercials? "If you would do that," he added, it might "force the sale of dolls up to a point where it will make it profitable for us to list more dolls."

It would have been simple enough. And yet Elliot turned him down. "There is no question that a ten second tag on one of our commercials would help Shindana sell more dolls," he replied, "but, unfortunately, it is not a practical thing for us to do. Shindana must make it on their own."

Perhaps Elliot's answer was in keeping with Bootstrap's spirit. But it was also dishonest. He knew that Shindana stood little chance without additional support. The toy industry, which had grown so rapidly in the first half of the twentieth century, was already concentrating the market among a few massive conglomerates. Bigger companies were swallowing midsize companies. Midsize firms were merging with slightly smaller ones. The tiniest concerns were mere chum. In 1958, the year before Barbie debuted, there had been about sixteen hundred toy companies in the United States. But by 1969, a year into Shindana's tenure, there were only a thousand.

Elliot knew these statistics. Just months before, he had recited them himself in a speech to Mattel's management association. The number of American toy companies was "decreasing every day, as the smaller companies either fade away or get acquired, and the remaining companies grow even larger," Elliot had told the crowd. "This, of course, bodes well for Mattel, if history teaches us anything."

He was right about the consolidation. He was wrong that it bode well for Mattel, or at least, for the Handlers' role there.

CHAPTER 12

THE SUITS

It became clear, almost right away, that Ruth did not like the new guy, even though she had been the one who hired him in the first place. Things had been going well for Mattel, almost too well. It had taken twenty years for the company to start doing $100 million in annual sales. But Mattel made it to $200 million in only three more. They ran factories in Hong Kong, Taiwan, Britain, West Germany, Portugal, Canada, two massive assembly plants in California, a third in New Jersey, and thanks to a new tariff loophole, one of the earliest maquiladoras on the Mexican border. They had, on average, some fourteen thousand people on payroll, and more at peak season. Barbie had become "the top-selling toy in toy-making history." But Ruth feared the company had grown too big, too quickly; that Mattel had primed investors to expect ever-accelerating returns, even while the company was, in reality, starting to slow down.

Ruth had been running Mattel like a small business, when in fact it was quite large, cumbersome, ungainly, and impossible for one person—someone whose training amounted to some night classes and the boot-camp of just figuring it out—to manage on their own. It was also a public company, and shareholders expected consistent growth. Even as Mattel posted profits, some on Wall Street had begun to tire of the toy industry's fickle cycles—the inconsistent alchemy of concocting hit toys, the too consistent droughts of seasonal sales. The company's stock had started to slip. The Handlers tried to smooth out their production year with sales incentives. They offered wholesalers discounts for buying early in the year. In 1967, they dreamed up what Ruth called a "revolutionary merchandising concept," branding each store that ordered the full catalog in advance a "Mattel All-Occasion Gift Center." The program's awkward acronym, MAOGC, distilled the executives' desperation to juice their sales: they pronounced it "Magic."

Even Barbie seemed to be reaching market saturation. That year, Mattel wowed Toy Fair with "Twist 'n Turn Barbie," the Jack Ryan–patented innovation whose newly flexible waist—"more humanoid than ever"—should have sold itself. But Mattel's marketing division feared they had maxed out America's Barbie budget. So they advertised the doll with a trade-in promotion: customers could swap in their old Barbies for a discount on the new one. For those five weeks, Ruth claimed, "there were more Barbie dolls traded in in this country than automobiles." Futurist Alvin Toffler saw this as a sign that Mattel was teaching "tomorrow's superindustrial" citizens "that man's relationships with things are increasingly temporary." But it likewise betrayed a fear that obsolescence was not reserved for objects. It could also come for companies.

It was all well and good that Mattel was profitable, but what Wall Street really cared about was EPS, or "earnings per share," which crunched how much money the company made for each of its stocks. This number was so important for investor confidence that, the previous summer, Mattel had rewritten its corporate mission statement to make increasing EPS its top priority, to "regain a favorable corporate image." But so far, it had not helped. Between 1965 and early 1967, Mattel's stock price had fallen from $40 to a low of $7. The brokers' disappointment was partly skepticism toward Ruth. Though she had always acted as Mattel's president behind the scenes, Ruth hadn't officially assumed the title until that year. In response, the company's creditors urged the Handlers to hire a strong business manager—someone to telegraph to Wall Street that, though a woman occupied the top office, their stocks were still in safe hands.

Over the summer of 1967, Ruth was saying as much to Mattel's personnel manager, and he floated a name: Wall Street wunderkind Seymour Rosenberg. He had been a darling of the financial press, earning a reputation as a "'money man' and merger-maker." A New York transplant in Los Angeles, Rosenberg was a patent lawyer by training. He once handled patents for none other than Howard Hughes, the eccentric aviator who had produced some of the biggest Hollywood movies of the twenties and thirties, then pivoted into the aerospace industry, cranking out airplanes and military fighter jets, and whose various compulsions included a "passion for secrecy." Rosenberg had gone on to work for Litton Industries, one of the hottest enterprises in corporate America.

Litton had started in 1953 as a relatively modest electronics company, selling communications and navigation tech, primarily to the U.S. Department of Defense. But its founders were early movers on America's mid-century trend toward consolidation. Soon, Litton began gobbling businesses like Pac-Man, inhaling twenty-three entities in eight years and "close to a hundred" within fifteen. "The U.S. is currently in the midst of the largest merger wave in its history," an article on Litton announced in 1968, "already twice the magnitude of any previous wave, and still on the upswing, with no sign of peaking."

The Department of Justice had a habit of interfering when two overly similar businesses tried to merge. The trick to avoiding antitrust regulations was to create a Frankenstein-like conglomerate, whose subsidiaries were nothing alike: grafting an oil processing branch onto a thermometer business and tacking on a girdle factory. By the sixties, Litton produced calculators, airplane guidance systems, typewriters, medical products, office furniture, and Stouffer's frozen foods. Executives proselytized about "synergy" and how the Litton empire was "meaningful as a whole," if not necessarily as a heap of component parts. They refused the word "conglomerate," in favor of the more forward-looking "technology company." (Though as even the business-friendly *Fortune* could concede, "considerable mental agility" was required "to perceive an impending technological revolution in some of the businesses Litton has bought—e.g. office furniture.") In fifteen years, Litton had amassed dozens of entities, forming, as one magazine put it, "a composite giant whose scope of industrial enterprise is truly awesome."

Rosenberg was seen as something of an architect behind Litton's rapid growth. A confidant of the founders, he had been promoted to the company's vice president of long-range planning and his long-range plan seemed to involve more subsidiaries. In the press, he claimed to have overseen "at least 100" such acquisitions in his thirteen-year tenure. Those acquisitions were often funded by stock, and Rosenberg had pioneered a new form of premium shares to facilitate the deals. It was the kind of invention that only people with wealth management advisors cared much about or even understood. But Mattel's hometown paper, the *Los Angeles Times*, had called Rosenberg's concept an "innovation in corporate finance." He had made a lot of people a lot of money. Los Angeles financiers loved him. Wall Street loved him even more.

When Rosenberg arrived at Mattel in September of 1967, Mattel's investors were pleased. Though he had a limited financial background, Rosenberg cut the profile of a Wall Street whisperer, and Mattel deployed him as such. He booked meetings with brokers and stock advisors, introducing them to management and touring them around Mattel's headquarters, so they'd go home and dash off reports on the integrity of Mattel's shares. The company's stock surged—climbing to over $36 in a week, almost back to its prior high.

But something about the forty-six-year-old struck Ruth as odd. Maybe it was how he parted his hair to slightly too far to the side. Or how he smiled with a slight sneer. He had the air of an adult Eddie Haskell, the two-faced schemer in *Leave it to Beaver* whose performative good manners gave cover for a casual cruelty toward those who knew him best. (Maybe he reminded her too much of herself: Rosenberg was extremely "secretive," she said, excessively covert for even the reticent toy industry.) "I never liked that man and never trusted him," her secretary agreed. Whatever it was, Ruth's dislike for the man crystallized only a week after he started work. When Rosenberg returned from a meeting in New York, she waltzed into his office, like she would with any new top hire, to help him get oriented. As Ruth later recalled, she debriefed Rosenberg on who to chat up for this financial matter, who to ask about that accounting concern. She sat and spoke for about fifteen minutes, talking with her hands, prattling on uninterrupted. Rosenberg sat back without taking notes. When she finished, he looked up and announced: "You won't do."

"What?" Ruth said.

"I said you won't do. To carry this company into its next stage of development, you are simply the wrong person. We are going to have to change things around here."

It would have been a brazen thing to tell any new boss, all the more so when that boss was the company's founder, who had been part of its public image for twenty-two years. But this was how Ruth, at least, remembered it. Though as the years went on, her story changed slightly. In these versions, Rosenberg had been even more explicit:

"You're a woman, you're Jewish, and your style is all wrong," he allegedly said. "If you were to deal with the investment community you wouldn't create the right impression."

This would have been odder still. Rosenberg himself was also Jewish. The patent lawyer, for his part, claimed he had merely relayed what Ruth already knew—that while he chatted up the financiers, the very analysts and investors whom he had been hired to charm, some had conveyed their doubts about putting a woman in charge. Maybe Ruth just remembered her own feeling of humiliation in her meeting with Rosenberg and fudged some particulars. Perhaps Rosenberg was dissembling when he claimed that he "did not share the analysts' concern." However it unfolded, it was obvious that Ruth Handler and Seymour Rosenberg were not fated to be friends.

What Ruth perhaps did not know was that, while Rosenberg had been working for Hughes, two of the billionaire's top deputies were accused of orchestrating an elaborate scheme of what you could call "creative" accounting, in which the Air Force had been overcharged millions of dollars. The company had been forced to repay the military $43.4 million, and the two deputies had been locked out of their offices upon order of the Air Force secretary himself. The disgraced pair had gone on to form Litton Industries, where they hired Rosenberg the very next year. Four months after Rosenberg left Litton, that company had suffered a financial scandal too: its profits collapsed by the multimillions due to "certain earlier deficiencies of management personnel." "If he's done nothing else, Rosenberg has to be called a genius," one reporter noted, "having left Litton before its earnings tumbled and its stock collapsed and having joined Mattel before its last surge."

But in his office that day, Ruth mainly sensed that her much-hyped hero had gotten off to an obnoxious start. Ruth stumbled out of his office, closed the door, and burst into tears. Elliot found her crying at her desk. "I'm going to fire that son of a bitch," she said. But she knew that she couldn't. "We've just created a furor on Wall Street about him,"

Elliot reminded her. "If you fire him, everybody will think he's uncovered some disaster here."

⁓

Rosenberg was tasked with balancing out the peaks and valleys of the company's seasonal sales. He made brisk work of it. Mattel had already made some minor acquisitions, like a school supplies producer called Standard Plastic in 1965 and some doll plants in Europe. But under Rosenberg's watch Mattel acquired several more. His targets were not other toy companies. No one wanted the feds to pay Mattel any more attention than they already did. But unlike Litton—whose acquisitions of unrelated industries spanned from missile navigation systems to frozen lasagna—there was at least a common theme. To "capitalize upon Mattel's ability to advertise to children," the company would stick to a single domain: the "World of the Young."

The toy maker went on a shopping spree. "We binged," Ruth later wrote, "there's no other word for it." The next summer, Mattel acquired Monogram Models, a purveyor of hobby products and miniature model kits. A year later, they added Metaframe Corp, a manufacturer of home aquariums. Then came Turco Manufacturing Co., a provider of playground equipment, and Audio Magnetics, a cassette-tape maker. Internally, they started a whole new enterprise, a top secret and "entirely autonomous" division codenamed the "Concord Project," devoted to developing a line of high-end electric organs. And soon, Mattel joined the circus.

Two-time Houston mayor Roy "The Judge" Hofheinz was a cigar-chewing orb of a man, who'd once served as the county's youngest judge. He'd just overseen the construction of the Astrodome—an eighteen-story covered stadium with a small city of similarly named "Astro-colonies" (the nearby Astroarena, the Astroworld theme park, the Astrohall theater, and four Astrohotels), which he called his "Astrodomain." To outfit the "Eighth Wonder of the World" with world-class activities, Hofheinz had pursued a controlling stake in the Ringling Bros. and Barnum & Bailey Circus.

The Judge had a thing for grand gestures, so when he summoned the Handlers to Houston, they were greeted by a limo and put up at one of his many hotels in a luxury apartment stocked with more food and drink than the Handlers "could eat in two weeks, let alone two days." A horse-drawn carriage toured them around the stadium. Hofheinz lit up the signboard to read "WELCOME RUTH AND ELLIOT HANDLER!" He treated the couple to dinner in an all-glass room at the height of the dome. He introduced them to two men in suits. One was investment banker Dick Blum, the husband of future California senator Dianne Feinstein. The other was Irvin Feld, a carnival barker of a publicist, who had, a decade earlier, planned the "Winter Dance Party," a frostbitten concert tour that ended in the plane crash that killed Buddy Holly. The incident became known as "The Day the Music Died," and Feld as "the cheapest promoter imaginable." But Feld had survived the scandal; he was now Hofheinz's co-owner in the circus.

The men wanted to build another theme park, this one not in Houston but in Orlando, Florida, to compete with a new complex called Disney World. Ringling's answer was "Circus World," a six-hundred-acre construction with a twelve-thousand-seat "big top" circus tent, a circus museum, an outdoor coliseum, an array of wild beasts from lions to tigers to leopards, and a penthouse restaurant overlooking the grounds from the cranium of a sixteen-story imitation-elephant modeled on the skeleton of P. T. Barnum's famous pachyderm "Jumbo." Hofheinz figured the complex could have some toy-related programming, which maybe Mattel would want to sponsor. But in the midst of Rosenberg's binge, Ruth had a better idea: they'd buy the circus outright. Thus the Barbie kingdom began hashing out the details to acquire the Greatest Show on Earth.

The only catch in Rosenberg's plan was that it put even more pressure on Mattel's stock. As he had done at Litton, Rosenberg had arranged for Mattel to pay for its new subsidiaries mostly through shares. In order to follow through on those deals, Mattel needed to keep its stock price up, while showing "spectacular gains" to keep investors excited. Rosenberg seemed to think the purchases would pay for themselves: adding new, profitable arms would juice earnings, which would in turn trickle into their stock.

But Ruth suspected they might need some help. "The monstrous growth was more than I felt able to deal with," she said. They needed to divvy up the company's responsibilities to keep everything under control.

Besides, Ruth was already thinking about her retirement. She did not plan to step back anytime soon, but she did want to groom her eventual successor. Rosenberg hadn't been the only energetic newcomer to the company. As Mattel professionalized throughout the sixties, the company had hired a series of striving young suits—all men, all white, most under forty. Arthur Spear, an orthorexic MIT engineer, so nervous he seemed to vibrate, had come from Revlon in 1964. The year after, Mattel had stolen Josh Denham away from his role at Miles Laboratories, the inventor of Alka-Seltzer. And when Rosenberg arrived, so did Ray Wagner, a staid veteran of Sears Roebuck and Co. Ruth called them her "young tigers."

The best way to find the candidate to replace her, Ruth felt, was to give the tigers their own turf and see who prowled best. In a process she called "divisionalization," Ruth broke the company into four fiefdoms: "Toys," "Dolls," "Games," and "Wheels and Wings." She doled them out to her most promising deputies. The idea was to divide and conquer, to ensure each sector of Mattel's operation got its due. In reality, investigators later reported, it meant Mattel "not only competed with other toy companies, but also with itself."

Bernie Loomis was not technically a "young tiger." At forty-five, he was a bit older than the new cubs and had joined Mattel a few years before they'd crawled on the scene. But he acted like one. Reporters often called him "Peter Pan," perhaps because it's also what he called himself. "I'm Peter Pan," he told *The New York Times*.

Loomis drew comparisons to all sorts of kid icons. He "has the girth of Captain Kangaroo," one article wrote, "and he's friendlier than the Friendly Giant." He later became a kind of legend in the toy world, the "Grandaddy of Concepts," the marketing mastermind behind *Star Wars* toys, Care Bears, and Strawberry Shortcake. But the epithet by which he was best known, the one that would get reprinted in his obituaries, was "The Man Who Invented Saturday Morning." And he earned it at Mattel.

Loomis had come to the company just a year after Barbie, and he had seen how Mattel had made her something bigger than a doll. "Pre-Mattel, there were no branded toys," he told one historian. But with its onslaught of related merchandise and its ongoing presence on children's television,

Mattel had turned Barbie into a mold that could bear infinite offshoots. He concluded that any successful toy had to be a "continuing concept"—something that enticed customers "to come back for additional items" within that toy line.

It was tricky to determine which toys inspired that kind of pull, but Loomis had observed one shortcut. Mattel had already tiptoed into the terrain of "licensing," or making toys based on pre-existing intellectual property, like TV shows. Loomis would become famous for his ability to spot which series would make the best toys; he coined the clunky portmanteau "toyetic" for concepts or characters that could translate easily into the domain of play. But in the late sixties, during divisionalization, he was struck by the idea that he could invert the relationship between toys and TV; that one could not only make toys based on successful series, but launch shows based on famous toys.

In early 1969, Ruth put Loomis in charge of the "Wheels and Wings" department, which included Mattel's latest hit, Hot Wheels. The line had been Elliot's idea, after he noticed his son's toy cars were "dull-colored" with "static wheels." He figured boys would prefer brighter models, with working axles so they could "live out the thrill of racing." (In reality, Elliot had also been "inspired" by a foreign toy—Matchbox cars from Britain had been on the market for fifteen years. "They had been in the business long before [us]," Ruth said privately.) When Hot Wheels hit the market, they became so popular that Mattel built a dedicated production plant—a facility so huge and so productive that it rivaled only Barbie in volume. If split off, *The Wall Street Journal* reported, Hot Wheels "would have ranked as the nation's second biggest toymaker all by itself."

Loomis seized on the cars' popularity. He pitched ABC on a thirty-minute Saturday cartoon called *Hot Wheels*. The show would feature a "typical all-American boy" named, aptly, Jack Wheeler, whose love of drag racing was outpaced only by his dedication to "to the advancement of law-abiding, safe driving practices." When the series debuted in September of 1969, *Hot Wheels* became the first toy-based TV franchise.

Ruth ran with the idea. If Mattel produced their own programs, they wouldn't have to settle for intermittent advertising. They could sell toys during the show itself and during commercial breaks. The company went on to sponsor a series of children's "minidocumentaries" for

CBS, a monthly broadcast studying the world "from the child's point of view," and the weekly series called *Hot Dog*. Most ambitious of all: Mattel cofounded a production company with Robert Radnitz, the "one-man Disney studio" behind family-friendly productions like *Island of the Blue Dolphins* and *My Side of the Mountain*. Together, he and Mattel planned to produce eight movies over three years.

Mattel produced toys, sure, but soon they would also sell year-round experiences—circus acts, theme park rides, movies, toys based on TV shows, TV shows based on toys, eateries stationed in giant elephants. They were the self-appointed leaders of the World of the Young.

There was only a minor snag. Mattel's dream of an entertainment empire was somewhat ahead of its time—so much so that it was not technically legal. There were still limits on how much advertising any one station could run, especially when the series were directed toward children. The *Hot Wheels* cartoon had barely hit the air before a competitor filed a complaint with the Federal Communications Commission, alleging the show blurred the line between advertising and conventional programming. Soon, the Federal Trade Commission began to investigate whether Mattel was using "deceptive advertising" that "unfairly exploits children.'" Then, the Department of Justice got involved, asking questions about Mattel's many acquisitions and sending two letters looking into "possible antitrust implications."

In public, Rosenberg dismissed the investigations as "routine." Mattel would "be cooperative in every way." The company couldn't be accused of mounting a toy monopoly, the executives reasoned. They were thinking bigger than any one market. The watchdogs were annoying, they thought, but Wall Street was the real worry.

CHAPTER 13

THE LEAKS

When I met Carol Spencer in Santa Monica, she was thinking about her legacy. She had retired from Mattel in 1998, after thirty-five years as Barbie's fashion designer. But in quitting her job, she had not moved to Boca, taken up pottery, finally learned Spanish, or any of the other things people do when they leave behind a nine-to-five. For Carol, quitting Mattel meant more time for Barbie. She'd spent the next quarter century as a celebrity in the Barbie fan community, giving speeches at big conventions or local clubs, where she was uniformly greeted by a round of applause. In 2019, she published her memoir *Dressing Barbie*. Even now, in her mid-nineties, she signs off her emails "Barbie love, Carol."

On the day of our lunch, she showed up in a baby-pink blazer adorned with a bejeweled Barbie pin. We'd planned to get burgers and then visit a pop-up exhibit in the Santa Monica mall. The installation, called "World of Barbie," pegged to the *Barbie* movie, offered a heavily curated tour through the doll's seven-decade history. There was no mention of *Bild Lilli*, or any of Mattel's more controversial creations, like the pregnant Midge or the black "Oreo Barbie" or "Earring Magic Ken," whose cock ring–like necklace made him briefly popular in nineties queer media.

Spencer had a reputation for speaking candidly—too candidly, some have thought. One collector had cautioned me that she'd "criticized Mattel so much that she had burned her own bridges." That was, in my experience, a rare quality among former Mattel staff, who seem to view their old employer with a mix of wariness and maybe Stockholmian loyalty. As we walked through the exhibit, Spencer did not disappoint, joking openly about *Bild* Lilli, Elliot Handler ("He enjoyed a good laugh, but he wasn't necessarily funny"), and the time she caught Jack Ryan "shacking up" with his secretary in the next lane over on the freeway.

But if Spencer spoke about Mattel more freely than most, that did not mean she was willing to reveal all its secrets. On our walk back to her car, she told me she was donating her papers to the Strong Museum, a massive archive of toy artifacts and ephemera, based in Rochester, New York. The museum had flown out a team of toy librarians to help organize her personal collection. But before they arrived, Spencer sorted it all herself, using a filing method that can be safely described as an archivist's nightmare: she removed every document stamped "CONFIDENTIAL" and set them all on fire. "Any pages that I have that are confidential," she said, "those get burnt up."

Few people, not just former Mattel employees, would relish handing over the detritus of their life for public inspection; among the willing, only the least bashful would do so without some trimming. Ruth had certainly trimmed. In the thirty-five boxes of her stuff at the Schlesinger, there are only oblique references to what she went through in the seventies—an ordeal that would get her pushed out of her own company and nearly send her to prison. She kept legal documents and secondary sources, but few of her own notes or reflections from the time. Ruth edited the story in her memoir as well. In *Dream Doll*, she depicted herself as the victim of a sexist frame job by the likes of Rosenberg and the young tigers; the oblivious executive presiding over a climate of "psychological warfare" among her subordinates; the sap who'd had the bad luck of being in charge during a series of unforeseeable catastrophes, making her the fall guy when everything else fell apart.

Spencer hadn't known Ruth well, she told me as we were leaving. The Design Center, where Spencer worked, was Elliot's domain, the creative side. And she'd had little involvement with the financial departments Ruth frequented. But the effort to steer the narrative of Ruth's professional demise had evidently started early. "They kept it very quiet," Spencer said. "I didn't know until I read it in the paper." All these years later, her sense was that Ruth's "young tigers were taking advantage of her. They were telling her that because she was a woman, she should take a back seat." She'd learned as much from reading Ruth Handler's own book.

It's true that, by the end of the sixties, the tensions inside Mattel had become palpable. The informal family atmosphere that had characterized the company's early years gave way to increasingly cutthroat corporate tactics. The division heads "became very possessive of the power I had delegated to them," Ruth would later observe. "They knew that one of them was to become president of the toy company."

Each sector was out for its own, and everyone else had to jockey for scraps. Operations head Art Spear clashed with newly empowered cubs, many of whom had once worked directly under him, and he "became bitter toward" Rosenberg. Often, Spear simply "worked behind his back." And no one resented the new, post-Rosenberg arrangement more than Yasuo Yoshida—who, as Ruth's right hand and financial translator for nearly two decades, had expected to get Rosenberg's job. Yoshida had always been a team player; when he appeared in the news, which was rare, it was usually for one of his recreational sports leagues—flag football, golf, bowling. But once he was passed over, Yoshida "became increasingly cool," Ruth observed.* He "started to pull away."

Ruth, meanwhile, was warring with Bernie Loomis over Hot Wheels. "I was fighting with Loomis to keep his quotas down to avoid glutting the market and overproducing our products," Ruth said. She began spending less time in the office. The 1970 season was about to start, and Ruth had a packed calendar for the new year. She was about to embark on a three-month tour across Europe, Asia, Australia, both Americas, with stops at seventeen international toy fairs.

In the future, Ruth would say that trip, so distant from the office and so consuming with the work of public relations, meant she could not possibly

---

*Rosenberg didn't make the transition any easier. The Litton alum's contract only required him to work three days per week because his wife had polio and needed home care. The rest of the work was to fall to a second-in-command, but Rosenberg refused to hire Yoshida for that role either. Ruth didn't fight for him, or even seem to understand, writing off Yas's animus as a race thing: "Yoshida, being Japanese, was concerned about an apparent loss of 'face.'" Instead, Rosenberg secured permission from his old boss Litton Industries to loan out a staffer named Frank Slovak for two days each week. He didn't last. When Rosenberg went on a work trip his first week, Yoshida stonewalled the new guy. When Rosenberg got back, Slovak said he had received "no cooperation from Mr. Yoshida, since Mr. Yoshida felt that should have received Mr. Slovak's job." He went back to Litton after just three days. Ruth never even met the man.

have known what had begun in her absence. How could she have known that, for example, within the next month, someone or several someones, would decide that the company's profits were not up to par, and that its earnings-per-share were doomed to disappoint Wall Street? How could she, with her busy schedule and her lack of business school background, have figured out that this person, or several people, would take it upon himself, or themselves, to do something about it?

In fairness to Ruth, she had other things on her mind. Years earlier, Ruth had been diagnosed with what was then called "cystic breast disease," a mostly benign condition so common that it's no longer considered a disease. But it gave her intermittent cysts, painful swelling, and knots of thicker tissue. Her older sister Sarah, the one who had raised her, had died of ovarian cancer in 1950. The cancer was spotted so late that when Sarah went into surgery, the doctors had taken a look and simply "closed her back up." The grief spurred Ruth to keep a close eye on her own various bumps and bulges, checking into a hospital the instant anything seemed too large. "If I was going to have to face the bad music, I didn't want to have to screw around first," Ruth said. "I just wanted to get it over with."

By 1970, Ruth had gotten so many biopsies she'd experienced the procedure's evolution firsthand: her first five had been surgical, full knock-out operations that left her with incision scars on the sides of her breasts. Her last was an "aspiration," a less invasive transaction using a needle to draw fluid straight from the growth. Biopsies had become a kind of routine, but the surgical procedure was invariably a "big fuss," requiring a multi-day hospital stay. Each time, Ruth had to sign a release allowing doctors to "immediately remove the breast," if they discovered any cancer. "You'd wake up, your chest tightly bound with bandages," she wrote, "and not know whether you still had a breast or not."

The first six biopsies had come back benign. But when Ruth found her seventh lump that June, it felt new and odd. It was harder, uneven, more rock than grape. When her doctor examined it, he didn't respond with the easy confidence of prior visits. She booked another biopsy three days later. She awoke in haze, still dopey from drugs and half-hallucinating. She could swear she saw Elliot standing over her bed in a jet-black suit, as if preparing her funeral procession. When she finally came to, her chest was bound, but she didn't need to ask if they'd found anything. Her left side felt like it had been doused in gasoline and set on fire. She'd undergone a "modified radical mastectomy"—a complete removal of the left breast, from skin to tissue to nipple. They'd carved out her chest muscles, chiseled the lymph nodes out of her armpit. The procedure left Ruth with permanent nerve damage. (The *International Journal of Surgical Oncology* would later call radical mastectomies effective but "frankly mutilating.")

She took five weeks of medical leave, healing at home, ping-ponging between depression and overt hostility. "My days were long, lonely, and black," Ruth remembered. Though some may have seen her as a chain-smoking backslapper, Ruth had always taken pride in her feminine presentation. Like Barbie, Ruth had assembled an extensive wardrobe, expensive, beautiful, and carefully thought out. "I was well built and my designer clothes showed off my body," she wrote in *Dream Doll*. The sustained sexual chemistry of her marriage was obvious to anyone who interacted with the Handlers, and especially to anyone who read their letters, which remained quaintly dirty. ("There's only one thing that could make me forget the heat right now," Elliot wrote from a sweltering trip to Japan.* "And that's a long session with you in an air conditioned room.") But now Ruth, who once pitched breasts as totems to womanhood, had been stripped of the very anatomy that defined her doll. She felt "de-womanized." No one knew how to talk about the surgery, so no one did—except Ruth, who periodically blurted out things like "I'd like to chop off parts of that doctor."

After the cancer scare, Ruth felt she was "losing control." When she returned to work in late July of 1970, the state at Mattel hardly suggested otherwise. "The four young tigers who now ran the product

---

*In another letter from that same trip, Elliot described how his hosts had offered him the services of a consort. He told Ruth that he'd declined: "These people probably think I'm not normal. I guess I'm the romantic type—I like my sex to be clean with a good warm feeling of love and emotion inside," he wrote. "Boy, you can tell my mind is not in Japan tonight—keep it in use honey—I'll warm it up when I get home."

divisions had become entirely too aggressive and freewheeling," she wrote later. "Each division vice president was doing his own thing in competition with each of the others." Ruth's top deputies assured her that everything—orders, profits, egos—was in check. But as inflation heated up the national economy and further ignited Mattel's sales targets, Ruth faulted them for their aggressive quotas. Others believed she bore the blame. "Ruth thought there was no limit to what Mattel could accomplish. She'd encourage unbelievably optimistic sales projections," a former Mattel market researcher said. "It was a game of hyperbole with us, but I think she really fell for it."

But regardless of who started it, Mattel's sales quotas kept soaring. So when the fire erupted two months later, it seemed almost on the nose, like some blunt omen that they'd flown too high.

Mattel's Mexican assembly plant, situated in the city of Mexicali, just four hours southeast of Los Angeles, had opened in 1967 as a fairly modest facility, with a workforce of about two hundred. But in under three years, it had grown into a tremendous complex spanning 323,000 square feet, its payroll growing in inverse proportion to that of Mattel's union staff in the States. The factory now employed some 2,700 workers—nearly all of them women under twenty-three, each earning some fourth of what Mattel paid their American counterparts. It had become Mattel's most important assembly facility, and would soon be "the single largest employer along the border." It was also a tinderbox—a warehouse full of flammable material, from plastics to solvents, lubricants to rubber. When the fire sparked a little after noon on September 30, 1970, it overtook the factory in a matter of minutes, leaving behind a pile of "ashes and twisted iron." Two workers were found dead in the rubble; two more were reported missing.

The fire incinerated everything else too: the structure, the tools, the toys. As Mattel's executive vice president of operations, Art Spear flew down to the site, setting up an enormous circus tent to sort through the rubble and see what could be salvaged. But the losses were "staggering." At the height of the toy year, when the company began preparing for the Christmas season, $4 million worth of inventory had been "completely destroyed." Meanwhile, the Mexican authorities were poking around about the employees' deaths. Legal settlements looked likely.

Mattel's holiday schedule devolved into chaos. The company was not on track to meet its aggressive targets; it might not even match the previous year's. Internally, the executives scrambled to find a solution, taking emergency measures to boost their bottom line. They were already conducting aggressive layoffs. They axed their employee profit-sharing plan, reshuffling a reserve of $2.6 million—money that would normally go to workers—back into cash. They cut back on royalty payments to Jack Ryan, who was still draining millions from their coffers.

It was in the midst of this that Bernie Loomis suggested a bolder idea: a strategy called "bill and hold," offering customers discounted prices on toys that Mattel wouldn't ship right away, not when those stores already had too much stock anyway, but later, in a few months. With "bill and hold," Mattel could say they had made a few more million in sales now, even if they didn't send anything off for some time—a perfectly standard practice, provided the sales eventually went through. If buyers could bow out of orders before they ever shipped, Mattel might put itself in a position to have claimed sales that did not, technically, exist. Whatever they did, Mattel's general counsel cautioned, it was too early to make any public disclosures. They should stick with "secrecy."

But Rosenberg was plotting Mattel's real deus ex machina, an endgame to his merger frenzy: Mattel would be bought itself. At Toy Fair that February, Rosenberg's Wall Street contacts put him in touch with some friends at Kinney Services, a young but massively profitable business with a keen interest in acquisitions. Started as a Manhattan mortuary operation, its founders had joined forces with an array of tristate area enterprises, assembling one of those Litton-esque conglomerates that spanned from funeral parlors to parking lots, talent agencies to the "Tiffany of cleaning companies."

Kinney came with some less-than-ideal baggage. Its subsidiary, a Jersey car lot operation called Kinney Parking, had been founded by several underworld personalities with not especially oblique ties to the mob. The parking business had shielded its ownership with a network of some forty shell companies, but its primary backer was known to be Emmanuel Kimmel, a notorious bookie with an active FBI file. As the

Bureau noted in 1965: "Kimmel is known to be a lifetime associate of several internationally known hoodlums."*

Kinney Services' unsavory associates had not stopped it from becoming a potent force in business. It had managed to acquire the publisher behind *MAD* magazine, as well as movie equipment maker Panavision and music industry titan Atlantic Records. Just a year or two earlier, Kinney had spent $400 million acquiring the assets of an entertainment company with a multi-hyphenate name. They'd called it something simpler: Warner Bros.

The Kinney executives wanted to ditch their unsexy subsidiaries, selling off the funeral parlors and parking lots, to blend their entertainment enterprises with Mattel, "capitalizing on the reputation of the West Coast outfit as a go-go concern." Kinney had "considerably more money" than Mattel. But Mattel, even with its troubles, had a "better image" on Wall Street. Their stock sold at a much higher multiple of their earnings, in part because investors still believed Mattel would continue to grow at the same rapid pace. The Kinney people envisioned merging Warner Bros. with Mattel, and re-entering show business together under the Mattel name. Mattel, of course, would benefit too. The arrangement could single-handedly solve all their financial shortfalls. "Our appetite was whetted," Ruth wrote. "It looked like we were going to make a deal."

By mid-May of 1971, spirits were high at Mattel. At their annual meeting, Mattel's attempts to soothe shareholders seemed only slightly strained. One division president approached the stage with a "four-man band of clowns," whose presence mainly seemed to serve his punchline: "We're the only business that doesn't mind if its employees clown around." The real clown was Irvin Feld, the president of Ringling Bros., who stumped for Mattel's long-awaited circus merger. Feld came in "like a high-powered press agent," *The Wall Street Journal* wrote, barking out

---

*During the Depression, the rumored bootlegger had set up one of the first numbers rackets in Newark. His partner, Abner "Longie" Zwillman, had been a major target of the Senate's famous investigative committee on organized crime; the news had dubbed him the "Al Capone of New Jersey." And the Jersey Capone, it seemed, was another suspected partner in Kinney Parking. But no one could quite confirm the parking lot's funders. And besides, Zwillman had been found dead in his mansion three years before the parking operation joined the newly merged conglomerate.

his "fabulous PR" scheme—parading nineteen elephants from a New Jersey suburb to Madison Square Garden. Feld's once-fatal thriftiness now served him well: New York's Port Authority, he told the crowd, "only charged me fifty cents an elephant to go through the Lincoln Tunnel."

For the grand finale, Ruth introduced Elliot's pet project, the top-secret device developed for years under the code name "Concord Project." Elliot thought it was going to be big, and physically it was: a complex electric organ whose array of bonus features had, over the past few years, only become more dramatic and expensive (it would retail for some $500). But when Optigan's president sat down to plunk its first notes, no sound came out. As one minute turned into several, the toy makers started to look nervous. The goal was to telegraph to shareholders that Mattel could overcome its struggles. It wasn't a great omen that no one had remembered to plug the organ in.

One week later, the Handlers convened a meeting at their beach house in Malibu. After three months of negotiating, Rosenberg had reached a tentative deal with the morticians-turned-movie moguls. And now everyone—a half dozen Mattel people, a half dozen Kinney people, almost as many miscellaneous suits—had arrived to discuss the details. The Handlers sat across from Rosenberg and Steve Ross, the former funeral parlor director who now served as Kinney's chief executive. Ross likely brought Kinney's executive vice president, Caesar P. Kimmel, the thick-jawed son of the storied bookie Manny Kimmel, who carried on the spirit of his father's legacy as a breeder of racehorses and Rhodesian Ridgebacks, a kind of lion-hunting dog he used for protection.

The big sticking point during negotiations had been the question of which company would "survive," or retain primary control once the merger went through. The contract outlined a compromise: Mattel would keep its name and continue to manage its operations. Ruth would stay on as the head of the toy company. But Kinney would take majority control of the merged conglomerate's board of directors. Steve Ross would serve as chairman, Elliot as vice chairman. Ruth had expected as much. Kinney was, after all, the bigger and richer of the two.

But as Ruth read over who would represent Mattel on the board—the members that would make up the minority votes—she noticed that Kinney had installed one of its own, a Wall Street investment banker who had spoken for the conglomerate during negotiations. The banker "was a bright and good man," Ruth wrote, but "he represented Kinney's interests, not ours." Odder still was Kinney's selection of president of the merged conglomerate, the man who would serve as the new entity's public face. Ruth had expected that role would also go to Steve Ross, who oversaw everything as far as Kinney was concerned. But instead, Kinney's board had selected a dark horse candidate, a man no one had expected, who had barely any role at the company and hadn't for years.

Ruth never named the man in her notes or memoir. Nor did the press; both companies were still publicly denying that they had any plans to merge. Ruth described him only as "nearly eighty years old and virtually inactive in Kinney affairs." But the man himself was not as important as what he seemed to represent to Ruth: a decoy, a dummy candidate meant to seem fairly innocuous, to convince Ruth to sign over most of her sway. At some point soon, she reasoned, this elderly man would have to step down. And she would have essentially no input in naming his successor.

This was a coup, Ruth thought. A ploy by Rosenberg to take the presidency himself, long after she could do anything to stop it. Elliot shared her suspicions. "How can this old man who is presently inactive," he asked, "be the president?"

Ruth took a less subtle tack, screeching: "This whole thing is a farce!" Clearly this organizational structure was not what they had intended at all. Ruth turned to Rosenberg. "You really fixed this up," she said. "We weren't told about this and you worked behind our backs."

Rosenberg walked straight out of the room. The next morning, Ruth ordered her secretary to lock him out of his office. If he dared to show up, she was to tell him to leave. She hounded one of Mattel's lawyers to sniff out whether Rosenberg had been "subversive." Ruth wanted to fire him, effective immediately. But the company could not yet skewer him publicly. Rumors were circulating that the Kinney merger had been aborted and that Mattel's near-term earnings were "turning sour." The coverage spurred a massive sell-off of Mattel stock, and its share price again plummeted. Rosenberg's new role, his only role, was to run defense in the press. "Mattel is alive and kicking," *The Wall Street Journal* reported in June of 1971. "That's the gist of a statement by Seymour Rosenberg ... in response to a spate of unfavorable rumors about the company."

CHAPTER 14

THE STRIKE

The 1971 season was not good for Mattel. As the executives prepared for the next Toy Fair, one vice president would try to joke about about how bad it was, leading the crowd in a rendition of "Auld Lang Syne."

Should old acquaintance be forgot
I should have stayed in bed
I needed 1971
Like I need a hole in the head.

At first, the executives blamed the fire; then they blamed the feminists, the "Mrs. Yenta[s]," marching down the streets. ("A real saucy bunch of ladies," the same vice president quipped from the Toy Fair stage. "I remember when street walkers used to be fun.") And less than a month after the Kinney deal imploded, Mattel began blaming the unions too. Their "restrictive policies" slowed "the productivity of individual workers," Ruth had heard in a speech that year. They provoked "excessive wage gains."

Though much of their American workforce was unionized, Mattel's aggressive offshoring had spread Barbieland across the globe. Barbie's body was built from ethylene refined from Saudi Arabian oil. The ethylene was processed into vinyl pellets in Taiwan, which in turn were injected into Barbie molds in plants from West Germany to Hong Kong. Japanese workers threaded her nylon hair, while Mexican workers assembled her friends and accessories. All the while, Mattel's American payroll shrunk. In the sixties, Mattel employed some four thousand members of the Rubber Workers International Union alone. By the end of the seventies, that number had dipped to just nine hundred. Mattel moved those jobs, and many others, to countries with favorable labor markets—which is to say, low-paid and largely unorganized. Even when unions were required abroad, Mattel often found ways to mute their influence. At the Mexico facility, for example, Mattel cut a "sweetheart" deal with a state-run union "without the workers' knowledge." When the staff still managed to strike, Mattel threatened to close the factory down.

But for all its efforts, over the summer of 1971, Barbie's maker still relied on some union workers. Perhaps more precariously, they still relied on union workers employed by subcontractors, whose bargaining agreements they did not control. The downside of outsourcing jobs abroad was that the toys, eventually, had to travel to the States. And so at eight a.m. on July 1, 1971 when fifteen thousand longshoremen from San Diego, California, to Bellingham, Washington walked off the job, Mattel found that many of their toys were stranded at sea. The strike dragged on for ninety-seven days. By September, Mattel's stock had fallen by 50 percent and seemed ready to plunge even lower. As one brokerage told *The Wall Street Journal*: "I don't think many investors realize just how bad the situation is and could be."

By now, Mattel's accountants had deferred so much, "squeezed" as much money as they could from various corners of the company, that they seemed to have hit a dead-end. The fire, the strike, the bad economy, increasingly attentive regulators, and increasingly vocal activists had all piled up together. Worse still, Mattel continued to grapple with the fallout of 1970's financial fixes. Bernie Loomis's "bill and hold" idea had put Mattel in an awkward position: in the end, customers canceled most of the orders. The result was that Mattel had reported over $14 million worth of "fictitious" sales—or about $107 million in today's dollars. Those sales now needed to be subtly subtracted from the current year's profits, so as not to attract outside attention.

For years, Mattel had been posting incredible gains each quarter. But it was now inevitable that the company would have to declare a deficit, its first since going public over a decade ago. The question was how big. They were down more than $15 million that quarter, or as Wall Street would see it, a loss of fifty cents per share. But Ruth and Rosenberg agreed that a loss of that size was "unacceptable." The accountants needed to do something, anything really, to get that number down by half. Yoshida was wary of their strategy—it seemed obvious that the loss had to be "artificially reduced" to hit the number they wanted.

The accountant eventually complied. But as he began preparing Mattel's annual report—their financial results for the entire year of 1971—Yoshida realized that they were in much worse trouble than he had recognized. Rosenberg had obscured their losses with some, to put it generously, unusual accounting practices to show consistent growth. Mattel had to admit another deficit, but subtly enough to avoid further questions. The company still could not suddenly acknowledge the full extent of the problems. A sudden return to normal methods would prompt questions from their auditor. They had to understate their excess inventory, and by extension the loss itself. The situation was so dire that Darrell Peters, Mattel's vice president of administration, refused to meet with the auditors altogether. A corporate marketing executive had to go in his place. He knew the numbers "were fictitious," Yoshida said. "He felt that was wrong."

Finally, in early 1972, Mattel announced that while its third quarter had been bad, its entire year had been worse. They reported their first ever year-long deficit—a pretax loss of some $55 million. The Handlers knew who to blame. "REASONS FOR BAD YEAR EXPERIENCE," they wrote in their notes. "1. Dock Strike."

The good news was: Rosenberg agreed to leave. He'd negotiated a generous exit package, requiring Mattel to pay him a salary of $60,000 for the next two decades. (A month later, he sold the vast majority of his Mattel shares, adding another $2 million.) Once he was officially out of his office, Ruth set about undoing essentially everything he had accomplished, shedding Mattel's overbearing executives and their overeager targets and combining the divisions once again. She fired Bernie Loomis, unloaded Rosenberg's acquisitions, and tried to hide any hint of unconventional accounting. She believed the company would do well in 1972, that whatever sly maneuvers they'd pulled over the past few years were behind them. Their joint film project with Radnitz was already bearing fruit—his first feature, *Sounder*, was about to come out. And they were already plotting a second, an adaptation of another children's novel, *The Witch of Blackbird Pond*.

By Christmas, toy sales seemed to have recovered from the economic blow of 1971, not just at Mattel, but everywhere. "The business came in late," one toy maker told *The New York Times*, "but then it came in like a bombshell." So, when the time arrived to announce Mattel's year-end results for 1972, preliminary estimates suggested they would report "satisfactory earnings." In February of 1973, Elliot put out a press release declaring a "definite turnaround."

But while the Handlers were in New York showing off their latest lines, they got a frantic call from several Mattel executives. So many accountants had left in the past year that the numbers had not been properly crunched. Elliot needed to retract his statement, they said. Mattel was not headed for a "definite turnaround." If anything, the numbers showed the opposite. So just eighteen days after his victory lap, Elliot walked it all back. The "troubled toy maker said it expects to report a 'substantial' operating loss of some magnitude," *The Wall Street Journal* reported—another $30 million in the red.

The Handlers had hoped that the year of 1971 would go down as one of Mattel's all-time worst, but then it was followed, in close succession, by 1972 and 1973. Ruth didn't know it yet, but she wouldn't like the five years that came after that either.

This was a new feeling for Ruth. The company had weathered crises in the past, but never so many, so acutely, at once. Regulators were asking questions; shareholders were filing lawsuits. One accused the Handlers, Rosenberg, and five other officials of insider trading, of selling off their stock before anyone else understood the coming collapse. Another, filed just two weeks after Elliot's announcement, claimed Mattel and its auditors had perpetuated "a fraud and deceit" upon the public.

Ruth needed a pause and some sun. She and Elliot left promptly for a Caribbean cruise. But even on the boat, she couldn't relax. When she returned to the office a few days early, she walked in on a meeting with what seemed like all of Mattel's bankers. The room's air of unease made it obvious: the Handlers were not supposed to be there. The meeting was secret. Mattel's bankers wanted to force a regime change. The real coup, Ruth realized, had not come from Rosenberg at all, but from unthreatening Art Spear, the anxious executive whose hands shook when he spoke. The verdict of the meeting: Ruth could no longer be trusted to run the company she had founded. The optics were bad—bad enough that in March of 1973, Mattel's board forced Ruth to resign. She could stay on as board co-chairman, but she surrendered the presidency to Spear.

The new, Ruth-less Mattel shed its subsidiaries fast. Optigan shuttered in May. Audio Magnetics was on the auction block by August. By January, Turco was in the can too. The toy company tried to sell the circus, but no one bit. Perhaps because, by the following year, Mattel had been hit by four more class action lawsuits, with Ringling playing a role in almost all of them. The circus shareholders were enraged that the merger had been funded by Mattel stock, which had fallen from $41 to $2 in just three years. Others claimed that Mattel had lied about its financial information when the circus merger went through, understating prior earnings to juice future growth.

Every colorful character from Mattel's past decade seemed to come out for their cut. Roy Hofheinz, who had courted the Handlers into the circus deal to begin with, joined one of the shareholder cases, calling for damages of over $40 million. Jack Ryan started suing over his royalties, claiming Mattel had shorted him by as much as $24 million. Nearly everyone was furious about Rosenberg's rosy severance package. "It seems that we are paying Mr. Rosenberg for his mistakes," one shareholder said, "and he's profiting tremendously."

Finally, in August of 1974, the SEC joined in. They charged Mattel, Ruth, and Rosenberg with "employing devices, schemes, and artifices to defraud" the public for at least two years. Perhaps it seemed like the Handlers' legal troubles could not get worse. But the couple continued to chisel below rock bottom. Barely a month into the case, Art Spear announced that Mattel had "discovered" further accounting irregularities. It became obvious the problems went deeper than the "definite turnaround" of 1973—that Mattel's stunning reversal was merely the "cumulative effect of prior accounting practices" suddenly "brought to a head." It now seemed that Mattel's rapid growth had been reverse-engineered, that the toy maker had set targets for itself—targets that would show the consistent, season-less growth that it had so long pursued—and reported those to the public, "whatever the actual figures turned out to be."

Under Art Spear's reign, Mattel seemed to be cooperating. But when Arthur Andersen, the independent auditor, quit over Mattel's refusal to turn over its unedited records, the SEC decided that perhaps some new management was in order. In October, the commission called on Mattel to install SEC surrogates on its board of directors and commission an outside investigation. The newly appointed board would hire two legal specialists, a special counsel and a special auditor, to conduct an aggressive inquisition into what exactly went wrong.

⁓

Ruth called the next few years her "Mrs. Invisible" period. She went to the office, but she had nothing to do. No one spoke to her. She began gambling almost every day, driving down to the casinos in Gardena, sometimes betting thousands at a time. She mused that she might end up like her father. Keel over one day at the card table, rigor mortised over a pile of chips. Maybe then the SEC would understand who really got stiffed.

She had worked so much for so long that the sudden freedom in her schedule seemed suffocating. She pored over classifieds, contemplating a day job to keep busy. But she couldn't imagine any department store would want a disgraced CEO manning its makeup counter. She took stray teaching gigs, lecturing at local colleges on topics like "entrepreneurship." Maybe her own advice sank in because eventually she followed it. She started a new business in a field well suited for the former Barbie founder: fake breasts. Her post-mastectomy life had been a brutal tutorial in the mediocrity of the prosthetic knocker market. The selection on offer was hideous; her first fake resembled an "egg-shaped glob." It was not designed to be worn on the left side, or the right for that matter, but to be interchangeable, like a shoe fit for both feet. The result was an awkward boulder that seemed to announce its artificiality, wherever it sat.

Ruth remained unoriginal in the naming department. She called her new corporation Ruthton. (Her breast brand went by something only slightly less literal: Nearly Me.) Ruthton had no ad budget, but it helped that its namesake was famous and now notorious. Ruth went all out on marketing. She went on television and tossed her cutlet to the host. She let retail executives feel her chest and guess which breast was real. She posed for *People* magazine with her blouse unbuttoned. She assembled a staff of mostly older women, many of whom had had mastectomies themselves.

Privately, Ruth was still furious. She maintained that she had not known nearly anything about Mattel's financial struggles, or the lengths some had gone to hide them—at least not until it was too late. She had been caught up in the "consumer" wars. She had been touring toy fairs and healing from cancer, all while assuming her staff could take care of the company. She believed that her former subordinates had, in fact, planned for Mattel to get in trouble, to put the company into a precarious position "so that a takeover could occur." She suspected Art Spear had been conferring with the Securities and Exchange Commission well before the charges, that he had "quietly, surreptitiously been preparing" to take over the company, clear his own name, and frame her for Mattel's failures. Above all, Ruth hated the special counsel, the SEC-appointed lawyer Seth Hufstedler, who struck her as a dull, joyless man and yet seemed to be the only person interested in talking to her. He interrogated her without sympathy. The whole thing struck her as a violation of due process and the very principles of the American Constitution. His investigation seemed designed to indict her as a liar.

Ruth was right in that regard. When the special counsel report came out in November 1975, it did not paint Mattel's erstwhile executive as an innocent and honest broker. The five-hundred-page report outlined a complex scheme, devised by Rosenberg, egged on by Ruth, to "show a pattern of ordered growth with regularly increasing sales," by issuing deliberately misleading and fraudulent financial statements, and then covering their misdeeds up by destroying "critical corporate records." His report indicated that the fraud may have started almost as early as 1968—just months after Rosenberg came on board.

The bill and hold sales had perhaps been Mattel's most egregious tactic, but by Hufstedler's account, they had deployed many others. They had recorded shipments in the wrong quarters. They had misused "annualization"—an accounting practice that spread expenses across the year, deferring multimillions in expenses to show smoother seasonal profits. They had eliminated their employee profit sharing plan without disclosing it, and added their insurance payout from the fire to income, also in secret. They had misestimated the costs of tooling and understated Jack Ryan's royalties by at least $1.9 million, and adopted an exceedingly liberal approach to "inventory obsolescence"—or determining which toys had fallen out of fashion and could no longer be sold at market rate. When Hot Wheels had "literally flooded" the market at the end of 1970, they had covertly issued "substantial credits" against the inventory. Internally, they called it "help money." They had sold off the unwanted cars at steep discounts but still recorded the sales at the higher prices. In one instance, they had recorded the same sale of Hot Wheels twice—an overstatement of $4.8 million. Ruth and Rosenberg had agreed to "let the error slide;" they needed the padding to meet their target. Their strategies were subtle—arcane-seeming manipulations of accounting math. But the tedium was the point. It's hard to write an exposé about something you need a CPA to understand.

The report enraged Ruth.* When the Department of Justice began investigating a possible criminal case, the Handlers did everything to stop it. Ruth and Rosenberg sued both the SEC and two DOJ attorneys to prevent the special counsel report from being admitted as evidence, calling Hufstedler an "impartial trier of fact."

Even when confronted with Hufstedler's meticulous disembowelment of her defense, Ruth maintained that she was being set up. She felt wronged by Rosenberg, Bernie Loomis, and Art Spear. Loomis—who had come up with the "bill and hold" idea in the first place—had not only emerged unscathed, he had been promoted, now serving as president of Mattel's competitor, Kenner Products. Just hearing his name sent her into a fury. Former Mattel staffer John Birdsall recalled one dinner during that time, when the old Hot Wheels head came up in passing. Ruth's face spasmed. "She slammed down her fork," he said, "and announced to the entire table: 'Bernie Loomis is a lying son of a bitch.'"

---

*It didn't soften the blow that, the same month the report came out, Mattel settled its five shareholder lawsuits for $30 million—what was then the largest class action settlement for any case involving corporate directors. Mattel responded by suing Arthur Andersen for neglecting its duty in failing to catch Mattel's own deceptions. The firm protested by filing its own suit, before eventually agreeing to chip in $900,000.

When the indictment came down, the grand jury charged Ruth and Rosenberg with ten counts of mail fraud, conspiracy, aiding and abetting, and filing false statements with the SEC. The indictment alleged a list of forty-five "overt acts" of fraudulent activity over a five-year period, as part of a conspiracy to "influence the market price of Mattel stock" and borrow money from banks. The fraud, prosecutors estimated, had cost shareholders some $256 million.

Loomis, it turned out, had flipped, becoming a state's witness in exchange for his immunity. But the key witness in the case against Ruth and Rosenberg was Yasuo Yoshida. In a searing grand jury testimony, Yoshida swore, under oath, that Ruth had not only known about and encouraged Mattel's financial deceptions, she had helped cover them up. He affirmed how, over the spring of 1972, Ruth had summoned him into her office and asked, as the prosecutor paraphrased, if they had "cleaned up" all their "past sins as far as the books and records were concerned." When he'd told her that there were still some documents that "might prove embarrassing," Ruth called in a member of Yoshida's team—someone who "would not look suspicious" revisiting old files. "We had a short discussion as to where the bill and hold documents were," Yoshida said. Then Ruth told the accountant "to quote 'purge the file.'"

Yoshida and two of his accountants pleaded guilty to a single charge each, walking away with $5,000 fines and two years of probation. But Ruth and Rosenberg denied all wrongdoing. At her arraignment, Ruth delivered an outraged, prewritten sermon reaffirming her innocence and comparing herself, rather bluntly, to Jesus. For too long, "I turned the other cheek as false accusations were hurled at me," she wrote. "Now, however, I find I cannot ignore these accusations any longer."

Her indignation had evidently waned by autumn when it became obvious the jury was unlikely to see it her way. Just days before their cases were about to go to trial, Ruth and Rosenberg struck a compromise, changing their pleas to *nolo contendere*—or "no contest." They would no longer fight the charges, but they would likewise not admit guilt. The plea would spare the two former toy makers the indignities, and press coverage, of a trial. But the prosecutors saw it as a cop-out. "If the *nolo contendere* is for all intents and purposes a guilty plea," District Attorney

Andrea Ordin told the *Herald Examiner*, "there should be unambiguous acceptance of responsibility."

At their final hearing in December of 1978, U.S. District Judge Robert Takasugi called Ruth and Rosenberg's crimes "exploitative, parasitic" and "disgraceful to anything decent in this society." He sentenced both executives to the maximum—forty-one years in federal prison. But neither would spend a night in custody. The judge immediately suspended both of their sentences. Takasugi's rationale was that both executives were unemployed, and both had medical expenses—Rosenberg, because his wife had polio; Ruth, because she was getting a second mastectomy. But his generosity fit in with a broader trend; as the United States Sentencing Commission later found, white collar criminals routinely "received less severe sentences" than others charged with theft, often getting off with "simple probation." Sure enough: Ruth and Rosenberg were each given five years' probation and an annual five hundred hours of community service.

Takasugi was not sympathetic to all of Ruth's pleas. She tried to pitch her for-profit breast project as a public service worthy of counting against her hours. As a gesture of her generous spirit, she pledged to donate free boobs to the needy. But the judge did not buy it.

"The very thing that I had worked so hard to do, an act that would help humanity," Ruth ranted, "was the very thing that was slapped in the face and rejected by the judge as non-worthy."

Her sentence should *cost* her money, not help her make it. On top of their probation, both Ruth and Rosenberg would also have to pay $57,000 in "reparations." But Ruth still approached her punishment with a business mindset. Mere months after her sentencing, she phoned up her accountants to ask if she could deduct her $57,000 fine from her taxes. After all, what were "reparations," if not another kind of business expense? She could try, they said, though there was a chance it was not, technically, legal.

When Ruth left the courthouse in December of 1978, she no longer had many ties to Mattel. Her few allies had fled. Elliot had quit, opting to return to a life of painting. Two years later, on Valentine's Day, the couple sold nearly all of their stock. But if Ruth could no longer control Barbie, she could try to control the story. She would maintain her innocence until she died in 2002. And over time, her role in the ordeal would be remembered variously as a sexist mistake or some benign tax problem. In the *Barbie* movie, Rhea Perlman renders Ruth as some cross between a bawdy ghost and a guardian angel, the wizened resident of a heavenly kitchen lodged somewhere in Mattel's headquarters. Her fraud case comes up only once in the film, as a punchline. "You're Ruth from Mattel," Margot Robbie's Barbie says. "Baby, I *am* Mattel," Perlman laughs, "until the IRS got to me—but that's another movie."

PART III

INTRO

In March of 1985, fifteen hundred corporate raiders and yuppie strivers—the kinds of Wall Street hard-chargers Tom Wolfe nicknamed the "Masters of the Universe"—filed into the auditorium at the Century Plaza, the luxury Los Angeles hotel where Ronald Reagan stayed so often some called it the Western White House. The room, organizers bragged, was worth a collective $3 trillion. "Practically every raider, would-be raider, and raider specialist was there," James B. Stewart wrote in *Den of Thieves*: publishing magnate Rupert Murdoch; Texas oil tycoon T. Boone Pickens Jr.; vending machine mogul Nelson Peltz; the billionaire Carls (Icahn and Lindner); and arbitrage artist Ivan Boesky, an unsettlingly serpentine man who called greed "healthy" and coffee "vampire's plasma." Beside them sat several emissaries from Mattel. They had come for the annual Drexel High Yield Bond Conference, though lately it went by another name: the Predators' Ball.

Their host was the biggest looter of all, so affluent and authoritative that this crowd knew him simply as "The King." Michael Milken was a bone-thin bond trader with a trapezoidal expanse of forehead. His suburban backstory seemed ripped from a Barbie box. A tanned native of Encino, California, Milken was the textbook Valley boy: king of his senior prom, his yearbook's "friendliest" and "most spirited," and head cheerleader of a squad whose roster included Sally Field. In college at Berkeley, he'd sat out the civil rights movement to focus on his fraternity and his investment portfolios. He never smoked, did drugs, or drank, be it alcohol, coffee, or soda. On Wall Street, he was secretive, and obsessive about image; rumor had it he owned almost every photograph of himself ever taken. Bald from an early age, Milken came with an array of headpieces. He intermittently paired a leather aviation cap with a toupee that looked perpetually ready for lift-off—one reporter, with the sensitivity of a Mattel copywriter, called it "a rug you could fly to Baghdad on." By the mid-1980s, Milken came to be seen as a metonym for American capitalism; his birthday was the Fourth of July.

An amateur magician, Milken often performed sleight-of-hand stunts for friends. But his biggest trick had been transforming this conference—once a dreary annual meeting about distressed debt—into a raucous four-day romp of slick video presentations, billion-dollar deals, and lavish partying, where pit-stained bankers could mingle with Barbie-ish escorts paid for by the host's firm. ("The conference has become," as one executive put it, "a gangbang.") Tonight was the grand finale. Every year, the event invited a secret celebrity guest. Last time: Frank Sinatra. This year, rumor had it: "either Michael Jackson or God." When the spotlight hit the stage, out came Diana Ross. It was a fitting choice. She was working on a new album called *Eaten Alive*.

Seven years ago, Ruth's financial ploys had gotten her expelled from the company she'd started in a garage. But soon after, sleaze became something of a norm. In 1980, Reagan landslid his way into the White House, bringing with him an avalanche of deregulation, diversification, arcane financial vehicles, tax breaks, and budget cuts. In his remodeled economy, the incomes of America's top fifth would spike by almost 50 percent, while those of the bottom four plunged. The men at Milken's conference had helped pioneer the art of the "hostile takeover"—a shareholder bid to take over a company, against the will of its leadership, and slash costs, which sometimes meant stripping it for parts. These corporate raids were often heavily leveraged, financed with vast sums of borrowed money, much of raised by Milken himself. The nation had entered the "Decade of Greed," and few embodied it better than Mattel's host at the Predators' Ball.

Milken had popularized a theory about the corporate bond—a kind of securitized debt companies issue to raise capital. Most investors preferred the highest-rated bonds, meaning those that came from "investment grade" companies with strong credit and stable balance sheets. Low-rated bonds, often from struggling companies, were risk-ier and thus less desirable—seen as "fallen angels," or junk. But with the risk came potential reward; investors could collect much more in interest. Milken proselytized for the fallen angels: the broke companies with bad debt, bad earnings, and bad ratings, but just enough promise of future health. In a matter of years, he transformed junk bonds from fringe investment vehicles to a billion-dollar market. Milken made so much that his firm, Drexel Burnham Lambert, let him leave Wall Street for Uncle Bernie's old street, Rodeo Drive. From his desk in Beverly Hills, he became, *The Wall Street Journal* mused, the "highest-paid employee in history." Only Al Capone could claim to top him, if you factored in inflation—though Capone, the paper noted, had been self-employed.

But as Milken worked his way up in the late seventies, Mattel had begun to look a bit like a fallen angel. After the fraud case, the leadership "had no friends," one executive told *Businessweek*. "Everybody walked away from them." Inventory was bloated. Morale was low. Mattel's stock had cratered to $2 a share, cheaper than some of Barbie's tiniest accessories. Their best seller after Ruth left was "Slime," an oozing green goo made primarily from guar gum, an antidiarrheal. It came in its own garbage can. The rescue effort thrust upon Ruth's replacement, Art Spear, one toy executive told *Fortune*, was like "the reassembly of a doll after it had been flattened by a truck."

The revival process involved two major projects. While the Handlers had been distracted by scandal, a little-known company called Atari had released Pong, the first commercially successful video game. Ruth's old foe Kinney, then renamed Warner Communications, had scooped up the business. By the time Reagan took office, it led the new field of toy electronics, while Mattel trailed with some dinky handheld devices (see: the Diet Trac, a "diet computer" that counted calories). The company had poured its resources into a more deserving rival with the "Intellivision," an elaborate home gaming system sold at a premium. The console alone retailed for $295, not including a much-hyped $550 keyboard, which would convert the device into an "Intelliputer." The Intellivision was a direct answer to Atari's popular console, which offered nearly identical games. But as the clunky portmanteau spelled out, the gaming device was explicitly billed as a sophisticate's toy: intelligent television. Mattel chose as its spokesman none other than George Plimpton, the patrician editor of *The Paris Review*.*

At the same time, Mattel tried to make up for an oversight in 1977, when one executive passed on the toy licensing rights for a new film franchise. He'd balked at the $750,000 asking price from a nobody director. Unfortunately for Mattel, the director was George Lucas. *Star Wars*–branded toys sold so quickly they upturned the entire industry. (The year prior, licensed toys only made up a fifth of annual toy sales; a decade later, they would make up 80 percent.)

In 1981, Mattel responded with its own space epic superhero: "an unbelievably ripped hombre," as designer Roger Sweet put it, so cartoonishly bulky it bordered on pornographic. ("Every boy—or man, for that matter," Sweet wrote in his memoir, "would love to have the kind of anacondas hanging from his shoulders that make people draw back in awe.") The result was a male form as exaggeratedly masculine as Barbie's was feminine, so juiced with testosterone it leaked into his name: He-Man. (Barbie, by contrast, only seemed to get girlier that year; "Pink & Pretty Barbie" came in head-to-toe tulle.) In a sense, He-Man was the fashion doll's inverse. If Barbie's mutability had allowed her to adopt infinite jobs and scenarios, He-Man's selling point was his specificity. The line came with a canon of pre-scripted lore, an elaborate space opera with Lucas-like narrative ambition, drafted by an author of the *Star Wars* novels. Mattel called the collection: "Masters of the Universe."

But Mattel's executives were mere mortals. He-Man sold well enough—later scoring its own TV show, then movies—but the next winter, the video game market collapsed. By late 1982, every toy company was hawking some gamified gadget, and often at prices much lower than the Intellivision. As game stocks crashed, analysts concluded that Mattel appeared "to be the most vulnerable." The company was danger-

---

*Mattel's pitch was not that its console was original, but that, with its higher-def imagery, the Intellivision was better at mimicking real life. In ad campaigns, Plimpton stood beside twin televisions, presenting side-by-sides of Atari games and Mattel's more detailed rivals. "You can see how much more realistic Intellivision looks," read one caption. The tagline: "Intellivision—The closest thing to the real thing."

ously close to defaulting on $349 million in loans. As *The Wall Street Journal* put it: "Mattel's greatest glory in recent years, the Mattel Electronics Division, has become its greatest disaster."

Milken had never been scared off by bad debt. The junk bond king was always hunting for some hint that a flailing business was undervalued—and he saw it in Barbie. "I believed in Barbie," Milken later recalled. "There's more Barbie dolls in this country than there are people."

Milken called up Art Spear and offered to personally invest $200 million in Mattel. The company certainly needed the cash; their loans came due in less than a year. But Spear had reservations: "We were concerned about who the shareholders would be." Spear meant Milken's clients, the so-called corporate raiders with a habit of hostile takeovers.

To pacify Spear, Milken teamed up with two private equity firms—backed by investors Lionel Pincus and Richard Riordan—who agreed to inject $231 million into Mattel's operation. The sum was enough to secure a nearly matching loan from the banks and safely avoid default. The way the press told it, Milken was merely an afterthought in Mattel's debt restructure. "The investor group is led by Warburg, Pincus," *The Wall Street Journal* reported, and "includes the investment banking firm of Drexel Burnham Lambert." The article omitted Milken's name.

By the time Mattel's executives showed up at the Predator's Ball that March of 1985, the company had already recovered. "It just took the ability to see the diamond hidden within Mattel," Milken said. The hidden gem, of course, was Barbie, and that year, she looked like one. The couturier Oscar de la Renta had just produced a line of four Barbie dresses. At the ball, Mattel hired "buxom models" to strut around in full-sized reproductions of the doll's designer gowns. Money seemed a faraway issue. This was the decade of Barbie's "Golden Dream" dress—the doll had, the box boasted, "that billion-dollar look."

CHAPTER 15

HOSTILE TAKEOVERS

Judy Shackelford was the kind of marketer whose talents were often described in the language of combat. "She would just brutalize people," former Mattel executive Bruce Stein said, admiringly—"beat the crap out of them." She'd joined the company in 1976, the year after Ruth left, and Shackelford had come to represent the founder's spiritual successor. The culture of the Sales Department "was very bare-knuckled, just kind of a rough and tumble humor," Stein told me. "They were gritty guys." But like Ruth, Shackelford was something of "a ballbuster." She was also an outlier, the rare woman among men, and an out lesbian at a company that had become one of the most prolific producers of heterosexual iconography in the world. "Those were the days when people thought no man would work for a woman," Shackelford said. "I was the one that had the machete in my hand to beat a path."

When Shackelford arrived at Mattel, she pitched herself as an answer to a question the company had been asking. As the C-suite wrestled with Mattel's identity beyond Barbie, the doll division had been wondering something else. Who was Barbie without Ruth? Parents had never played a major role in Barbie's public life, but now even behind the scenes, she was something of an orphan. The doll had not only left the custody of the Handlers, but also that of her other ostensible inventors. Her clothing designer Charlotte Johnson, struggling with Alzheimer's, retired in 1980. And after years of bitter litigation, Mattel finally cut ties with Jack Ryan, sealing his departure with a $10.1 million settlement. Barbie was no longer the brainchild of a single woman; she was in the hands of a whole host of business school graduates and consultants, who all had other things to do. "Nobody was running Barbie for a while," Shackelford told me. "Quite a while actually."

The designers kept designing, but without much oversight, which helps explain some missteps. In perhaps a weird hat-tip to Ruth's second life, Mattel had released "Growing Up Skipper," a version of Barbie's little sister who, with the twist of her arm, could "sprout" breasts. The doll outraged the organizers at NOW. Maybe Mattel could atone, NOW wrote in a letter, by making a male doll whose junk also grew on command. "Of course, we didn't take them seriously," Mattel's spokesman told *The New York Times*. And yet the company showed up at Toy Fair the next year with "Baby Brother Tender Love," an "anatomically correct" doll, down to a plastic scrotum. At last, Ruth could see, if only from afar, how the public responded to a real bulge. (The answer, it turned out, was with death threats.)

The great revelation of Mattel's mistakes was that they hardly seemed to matter. Barbie had weathered Ruth's trial all but unscathed, her line single-handedly raking in some $100 million only a year after Skipper's precocious puberty. Even before Milken's investment, the once middle-class-coded doll seemed to ascend tax brackets. The fifties cheerleader became a celebrity with SuperStar Barbie (the "SuperSize" version stood some six inches taller than the standard dolls), an it girl who got papped ("She oughta be in pictures!" read the box for Fashion Photo Barbie. "And she is!"). She protected her assets with "Fur and Jewels Safe," an alarm-sensitive storage system for toy valuables hidden behind an "oil" painting of the SuperStar herself. The doll's success seemed to radiate off her; unlike their pouty predecessors, the SuperStar Barbies smiled.

But Shackelford saw an opening. She went to her boss: "I said, 'Why don't you let me run Barbie?'" She was almost surprised when he agreed. He gave her an assignment: increase the sales of Barbie's accessories.

Shackelford thought about it. She imagined she was a parent, going to the store to buy a birthday present. *Was she going to buy an individual outfit?* Probably not, she thought. She was going to buy a doll. That was the problem; many of the girls who might want a Barbie already had one. Mattel had sold some 115 million Barbie dolls since 1959 and the market seemed near saturated. And though the line had chugged along with some four or five new dolls each year, they were all pitched at the general consumer, the "Everygirl," or at least Mattel's assumption of who she was. Shackelford needed to give girls reasons to buy more than one. She thought: "I'm going to make all sorts of different kinds of Barbie dolls."

A simple idea: more dolls. And yet, no one had suggested it. Shackelford and her team drilled down into the particular reasons a child might want a doll, dividing Barbie's potential customer base into niche demographics and designing dolls to appeal to those groups. She debuted what was known as a "segmentation" strategy: in lieu of specialized accessories, Mattel would sell specialized dolls. The upsides were straightforward. As M. G. Lord wrote, "Because the costumes were sold on dolls, Mattel could charge more for them."

The first batch was aimed at particular "play patterns": a *glamour* doll, who came with an elaborate dress and primping accessories; a *lifestyle* doll, who came with athletic gear; a *hair play* doll, whose locks could be fashioned in a variety of dos. Then came "Dolls of the World," a collection of international Barbies, though Mattel's interpretation of "the world" initially seemed to mean Europe, debuting with "Parisian Barbie," "Italian Barbie," and "Royal Barbie," who was from England. The year after brought "Scottish Barbie," who wore plaid, and "Oriental Barbie," who served as doll emissary not for a single country or city like the others, but an entire continent. Even then, she managed to remain somewhat Eurocentric: "Oriental Barbie" was from Hong Kong.

The biggest change to the catalog that year had been conceived by Kitty Black Perkins, Barbie's first black fashion designer. She'd joined Mattel the same year as Shackelford and had been lobbying since her arrival for a Black Barbie, not another Christie or Francie or Talking Julia—not another black friend or supporting character, in other words, but a version of Barbie herself. Shackelford agreed. Two decades after Barbie launched, Hispanic Barbie and Black Barbie appeared in the 1980 catalog, the latter sporting a scarlet disco wrap dress, inspired, Perkins said, by Diana Ross.

In essence, Shackelford was reproducing the entire Barbie operation in miniature, multiple times, building out an army of more detailed Barbies, and "creating whole worlds around them." It was something Ernest Dichter, the motivation researcher, might have wanted to unpack. But marketers in the eighties had dropped their sheen of academe, looking less to Freud than Sun Tzu or the Prussian general Carl von Clausewitz. "Marketing warfare was really the key," Shackelford said. Businessmen had started to sound like grizzled generals digging foxholes on the Western Front. "A company's advertising is its 'propaganda arm,' its salesmen are its 'shock troops,' and its marketing research is its 'intelligence,'" Ravi Singh and Philip Kotler wrote in *Marketing Warfare in the 1980s*. "There is talk about 'confrontation,' 'brinkmanship,' 'superweapons,' 'reprisals,' and 'psychological warfare.'"

The latest term of art was "flanking," the offensive maneuver of assailing an enemy from the side, rather than head-on, in the hopes of finding a weakness. Companies could introduce a niche product to find an edge against a rival, rather than attack with a direct competitor (as when Kimberly-Clark introduced Huggies, a disposable diaper with an "hourglass" shape, rather than the clunkier rectangle, an oblique attack on Pampers). Businesses could also flank themselves defensively—strengthen their sides with peripheral products to foreclose a rival's point of entry (as when Pampers made its own hourglass diaper, Luvs). "In marketing," a former Mattel executive said, "you want to 'flank' your brand, so there's very few areas of access for competitors." Shackelford's segments doubled as "flanker brands," expanding Barbie's reach, while ensuring no one else beat her there.

⁓

Over the fall of 1985, Judy Shackelford got a call from an inside source. One of the sales guys had been chatting up some buyers for big box stores like Walmart and Toys "R" Us. A rumor was going around. Hasbro, the Rhode Island operation behind G.I. Joe and Mr. Potato Head, had spent years developing a new toy—a fashion doll designed to compete with Barbie. "I didn't like that," Shackelford said. She wanted to know the details: What kind of doll? Would she have a job? Would she have accessories? When would she hit the market? He wasn't sure. She rang up salesmen from California to Hong Kong. One called back later that week. "He said: *Juuuuudy, I know what it is*," she later reenacted. "*She's a rock star.* And I said: that's all I need to know."

Under normal circumstances, this news might have barely registered on Mattel's radar. For years, Mattel had rested comfortably at the top of the toy industry, while Hasbro hovered among the midsized corporations. Hasbro had spent decades trying to find some rival to Barbie—a "super fashion model" named Leggy, a line of *Charlie's Angels* figurines, a collection of hippie dolls called the "World of Love" (their names: Love, Peace, Flower, Soul, and Adam). None had lasted a single presidential term. But while Mattel whiffed on electronic games, Hasbro had stayed focused on conventional toys, surviving the crash with positive cash flow. While Mattel was being bailed out by Michael Milken, Hasbro had acquired Milton Bradley, another major toy company, bringing its annual sales to $1 billion. That summer, *The New York Times* reported that Hasbro was poised to "snatch the No. 1 industry position from Mattel Inc."

The prospect of a Hasbro Barbie amounted to a greater threat than the average knockoff. Shackelford summoned a "war council," whom she called her "Pink Berets." Her marching orders: Mattel was going to have a rock star too. And they were going to beat Hasbro's to market.

It was the fall of 1985, and Toy Fair was in February; they had to act nimbly. Over the next sixteen hours, the troops inventoried everything music-related the company had on hand—"every guitar, every musical instrument, every piano, every keyboard, every outfit," Shackelford recalled. By the next day, they had a mockup of a new musical doll. They drew up a packaging design and a marketing campaign. They would commission renowned producer Giorgio Moroder—the Italian "Father of Disco" who'd written for everyone from Donna Summer to David Bowie—to compose pop ballads for Barbie's new band. They sent the doll off for production. Mattel was fighting its usual eighteen-month delivery times. Shackelford produced "Barbie and the Rockers" in four.

The Hasbro project in question, in the works for three years, was "Jem and the Holograms," an all-doll girl group, complete with seven characters, a real album, and a number of high-tech accessories, like a yellow hot rod that doubled as an FM radio. Hasbro's display at Toy Fair looked higher budget than some off-Broadway musicals. The company had built a life-sized recording studio in its Madison Avenue display room and hired a young actress to play Jem's full-time secretary, "Jewel." As part of the presentation, Jewel would reach to pull the studio's blinds, at which point the whole set would part like a dollhouse to reveal a hidden gallery. "The room's walls disappear, revealing a series of other rooms," one reporter observed, scored by deafening rock and lined with flashing TVs.

Like He-Man, Jem was going to get her own cartoon. As the marketing copy put it, Jem was really "Jerrica Benton, a savvy Eighties career woman" who had inherited her father's music label (as well as his nonprofit, "a shelter for homeless girls"). Thanks to a supercomputer named "Synergy," which could project holographic images through a pair of techno-magical earrings, Jerrica could transform into her secret rock star alter ego, Jem, "a truly outrageous rock singing sensation." The story's villain would be "an evil competitor" who tries to rig a battle-of-the-bands contest by forming his own doll-based group. His ultimate scheme was "to gain control of Jerrica's company."

In the TV show, Jem would invariably overcome her competitors' attempts at sabotage. In real life, Hasbro wasn't so lucky. After Toy Fair, analysts predicted Jem would have a "credible first year," perhaps making some $40 million by Christmas. Mattel was expected to rake in up to three times that off Barbie and the Rockers alone. "We had that thing put together, and we shipped earlier than they did," Shackelford said, giggling. "The whole world thought they copied us."

Hasbro's leadership knew exactly what had happened. "Everybody knows everything they use for 'Barbie and the Rockers' is all old Barbie parts," Senior Vice President Stephen Schwartz told a reporter. But Mattel played coy in the press, insisting Barbie's timely entry into the music industry was pure coincidence. "It couldn't be" a response to Jem, a Mattel spokeswoman told *The Boston Globe*. "The toy industry is very secretive and the development cycle is so long that they were just coincidentally being developed at the same time."

⁂

Barbie and Jem's battle of the bands was textbook flank warfare. If Jem was, as one outlet put it, "clearly meant to be the Barbie doll of the late 1980s," she was also subtly and strategically distinct—hip where Barbie was stodgy, personified where Barbie was blank. "Whereas Barbie is a one-dimensional character," Hasbro's marketing chief said, "we designed Jem with a sophisticated personality"; she was "capable of meaningful relationships with others." Schwartz put it more bluntly: "Jem happens to have pink hair and makes Barbie look like Phyllis Schlafly."

But Hasbro had made some strategic errors. The company had intentionally designed Jem to stand an inch taller than her rival, forcing customers to buy her proprietary clothing, rather than upcycle Barbie's old wares. The added material for a larger doll with larger clothes translated into higher costs. "The result," as G. Wayne Miller wrote in *Toy Wars*, "was a retail price that Mattel could easily undercut with Barbie." In December, when *Playthings* magazine ranked the year's top toys, Barbie and the Rockers sat comfortably in the top three; Jem did not even make the list. She and the Holograms glitched out after two years.

Hasbro should have known this would happen. Much of Mattel's catalog looked like a cautious two-step with potential competitors. When a rival identified a niche Barbie had not entered, Mattel often put out a new Barbie in the same mold. Back in the sixties, the U.K. company Pedigree released a doll called Sindy—a younger fashion doll with mod style and less "offensive" proportions (without, as Pedigree's managing director put it, Barbie's "damn great bosoms"). Just as Sindy's sales inched toward one million, Mattel responded with Francie—Barbie's British cousin, with the slighter frame. In 1971, the Topper Corporation dropped "Dawn," a six-and-a-half-inch pageant queen whose ability to walk scored her a write-up in *The New Yorker*. The next year, Mattel had "Walk Lively Barbie," who could strut down a runway. And the same year LJN Toys Ltd. made a Brooke Shields doll, whose "Suntan" version arrived in a yellow swimsuit, Mattel put out a line of "Sunsational" Barbies, which came in a darker bronze. Hasbro itself had been on the wrong side of a Mattel flank before; their *Charlie's Angels* line had clashed with Superstar Barbie, who sported Farrah Fawcett's signature hairdo. Hasbro tried to topple Barbie again a few years post-Jem, with "Maxie," who shared Barbie's height and open-ended play pattern. Mattel answered with "Jazzie," Barbie's "cool teen cousin." As stock analyst Sean McGowan told *The New York Times*, she was "a direct shot at Maxie."

No one was immune to Mattel's mimicry, not even old friends. "I knew I couldn't out-Barbie Barbie," Bruce Stein told me over coffee. Stein had spent nearly three years working with Shackelford. She had taught him all the tricks. The year after Jem's launch, he'd left the company to become a vice president, then president of Kenner Products, a midsized toy firm best known for the Easy-Bake Oven. His solution to Mattel's prolific flanking was to create a fashion doll that Barbie couldn't replicate—not by producing an original toy or identifying some new subsegment, but by licensing a well-known entity that itself stood in for the kind of stereotypical femininity that Barbie had come to represent. "We have a concept [Barbie] really can't be," Stein told the Toy Fair crowd in 1991. He had licensed the Miss America pageant.

Kenner's line of Miss America dolls included five contestants with plucky biographies and names right out of *Drop Dead Gorgeous*—Devon, Tonya, Blair, Raquel, Justine. The five beauty queens were safe, Stein thought, because only Kenner owned the toy rights to the seventy-year-old property. But he was wrong. Mattel not only debuted a new pageant doll the same year—"American Beauty Queen Barbie"—but also waged a public battle, accusing three of Kenner's five contestants of imitating Barbie. As the *Washington Post* reported: "Barbie says Miss America ripped off her head." Stein was furious. "I was really upset," he told me. "You know, we were a small company. Mattel could crush us."

It did: Mattel reported Kenner to U.S. Customs for copyright infringement and got a shipment of ninety thousand Miss America dolls seized at the border. Kenner promptly sued Mattel in federal court to wrest the girls—Devon, Tonya, and Blair—out of captivity. Allowing Mattel to force the seizure of the dolls without proving they were pirated, Kenner argued, amounted to unfair competition.

But Mattel was backed by a "heavyweight coalition of business interests"—a smattering of corporations and trade groups with keen interest in expanding Customs' power to crack down on foreign knockoffs. Any court intervention, they countered, could undermine the agency's authority over the border. Both the district court and the court of appeals decided to hold off until Customs administrative proceedings were completed—a process that would take months, all but ensuring the detained dolls would not be released before the Christmas season. The two companies settled the following summer, with Mattel allowing Stein to use one of the three heads, if he decapitated the two other dolls. But by then, Barbie had already won. "The entire success of the Miss America line of dolls," as one paper put it, "depended on its launch." Barbie has survived "an army of imitators," *Time* magazine wrote, though in a sense, she'd done it by forming one of her own.

⸺

The media often compared Jill Barad to Barbie, which made sense the second you saw her. The Mattel marketer also started out as a model. She had the kind of face that you could swear you'd seen in that one movie, and if that one movie had been a 1974 Dino De Laurentiis mob flick called *Crazy Joe*, you would have been right. Her father directed after-school specials, and in the seventies, Barad had scored a bit-part playing a beauty queen who became "Miss Italian America." But acting struck her as "just superficial," she said, so she moved on to cosmetics, then advertising. As an adult, Barad seemed to style herself after the Mattel catalog. She understood the appeal of a well-placed accessory. Her signature was a bumblebee pin, a gift from her mother. The broach, Barad liked to say, symbolized the power hidden within even the unlikeliest creatures. Despite their small wings, bees can fly. They can also sting.

Mattel had hired Barad in 1981, and in a year, she'd flown straight to the top of Barbie's marketing team. She had a natural feel for design, with strong opinions on Barbie dos (wear "fancy clothes") and don'ts (wear orange lipstick). "She's a really creative product person," one executive told me. She'd helped the doll break the "plastic ceiling" with 1985's "Day-to-Night Barbie," a business executive who could transition from chic skirtsuit to evening attire. But Barad inspired the same kind of divisiveness as the doll she sold. Colleagues joked about her middling grasp of math. Rumors proliferated that she had "used her good looks to her advantage," one paper put it, a critique very much of its time. The real issue, several former colleagues said, was that she seemed to share Ruth's tendency to take credit. "She's stolen ideas from other people," a former Mattel marketer told me. "If she likes an idea, she'll push it as her own."

As a marketing director, Barad worked under Shackelford, then Mattel's executive vice president of marketing and product design. Shackelford was, in her words, the "highest-ranking female executive in the world," and Barad became her right hand—her top soldier in segmentation, her deputy in the Jem war. Their work so intertwined that, from the outside, it was easy to confuse who had done what, though the media was often confused in Barad's favor. When the press finally figured out what happened with Barbie and the Rockers, *The Wall Street Journal* reported: "Barad's team managed to produce the doll in just four months." *Bloomberg*, meanwhile, would credit Barad with executing segmentation "beyond anyone's wildest dreams." And Barad would give interviews about her inspiration for one of Barbie's most famous ad campaigns—"We Girls Can Do Anything, Right, Barbie?"—though Shackelford maintains it was a team effort. "She was an instrumental part of it, but she certainly shouldn't be taking credit for it like she made up the whole thing," Shackelford said. "She didn't."

Barad, one executive said, "marketed herself as the Barbie guru." And at a good time. The company was no longer a mom-and-pop, the kind of place easily associated with its founders, with maybe one or two people. Mattel had become a faceless multinational, a financial entity so large it seemed to sustain itself. And the new corporate environment was more cutthroat than ever before. When Art Spear stepped aside as chairman of the board in 1986, he nominated, not one successor, but three—a triad executive committee who would, in the spirit of the eighties, compete against one another for the top job.

Within a year, one dog had eaten the others. The winner, John Amerman, was the "central casting CEO," a former vice president told me—white hair, white shirts, and yellow ties he never loosened, even on airplanes. He always kept three dimes in his pocket for good luck. It should have been a celebratory year; in 1987, Mattel secured one of its most lucrative licenses—the rights to produce Disney's preschool toys. But just six days later, the market crashed in the financial panic known as Black Monday. Over the next year, the company cut its workforce by 20 percent, eliminating some six hundred domestic jobs and consolidating Barbie's two factories in the Philippines. When the Filipino union struck in protest, Amerman simply shuttered both plants, laying off nearly four thousand workers. But if workers were dispensable, Barad had made herself essential.

Amid the shake-up, Mattel's C-suite decided to split Shackelford's jurisdiction in two—spinning off marketing and product design into separate roles, letting Shackelford keep the latter, while giving the former to someone else. It was a demotion, Barad told her boss, which, in fairness, it essentially was. Barad suggested they could resign together, form their own toy company. "She led me to believe she was leaving and would, but she was evasive enough," Shackelford said. Instead, when Shackelford quit, Barad stayed. That August, Mattel announced a promotion. Barad had taken over a new role: Shackelford's.

On Barad's watch, Barbie seemed to break a new sales record each year. "Barbie's flame will never dim," a *New York Times* column declared in 1989. "She has something more important than magic powers or rhinestone garments; she has tremendous breasts." The same year, neocon Francis Fukuyama declared the end of history, predicting the "unabashed victory of economic and political liberalism," brought on by the "ineluctable spread of consumerist Western culture." Barbie stood squarely with the victors. As the Berlin Wall fell that fall, Barbie began her march east, taking over the stores of the former Soviet Union in a gesture that became, Russian poet Tatyana Voltskaya wrote, "a symbol of perestroika."

The outlook was bleaker for Barbie's friend Michael Milken. That same year, he was convicted on charges of securities fraud and racketeering by a young prosecutor named Rudy Giuliani. The allegations painted the picture of an ultra-secretive clan of Wall Street insiders who manipulated stock prices to enrich themselves at the expense of the public.* Milken later pled guilty to six charges, and a judge handed him ten years in federal prison alongside $600 million in penalties.

But executives at Mattel, along with many on Wall Street, rallied around the fallen king. Mattel's new CEO Amerman joined a coalition of ninety executives who took out full-page ads with the headline "Mike Milken, We believe in you." Former Mattel vice president Tom Kalinske,

---

*Mattel made it into the complaint. The traders had allegedly hidden their stake in Barbie from their fellow investors in what prosecutors called a "stock-parking agreement," meaning a stake illegally acquired on behalf of another to conceal their involvement. Prosecutors alleged that Milken and his brother had not disclosed the scope of their Mattel investment. The charge was later dropped when Milken's brother agreed to a plea deal.

one of Spear's would-be successors, went a step further—penning a full-throated defense of Milken in the *Los Angeles Times* headlined: "Milken Deserves Much Praise."

By the end of the eighties, Milken had become an emblem of something larger than himself, and that mythos was tied to Mattel. "Michael Milken has often been depicted as the symbol of the 1980s," *The Wall Street Journal*'s op-ed page wrote, "the Master of the Universe presiding (with Ronald Reagan) over the decade of greed."

CHAPTER 16

THE COLLECTORS

The man camped out in front of the late registration desk at the Hyatt Regency Orlando was named Ken. He wore a goatee and a Barbie T-shirt. He also carried a king-sized pillow, as he'd been sitting there since dawn.

I'd been in Florida for less than twenty-four hours, and this was my second Ken. It was July, and the hotel was hosting the National Barbie Doll Collectors Convention, the doll world's version of Bonnaroo or Burning Man, an annual pilgrimage for connoisseurs who see Barbie not as a children's toy, but as something closer to how she is often categorized by the U.S. Copyright Office—a work of art, one worth paying thousands of dollars to own, and sacrificing entire rooms of their homes to display. Many of these enthusiasts, I learned, had been drawn to the Barbie extended universe because of the names they had in common. According to the program, there were at least two other Kens, a Kendall, a smattering of Kellys and Christies, and twelve Barbaras in attendance, seven of whom were dedicated volunteers. I'd met a Barbie yesterday, and I suspected there were more. The program only included official registrants, and specifically those who had secured their tickets on time. But as Pillow Ken and I could attest, along with the rest of the crowd lined up behind us, not everyone had made the cut.

Frankly, it was pretty hard to make the cut. The convention sells out almost instantly. Each confab ends with ticket sales for the next, and regulars snatch up their seats right away. But here, almost everyone is a regular, leaving little room for impromptu planners or uninitiated reporters. There is a waitlist, though only the earliest birds stand a chance of flying off it. I had signed up for my slot the previous September. But when the conference kicked off on July 4, my would-be registration was still wallowing in standby obscurity. It was only when a Barbie forum poster told me that Orlando locals could, occasionally, scoop up the tickets of any no-shows that I decided to fold myself into a Spirit Airlines middle seat and pray for a late-breaking scheduling conflict. Which is how I wound up waiting with Ken.

One consolation: even the ticketless had plenty to do. The convention, then in its forty-second year, is governed by several traditions, none so treasured as a ritual called "room shopping." Attendees come up to a week in advance to convert their studio suites into small pop-up emporiums, lined with doll displays more elaborate than FAO Schwarz at the holidays. The hotel's upper hallways were dotted with propped-open doors, the rooms so inundated with pink decor that the entryways seemed to glow. Some fans come for this feature alone; it's the only place vendors can sell unofficial paraphernalia, like risqué off-brand outfits or anything related to *Bild* Lilli. Migrating between bright pink rooms amounted to a crash course in collector argot: *NRFB* for "Never Removed From Box," *OOAK* for "One Of A Kind," and *No. 1* or *Ponytail* for the much-desired first-edition Barbie, produced for little more than a month in 1959. But a ticket was the key to everything else—the annual Barbie fashion show, the daily banquets where organizers give away more merch than Oprah, the doll-hair threading workshops, the auction where custom Barbies sell for upward of $20,000, the ceremony for the annual "Barbie's Best Friend Award," and the seminars on everything from collectors' insurance to "Making Doll Size Tropical Drinks."

"We've had people try to bribe us and everything," the woman at the desk said. Bribery, it turned out, was not necessary, though an NDA was. Ken and I forked over the requisite $475, and I slipped the legal paper into my pocket without signing it. It was a good time to be obsessed with Barbie. Greta Gerwig's movie was scheduled to come out in three weeks, and one would have been hard-pressed to find a sentient creature on American soil who had not heard something about it. The promotional campaign had gone well beyond trailers and billboards. The past six months had brought an unrelenting flood of Barbie-related merchandise, from washable rugs to limited-edition fuchsia Xbox controllers, to a low-calorie pink lemonade, to a line of "on-chain virtual collectibles" designed to "empower women" to "explore Web3." The doll was on Gap apparel, Starbucks cups, Superga shoes, and Funboy pool floats; she was at Primark, Bloomingdales, a dedicated Amazon store, two pop-up cafes in New York and Chicago, an immersive museum in Los Angeles, and a boat cruise around the Boston Harbor. The Barbie logo had plastered itself on so many products that a visiting extraterrestrial could reasonably conclude that America had at last heeded King Camp Gillette and handed its operations to a single hulking megacorporation with a thing for pink. It was an exercise in what branding strategists called "culture jacking," and the culture of the Barbie convention had certainly been jacked. You could barely walk to the bathroom without being stared down by a cardboard cutout of the movie's multi-Barbie cast.

Though BarbieCon was perfectly timed for the press rollout, it had barely registered amid the daily coverage of Barbie brand activations, the casts' archival Barbie outfits, or the box-office race against a movie about the atomic bomb. Unlike most aspects of Barbiemania, this event is not technically orchestrated by Mattel. The five-day festival is painstakingly put on by various collectors clubs scattered around the country. But Mattel still plays a crucial role in the programming. A small clique of lanyarded staffers roam the grounds like celebrities—sitting at a special front table during meals, giving speeches with exclusive sneak peaks of forthcoming lines, holding court at a designated meet and greet, where collectors line up along literal red carpets, clutching doll boxes like offerings, pointing out different designers like subjects waiting for the king.

Mattel was also one reason for the convention's low public profile. As an official Barbie licensee, the convention was subject to certain corporate stipulations. When I'd reached out for a press pass, my requests had been forwarded straight to Mattel's Communications Department. They were promptly rejected. I pitched a piece to a national newspaper, who reached out again on my behalf—no dice. Mattel's uninvolved involvement in the convention is an emblem of its complicated relationship with Barbie's most devoted fans: collectors who love Barbie, but also spend every free moment studying the kind of historical trivia any public relations department would prefer to be forgotten.

Collecting, less science than religion, has only a distant relationship with rationality. "There is just a fascination about the Barbie doll that defies description," said Sibyl DeWein, a pioneer of the hobby who became known as the "Dean" of Barbie collecting. "We call it 'The Barbie Mystique.'" There is, even among the most arcane or absurd collections, something spiritual going on. Collectors—in their attempt to impose order on chaos, to grasp the entirety of something, to construct a perfect archive of the past—become, as avid object-gatherer Walter Benjamin put it, "interpreters of fate." It is a kind of ritual, essentially iterative; collecting is something one simply does, and does again. Each acquisition invites a hunt for the next. For the book collector, "not only books but also copies of books have their fates," Benjamin affirmed. "And in this sense, the most important fate of a copy is its encounter with him, with his own collection."

So it's perhaps unsurprising that Barbie, a copy whom Mattel kept copying into new costumes, new professions, new worlds, became a collector's item almost as soon as she hit the market, and well before anyone unafflicted by the hobby would consider her something of value. In the early sixties, there was no infrastructure or community or received wisdom for Barbie collecting, the way there was for stamps or baseball cards or rare coins or even older dolls. The first devotees were autodidacts, making their own records of release dates, niche trivia, and manufacturing idiosyncrasies. By 1969, there were enough of them to form a group: the Barbie Collectors Club of California. Based just a few miles from Mattel's headquarters, the chapter was the first and then only of its kind, and welcomed stragglers from elsewhere. DeWein joined as a "member-at-large" from her home in Tennessee. Through the club, she struck up a correspondence with another collector named Joan Ashabraner. In 1977, they published *The Collectors Encyclopedia of Barbie Dolls and Collectibles*, the first book on Barbie, whose insights on the particulars of early molds—the distinctions, say, between a No. 1 and a No. 3— became so vital to the still-nascent scene that insiders nicknamed it "The Barbie Bible."

Armed with the Bible, the adherents of Barbie's creed organized quickly. In the Bronx, a woman named Ruth Cronk founded a collectors club with its own media arm. Cronk initially ran a somewhat renegade operation—sneaking a friend into Toy Fair posing as a buyer, calling her monthly publication the *No Name Newsletter* to avoid becoming the next docket entry on Barbie's extensive list of lawsuits. But Mattel's executives, whom DeWein had contacted during her book research, were starting to pay attention to Barbie's adult fans. In a canny gesture of allyship, they granted select collectors permission to use the Barbie name—the *No Name Newsletter* became *The International Barbie Doll Collectors Gazette*; over in California, a collector named Dori O'Melia started another fanzine, *The Barbie Bulletin*. Soon there was *Barbie Talk*, *Barbie Penpals*, *The Barbie Companion*, *The Barbie Network Newsletter*, and the similarly named *Barbie News Network*. These homespun zines gave way to more professional products, the glossy magazines like *Barbie Bazaar* and *Miller's Barbie Collector*.

Mattel kept apprised of the collectors' work. In 1980, when Cronk organized the first convention at the Travelodge Hotel at JFK Airport, Mattel sent souvenirs: gold-plated "Mini Barbies" (a nod to a collector favorite, the tiny meta-Barbies that had come with the 1965 Skipper ensemble "Me 'N My Doll"). The first convention drew only about a hundred fans. But Mattel's head of licensing Beverly Cannady came too. Her presence was a signal that this assortment of mostly older women were more than hobbyists; they were a burgeoning market. "That first Barbie convention?" Cannady wrote in a letter to Cronk. "What an eye-opener for Mattel!"

But no one brought more attention to the cause of Barbie collecting than an elusive club kid who appeared, as if from nowhere, in eighties Manhattan.

᠅

There are several mysteries about BillyBoy*, foremost his name, which is spelled with an asterisk and which he insists is his sole legal appellation—"That's what it says on my Social Security card," he told the *Chicago Tribune*—but which the occasional baffled reporter nevertheless shortened to the simpler "Mr. Boy." There was also the matter of his age; he told those same uneasy writers that he had been born six thousand years ago, and also in 1960—in either New York, or somewhere south of Poughkeepsie, but east of Nantucket, or Egypt. He had been found as a baby, sailing down the Nile, or abandoned on a doorstep in a "lime-green groovy vinyl basket, with a little shoe hat perched on my head and a little Barbie in my hand, wearing an enormous '40s cocktail ring." Alternatively, he had been an accident, the unplanned child of an Austrian man and an "Egyptian beauty," who had dropped him off at a Staten Island orphanage, where he was adopted by a cowboy and a professional gambler. BillyBoy*'s attitude toward accuracy resembled that of *Simpsons* lawyer Lionel Hutz ("But what is truth, if you follow me?")—which perhaps made him a natural ally for Mattel.

What can be said with some confidence is that by his mid-teens, BillyBoy* had left his adopted home and driven around the country before moving into downtown Manhattan's Chelsea Hotel. He started a series of businesses specializing in haute couture, selling garments like a tuxedo accented with a plastic lobster, or a leather jacket with dinosaur spikes. He befriended a litany of art world, fashion world, music world bold-name somebodies, from Jean-Michel Basquiat to Keith Haring, Sid Vicious to the Ramones, William Burroughs to Andy Warhol. He was also rapturously obsessed with Barbie. His collection had trailed him since he fled home, having—allegedly—"purchased a 1950 black Cadillac limousine with a gray mohair interior" and "filled it up with Barbie dolls." By his mid-twenties, he claimed his stockpile numbered somewhere near eleven thousand.

BillyBoy* was eye-catching: a skeletal six-four, with an oblong face always hidden by circular shades, and a hairstyle that changed as frequently as his favorite doll's. He caught the eye of increasingly prominent magazines; in *ELLE*, the artist was photographed with a Barbie perched on his shoulder "like a little bird." When a copy wound up at Mattel, the company reached out. "At the time," wrote Jean Pierre Lestrade, BillyBoy*'s partner and an artist known as Lala, "Mattel executives in general had very little awareness, if any at all, of a potential adult collectors market."

This too, of course, was not quite true. Mattel did know collectors, but none like BillyBoy*. As Lala recalled: "I remember that he used to go to board directors meetings, with his slicked down platinum white blonde pre-war styled hair dressed in slick black vinyl, sometimes wearing a casual wool miniskirt by Mary Quant over black wool leotard—and smothered in exotic and rare jewels."

Unlike the convention organizers, whom Mattel merely encouraged, BillyBoy* crossed over from enthusiast to employee. He joined forces with the company and embarked upon a series of elaborate projects aimed at endearing the dolls to adults—mocking up designs for new lines; writing the first book about Barbie aimed at a wider audience (*Barbie: Her Life and Times*); and, in 1984, organizing a peculiar and expensive nationwide tour. The latter came out of BillyBoy*'s belief that Barbie was not just a symbol of America's evolving ideas of womanhood, but a nearly year-by-year chronicle of high fashion, both in the States and abroad. He saw his Barbies as contiguous with his collection of vintage haute couture—and his tour endeavored to put the two in dialogue: he restaged a landmark exhibit from 1945, called "Le Petit Théâtre de la Mode," a touring fashion show and a collaboration between the biggest names of French couture—Hermès, Balenciaga, Lanvin, and fifty others. As fabric remained scarce after the war, the designers had modeled their clothes in miniature, using terracotta dolls.

For his version, BillyBoy* recruited many of the same designers and as many of his own high-fashion friends—Balmain, Christian Dior, Christian Lacroix designed Barbie ensembles. Yves Saint Laurent himself designed sixteen outfits. The garments were embroidered with so many jewels that when the exhibit came to New York, the display was surrounded with armed guards. BillyBoy* called it the "New Theater of Fashion," or the "Nouveau Théâtre de la Mode."

The first installation had raised money for war relief—underscoring, as art historian Juliette Peers observed, the "confluence of patriotism, propaganda and French couture" embedded in the figure of the fashion doll. BillyBoy*'s revival, in a sense, carried on the nationalist spirit, only the nation was Barbieland and the money went to Mattel. It further inscribed Barbie in the world of high art—a subtext that became text when the tour culminated in a lavish party, mobbed by models and artists and celebrities, at which Andy Warhol unveiled a new painting. He had undertaken to paint BillyBoy*, whom he saw as "the last SuperStar." But BillyBoy* had told the pop-artist that he "was not very interested in having his own portrait done," Lala wrote. "He'd rather have one of Barbie." Besides, he said, borrowing Flaubert's apocryphal line about *Madame Bovary*: "Barbie, c'est moi." When Warhol revealed his new work, the crowd beheld a tableau of Barbie's SuperStar grin against a blue backdrop. The title card read: *Barbie, Portrait of BillyBoy**.

Jill Barad embraced Barbie's new status as a symbol of pop art, the collapse of culture and commerce embodied by Warhol's work. (She would later commission a second Warhol portrait for Mattel's headquarters in the company's signature red.) The year after BillyBoy*'s exhibit, Barad's Barbie division began catering to collectors—1986's "Blue Rhapsody Barbie" was the first of Mattel's "collector dolls," premium figurines designed less for children than adults. As with Barbie's other segments, these dolls had a noted sales advantage. Because they were limited-edition, and made from quality material, Mattel could charge a much steeper price. The "Happy Holiday Barbies," a line of exclusive dolls that went on sale each winter starting in 1988, were marked up by more than 300 percent. "Mattel had no intent to market to adults," the company admitted in an employee handout, "but collectors were making the company an offer it couldn't refuse."

But Mattel's most pointed effort to reposition Barbie as something art-like was a subtle change on her box, the kind of alteration kids would ignore but collectors would love. For decades, the designers of individual Barbie dolls or ensembles lingered in obscurity, unless they happened to have a patent. But Mattel began crediting the doll's designers—an attempt to create a celebrity culture around their in-house artists. Collectors would come to know designers like Carol Spencer, Kitty Black Perkins, and Carter Bryant. When BillyBoy* put out his own specialty doll, "Feelin' Groovy Barbie," also in 1986, he became the first to sign his work. "Designed by BILLYBOY*," the box read, "internationally famous designer."

⁂

"You can tell it's not an original," Glen Offield told the crowd, "if you look at the lips closely." Some two hundred avid collectors were seated in the theater of the Niagara Falls Convention and Civic Center, craning to see Offield, a lean, flanneled man, whose head hair seemed to have fled to the dense brush above his lip. He was holding up what appeared, to the untrained eye, to be an average Barbie. It was July of 1992, and this crowd was just a sampling of the hordes who'd descended on the "Honeymoon Capital of the World" for the twelfth annual collectors' convention. (This year's theme, aptly: "Barbie's Wedding Dreams.") Offield was leading a seminar on "Barbie-doll fraud detection," and he had already detected one. A woman in the crowd had brought a specimen—a doll for which she'd coughed up thousands, only to find it was a fake. The tell was in the spittle-like sheen, he explained: "Mattel doesn't use high-gloss paint."

Offield was an authority in the Barbie collecting economy: a frequent contributor to fan magazine *Barbie Bazaar* and an institution at Barbie events for nearly as long as Cronk. When *Smithsonian* had photographed Barbie for her thirtieth anniversary, it was Offield's collection on the cover. And for good reason: his was among the largest and most valuable in the world. His holdings, which spanned somewhere between five and seven thousand dolls, went beyond the classics one might recognize from catalogs, or the short-lived niche releases. He had acquired the private archive of Barbie designer Charlotte Johnson; he had courted Mattel titans for rare handmade samples—singular demo creations, like the talking Barbie built with a clear plastic torso, to show off her speech mechanism. Offield's most prized possession was the only model known to exist of Becky, a never-released Barbie friend from 1971. Another collector once offered him $20,000 for it, but Offield refused. His Barbies were worth more to him than money, than most things really, maybe than being alive. "If I had a fire in my house, I'd just stay," he joked during his seminar. "They would find a skeleton in a clump of plastic."

This proved to be less of a hypothetical than Offield could have intended. About three months after the Niagara convention, the collector came home to find there had been a fire in his house. In fact, there had been two. Over the weekend, while he had been away at another doll show, someone had broken in, doused his home in gasoline, and set the place ablaze. When the first went out too quickly, they'd come back the next day to burn the rest. By the time Offield returned, what remained of his property had been bandaged in police tape. But in the wreckage, there were no clumps of plastic, no melted torsos, no Becky—his Barbies had disappeared. "Somebody knew exactly what they were doing," a fire department investigator told the press.

The theft of Offield's collection, estimated to be worth some $1 million, was "perhaps the largest Barbie doll heist in the nation's history," the *Los Angeles Times* reported. When the San Diego Police Department opened an investigation, the saga of the "Barbie bandit" became national news—attracting the attention of papers from the *Orlando Sentinel* to *The Sun*, a *Bild*-like British tabloid, which ran an item on the caper. *Spy* magazine ran an eight-page spread on the scandal. "Barbie, America's Favorite Plastic Sex Symbol, Was Recently Kidnapped," the subhead read. But if the heist was, on some level, a testament to Barbie's ever-growing desirability, it quickly became the kind of salacious story Mattel did not want.

As the investigation progressed, attention turned to the collector's life outside of Barbie: he worked as the art director for "Another Video Company," a film studio in San Diego specializing in gay porn. His boss, a prominent real estate agent named Bruce Scott Sloggett, was also Offield's landlord, who had, it turned out, been house-sitting the weekend of the fires. But during the police inquiry, Sloggett had mysteriously disappeared. About a week into the search, one of his staffers called in with a tip claiming the porn producer was still in town. The staffer had, to avoid being evicted, threatened to come forward about the missing Barbies; Sloggett had bombarded him in the shower and shoved a 9mm revolver in his mouth, chipping a tooth. It was enough to secure a warrant to search Sloggett's villa, where they found the realtor lying low amid his own array of toys: two safes stuffed with jewelry, a library of several hundred porn flicks, and a stash of BDSM equipment to rival Jack Ryan's—whips, chains, and a sauna with a built-in sex swing.

Sloggett had, it turned out, been collecting crystal meth; he had several ounces at his house. On top of the assault, the cops booked him for possession with intent to sell. A week later, Sloggett was dead—after posting bail, the realtor swallowed a fatal combination of meth and morphine. The friend who found him mentioned in passing that Sloggett kept a storage unit under a nearby freeway. When the detective broke in, they found a yellow refrigerator surrounded by packing boxes stacked "floor to ceiling," bearing labels for "bottled water" and "cherries." In fact, they were filled with Barbies. Sloggett, it emerged, had fallen into debt—his business was failing; he owed money over real estate deals—to pay it off, he'd made arrangements to scalp Offield's collection abroad. It was the natural by-product of Barbie's asymptotic approach toward being a work of art: she had become collectible, valuable, something to steal.

The Offield heist, extreme as it was, seemed to capture the complexities of courting Barbie's grown-up fans, whose incursions into Barbieland necessarily brought some of the baggage of the adult world—sex, drugs, crime. They loved Barbie as much as any child, maybe more. But they were also independents, less compliant and malleable and virginal than one of Barbie's blank friends. Adults, unlike kids, could raise real complaints. They could organize. They had their own desires. Unlike Barbie, they had real lives.

Maybe the first sign of trouble had come when Andy Warhol died, a year after painting Barbie's portrait. BillyBoy* had already been souring on Mattel, with its corporate hesitation to fully realize his designs. He "could not stand Barbie's smile," for one. He'd wanted his dolls rendered with closed mouths and "Anna May Wong" black hair. He claimed Mattel had dismissed many of his designs as "too lavish to produce." Warhol's death seemed to mark something ending. BillyBoy* put his Barbies in basement storage and stopped collecting; eventually, he even sold the portrait, auctioning it off at Christie's for more than a million dollars.

If BillyBoy* had simply returned to jewelry-making or clothes collecting, Mattel might have greeted his departure amicably. But BillyBoy* did not just quit, he had introduced a doll of his own—an "anatomically correct" fashion model with an angular black bob, a closed mouth, and the kind of luxe wardrobe that Mattel would have never approved. (She was created, Lala explained, "basically out of desire to express his ideas fully.") Her outfits—couture shapes hand-sewn from "wool tweeds, silk prints, satins and rich brocades"—retailed for anywhere up to $700. Her dollhouse, built by French cabinet makers, sold for $20,000. Even her name seemed expensive. It looked like a mistyped Roman numeral: Mdvanii, pronounced *med-vah-nee*.*

Billyboy named her for Isabelle "Roussy" Mdivani, who once, he later wrote, "came to me in a dream." Roussy was an eccentric Georgian aristocrat and sculptor known

BillyBoy* was tired of being seen as "the wacky designer." He billed Mdvanii as an intellectual's doll. ("She can wear fabulous necklaces of uncut stones and still understand existentialism," he told the *Times*.) But he couldn't help himself. When he introduced Mdvanii's friends, he gave them names like: Dheei, Rhogit-Rhogit, Zhdrick, Tzulli, Muio-Bix, Jobbi, and Ouimi.

Mattel could not have welcomed BillyBoy*'s alt-Barbie, wacky or otherwise. Their relationship devolved into legal disputes, the precise terms of which remain as mysterious as BillyBoy*'s birth. On the couple's blog, Lala later claimed, obliquely, that Mattel had made "unfair and arbitrary decisions," certainly some related to copyright. But BillyBoy* has not spoken publicly about the terms of his separation, having decided in 1993 "to refuse all interviews and media appearances." (One former Mattel Collections designer, who had her own copyright dispute with the company, concluded after several failed attempts to reach him: "He got the NDA.") At one point, Lala tried to write about BillyBoy*'s work in *Barbie Bazaar*, but the article was killed. The editors told him that "Mattel forbid the publication."

BillyBoy* was just one collector, but Barbie's adult fan base grew exponentially into the nineties. By the middle of the decade, collectors estimated their numbers hovered around 250,000 people worldwide. Mattel's collectors' lines netted $35 million in 1993, then $220 million three years later. But the collectors did not always approve of Mattel's increasingly corporate culture. Many of them had been drawn to Barbie for the handicraft of the early clothes, and some started to complain that quality had been sacrificed at the altar of efficiency.

For a time, in the mid-nineties, it seemed that every holiday season brought some new scandal. There was the "Poodle Parade Barbie" debacle of 1995—a reissue of a beloved 1965 doll, whose hair had originally fallen into soft curled bangs. The hair on the new version jutted out from her forehead like the shelter of a bus stop; it looked, outlets reported, like it had been "trimmed with a chainsaw." Then there was the new Francie, a

---

for her throuple with Spanish artist Josep Maria Sert and his wife, Misia Sert, as well as for traipsing around Paris with, a relative recalled, "two monkeys dressed in rich Oriental brocades."

revival of the slighter sixties doll, which BillyBoy*, years earlier, had told Mattel was a fan favorite. The 1996 Francie's shoes had been manufactured too small; they split if anyone tried to put them on her feet.

Those paled in comparison to the fiasco of Holiday Barbie, which in 1995, had become so valuable that stores across the country experienced a shortage. (Some at Mattel speculated that collectors were hoarding the dolls for resale on the lucrative secondary market.) Barad increased production each year and in 1997 tripled the original quota, flooding the market with three million Barbies in Christmas-colored chiffon—and spoiling the resale market. Collectors were furious. "If De Beers let loose," one told the *Journal*, "the price of diamonds would plummet."

The collectors were souring too at the company's efforts to control how adults engaged with the doll. They bristled at Mattel's refusal to lend the Barbie name to unsanctioned events, including a Michigan children's fundraiser called "Barbie Grants a Wish Weekend," and at the cease-and-desists sent to independent doll artists, like several furriers who sold Barbie-sized minks. "Mattel has taken action after action that is hostile to our group," a collector named Priscilla Wardlow said. "They are stealing our hobby. We want our hobby back." When longtime collector Joe Blitman pushed his book, *Barbie Doll and Her Mod, Mod, Mod, Mod World of Fashion*, Mattel barred him from using several of his own photos, because they depicted the doll beside sleeping pills or champagne. But Mattel's logic made little sense to people who knew the Barbie catalog better than many employees. The company could not prohibit pictures of alcohol on moral grounds, one club leader pointed out to reporters. They had long sold Barbies with wine-serving sets.

The final straw came that spring, when Mattel attacked a Barbieland institution—*Miller's* magazine, which had published an excerpt of Blitman's book (and had, until then, been running a series on *Bild Lilli*). The outlet was one of two glossy magazines centered on Barbie. But unlike its rival, *Barbie Bazaar*, *Miller's* was independent, unlicensed, and prone to subtle critique, mixing photospreads and price lists "with barbed product reviews and occasional satire." The lawsuit, filed in Los Angeles federal court, alleged trademark and copyright violations, demanding the founders, a married couple named Dan and Barbara Miller, pay monetary damages and cease publishing articles with "false or disparaging statements." During the proceedings, Mattel's lawyer allegedly said: "We want the Millers' house."

After three years of scandals, the fan clubs were prickly. "Online Barbie chat groups buzzed about First Amendment rights and what collectors viewed as Mattel's Big Brotherish behavior," *The Washington Post* reported. A Chicago collector named Ian Henzel tried to "focus" the rage, building a website called "PINK ANGER" and calling for a "pinkout"—a pledge to boycott Barbie for thirty days. The pledge spread across the internet, onto other continents, translated into German and Japanese. In a sign of solidarity, bloggers replaced the B's in Barbie's name with asterisks, writing "*ar*ie" in online forums. Participants inundated Mattel with complaints scrawled in pink letters—an influx so color-coordinated that it became part of the publicity, nicknamed the "Pink Tidal Wave." "It's just like the sixties," said collector Norita Bergmann, who'd previously clashed with Mattel over the name of her Michigan-area club. "It's us versus them."

In the press, Mattel downplayed the boycott's impact on Barbie's $1.7 billion in annual sales. And perhaps they were right. But the executives took it seriously enough to meet with the movement's leaders. In mid-May of 1997, three Mattel vice presidents hosted an unprecedented summit with the top organizers of the Pink Wave. The protestors tapped two delegates to represent them. And yet, after six hours of negotiating, the parties left without resolution. "They want everyone to go away and be happy in Pink Land," collector-side negotiator Sandi Holder said.

The press covered the conflict with condescension, dismissing the collectors' concerns as the quibbles of middle-aged women upset over "bad hair" and "chintzy shoes." But the core of the boycott was a fight over corporate censorship and an independent press. "This isn't about saccharine-smile blond fashion dolls dressed in pink, polyester, Velcro-clad clothing," collector Melissa Pitman insisted. "To us, it's about freedom of expression." And it was precisely that point on which Mattel was most resistant. "Who better to control the image of Barbie," Mattel spokesman Sean Fitzgerald asked, "than those who developed the image of Barbie?"

The executives eventually offered collectors new shoes for Francie, and replacement heads for Poodle Parade Barbie, at no additional cost.

They would not, however, drop the case against *Miller's* magazine. Mattel "loves the collectors," Jill Barad assured shareholders at the annual meeting that spring. But they could not interfere with Barbie's public profile. "What I do in my job, first and foremost," she said, "is protect Barbie."

Mattel made its point. The court found in their favor, ordering the Millers to pay nearly $35,000 in damages—an insignificant sum for a multibillion-dollar corporation, but not for an independent magazine. The outlet had stopped publishing before the verdict and after it, never resumed. For some, it sucked the pleasure out of the hobby. Even among those who kept at it, some uneasiness remained. At the height of the Pink Wave, Pitman had asked a pressing question. "This is about big business squelching my right to say and read and write whatever factual information I choose," she said. "If Mattel succeeds in this action against the Millers, who is next?"

CHAPTER 17

THE *BUDDENBROOKS* CYCLE

In 1993, a twenty-five-year-old named Igor Vamos spent the summer in his parents' basement doing corrective surgery without a scalpel, or, for that matter, a medical degree. He was the head of a guerrilla group whose members spanned from teens to octogenarians. They were mercenaries mostly, hired hands he found through relatives or whoever. He met one of them at a twenty-four-hour Kinkos, scanning zines in the middle of the night. All operated under code names, like "Leptus Face" or "The Arm."* Vamos went by "The Conductor."

The year prior, Mattel had introduced Teen Talk Barbie, whose digital talking mechanism enabled each doll to recite a random 4 of 270 pre-recorded sentences. One of them was: "Math class is tough!" (When the American Association of University Women slammed the line as sexist, the company countered that she also could say: "We should start a business.")

Vamos had read about Teen Talk Barbies. He thought they were so funny and stupid. He spent months stocking up on Barbies and G.I. Joes, disemboweling them in his subterranean workshop and swapping their voice chips. He would solder the subjects back up and ship them off to operatives across the country. Recruits would inspect his shipments, file "patient reports" to track inconsistencies, and slip them back onto toy store shelves. He called this process "shopgiving."

---

*An incomplete list of known code names: The Tuba Man, Fifi Le Femme, Shoeless Joe, Okeechinpo, Wonder Woman, Wonder Girly, Zorro, Talkin' Tina, The Cleaner, Operative UHQ, Milquetoast, The Woolverine, The Eye, Madam X, Devastator 5100, The Unknown.

That Christmas, a seven-year-old boy in San Diego opened his G.I. Joe, only to hear him purr: *Let's plan our dream wedding!* Little girls discovered their Barbies had deep baritones and spoke in vaguely threatening axioms: *Dead men tell no lies.** The Conductor released a video taking credit for the mass doll exchange. It was shot to look like a hostage film—with ransom note graphics and B-roll of dolls operating on themselves. "I'm Teen Talk Barbie, the spokes-doll for the B.L.O.," one chirped. "That stands for the Barbie Liberation Organization."

Given Mattel's history, one might have expected the company to sue. The Conductor did. A paralegal friend told him: "They will litigate until you lose your pants." But if Barad or Amerman or anyone had wanted to, it would have been hard to know who to serve. Vamos's spokespeople identified themselves only as "Barbie" and "Joe." In the press, toy executives acted as if they'd been mailed anthrax. "I've got a very strong negative feeling," one told *The New York Times*, "about terrorist acts against children." Vamos loved that. He'd paid for the stunt with an art grant from New York state. "Publicly funded terrorism," he said.

It was not the doll's first time going under the knife in the name of art, Barbie-related art being, like collecting, nearly as old as its subject. (Future members of the Beach Boys put out the single "Barbie" in 1962, under the name "Kenny and the Cadets.") But if collectors idolized Barbie as she is—"never removed from box"—this other adult audience tended toward something more like dismemberment, lifting parts, synthesizing some new whole, at times more literally than others. As early as 1967, conceptual artist Adrien Piper was dissecting Barbies in her "Barbie Doll Drawings," simple pen illustrations of dismantled doll limbs. In the seventies, photographer Cindy Sherman began shooting deconstructed Barbies and other mutilated dolls. Around the same time, Barbie became the namesake of a Marge Piercy poem. "Everyone saw a fat nose on thick legs," went one line. Later: "So she cut off her nose and her legs / and offered them up."

In the late eighties and nineties, the doll seemed to multiply across

---

*Vamos also experimented with a hybrid Barbie and "Seymour Butts" doll the latter of which, a patient report noted, "farts, belches, hacks, vomits." But an operative determined that the "sounds could be better," and that, despite his $19.99 price point, Seymour was "a rather low-quality fellow."

artistic mediums—making cameos in novels like Alice McDermott's *That Night* and Barbara Kingsolver's *Pigs in Heaven*, getting spoofed in movies like *Weird Science*, taking new shape in sculpture and figurative painting. "Barbie has been reimagined in versions of Marcel Duchamp's *Nude Descending a Staircase*, in pastiches of Edward Hopper's dystopian cityscapes, as Edouard Manet's *Olympia*, as the *Venus de Milo*, and as Botticelli's *Birth of Venus*," two legal historians observed. Cyberpunk pioneer Rudy Rucker named a character in his *Ware* tetralogy "Kendoll." Comedian Jeffrey Essmann played a teetering, alcoholic Barbie in his one-man show *Artificial Reality*. *The Simpsons* spent an entire episode spoofing Teen Talk Barbie in "Lisa vs. Malibu Stacy." Exhibits popped up in museums from the Smithsonian and MoMA to the Oakland Museum and London's V&A. Photographer Scott C. Schulman shot the doll undergoing durability tests with increasingly torturous sounding names—"The Bite Test," "The Leg Pull," and just: "Flammability."

"Barbie's miniature life reflects what has been called the *Buddenbrooks Cycle*," *The New York Times* wrote in 1991, "in which the first generation makes the money, the second contributes to the civic good, and the third becomes artists." A solid recap, though notably, the entrepreneurs and artists of Thomas Mann's generational epic do not hold one another in especially high esteem. "Every businessman is a swindler," one theater-lover says. His businessman brother spits back: "You're an abscess, an unhealthy growth on the body of our family."

⁓

Todd Haynes was in grad school when he made one of the most famous Barbie works, a winking but sympathetic study of the Carpenters frontwoman, Karen Carpenter, shot, as one critic observed, "in the manner of Douglas Sirk's melodramas."* *Superstar: The Karen Carpenter Story* charted the seventies singer's rise to fame and untimely death in 1983 after a prolonged battle with anorexia, which Haynes reenacted with Barbie dolls. As the singer becomes increasingly emaciated, the Karen Barbie begins to lose literal chunks of plastic from her face and arms.

---

*Haynes was a Sirk fan; his fifties period piece *Far from Heaven* later paid homage to, among others, *Imitation of Life*.

Haynes screened the film in 1987 at scattered festivals and indie venues, but after two years, it all but disappeared. The forty-three-minute short has since become a cult classic, not just the most famous work of unsanctioned Barbie art, but "perhaps the most famous nonpornographic bootlegged video" of all time. Even now, when pirating films requires little more than a media player and a search engine, the accessible versions have a samizdat feel. (One available copy features a birthday message from whoever originally taped it: "HAPPY BIRTHDAY BILL / LOVE SEAN").

The lore of *Superstar* has as much to do with Haynes's battle to screen it as Carpenter herself. Haynes and his team made efforts to shield the film from litigation—reaching out to the singer's label for permission, avoiding any explicit references to Barbie, describing his mechanical cast in marketing materials as "Barbie-sized dolls." He wasn't lying. The dolls were a mélange of used parts scavenged from thrift shops and remolded past the point of brand legibility—the Dionne Warwick doll had reportedly been Frankensteined from a Barbie-like body and the head of an off-brand Michael Jackson.

Even so, it wasn't enough to evade Mattel's notice. The film broke an internal consensus: that Barbie could not appear in a movie. When it came to cinema, the toy company was "always overprotective of the Barbie franchise," Barbie's former marketing director told me. "If somebody plays Barbie and if that person shoots up heroin or whatever, it's a negative reflection on Barbie."

Mattel had commissioned plenty of derivative works—from the Random House books to a line of records called *Barbie Sings!* to a direct-to-VHS dance tape featuring Paula Abdul. But the company did not want to impede Barbie's open-ended fantasy by attaching her to any one story, and thus transform her from adaptable archetype to particular character. The earliest Barbie books had been allowed some creative liberties—filling in details on her parents or hometown—but there was little continuity. And the stories were constrained by the Mattel catalog. Their illustrations, for example, had to "utilize Barbie's costumes whenever possible," as Random House editor Robert L. Bernstein warned an artist in 1963. "Mattel is very particular about Barbie."

By the eighties, any backstory elaborated in the books had largely been discarded. The sanctioned projects were usually as empty as their protagonist, sparse on particularizing details or borrowed from stories so familiar—*King Arthur* or *Arabian Nights*—that they announced themselves as myth. When *Barbie* magazine depicted the doll in "protodramas"—short stories told in pictures—their narratives were episodic, offered without context or personal history. The staff could not portray Barbie's family, save Skipper, who was for sale. "Barbie has no biography to be passed on," editor Karen Tina Harrison told M. G. Lord. "Barbie simply is. No one knows where she came from or how she got there."

Mattel-approved artists often had to cannibalize material the company had already produced. The photodramas were "always based on a product of some kind," art director Pegi Goodman told me, which is not to say they could not be creative. Bernard Maisner, a graphic designer who was introduced to me as the "Hand of Barbie," designed Barbie's penmanship for the magazine's advice column. Maisner also moonlights as a hand actor—he did handwriting for Daniel Day Lewis's Newland Archer in *The Age of Innocence* and Johnny Depp's Ichabod Crane in *Sleepy Hollow*. His process, he explained, calls for an intensive character study, examining the stroke and shape of their script until he can duplicate it on command. He spent weeks in the Library of Congress studying old letters to prepare for his scene as the hand of Lee Harvey Oswald, who switched, unpredictably, from cursive to print. Barbie, of course, had no old letters, nor much of a paper trail. Maisner made her typeface from the letterforms of old logos.

But for Mattel to tolerate a reproduction of Barbie, it had to be, as Bernstein put it, "as identical to the doll as possible"—a perfect likeness, an authentic, sanctioned copy of its copied doll. Perfect, not only in its aesthetic faithfulness to the doll itself, but existentially: Barbie could not be flawed. Barbie solved problems—a friend's heartbreak or wardrobe crisis—she did not have them herself. "Only glamour could befall Barbie," Harrison said. This quality seemed to rub off: when a Barbie comics writer sent the doll to a homeless shelter, Mattel forced her to "de-grit" the scene—redecorating the facility with lush carpet, outfitting the residents in designer clothing—so it wouldn't "scare" children.

Live-action adaptations seemed particularly risky; they would give the blank doll a human face. A few months before *Superstar* came out, the company had scrapped plans for a "Barbie TV Magazine," partly over concerns that no actress could approximate the doll's unblemished generality. Sharon Stone's attempt to pitch a movie, a few years later, earned her "a lecture and an escort to the door." Around the same time, Mattel barred Barbie from appearing in *Toy Story*.

Haynes had doubly erred: casting Barbie in an unauthorized movie and linking the immortal doll with not merely sickness but death. In 1988, Mattel began inundating his producer with copies of various Barbie patents and legal letters. At one point, representatives even showed up at Haynes's office. Mattel never pursued legal action, but the company didn't need to. Karen's brother Richard did it himself in 1989 (not coincidentally, the year he produced his own TV special, *The Karen Carpenter Story*). Haynes had not succeeded in licensing the music, and the combined legal threats of the Carpenter estate, the Carpenter label, and Richard's publisher forced the film underground. Richard even called on Haynes to recoup remaining cassettes from retailers and destroy them.

It was a demand Mattel could appreciate and was maybe even inspired by. Though perhaps someone should have noted the side effect: Haynes's movie became all the more alluring because of the scandal of it being suppressed.

꒰꒱

The adult interest in Barbie foreshadowed a change at Mattel. The toy industry was then getting acquainted with a trend that would get repeated in so many articles and market research studies that it would get its own acronym: KGOY, or "kids getting older younger." The concept was so simple as to be self-explanatory, and the marketers of the nineties were not the first to notice it. Thirty years earlier, the *Esquire* writer who'd asked Ruth about "Freudian" marketing had argued that the grade-schoolers of the sixties were both more sophisticated and more primitive—profligate drug users and criminal geniuses but also "post-literate," prone to communicating in an "esoteric, multi-leveled, and intricate" blend of gestures that bordered on "telepathy."

The article, absurd then and now, was borne out in at least one respect, decades later: children were literally maturing faster. Studies showed that children were going through puberty earlier—with some girls developing breasts as young as eight. These biological changes seemed to coincide with a cultural shift: children's tastes matured faster too. Perhaps because of the instant availability of adult culture through television and the internet, kids began tiring of their childhood toys more quickly, sidelining dolls and action figures for teen accessories like Walkmen and computer games. Girls who once bought Barbies until age ten were starting to tap out at five. This trend, also called "age compression," became "the core challenge facing the toy industry," one analyst told *The Washington Post*. "And it's magnified with Barbie."

The task facing Mattel's executives was to make Barbie appealing to girls who now saw themselves as too old to play with dolls. In 1990, the company started supercharging Barbie's stable of licensed goods, introducing more products aimed at teen girls—human-sized clothing, bed sheets, trading cards, cookbooks—accessories to that could escort Barbie fandom into adulthood. They called it the "Barbie Style." The goal was to create a market around the *idea* of Barbie, one that could rival, or even outstrip, the physical doll. The only problem was that, by that point, most Americans already had an idea of Barbie, and it was not necessarily the one that Mattel was going for.

By 1995, Barbie's likeness was everywhere, her name inserted into more songs than could fill a trunk load of cassettes. David Bowie had named-dropped her in "Young Americans." Joni Mitchell had crooned about a "perfect air-brushed angel" who is "like a Barbie doll." The Lunachicks's "Bitterness Barbie" imagined the doll balding, post-mastectomy, while Rick Monroe gave her a drug habit in "Barbie's Got a Jones."

Many of these Barbie art projects shared a common theme. Mattel had made the doll easy to adapt, a template that could be altered for any scenario. Thus: Fat and Ugly Barbie, Big Dyke Barbie, Mentally Challenged Barbie, HIV-Positive Barbie, Suicide Bomber Barbie, Exorcist Barbie, *Carrie* Barbie, and Klaus Barbie Barbie—modeled, with perhaps unintentional accuracy, after the Nazi who spent three decades in the Americas, hiding under a pseudonym. A group called the Barbie Disinformation Organization stamped home-printed stickers on boxes across the Northeast, transforming "Barbie's Stylin' Salon" into "Barbie's Lesbian Barber Shop," which gave the doll a mullet. "The Barbie Liberation

Organization has inspired a wave of Barbie knockoffs and 'adjustments' all over the world," *Mother Jones* reported. Some of these adjustments were physical: Cindy Jackson would set the Guinness World Record for most cosmetic surgeries, after going under the knife thirty-one times to become the first human Barbie doll. "Barbie was the blank canvas I filled in," she told CBS.

Amid the flood of off-brand Barbie work, Mattel disseminated some of its own—commissioning the coffee table book *The Art of Barbie* in 1994, and sponsoring, the year after, a New York exhibit called "Art, Design, and Barbie: The Evolution of a Cultural Icon." Between the two undertakings, Mattel solicited nearly two hundred pieces from artists like *Looney Tunes* cartoonist Chuck Jones and LeRoy Neiman, the so-called "Holiday Inn expressionist" whose fluorescent paintings of athletes managed to rival Barbie in both obscene popularity and critical revulsion.

These works were, in relation to the swelling repository of Barbie artifacts, merely the topsoil of a towering midden; the cleanest, most presentable pieces handpicked to present Barbie in the most flattering, most commercial light. (Aptly, the exhibit was installed in a high-rise at the World Financial Center.) The standards were so specific that the company at times took issue with even its own selections. Executives "were horrified" when Nancy Burson, a photographer best known for digitally morphed portraiture, presented her contribution to the book: *Aged Barbie*, a black-and-white portrait of the original Ponytail, with crow's feet. Mattel pulled it from *The Art of Barbie* manuscript. The artworks that made it into the book and the exhibit were so heavily policed that even the artists themselves could not use them. When former Mattel Collections designer Anne Zielinski Old asked to sell prints of her Barbie illustration and donate the proceeds to an AIDS charity, Mattel denied her request.

But for all its efforts, Mattel misunderstood the public's interest in the idea of Barbie; an artwork that "only glamor befell" was not especially interesting. The New York exhibit was panned as toothless and dull. Barbie historian M. G. Lord slammed the show as "a vapid collection of glittering junk," an "advertisement" redolent of "a three-dimensional corporate annual report." The exhibit, it turned out, had also lost contributors over heavy-handed censorship. Curator Steven Dubin quit after objections to his catalog essay. "Mattel's public relations representative returned my essay, sanitized in red pencil," the media studies professor wrote. "Among other things, I discussed sex, death, and lawsuits."

CHAPTER 18

PRESIDENT BARBIE

The field of presidential hopefuls should have been getting smaller in July of 1992. The major parties had picked their nominees—Arkansas governor Bill Clinton on the Dems' ticket, incumbent George H. W. Bush on the GOP's. Ross Perot, the squat Texan billionaire running as an Independent, had temporarily dropped out. But that month, two inanimate objects and one cat entered the race. Russ Troll, a four-inch doll, rolled out his platform with a series of bumper stickers, a toll-free constituent hotline, and a campaign poster of his rainbow-haired head etched onto Mount Rushmore. Then came Morris, the feline mascot of pet food brand 9Lives, who announced his "cat-didacy" with a press conference at New York's Winter Garden Theater, the decade-long home of Broadway musical *Cats*. (His spokesman, a twenty-four-year-old Adam McKay in a plastic cat nose, contrasted "fat-cat" politicians with Morris's innate "animal magnetism.") The remaining candidate, neither thirty-five nor precisely American, kicked off her campaign the old-fashioned way: with ads.

President Barbie's hair was coiffed in a news anchor bouffant. Her arm was perpetually bent for a welcoming wave. Her wardrobe—a red pantsuit with gold lamé accents and a "star-spangled inaugural gown"—conveyed professional decorum without sacrificing sex appeal. She boasted extensive military experience, with stints as a naval petty officer, a Marine Corps sergeant, and an Air Force pilot during the Gulf War. She'd already garnered a substantial base—that year, by Mattel's count, a new Barbie was selling roughly every two seconds—though few of her supporters could vote. Her campaign managers had conducted robust toy-store exit polling to develop a platform that skirted hot topics like "the abortion issue" in favor of promises to champion world peace, racial harmony, and free ice cream. Her first endorsement came from a billion-dollar corporation: Toys "R" Us had, as one paper put it, "an exclusive contract with Mattel to sign Barbie up for personal appearances in homes at about $20 a pop." She even had the start of her first political scandal. Voters had not yet learned, another paper joked, that "Ken, Barbie's preppy pal, was appointed to the Coast Guard during the Vietnam War."

The campaigns were stunts, of course, joke marketing that satirized the familiar genre of platform rhetoric while tying a product to a year's worth of national news. But they also tapped into a certain cynicism about politics, and its decreasing distinguishability from big business.

Barbie's bid for one of the world's highest offices bordered on redundancy; the doll had never been more powerful. Unlike prior conflicts, the Gulf War, short and televised, had accelerated sales of military toys; Barbie's Pentagon-approved uniforms had flown right "off the shelves." Former secretary of defense Harold Brown, a former nuclear weapons designer who'd run the Pentagon under Jimmy Carter, had joined Barbie's board of directors. Barbie herself was on track to hit $1 billion in annual sales, thanks in part to "Totally Hair Barbie," a hair-play doll whose Rapunzelish mane had made her Mattel's fastest selling toy of all time.

The credit had gone to Barad; barely two weeks after Barbie hit the campaign trail, she became Mattel's president.

When Clinton won that fall, it seemed that Barbie had too. At the inauguration, *The New Yorker* compared the first lady's "tinselly gold scarf" to the "one that the Barbie for President doll wears." Clinton had promised to form a "new covenant" with the American public, dispensing with the trickle-down economics from which Barbie had benefitted. But Clinton's "New Economy" would look a lot like the old economy. At the dawn of the decade, "there was a sensation, mostly unspoken, that the vibe of the eighties would robotically continue," Chuck Klosterman wrote in *The Nineties*. Financially speaking, they seemed to. Reaganite deregulation accelerated, not just domestically, but internationally. And thanks to Reagan's weakened antitrust enforcement, the merger boom that dominated eighties finance spread to other industries—"Big Mergers Get Bigger in the '90s" read one headline. "The most powerful political forces in our society," Naomi Klein wrote in *No Logo*, "are as likely to be multinational corporations as politicians."

The toy industry in particular seemed to be "playing monopoly," *The Wall Street Journal* reported, with the three largest American toy makers—Mattel, Hasbro, Tyco—acquiring more than a dozen competitors in the first half of the decade. Tyco bought View-Master, then Matchbox. Hasbro bought Tonka. Mattel alone scooped up Mexican toy maker Auritel, sports toy company Aviva, Uno-maker International Games, Kransco (maker of both Hoola Hoops and Frisbees), Scrabble manufacturer J. W. Spear, the license for eighties fad doll Cabbage Patch, and—in a $1.2 billion dollar deal—the infant gear behemoth Fisher-Price.

By 1994, the traffic of international toys had become more of a carpool, with just five companies accounting for 60 percent of the business—a shift partly owed to Barbie's campaign backer, Toys "R" Us. The so-called supermarket for toys had itself spent the eighties cannibalizing the corner store, establishing itself as the big box destination for all things play. "The predominance of Toys "R" Us is unprecedented," two toy historians wrote in 1990, "and everyone assumes it is permanent." Because Toys "R" Us ordered toys every month of the year, seasonality seemed nearly a thing of the past. "They would make an event out of Easter. They would make an event before summer," Bruce Stein said. "So you could keep loading them with product." The industry had never been closer to a Christmas in July. And Mattel's balance sheet looked like an upward arrow—growing almost 15 percent per year.

"On a relative basis," one stock analyst said of Mattel, "they're eating the industry's lunch." In fact, they tried to. One momentous week in 1996, Mattel tried to buy Hasbro, mounting a $5.2 billion "bear hug"—a nominally friendly bid with a less-than-veiled threat to turn hostile. ("Barbie proposed to G.I. Joe and she won't take no for an answer," wrote the Associated Press.) The hypothetical mammoth, which the press nicknamed "Mat-Bro," would have controlled nearly a third of the toy market. "It could be the apocalypse of the industry," one sales rep said.

Hasbro's CEO rejected the offer as "patently absurd," rallying an opposition that spanned from Steven Spielberg to several congressmen—including a Kennedy, Ted's son—who alerted the DOJ. Then, as quickly as it had started, Mattel withdrew the offer after just nine days, blaming Hasbro for going "scorched earth" in the press. In the aftermath, Amerman looked for something else. "There is no question in my mind," he wrote in an internal memo, "that there will be additional acquisitions and/or mergers." He found one. By the end of the year, Mattel bought Tyco.

Among Clinton's first acts as president-elect was to invite Jill Barad to Arkansas for the "Clinton Economic Conference." She showed up in a pink pantsuit, with her bumblebee pin. Mattel had always been aggressive about cutting labor costs, but under Clinton, it would become a ruthless advocate of demolishing obstacles to global trade. For six years, the member nations of the General Agreement on Tariffs and Trade (GATT), a post–World War II treaty designed to encourage international commerce, had been negotiating a new pact that would, as Clinton's trade ambassador boasted, "bring down more barriers further than any trade agreement in history." Critics warned that the new deal, which created the World Trade Organization, would give corporate allies greater power to "pre-empt the regulatory authority of government agencies."

One of the most pressing questions for the U.S. was whether China could remain a "most favored nation," a vaunted trade status which allowed for lower tariffs. Since the Tiananmen Square massacre of 1989, a suite of human rights abuses had triggered backlash on the left and center. During the campaign, Clinton had accused Bush of "coddling dictators," by vetoing legislation that would have conditioned China's trade status on compliance with modest human rights standards. Barad saw it differently. The Barbie empire had been built on cheap foreign labor. (Or as she told the conference: "It wasn't until we went to lower cost sources, that in fact we were able to dominate the world-wide toy market.") Hindering those imports would upend Mattel's business model. "Though I know, President-Elect Clinton, we are all very, very concerned with the human rights situation in China," Barad said, "we would hope there is another way to address this situation that would not affect American industry."

It was not the first time Mattel's demand for low-paid workers would ally the company with repressive governments. When Clinton considered imposing tariffs on Indonesia in 1993, over the Suharto regime's crackdown on labor rights, Mattel rushed to defend the status quo. Punishing Indonesia, Mattel argued, risked pressing Western values upon another cultural tradition. It would also, as Amerman wrote to Clinton's trade head, "severely impair Mattel's competitiveness"—or at least its Barbie factory in Bekasi. Mattel found an ally in Henry Kissinger, who echoed the company's case for sidelining human rights. Clinton listened. Before his first midterms, Clinton had broken with his party to "delink" China's trade status from its human rights record. The same year, he announced a $40 billion trade program with Indonesia. The new GATT pact was finalized in December of 1993, making it even cheaper to import toys from abroad. A Mattel trade consultant told the *Journal*: "Barbie is the big winner here."

But no nineties policy whet the appetites of big business more than the North American Free Trade Act, or NAFTA—a proposal to establish the largest free trade zone in the world by effectively removing all barriers between the U.S., Canada, and Mexico. Reagan had proposed the pact during his first campaign in 1979, and when Bush Sr. revisited the idea a decade later, many feared it would offshore American manufacturing jobs so suddenly that the country would hear, as Ross Perot memorably put it, a "giant sucking sound going south." But Mattel quickly took up the cause. NAFTA would really *benefit* American companies, a spokesperson told *The New York Times*, by lowering the costs of business. Besides, the reasoning went, Mattel couldn't fire American manufacturing workers. They no longer had any.

When Clinton picked up where Bush left off, Mattel became one of NAFTA's loudest corporate boosters. Fermín Cuza, the company's vice president of government affairs, also chaired the NAFTA advocacy committee for the industry's most influential lobbying group, the American Association of Exporters and Importers. (Its stated goal: to "eliminate regulatory and legislative friction to trade.") Cuza went on the offensive—granting interviews with major outlets and testifying before the House of Representatives. With the optimism of a hippie leading a drum circle, he told the committee that the pact would "foster a spirit of cooperation"—a warmth that could spread to other perennial problems, from "drug trafficking" to "the environment." This would all redound to the American worker, Cuza argued: "NAFTA could actually save U.S. jobs that might otherwise be lost to offshore production."

But after Clinton signed NAFTA in late 1993, Mattel did the opposite. The company may not have had any American workers left to fire but its new acquisitions did. And before NAFTA's first birthday, Mattel announced plans to put one thousand of them out of work. The executives soon shuttered a Fisher-Price plant in Upstate New York, citing "increased company imports from Mexico." It's not that the company was short on cash. The same quarter, Mattel told shareholders its net sales had summited to $3.2 billion, making 1994 the "sixth consecutive year of record sales and earnings." As a reward, Mattel's top five executives pocketed more than $12 million in bonuses.

Mattel had made itself one of the "poster children of NAFTA," but it was not alone reversing course. A Public Citizen study of sixty-six pro-NAFTA companies found that nearly all had broken promises to create American jobs. As one headline summarized: "Job Losses Only Thing NAFTA Created." In reality, NAFTA helped create something else. As tens of billions of American dollars flooded across the border, Mexico plunged into an economic panic, sending the government careening toward sovereign default. Clinton scrambled to orchestrate a $20 billion bailout. "The United States is now looking like Mexico's junk-bond financier," *The New York Times* opined. "It's the sort of deal Michael Milken would understand."

───※───

Li Qiang was twenty-five when he saw a man light himself on fire. It was early 1997 in Zigong, a city in China's Sichuan province known for what has been found under its surface: dinosaur fossils and salt. The man had been laid off from the Salt Company, where he and his wife had worked for twenty years. "With a lighter in his hand, he poured gasoline around his body and up the steps of the municipal building," Li later told a legislative commission on U.S.-China trade. "I can never forget his desperate face." The police intervened; the man survived; and Li, a student getting by off a small construction supplies business, began working with labor rights groups to help workers address grievances. For three years, he salted factories—getting jobs, then organizing the staff—until he started to fear it would land him in jail. With a fake passport, he fled to Thailand, then the U.S.

There is a video of Li on C-SPAN, shot one month after he arrived. A congressman had organized a press conference to oppose the U.S.-China Relations Act, which would make China's free trade status permanent. Li—hair tousled, button-down mussed, looking like a skater costumed in business casual—holds up a Farberware can opener. At his old factory, his team made fourteen hundred of these per day, he says through an interpreter, while standing for thirteen-hour shifts. At night, management paid them $40, to split between all twenty-three workers. "Do you know what these multinational companies are doing?" he asks. "They are treating Chinese workers like machines."

He points to his blue shirt, his green tie: "I have never seen a tie before in my life. My pants, my shoes, my shirts are all new here. But they are all made in China. There's no way I cannot buy these clothes. I find myself supporting those people who are exploiting my people." Abruptly, he announces: "I am finished," and leaves the podium. The room is silent, even by C-SPAN standards. Clinton signed the bill five months later.

Li is now in his fifties, a father of two based in New Jersey. He is the driving force behind China Labor Watch, a nonprofit he started a few months after the conference. Each year, Li sends teams of undercover investigators into the Chinese factories of multinationals, posing as workers to survey conditions unglamorized for corporate audits. For two decades, he has published exposés on factories supplying Amazon, Disney, and Ivanka Trump's shoe brand, where one manager assaulted a worker with the heel of a stiletto. His online archive has been hailed as "one of the few public sources of information about what goes on inside the world's largest manufacturing hub." And many of its reports—almost one a year—are focused on Mattel, with whom, Li told me, he has "a personal feud."

The feud dates back to 2011, when Hu Nianzhen, a worker at one of Mattel's subcontractors in Shenzhen, walked off the roof of the factory and fell to her death. Li learned that Hu had been tormented on the job—harassed for bad eyesight, scheduled for eleven-hour shifts, seven days a week. Her family, China Labor Watch reported, was barred from seeing the body for "security concerns"; when they returned in the evening to burn incense nearby, security beat them up, sending several relatives to the hospital. Mattel conducted an internal investigation, concluding that Hu's case had been an "isolated event." But from then on, Li "just started to doubt Mattel's credibility."

There was no China Labor Watch in the mid-nineties, though others had peered into the far-flung factories of American business. A decade before the GATT pact, Barbara Ehrenreich and Annette Fuentes had written about a Mattel facility in the Philippines, nicknamed the "motel" ("because we are often told to lay down or be laid off"), where management offered "prizes to workers who undergo sterilization." (This was not why the company halted its operations there in 1988; but because of a hike in the minimum wage.) But as the barriers to trade evaporated, more stories of labor abuses seemed to break through. *Harper's* published the pay stub of a girl in Indonesia who sewed Nike sneakers for $1.03 a day; a labor group revealed that Kathie Lee Gifford's line of Walmart clothing was stitched by Honduran tweens working twenty-hour shifts. Anti-sweatshop activism coalesced into an international movement. By 1996, even the business-friendly *Wall Street Journal* was running a serialized profile of a girl in Guangdong who bruised her hands stabbing hair into Barbie heads.

That Christmas, reporters at *Dateline NBC* aired a segment about a Mattel supplier in Indonesia, where kids as young thirteen sewed Barbie clothes until eleven p.m. The *Dateline NBC* segment caught the company "off-guard." In response, Mattel laid out what it called its "Global Manufacturing Principles," which officially banned hiring anyone under sixteen. "Simply stated," Barad said, in the 1997 announcement, "Mattel creates products for children around the world—not jobs."*

Mattel was not alone in adopting its own code of conduct. By the late nineties, Naomi Klein wrote, "the entire sweatshop issue had degenerated into a maze of warring codes." For the most part, these were glorified press releases injected with rosy idealism, "hybrids of advertising

---

*It seemed less simple the following spring, when a union put forward a shareholder proposal to link executive pay, including Barad's, with child labor compliance; Mattel's board called it "redundant," urging voters to reject the motion, which they did.

copy and the *Communist Manifesto*," Klein wrote—nonbinding, unenforceable, and drafted without input from the workers they concerned. Mattel's was an outlier, not in the rules it imposed, which were boilerplate, but in its enforcement. Mattel pledged to regulate not only its own factories, but its contractors and suppliers, subjecting them all to scrupulous monitoring—which, unlike most voluntary audits, which were internal and private, would be conducted by an independent third party and published for the public to read. "It was totally unprecedented," CUNY management professor Prakash Sethi said. "There just weren't any systems of its kind."

He would say that—he was running it. The *New York Times*, at least, seemed to agree, claiming that Mattel, in 1998, began subjecting its factories to "an unparalleled degree of oversight." But like any politician, Barad remained sensitive to public image. Despite promising to enforce the code across suppliers, the company never gave its auditor access to its licensing partners, arguing that the investigations should prioritize Mattel-owned facilities. But those proved tricky too. After the first round of audits uncovered extreme fire hazards at a Mexican plant, Mattel executives exerted "considerable pressure" on the investigators to modify their report. "The companies seem to be more willing to show to the public that they are doing something," Li said, "instead of actually changing anything substantial." The problem is that eventually, the public looks away.

⁂

It was Barad who brought Ruth Handler back into the fold, or at least she took credit for it. "I brought Ruth back after years of exclusion," Barad said. (Ruth remembered the initial invite came from John Amerman.) The ousted executive returned to her old headquarters in 1991, the year Jack Ryan died. Three years later, Barad made her a Mattel spokeswoman, and four years after that, a Barbie "Ambassador of Dreams." Enough time had passed to forgive Ruth's fraught history. Or maybe Barad sensed that she was about to repeat it.

Like Ruth, Barad became CEO at an inauspicious time. When Amerman tapped her in August of 1996, Mattel's sales had started to slow. The Mat-Bro merger had failed. Sales at Fisher-Price were sinking. The company had just reported its first flat quarter in eight years. And an ex-employee had filed a whistleblower lawsuit, accusing the company of systematically inflating its earnings in a scheme that sounded a lot like the one that had gotten Mattel's last woman president pushed out.

A former senior vice president named Michele Greenwald claimed she had been fired after informing her bosses of an illegal accounting maneuver. As she told it, Mattel owed its titanic annual growth in part to so-called "push programs"—covertly offloading merchandise onto retailers at the end of the quarter, in exchange for future "free goods." The pressure to hit targets had escalated into 1994, she claimed, when Mattel secretly deferred a $19 million debt to Disney, inflating its earnings by 15 percent. (Greenwald produced a Mattel PowerPoint slide which referred to "manufactured" earnings and Disney-related "accounting games.") Mattel called the lawsuit "unwarranted and baseless," commissioning an investigation from a former SEC lawyer, whose report later cleared the company of all wrongdoing.* But soon after, the company quietly disclosed a $15.1 million charge to the SEC, for correcting its transactions with Disney. ("Ms. Greenwald," her lawyer said, "feels vindicated.")

At the same time, Mattel had started attracting unwanted regulatory scrutiny. The Federal Trade Commission had been investigating the toy world for two years, and in 1996, it charged Toys "R" Us for orchestrating an elaborate price-fixing conspiracy with some dozen toy makers, including Mattel. (Mattel denied wrongdoing, but settled a related lawsuit brought by the attorneys general of forty-four different states for $8.2 million.) In response to the case and the growing threat of Wal-Mart, Toys "R" Us stopped ordering toys with its prior zeal. As a result, a Dartmouth case study observed, "Barbie could no longer grow at 15 percent a year or more." In fact, Barbie sales were falling for the first time in years.

Like Ruth, Barad tried to make up that revenue with acquisitions—Tyco, then Barbie competitors American Girl Doll and Polly Pocket. But

---

*A judge granted Mattel a win when he ruled that Greenwald did not qualify as a whistleblower. "There is nothing in the record that she ever reported anything to anybody until after she was terminated," he wrote. "I'm not disputing whether a public policy issue is involved, but you have to put your lips together and blow and Michelle Greenwald never did that."

in an increasingly consolidated toy market, Barbie's fate was tied up with that of Toys "R" Us. In March of 1998, the toy chain dropped a bomb. To keep up with Wal-Mart, it was simplifying its maze-like stores—and slashing annual inventories by half a billion dollars. The reaction across the toy stock market was immediate. Hasbro lowered their earnings forecast right away. But not Mattel. "Jill would not take the number down," one executive told me. "She said, 'We'll get clobbered by The Street.' But you know, there's your truth and God's truth, and your truth doesn't count."

Eventually, she took the number down, twice. In September of 1998, Mattel cut their expected earnings growth in half; then, three months later, they dropped it even lower, declaring a revenue shortfall of $500 million. The about-face did not help Mattel's situation. "Cutting guidance twice in the same year is an indication that you don't really have a handle on the problem," analyst Sean McGowan explained. "It says you didn't do a good job the first time or things are getting a lot worse."

CHAPTER 19
SEX, DEATH, AND LAWSUITS

With all this going down, one might think Mattel wouldn't have bandwidth to care about a middling Eurodance song produced by a Danish-Norwegian pop group. And for a time, it seemed the company did not. "Barbie Girl" came out in March of 1997, a tertiary track on *Aquarium*, the studio debut of European bubblegum band Aqua. Keyboardist Søren Rasted, inspired by seeing some vintage Barbies at a Copenhagen kitsch exhibit, had wanted to spoof "the 'plastic' world of Barbie and Barbie-like people"—a goal he executed with edgeless literalism. (The hook: *I'm a Barbie girl, in the Barbie world. Life in plastic, it's fantastic.*) Lyrics were not key to the group's appeal; their sole prior release was a reggae dance cover of "Itsy Bitsy Spider."

At least one Mattel executive seemed to like it. "I think it is a funny song," the executive said on Danish radio. "If there are such funny and good songs about Barbie, we're all for it." But after a limited U.S. release of 340,000 copies sold out in a single day, someone at Mattel evidently changed their mind. The company sued Aqua's label, MCA Records, claiming the song associated Barbie with "antisocial themes such as promiscuity, lewdness, and the stereotyping and ridiculing of young women." The complaint cast the music video, which featured a scene of the band playing with mannequin limbs, as a sinister storyline about "the KEN doll dismembering the BARBIE doll by pulling off her arm." As Richard Carpenter had with Todd Haynes, Mattel called for all existing copies of the single to be recouped and destroyed.

To the outside observer, the case could seem like a textbook First Amendment issue—the song a straightforward parody, its lyrics protected speech. But there were some reasons for Mattel's lawyers to think they had a shot at editorial control. A year before, the Dr. Seuss estate had sued Penguin Books for publishing *The Cat NOT in the Hat! A Parody by Dr. Juice*, a novelty children's book which told the story of the O. J. Simpson trial in Theodor Geisel's signature rhyming style. ("One knife? Two knife? Red knife. Dead wife.") The publisher defended the book as parody, but the Ninth Circuit sided with Seuss. The judge, a Reagan appointee, drew a distinction between "parody," which directly critiqued the copyrighted work, and "satire," which used the copyrighted work as no more than a "vehicle to poke fun at another target." (The notion that a work could mock two things at once seemed, to this judge at least, an artistic impossibility.) The book's true target was the Simpson trial, the judge concluded—not Seuss; thus imitating the author's rhyming scheme and illustrations was not protected "fair use," but an advertising gimmick designed to "to draw consumer attention to what would otherwise be just one more book on the O. J. Simpson murder trial."

The Seuss ruling, which Mattel cited in its case against Aqua's label, seemed to open the possibility of distinguishing the company's conception of its popular doll from how she was seen by the public, erecting a legal fortress around the former to exclude the latter from First Amendment protection. Through this lens, Aqua's song could be construed as a send-up, not of Barbie the doll, but of the bimbo consumerism she had come to represent, rendering any use of the Barbie trademark a mere gimmick—satire liable for suppression. Mattel had always been protective of its billion-dollar doll. But in the mid-nineties, the company sought a virtual monopoly on her public image, even, or perhaps especially, as Barbie's grip on the fashion doll market began to weaken. The Aqua case was just the highest profile in a spate of lawsuits against Barbie-related works, each more absurd than the last. Mattel's cease-and-desists were so prolific that the "standard cultural studies conception of Mattel" became that of "an intellectual property bully."

With Barbie, Ruth had once said, Mattel tried not to set trends but follow them, so that Barbie could "reflect the world around her." And in the abstract, it could seem that Mattel's legal crusade upheld that credo. The *Seuss* ruling followed several decisions in the twilight of the millennium that seemed to have raked the complex landscape of intellectual property law toward trademark and copyright owners. "The signal feature of the intellectual property system of the late twentieth and early twenty-first centuries," legal historian Dan Hunter wrote, is that it is "not really a system of incentives, but rather a technology of control."

And yet in truth, Mattel's aggressive litigation strategy was not just a means of adapting to a new corporate reality, but a way to actively shape it; its censorious cases, even those that did not prevail, as one attorney observed, affected "a slow erosion of the entrenched copyright and trademark laws against large corporations." In the war on the public domain, Mattel was not a soldier. It was a general.

The same year Mattel sued Aqua's label, a graduate student was sifting through the Mark Twain archive at Berkeley, and came across an unpublished manuscript titled *The Great Republic's Peanut Stand*. In his later years, Twain, dead broke after pouring his fortune into ill-conceived inventions like an exceedingly complex proto-typewriter with some eighteen thousand parts, became an advocate of stringent copyright protections—testifying before the Congressional Committee on Patents in his signature white suit, and trying, vainly, to trademark his own name.

The manuscript, his only extended treatment on the subject to which he devoted much of his non-writing life, was composed as a Socratic dialogue between a "Statesman" and a "Wisdom Seeker," a less than subtle stand-in for Twain himself. The Statesman advocates for the founders' conception of copyright—as a balance between the rights of the author, who needs compensation to incentivize creation, and that of the public, whose ability to flourish demands access to information and ideas. The "Wisdom Seeker" has a different idea: "I would amend the law and make copyright perpetual." His model would still benefit the public, he argues, by saving books that would otherwise "be hustled to death and flung away at the end of the term under the present evil system." But it would also redound to the author, who would get eternal "ownership in his property in place of a mere leasehold."

Twain's idea does not sound so radical now, when copyright is so jealously guarded that Disney can bludgeon a daycare in Florida into removing an unsanctioned mural of Minnie Mouse. But, as the grad student cultural historian Siva Vaidhyanathan later wrote, "copyright in the

American tradition was not meant to be a 'property right,'" at least as the owner of a car or blender might understand the term. "If nature has made any one thing less susceptible than all others of exclusive property," copyright skeptic Thomas Jefferson once mused, "it is the action of the thinking power called an idea." Jefferson saw the patent as a state-created monopoly on thought, an "embarrassment" the founders should ditch to "better guard our citizens against harassment by lawsuits."

The Constitution, however, had allowed for Congress to grant authors and inventors a "limited" monopoly on their work. The first state copyright statute—humbly titled the *Act for the Encouragement of Literature and Genius*—set the terms of that limit in 1783: fourteen years, renewable for another fourteen, at which point the work would belong to the people. Trademarks, meanwhile, served a different, but also circumscribed purpose: to dispel any confusion as to the source of a given product. The little circle beside a brand name was supposed to ensure that some customer seeking a Hoover vacuum would not open their new package to find an air pump attached to a funnel. But its impingement on any freedoms of expression was confined to this narrow task. "Whatever First Amendment rights you may have in calling the brew you make in your bathtub 'Pepsi,'" one judge wrote, "are easily outweighed by the buyer's interest in not being fooled into buying it."

The phrase "intellectual property," in its modern sense, is a post-Barbie invention—its first known use was in 1967. The new term to describe the nexus of copyrights, trademarks, and patents came into vogue just as the law was starting to treat them more like property, and specifically a kind over which the owners' power was almost absolute. Until the mid-twentieth century, many jurists harbored Jefferson's suspicion of conceptual monopolies; even in the seventies, well after Marx sued Mattel, federal courts could be outright "hostile to patent owners."

That hostility evaporated in the eighties, when "more infringement cases were being decided in favor of patent holders." Copyright terms grew longer—from fourteen years, to twenty-eight, then seventy-five on works for hire.* While Mattel was suing MCA, and Vaidhyanathan was

---

*In 1978, the U.S. Copyright Office adopted separate sets of terms for works created by *individuals*, and those created as *work for hire* (as well as those published anonymously).

reading Twain, Clinton extended it again to nearly a century. Trademarks too became more capacious, protecting a brand name not just where there was a likelihood of confusion (as, among sodas, for Coke), but in other fields (as in T-shirts that say "Coke"). The Federal Trademark Dilution Act of 1995 nationalized limitations on "trademark dilution," or any use that might blur the "distinctive quality" of the mark. And corporations like Mattel began arguing that they could trademark even basic sensorial experience: "scents, sounds, and colors"—like a particular hue of pink.

The entertainment industry and its conglomerates had played a central role in orchestrating these shifts. Critics nicknamed Clinton's 1998 copyright extension the "Mickey Mouse Protection Act," because Disney had lobbied for it so aggressively. But the real name was hardly better: the "Sonny Bono Copyright Term Extension Act" was named for Cher's late ex-husband and singing partner, who, as a Republican congressman, had cosponsored the original bill. ("Actually," his widow told Congress, "Sonny wanted the term of copyright protection to last forever. I am informed by staff that such a change would violate the Constitution.") Mattel adopted another strategy for protecting its IP—corporate lawyers call it "litigate to death."

At any given moment, Mattel's security director once boasted, the company was juggling "as many as 100" infringement investigations around the globe. These probes were often aimed at Barbie knockoffs—not every Jem needed to be outflanked. They could also be sued.

Mattel filed suit in fourteen different countries to stop Swedish doll Petra from being pitched in advertisements as Barbie's "friend." When Radio City Music Hall released a Rockette figurine, Mattel took them to court for cancan-ing too close to Barbie's copyright. An undergrad named Claudene Christian got served over her line of college cheerleader dolls (Mattel also tried to have her shipments seized and released its own co-ed booster: "Virginia Tech Barbie"). And when Hasbro gave the U.K.'s Sindy doll a Barbie-ish makeover, Mattel's lawyers descended on European courts

---

These terms refer to the latter, but the former grew longer as well—from the author's lifetime, to the author's lifetime plus fifty years, to the author's lifetime plus seventy years.

like warbirds at Normandy—seeking an injunction on Sindy's home turf, then broadening out to Belgium, Holland, Germany, Greece, Denmark, Spain, Hungary, and Turkey, over to Australia, then New Zealand and Hong Kong. Each time Sindy alit on a foreign port, Barbie's counsel seemed to have beat her there with briefs calling the Brit a counterfeit.

The press covered Barbie's disputes like the teen dolls were fighting in Jell-O. "It's the Big Battle of the Toy Blondes," ran one headline. "Barbie's Barbs Hit Sindy for Six," went another. An apparent plurality of articles involved the word "catfight." The court transcripts were hardly less salacious. Barbie's defenders called Sindy an "unwanted twin sister" and a "suburban nothing." Amid the French proceedings, G. Wayne Miller reported, the gendarmerie "arrested the manager of Hasbro France—a mild-mannered gentleman, by all accounts—in his office on a criminal charge of counterfeiting."

Only a few years earlier, these cases might have been harder to win. "Until the mid-1980s," legal scholar Orly Lobel wrote, "toy companies generally lost when they sued a competitor for producing a similar-looking doll." Copyright law is bound by what's called the *idea-expression dichotomy*: no one can own an idea, only its specific expression. (Anyone can write about a blasé rabbit, that is, but if his name is "Bugs," Warner Bros. may have a problem.) And yet ideas and expressions are not always easy to detangle. Courts devised tests to distinguish the stock traits required to convey an idea (a rabbit's large ears), from those owed to artistic license ("What's up, Doc?"). But these tests were "of necessity vague," one doll ruling observed in 1966. Absent direct evidence of copying, the judge was left with their eyes: Would the average observer see a "substantial similarity" between the two works?

Toys in particular proved tricky, Lobel has argued, as they were so often replicas of real-life artifacts—a model airplane, a toy soldier, a doll—whose features, in the courts' view at least, served little purpose other than conjuring those objects. The component parts of a miniature seemed more utilitarian than artistic—too generic to constitute protected expression. They belonged to the realm of ideas, the collective database of common concepts. "To extend copyrightability to minuscule variations," the Second Circuit wrote in a toy case from 1976, "would simply put a weapon for harassment in the hands of mischievous copiers."

Toy companies developed strategies for making their products especially distinct. Hasbro gave G.I. Joe an unusual facial scar because, the creative director quipped, there was "no other way to trademark the human body."* Mattel too made changes to Barbie's physique. Upon releasing SuperStar Barbie in 1977, the company copyrighted her newly smiling head as a sculpture—a work of art whose composition could be protected as one might a drawing or comic strip. And in case after case throughout the eighties and nineties, Mattel argued that the Sindys of the world had effectively plagiarized Barbie's face—not just the generic idea of it, but its specific expression—from the arch of her eyebrows to the span of her philtrum, the elements of what one outlet called "her eternal look of compliant joy."

Barbie's rivals returned to the old standard: Mattel was trying to own "the ineffable"—the feminine ideal. "The faces of fashion dolls must have the pretty features expected of most fashion models," read one filing, "along with the standard features of most dolls." But beause of lawsuits like Mattel's, the conversation was becoming more complicated. The courts began adopting increasingly specific metrics. Toy features no longer seemed so easy to write off as generic ideas. Toy makers pointed to increasingly subtle similarities to prove they had been copied.

Mattel's trials devolved into a meticulous scrutiny of doll physiognomy. "Barbie has very little chin," one rival argued, "her jaw is short and protrudes forward, making her look as if she has an overbite." Mattel, meanwhile, compared dolls' cranial shapes, shaving the crowns down to the scalp and purging their makeup with paint remover. They toted the naked heads to court in egg cartons. In Sindy's trials, the parties scrutinized the length of her thighs, the shade of her eyelids, the slighter pitch of her bust (the "main thing" anyone would notice, her lawyer argued, if looking at the dolls "without any clothes on"), and the fathoms of her nasal cavities. "If one looks up the noses of Barbie and Sindy from underneath," the latter's sculptor testified, "one can immediately see that Sindy has a much more pointed nose with deeper nostrils."

Mattel often settled—as it did with the Rockettes doll and Sindy. (Hasbro eventually presented Jill Barad and her team with a briefcase of "five

---

*This was its own failure of expression: he likely meant copyright.

distinct, disembodied Sindy heads" to choose whichever they felt "was a comfortable enough distance from Barbie's features.") But in the process, the onslaught of cases subtly expanded the expressive features that could be protected by copyright. Before Mattel settled with Radio City, for example, the company notched a kind of victory at the Second Circuit. A lower judge had decided in favor of the music hall, finding that the differences between Barbie and "Rockettes 2000" were "beyond genuine dispute" (while the Barbie doll is "virginal," he had written, the latter "may need Botox in not too long a time"). He had reasoned that Mattel could not copyright the "central features" of Barbie's face—"an upturned nose, bow lips, wide eyes"—because they represented an "idea" of a kind of doll face. But the Second Circuit rejected his opinion. While the judicial panel agreed the "central features" represented *ideas*, they ruled that those features could be expressed in subtly different ways. To merit copyright protection, they wrote, a feature "need not be particularly novel or unusual." It need only reflect a "minimal degree" of creativity—"even a slight amount will suffice."

When the "Barbie Girl" case wound up before a Ninth Circuit judge named Alex Kozinski, one could be forgiven for assuming that Mattel had found a sympathetic audience. Another Reagan appointee, Kozinski had been a "fervent capitalist" since fleeing Romania in the sixties. He'd been "bought off by cheap consumer goods," he joked, and as a judge, imposed few limits on how businesses made them. (His wife had worked for Reagan's FTC, he said, and "never saw a merger she didn't like.") He was also "a prominent defender of the right of owners to use their private property as they see fit."

But Kozinski—an avid snowboarder who assembled computers for fun, reviewed video games in *The Wall Street Journal*, and periodically sent crass jokes to an email list of several hundred—was somewhat idiosyncratic. When it came to intellectual property, he often sided against IP owners. His first year on the Ninth Circuit, he'd dissented when the court ruled that a tournament called the "Gay Olympics" infringed the U.S. Olympic Committee's exclusive right to the latter word. Forcing the event to rename itself the "Gay Games" amounted to a serious "infringement of personal liberties," Kozinski wrote. And in 1992, after New Kids on the Block sued a group of newspapers over several reader surveys ("Which

Kid is the sexiest?"), Kozinski sided with the papers. The surveys were a signal case of what he termed "nominative fair use"—using a trademark to describe its subject. "One might refer to 'the two-time world champions' or 'the professional basketball team from Chicago,'" he explained, "but it's far simpler (and more likely to be understood) to refer to the Chicago Bulls." If a trademark owner could sue anytime someone used the name, they could effectively "deplete the stock of useful words."

When he got the Aqua case, that seemed to be precisely what Mattel was trying to do. "If this were a sci-fi melodrama," Kozinski wrote in his Aqua opinion, "it might be called Speech-Zilla meets Trademark-Kong." The company had argued that Aqua, aiming to parody not Barbie per se, but a certain kind of superficial femininity, could have instead named its song "Party Girl."* Kozsinki didn't buy it. "Words and images do not worm their way into our discourse by accident; they're generally thrust there by well-orchestrated campaigns intended to burn them into our collective consciousness," he had written of trademarks in 1994. The corporations behind those campaigns thus ceded some of their control. Kozinski sided with MCA, ruling that Barbie had become a part of the common tongue. "The parties," he concluded, "are advised to chill."

Mattel did not chill. "They did exactly the opposite," Kozinski told me. The company appealed to the Supreme Court. The effort failed to get the court's attention, though it brought the case to everyone else's. The lawsuit became a national story. But rather than take a break from litigation, Barbie seemed to spend the late nineties looking for smaller artists to sue. There was the case against Paul Hansen, the San Francisco artist behind parody dolls like Drag Queen Barbie (Ken in heels) and Trailer Trash Barbie, whose box read "My Daddy Swears I'm the Best Kisser in the County." Hansen made about $2,000 off the dolls; Mattel demanded damages of $1.2 billion.

---

*Mattel's lawyers also argued that the song created a likelihood of confusion among customers, who might assume it had emanated from Barbie herself. Their evidence on this front spanned from a smattering of customer emails, a single fax from the United Arab Emirates, and the testimony of an expert with a "proprietary scoring system" called the "VALMATRIX," who promised to definitively crunch "whether or not confusion occurs." An earlier judge had called his mysterious methods "devoid of probative value" and "vague at best."

Next came Thomas Forsythe, a largely unknown Utah artist whose photo series "Food Chain Barbie" staged the doll naked, in apparent "danger of being attacked by vintage household appliances." The project netted him a grand total of negative $1,553.89. But Mattel kept him in court for five years. A Barbie dealer in Ohio made the mistake of writing a joke in his catalog: "If there were an ugly contest, Elizabethan Queen Barbie would definitely win." Mattel's laughter took the form of another drawn-out lawsuit. The dealer eventually agreed to describe Barbie only as "wholesome, friendly, accessible and kind, caring and protecting, cheerful, fun loving, talented and independent."

These were cases designed to squash, not to be won, and frequently Mattel didn't—a judge forced Barbie to pay Forsythe's $1.8 million in legal fees, a feat then "virtually unheard of" in intellectual property. When the company sued British artist Susan Pitt, who reworked SuperStar Barbies into a line of bondage-themed "Dungeon Dolls," she prevailed even while representing herself *pro se*. (The dolls had been sufficiently transformed, a judge reasoned: "To the Court's knowledge, there is no Mattel line of 'S&M' Barbie.") But Mattel could still eke out victories by simply exhausting its opponents. Despite losing on the merits, Mattel secured a $750 default judgment against Pitt after she missed a subsequent hearing. The judge overseeing the Hansen case, meanwhile, got so frustrated with Barbie's antics, he confronted her attorney in court ("Look, ma'am, have you ever had in your experience a defendant who has laid down and played dead like this one has?"). He granted a partial summary judgment against Mattel "for not having a sense of humor." Even still, Hansen settled, agreeing to stop selling any dolls that imitated Barbie's body shape, facial features, or packaging. He could not afford an appeal.

Mattel had been litigious since before Barbie was born. But its strategy seemed to have evolved. The company had not stopped Richard Peabody from publishing a literary anthology called *Mondo Barbie* in 1993. But six years later, they were suing independent publisher Seal Press over *Adios Barbie*, a collection of feminist writing which only mentioned the doll in a single essay. (It later appeared under a new title: *Body Outlaws*). Mattel is "waging one of the corporate world's most aggressive trademark wars," *The Wall Street Journal* reported in 1998. Something had changed. What?

CHAPTER 20

MASTER OF YOUR DOMAIN

Over the spring of 1994, the future had not begun yet, at least according to W. Joseph Campbell, who wrote the book *1995: The Year the Future Began*. But a small subset of the population was getting glimpses of it. Less than a third of American households had a computer, and only about 25 million of their occupants used one to access a newfangled thing called the internet. Though the American Dialect Society had named "information superhighway" its word of the year in 1993, "World Wide Web" was more of an information backroad with tolls—a network of news sites, proto-blogs, and forums accessible through dial-up services and text-based programs like Usenet.

That April, on a Usenet forum called *Alt.folklore.computers*, a woman in Miami started a thread soliciting takes on Barbie. "Tell me about your opinion surrounding her stereotypical image, as well as where you think she will be in the future," she wrote. The message reached a third-year student at Harvard Law School, who responded with a joke:

> Speaking for myself, my niece can't get enough of Hacker Barbie's Dream Basement Apartment! The pink Sun workstation in the corner, the little containers of takeout Szechuan scattered across the floor, her 'Don't Blame Me, I Voted Libertarian' t-shirt. . . . To me, the most realistic thing is how if you put her in the chair in front of the monitor, she'll stare at it for hours without blinking.

It was "just a ten-second joke," the law student told me. He's now a lawyer in his fifties, specializing in complex civil litigation, like antitrust and intellectual property. But his offhand comment went viral, or as viral as Usenet could get—aggregated in meta groups like *Alt.humor .best-of-usenet* and inserted in posters' signatures. A high-profile Java programmer reached out and asked if she could borrow the idea, then made a dedicated blog called *Hacker Barbe's Dream Basement Apartment*—intentionally misspelled, to "keep Mattel from getting upset." Within a month, someone else had lifted the concept, circulating a fake press release for "Hacker Barbie," which came with her own X terminal and an endorsement from "Naomi Wuuf," who swore the doll would "terminate the notion that women are inherently inferior when it comes to mathematics." The release also got reposted—everywhere from *Alt.fan .tom-robbins* to *Soc.culture.kuwait*. "That was somebody's attempt to make a longer, comic piece out of it," the lawyer said. "I didn't think it really worked. But you know, it's not like I had any IP in it."

Mattel did. And when the future got going in 1995, the toy firm finally logged on—setting up its first-ever product website that October. Barbie was planning to enter cyberspace herself with a proprietary software called *Barbie Fashion Designer*. Soon, Mattel launched Barbie.com, an online retailer that the company insisted was "the official source of information on Barbie." But Barbie was already on the internet, just not via Mattel. "While these projects may mark Mattel's first official foray into personal computing," *The New York Times* reported in 1995, "Barbie already has a following among computer users who browse the Internet's World Wide Web." There were collector fan sites, digital art portfolios, critical theory disquisitions, comment sections, blogs, and of course, newsgroups on Usenet. Barbie had never been so reproducible. The mimetic powers of, say, an unsanctioned sculpture or a portrait were multiplied when that artist could post a picture of it online.

To institutions outside the early tech world, the internet seemed like an instrument of intellectual property chaos. "The Net was built without a central command authority," *Time* magazine wrote in 1994. "That means that nobody owns it, nobody runs it, nobody has the power to kick anybody off for good. There isn't even a master switch that can shut it down in case of emergency." Clifford Stoll, a Berkeley astronomer famous for catching a notorious German hacker, called it "the closest thing to true anarchy that ever existed."

Mattel's answer to anarchy was to smother it in a thick layer of cease-and-desists. Among their many targets: an artist who made handbags from recycled magazines; a collagist who pictured Barbie "visibly pregnant"; a teenager named Barbara who started a parody zine called *Hey There Barbie Girl!* and an off-off-Broadway show, which featured a scene of the doll attempting a jumping jack and falling down. There were the fan sites like "Barbie of the 90's" or "The Plastic Princess Page," which taxonimized Barbie outfits, and "The Barbie Chronicles," which inserted Barbie into famous paintings, like *Whistler's Mother*. Austrian artist Franz Wassermann got hit for his site "Barbie Und Ken sind HIV-positiv," which needs no translation, as did sites featuring a "Politically Correct" Barbie and a photo of Barbie being carried like a sultan by guys in gimpsuits titled *Mistress Babs: The Queen of All She Surveys*. Even "Hacker Barbe," with her intentional misspelling, was not spared. In December of 1997, the Dream Basement Apartment was served with a cease and desist.

"We will protect our trademark," said Mattel spokeswoman Lisa McKendall. "If it's unauthorized in print or on the Web, we will act." And yet it was the Web that posed the real threat—as a former "Miss Nude Canada" could attest. She had performed under the stage name "Barbie Doll Benson" for sixteen years. But as one paper observed, "only when she produced a Web page did Mattel complain."

Mattel's onslaught worked better online than it did against individual artists like Forsythe or label-backed bands like Aqua. For many minor posters, the mere threat of litigation was enough to squash unwanted work. And Mattel often succeeded in court when it came to the most controllable aspects of the internet, like domain names—an early source of corporate panic.

Mattel reserved many Barbie-related websites in addition to the one it actually used (Barbie.com), including Barbie.net, BarbieDoll.info, BarbieDoll.net, and BarbieWorld.com. But it fought for several more, from clothing shops to a porn site called "Barbie's Playhouse" to—

BarbiesShop.com
BarbiesBeachwear.com
BarbiesClothing.com

BarbiesPlayen.com [sic]
Barbie-Club.com
TheBarbie.com
TheBarbys.com
Barbie21.com
DreamBarbieDoll.com
ChinaBarbie.com
BarbiesGrill.com
BarbieToy.com
BarbieRetro.com
Barbieborza.com
Barbiej.com
Barbiedoll-A.com
CaptainBarbie.com
Barbiegallery.com
QuieroBarbie.com
QuieroKillerBarbies.com

—and even just TheBarbies.com, "despite it being a small group of women who liked to play videogames." Not all of these efforts succeeded, though many did. Corporate panic over so-called cybersquatting was so strong that in 1999, it prompted action from both Congress and the United Nations. The resulting regulations—including the "Anticybersquatting Consumer Protection Act"—did not protect consumers so much as IP owners, enabling Mattel to take over several more addresses and become known as "one of the most vociferous and energetic of corporate censors in cyberspace."

But Mattel didn't understand some basic things about the internet, as evidenced by its campaign against a man named Mark Napier. Napier was an early web artist, who played with digital formats like hypertext. In 1996, he created a website called "The Distorted Barbie," which aimed to deconstruct the doll both literally and figuratively, combining a series of heavily altered images of Barbie faces with a page of public comments from visitors sharing their own analyses of the doll. One user sent in what they described as "AN ACTUAL LETTER FROM THE ARCHIVES OF THE SMITHSONIAN."

Thank you for your latest submission to the Institute, labeled "211-D, layer seven... Hominid skull." We have given this specimen a careful and detailed examination, and regret to inform you that we disagree with your theory that it represents "conclusive proof of the presence of Early Man in Charleston County two million years ago."... The specimen looks like the head of a Barbie doll that a dog has chewed on.*

When Mattel got wind of the Napier site, they sent a cease-and-desist to his internet service provider (ISP). The ISP wanted Napier to take the page down, but instead he scrubbed Barbie's likeness from his website—not by removing the images wholesale, but by distorting them "to an extreme," pixelating the portraits until they no longer resembled any one specific doll. Even that wasn't enough. Mattel's lawyers saw the use of the Barbie name alone as dilution.

Napier, however, was not without recourse. The internet had given him a platform, and he used it—posting Mattel's letter online and creating a kind of diary of Mattel's IP abuses. He also had allies. The editor of a zine called *Enterzone*, a man named Christian Crumlish, had published a version of The Distorted Barbie and got his own tersely worded letter from Mattel's lawyer, William Dunnegan. But unlike Napier, Crumlish had no ISP. There was no one to pressure him to take anything down. And as Napier live-blogged his censorship struggle, Crumlish lent a hand—contacting lawyers, reporters, and civil liberties groups like the ACLU and the Electronic Freedom Frontier. He created a zine feature called "The Daily Barbie™" which broadcast regular updates to his readers, while breaking down the particulars of trademark statutes and copyright law.

The saga found an audience, a public newly soured on corporate

---

*The letter, which went on at length about why the Barbie head could not be a fossilized skull bitten by "ravenous man-eating Pliocene clams," was not, in fact, an "actual letter" from the Smithsonian. It was a piece of short fiction written by Harvey Rowe, a medical student in Charleston, South Carolina, in late February 1994. Rowe sent it to a few friends, who in turn passed it on until, like Hacker Barbie, it became a kind of comment-section copypasta. The so-called "Fossil Barbie" letter eventually attracted enough attention that the Smithsonian sent out a press release denying responsibility.

censorship. McDonald's had recently sued two Greenpeace activists over a pamphlet called "What's Wrong with McDonald's," in a U.K. case that came to be known as "McLibel." And that very fall, the venture-backed online retailer "EToys" was suing a European performance art group behind an elaborate parody corporation, which sold fake "shares" at the URL etoys.com, and predated the toy retailer by four years. But as corporations got bolder, copyright scofflaws did too. Flouting cease-and-desists had become a point of pride, "a unique form of legitimation," a badge to be shared and shown off. "The lawyer's cease-and-desist letter has become a mark of authentication that alerts Web surfers that the satires, parodies, and corporate muckraking they have located are indeed 'the real thing,'" legal anthropologists Rosemary Coombe and Andrew Herman wrote. "In short, the letter of the law is engaged in a dance of mimicry that authorizes its own alterity."

Crumlish's blog drew enough readers that he opened a comment section of his own for onlookers to weigh in. He heard from other targets of Mattel's crackdown—a friend of "Trailer Trash Barbie" designer Paul Hansen; a zine called *Urban Desires*, which, in addition to publishing the juvenilia of future *Radiolab* host Jad Abumrad, had gotten in trouble for running essays on Barbie; and the maker of a tatted, herb-smoking doll named "Feral Cheryl," who claimed Mattel had lifted her idea during Barbie's brief and controversial flirtation with tattoos. The comment section soon broke out of its silo of digital freedom nerds, attracting the attention of Barbie fans and collectors, some of whom had only a tenuous grasp on what the site was originally about:

> **"NONE OF YOUR FUCKING BUSINESS," on Nov. 27 1997**: i think that who ever wrote this is a sad excuse for a human being, and [sic] if you"ve [sic] got a problem with her, then bite your ass!!!!!!!! and leave my barbie alone.
>
> **"Mbloom" on Dec. 1 1997**: I think Barbie is a bitch who used to much "plastic surgery." She has too many acessories and houses especially! E-mail me for a date or a chat over something!
>
> **"S*****n@golden.net.au" on Jan. 30 1998**: Hi my name is Elizabeth and I am 5 years old. I love barbie so much I think you

should make more barbie"s [sic] Could you please send me a special picture of barbie. thanks

But between the spam and the caps-locked shrieking, an organization started to emerge. About a week into the fight, Crumlish received an anonymous call to action titled *Fighting Corporate Censorship with a Meme*. The manifesto called Mattel "a mega-corporation hunting mosquitos with an elephant gun," and suggested a tactic to "drive Mattel lawyers crazy: turn the Distorted Barbie site into a free-travelling meme."

The word "meme" was still niche enough in 1997 that commenters needed a definition. ("I'd say it's an analogy to a gene, in the realm of ideas," Crumlish wrote, "a self-perpetuating concepticle.") But the manifesto laid out precise instructions, detailing how to create digital "mirrors," exact replicas of Napier's original site:

> Place copies of the site all over the net, then sit back and wait for Mattel to find them. When the company asks us to cease and desist, we will. But by that time, dozens more copies of the site will have sprung up elsewhere to take its place. The lawyers' bogus squirrel hunt will turn into an endless, crazy-making pursuit of a target that multiplies exponentially by digital mitosis.

The missive included copies of Napier's original artwork in several file formats, and soon the digital mirrors spread, popping up in other zines, from something called *The Lard Enquirer* to the blog behind a semi-well-known, if rudimentary clip game called "Slap a Spice Girl." The protest movement got written up in *Wired* magazine, and on tech blogs like *NetSurf*. Napier's saga was covered by *The Wall Street Journal*, while Crumlish went on radio stations like KPFA. At one point, Crumlish created a custom signature, called a ".sig virus," so the Distorted Barbie meme could spread across the web:

> The Distorted Barbie questions the effect of a girl doll on society ... but Mattel told Enterzone to remove the page.... Want to help? Copy me into your .sig–the Barbie meme .sig virus

Napier had briefly considered filing a class action lawsuit on behalf of all the Barbie artists being censored by Mattel. A lawyer told him it wouldn't work because "each site treats Barbie somewhat differently." But in a sense, it didn't need to—Distorted Barbie's audience was already acting as a class, replicating the blog faster than Mattel could keep up.

Jill Barad was keenly aware that the digital revolution would change everything. Computer and video games had also exploded, and Barbie was ill-positioned for the dot-com boom. Her sales were still growing—they would peak in 1997, with sales of $1.8 billion—but at more of a crawl than a sprint. As Toys "R" Us gutted its inventory, Barad needed a new growth story to sell Wall Street. The thinking was: "Mattel has to get into digital businesses," said Bruce Stein, then serving as Mattel's COO. The company had to assert itself online so Barbie could surf the net just as she'd ridden every other cultural wave. "All of us, including Jill and I, thought that this was the right strategy." The only problem: it "never got executed"—because the digital business Barad found was The Learning Company, and its chief executive was Kevin O'Leary.

These days, Kevin O'Leary is best known as the bald head from *Shark Tank* who calls people "cockroaches." But over the fall of 1998, he was best known as the chief executive of the digital gaming company behind titles like *Reader Rabbit* and *Carmen Sandiego*. As with many of his businesses, O'Leary did not found The Learning Company, he negotiated his way into it. He'd founded a different corporation, an edutainment brand called SoftKey in 1986. O'Leary's strategy was to buy up other popular companies, gut their research and development departments, and slash their sales prices. This proved profitable, and SoftKey went on an acquisition spree, scooping up over twenty companies in a matter of years—and culminating in a $606 million hostile takeover of The Learning Company in 1995. Two of O'Leary's mergers ranked "among the 10 worst U.S. acquisitions" of the mid-nineties, but it was an era of quantity, not quality. The Learning Company soon emerged as the second largest consumer software brand in the world. The first was Microsoft.

If you took a broad view, Barad's strategy almost seemed sound.

"The Learning Company was a Hail Mary in the year that Toys 'R' Us reduced their volume," Stein explained. "Since you couldn't get all of that volume back from Toys 'R' Us's reduced orders, you could change the story by saying our new growth is going to come from digital." Plus, if digital games were the future, Mattel needed a share of the market without starting from scratch. If The Learning Company had been what it claimed to be, the acquisition could have solved two Mattel problems in one deal. But as many warned Barad at the time, O'Leary's conglomerate was more like a "house of cards."

The red flags were obvious if you knew where to look. For one, it was a favorite among short-sellers—investors who bet that a company's stock will fall. "The short-sellers knew that the Learning Company had been aggressive with its books for years—years before it was bought by Mattel," finance journalist Herb Greenberg wrote in 1999. As with Barbie, its sales had slowed, reporting annual net losses several years in a row; by December 1998, its accumulated deficit topped $1.1 billion. There were rumors, later levied in shareholder lawsuits, that TLC was "channel stuffing," or deliberately sending retailers more product than they could sell and recording it as revenue. O'Leary's executives furiously denied any accounting games. But it didn't look great that O'Leary's auditor, Arthur Andersen—the same firm that had missed Ruth's fraud in 1973, and would shutter over its role in the Enron scandal—had objected to the company's financial controls. Or that after raising its objections, the firm had been fired.

Many of Barad's colleagues were baffled by her choice. Two executives, including Bruce Stein, left shortly after the proposed deal went public. But Barad pushed ahead anyway, finalizing the acquisition that May in a stock deal worth $3.8 billion.

For a moment, it seemed like it might pay off. Or at least that's what *The New York Times* said in September, when it included the sale on a list of Mattel's "wise purchases that will pay off." But almost exactly one month later, both Mattel and the *Times* list looked distinctly unwise. On October 4, Mattel disclosed that The Learning Company "had incurred millions of dollars of product returns and bad debt write-offs," shareholders later wrote in a legal filing. Mattel had predicted TLC would turn a $50 million profit in the fall. Instead, it would result in a loss of some $100 million that quarter alone.

The internet had sped up the spread of information, and news of Barad's bad deal spread like a virus. Barbie spent the end of the millennium in financial free fall. On October 5, Mattel's stock plunged to $11; the first shareholder lawsuit hit two days later. By October 8, *The Wall Street Journal* reported that Barad was "fighting to hold on to her job" and that the company still didn't know "the full extent of the problems." Another lawsuit arrived on October 25, and by November 7, Barad had, per the *Times*, "gone into hiding." By November 11, O'Leary was fired, just months into his three-year contract. When Mattel released its annual report that Christmas, Barad had to confront the crisis. "The bad news for 1999 unfortunately has overshadowed the good news," read the first sentence. "We are all painfully aware of the negative effect the acquisition of The Learning Company . . . had on our results."

By February, Mattel was hemorrhaging $1 million a day and desperate to offload its billion-dollar albatross. But Mattel couldn't even sell the company. They gave it away—handing it to a private equity firm to strip for parts, in exchange for "an undisclosed percentage of future profits." When the PE firm finished, what remained of The Learning Company was worth at most $80 million—or just 2 percent of what Mattel had paid. A former executive told me, "If it wasn't for Enron and probably AOL–Time Warner, it'd probably be the worst corporate merger in history."

In an apt twist for the internet's top litigator, Mattel was forced to resolve its shareholder lawsuits in a "mega-settlement" of $122 million—then the twelfth largest of its kind. Perhaps Barbie could recover, but Barad got litigated to death. The company's second female CEO was pushed out early into the new millenium, though she had a cushy landing pad. The board sent Executive Barbie off with $26.4 million in cash, a monthly payment of over $105,000 for the next decade, a $5 million life insurance policy, a $78,000 country club membership, and forgiveness on the $10.5 million in loans Barad had borrowed from Mattel, a third of which had paid for her house. One analyst called it a "$50 million kiss goodbye."

PART IV

INTRO

Mark Twain was in a town called Angels Camp, California, when he heard the story that would make him famous. A degenerate gambler in town, who would bet on anything—from horse races to cat fights to whether his friend's sick wife would die—once spent three months covertly training a frog, just so he could bet that his frog would jump highest. His hustle worked; his frog became the best jumper in the county. But eventually, the conman was outconned: a stranger took his bet, then quietly filled the gambler's frog with lead shot. When it came down to it, the trained frog lost.

Twain repurposed this anecdote, about a real man with a real frog, into a short story called "Jim Smiley and His Jumping Frog," only there was a twist. In Twain's version, a friend tells the narrator to find information about a reverend named "Leonidas Smiley," so he asks an old bartender with a reputation for yarns, who in turn, mistaking Leonidas Smiley for Jim Smiley, relays the original story about the jumping frog. The narrator sits through the bartending geezer's long-winded tale before he confirms his hunch: that there is no Leonidas Smiley, and the whole ruse was a prank to get the bartender to "bore me to death with some exasperating reminiscence of him as long and as tedious as it should be useless to me."

When this story came out in 1865, the literary world loved it—Twain's dry send-up of deception and storytelling in the lawless West. Though not everyone was amused. A writer overseas translated it into French just to prove to his countrymen that it wasn't as funny as everyone said. Only the Frenchman had mixed up the story, leaving out

Twain's frame narrative. The translated version starts and ends with the bartender's yarn; there is no Leonidas, only Jim. When Twain heard about the translation, he felt he'd been hustled. "Even a criminal is entitled to fair play," he wrote, "and certainly when a man who has done no harm has been unjustly treated, he is privileged to do his best to right himself."

Twain righted himself with a book which prints the story three times: first in the original English, then in the French, and last in English again—Twain's own re-translation from the French, as the subtitle reads, "clawed back into a civilized language once more by patient, unremunerated toil." The third piece is a goofy document—the Progressive Era version of a bad Google translation, riddled with grammatical errors and alien constructions like "I no me recollect not exactly." It both is and is not the story the reader has by then come to know, a clumsily plotted copy of a copy of a copy.

But there is a fourth version. In a coda at the end, Twain explains that, although he had heard this frog bit from a real man, relaying what he understood to be a real story, it had come to his attention that the frog tale was in fact much older—a Greek fable written by a Greek author some two thousand years before anyone bothered with this supposedly skilled frog from northern California. Twain reprints that story too, this time in a good English translation ("Greek makes me tired"), and poses a question:

> Now, then, the interesting question is, *did* the frog episode happen in Angel's Camp in the spring of '49, as told in my hearing that day in the fall of 1865? I am perfectly sure that it did. I am also sure that its duplicate happened in Boeotia a couple of thousand years ago. I think it must be a case of history actually repeating itself, and not a case of a good story floating down the ages and surviving because too good to be allowed to perish.

This line would itself get twisted. For years, poorly sourced newspaper stories and online aphorism aggregators would attribute to Twain the maxim that "history never repeats itself, but it does often rhyme." (In reality, this quote, appropriately, seems to stem from a range of sources all of which said slightly different versions of the same thing.) But in Barbie's case, Twain's book makes for the better analogy. The basic story, of a secretly stolen doll, reappears throughout Barbie's seven-decade history, not repeated or rhymed, so much as sloppily translated into new contexts, each iteration somewhat stranger and stupider than the last.

As it turned out, Twain had not chanced upon two identical frog stories taking place two thousand years apart. The Greek story was a knockoff of sorts. As Twain explained in yet another coda, the story had been written in ancient Boeotia but in contemporary England. A British professor in Twain's own time had lifted the latter's tale and "transferred the incident to classic Greece." He had not mentioned his source, assuming Twain's short story to be so famous that the homage would be obvious. The British press excoriated him for the apparent plagiarism. But Twain, for all his love of copyright, didn't blame him. He had stolen the miner's tale too.

CHAPTER 21

HOUSE ON FIRE

> I'm not sure I can take seriously a case about dolls. Honestly, I mean, pieces of plastic. . . . If I were on the jury, maybe I would learn more about it and then it might be important to me. But it might not. I might still decide that—Why were we here? Why are we all here? It's a doll.
>
> —Prospective Juror, *Mattel v. MGA*

In May of 2001, almost exactly forty years after Marx sued Mattel, Rolf Hausser reappeared in Barbie's life like a long-lost cousin short on cash. He was in his nineties, too arthritic to play tennis or violin. His company had gone bankrupt in 1983. His brother died soon after. The surviving Hausser was living off the inheritance of his wife, Lilly, writing a memoir (about how "politics influenced my life" in the thirties) and pickling in resentment. Four years earlier, he had been contacted by Dan Miller, of *Miller's* magazine, who was writing about *Bild* Lilli. When Miller sent him a copy of the 1961 lawsuit, Hausser had responded with surprise. He had not known about any lawsuit, he said. He remembered licensing *Bild* Lilli to Louis Marx in 1960. He remembered selling *Bild* Lilli to Mattel in 1964. But that a legal drama had played out between those poles was, he said, news to him.

That spring, Rolf sued Mattel again, or maybe for the first time. He alleged in German court that "the Barbie doll was an exact replica of the Lilli doll," but this time, he did not claim patent infringement. He claimed fraud. When the Haussers sold Mattel Lilli's rights in 1964, Rolf said, they had been deceived. Though Louis Marx had purported to represent both companies in the lawsuit, he had not complied with the "reporting requirements" of their contract—namely, telling the

Haussers that they were party to an American lawsuit. When Mattel later reached out about the sale, Rolf thought they had merely decided to do the right thing. He claimed Paul Guggenheim and his associates had "deliberately duped" him, making Barbie seem less successful than she had become. Had he known Barbie's real sales data he said, he would have never agreed to a small lump sum, but royalties for every doll sold. "Only after many years of having 'the wool pulled over its eyes' in the worst way" by Mattel, Rolf's lawyer wrote, did the company "learn of the exact circumstances of this deception."

If Rolf's story was true, or even partially true,* it didn't matter. Most of the people who remembered the first case were dead. And a year into the second, Ruth Handler would join them. Her death in April of 2002, at the age of 85, seemed to make it official; the past had been buried. Mattel contested Rolf's case and won. Hausser's lawsuit was merely a too-late attempt to gain "a perpetual ownership interest" in a global doll empire—a doll on which he had, at best, only a distant claim, Mattel's lawyers wrote the month Ruth died. It was a funny thing to say. As it happened, they were gearing up to do the same thing.

The new millennium had gotten off to a rough start at Mattel. The company's share price could have gotten it shelf space at Dollar Tree. The board was mired in lawsuits. The Learning Company had been hauled off to the finance equivalent of the junkyard. As Mattel floundered, Disney had killed its contract with the company and given the lucrative license to Hasbro. Jill Barad had been replaced by Robert Eckert, a staid, forgettable suit whose mien was less Executive Barbie than Lunch Meat Ken; he'd spent the past two decades overseeing Oscar Mayer wieners and Kraft cheese, where he'd once invented a salad dressing for baked potatoes. When reporters reached out to his old high school and college classmates,

---

*Mattel denied furnishing fake sales data—being a public company, that information "was readily available." They likewise insisted Hausser had to have known about the first lawsuit, citing a letter to Dan Miller about the case in which he'd written: "I have no old documents but I remember exactly this matter" (emphasis Mattel's). Though notably, Miller himself confirmed Rolf's account, writing that "Rolf told me that he never knew of the existence of the suit until June of 1997!" At the very least, records show that in the original case, Marx did get permission from the court to respond to interrogatories on the Haussers' behalf.

few remembered him. "You never would have predicted that I'd be a CEO someday," he told an interviewer. "I guess no one else would have, either."

This new guy promised to create a "leaner and meaner" Mattel, which he went about with dull predictability—slashing expenses wherever possible, moving more production to Mexico, laying off hundreds, shutting down Fisher-Price's last domestic plant, a factory in a Kentucky town with just under a thousand workers. The stripped-down company shied away from investing in any idea too far afield. "The downside of this conservative approach," *Businessweek* wrote in 2002, "is that Mattel could miss the blockbusters." Actually, it already had.

Amid the restructuring, Eckert had been blindsided by the arrival of a new line of fashion dolls from MGA Entertainment, a company with little experience in the doll market, or in girls' toys at all really. The newcomers hit the scene in May of 2001, the same month that Hausser filed his lawsuit. They had big heads and big feet and what many lawyers would call "attitude." By the end of the year, these dolls—Bratz—had already become the biggest threat to Barbie in half a century, leading what Mattel executives would call, with full-throated hysteria, a "Barbie genocide." Before Bratz's third birthday, the head of girls' toys would circulate what came to be called the "House on Fire" memo:

> The house is on fire ... Barbie is losing key attribute ratings with girls ... Bratz is gaining share with core five- to eight-year-olds ... We must do some things different around here. Fight fire with fire. No other brand in history is as emotionally meaningful to girls and women as Barbie. In spite of this, a rival-led Barbie genocide rapidly grows.

The solution, the executive concluded, was to marshal "all the talent, power and history behind the Barbie brand" into a counterattack that is "brilliant, tactical, aggressive, revolutionary and ruthless." Who had time for Hausser's ancient pleading when the very doll on which he claimed a stake was getting slaughtered in the marketplace? "This is war and sides must be taken," the memo read. "Barbie stands for good. All others stand for evil."

In August of 2002, Robert Eckert received an anonymous letter. "Dear CEO," it read. "I have information that I think Mattel should investigate." Eckert was a high-profile man, who got a lot of mail, and more than the average's person's share of anonymous letters—maybe a dozen every year, he later said. He viewed them with a "little jaundiced, skeptic eye." The sender could be anyone: a disgruntled customer, a crazed Barbie hater, a paranoid shareholder. But this one was interesting, in that it promised secret information on a subject of immense sensitivity at Mattel. Specifically, the letter claimed that Bratz had not, as the public then believed, originated with their manufacturer, MGA Entertainment. As the letter told it, they had been created at Mattel, and by one of Barbie's own people, a former designer named Carter Bryant. While still in Mattel's employ, the letter read, Bryant had "worked out a deal with MGA" to develop the dolls in secret.

Mattel employed tens of thousands of people—engineers, inventors, graphic designers, hair rooters, face painters, seamstresses, assembly line workers—most of whom operated in relative anonymity. But Carter Bryant was a name any attentive collector would know. He had been one of the top designers in the Barbie Collectibles, producing high-end fashions like the elaborate lavender charmeuse of "The Orchid Barbie," and the old glamour gowns in the Barbie's "Hollywood Movie Star" series. Like BillyBoy* before him, Bryant had signed one of his Barbies' boxes. The first installation of Barbie's "Grand Entrance Collection" included Bryant's headshot, artist bio, and a brief letter. "I'd like to welcome you to the delightful world of Barbie doll collecting," the box read. "With warm regards, Carter Bryant."

Bryant was ten years younger than Barbie, born in Southern California to a family who rarely spent more than three or four years in a place before picking up for somewhere else: Washington State, the Alaskan town of Soldotna, California again, Idaho. In the early nineties, the Bryants briefly "spent some time in Saudi Arabia." Bryant's constant was an interest in art—building "marionettes from papier-mache," drawing the toys his parents couldn't afford. As a teen, he mulled various careers in the arts—fashion designer, after he became obsessed with the photo spreads in *Vogue* and *Harper's Bazaar*; comic book artist, after he won a contest for drawing *Archie* characters; and for a moment, lyricist. In the late eighties, he copyrighted a baker's dozen songs. One of them was called "Talk Is Cheap."

Carter Bryant had wanted to study couture, but the world of human-sized fashion design seemed to charge a hefty entry price. He got into Parsons School of Design in 1993, but the tuition was too steep, even with loans. He enrolled instead at Otis College, an art school in Los Angeles, but after a few semesters, his small scholarship could not counteract his mounting debt. Over Christmas break of 1994, he moved back home with his parents, who were then living in Missouri, and set his sights on something smaller scale. He had always been "one of those weird kids that liked Barbie as a boy," he recalled in court transcripts. Her costumes seemed to come straight from the runway, and some of her designers had gone on to design for human women. After a few months in Missouri, he sent a small portfolio to Mattel, and they gave him a trial assignment: sketching Barbie as a superhero. He got the gig.

When Bryant moved to California and began working for Mattel, he seemed to see Barbie the way Ruth had: as a blank canvas on which he could design whatever he wanted, whose litany of jobs and parties would provide endless opportunity for new and elaborate gowns. "Because Barbie can be or do most anything," he later wrote on the Grand Entrance box, she "offers the designer an unlimited opportunity for artistic expression." But Bryant quickly learned that while maybe Barbie could do anything, he could not. At the Design Center in El Segundo—a 180,000-square-foot converted air hangar lined with cubicles—he spent much of his time navigating a bureaucracy about as glam as the DMV. In that first year, Bryant was designing for the Barbie "Main Line," and he wasn't coming up with ideas so much as executing others'—his additions limited to what "fit into a preconceived marketing concept." He wasn't designing the elegant dolls he'd grown up on, but rote "gidgets and widgets" with overly complicated mechanisms, humdrum outfits, and depressing commercial tie-ins—like "Avon Barbie," a collaboration with the door-to-door peddler of lipstick and body wash. By 1997, he was frustrated and homesick. He took a six-month leave of absence and moved back to Missouri. Bryant kept working for Mattel part-time, but some of the assignments seemed like caricatures of the corporate culture—at one point, he was told to sketch a bejeweled Barbie stapler. On April 15, 1998, he gave Mattel notice and resigned.

It was on his time off, he would claim, that Bryant first came up with Bratz. He was living at home in Kimberling City, Missouri, working at an Old Navy, when he drove by Kickapoo High School, Brad Pitt's alma mater. He was nearly thirty at the time, far enough away from his own teendom to have lost touch with kid fashions. These students struck him as so different from Barbie—edgier, with tighter tops and big, baggy jeans. They had backpacks and Walkmen and dangling earbuds. They weren't just white, but black, Hispanic, and Asian. As he flipped through teen magazines, he saw a cover of the Dixie Chicks, headlined "Chicks with Attitude." One girl seemed to stare out of a Steve Madden ad, her fist clenched, her proportions distorted to highlight gigantic shoes. In an ad for Paris Blues jeans, a model with big eyes, a big head, and pouty lips, looked like "she own[ed] the world." He sketched out drawings of four characters he called Jade, Lupe, Hallidae, and Zoe. "Meet the Bratz," he wrote, though at first the only person who met them was his mom. She thought they were so cute she showed her husband, then her friend Jeane.

Bryant had been working on several projects during his time off—a doll named Sabrina with detachable hair, and a line of cartoon greeting cards called "Rainy Day Rascals." He moonlit for Ashton-Drake, maker of the Barbie rival "Gene."* But his full-time job applications went nowhere, and after a few months, he moved back to L.A. to return to Mattel. He started his second stint on January 4, 1999, this time on the more creative Collectibles line. Just that New Year's Eve, he'd shown the Bratz to his on-again, off-again boyfriend, but now he put them away. He knew the designs would never go anywhere in the Barbie department.

But Bryant still thought of Bratz intermittently. During one bout of frustration, he sent the sketches to a company called Alaska Momma—a talent agency for artists based, bafflingly, not in Alaska, but in New York. That went nowhere, so in the early months of 2000, he showed them to an old colleague named Veronica Marlow. She was a fashion doll consultant, and she thought she knew a company that might be

---

*The doll was created by Mel Odom, the commercial artist whose angular, pinup-like illustrations of men regularly appeared in eighties *Playboy*, and who, among other things, painted the original face of Billyboy*'s Mdvanii.

interested. In August of 2000, it was Marlow who put Bryant in touch with MGA Entertainment, which is how he wound up, later that fall, in the office of Isaac Larian.

Isaac Larian is a chatty guy, the kind that makes for a great conversationalist, and an unruly court witness. The kind who makes words and sentences seem like so many dishes at a buffet, to try out and savor, without stressing too much if one or two undermine or overwhelm or clash with the others. He was born in 1954 to a Persian-Jewish family in Kashan, just south of Tehran. His father ran a textile shop, which Larian would claim was small and went bankrupt, though his brother has said it left the family rich enough to provide the start-up capital for their company. As a kid, Larian got into strength training, not using dumbbells, but bricks—becoming so strong he beat up his grade school bully. His next fight was getting out of Iran. In 1971, at age seventeen, he borrowed money from his family to buy a one-way ticket to America, with just $750 and a yellow blanket. He worked the night shift as a dishwasher in a Lawndale coffee shop, getting a degree in civil engineering from California State University, Los Angeles. During the Iranian Revolution in 1979, he arranged for his oldest sister, then brother to join him in the States. His parents were harder to relocate. "I arranged for my parents to leave through Afghanistan and Pakistan on camels and cars with my little sister," he said, "then they went to Austria, and then they came to the USA as refugees."

That year, he and his brother, Farhad, started a business called Surprise Gift Wagon, a mail order service for middling Korean brassware, run out of Isaac's Ford Phoenix. In 1982, the Larians quit snail mail for the digital age, rebranding as an importer of consumer electronics. They got into toys almost by accident: in 1987, they became a distributor for Nintendo, and later adopted a new name, Micro-Games America Entertainment, or MGA. MGA was not an international player on par with Mattel. It was small, family run, and private. They had a few hits, like the "Singing Bouncy Baby" in 1997, but they also had bad luck, filing for bankruptcy that same year. The most powerful man in the toy business, the Wal-Mart buyer, wouldn't give MGA the time of day. Larian would often fly to Dallas, then take a small plane to Wal-Mart's headquarters in

Bentonville, Arkansas, make his pitch, and come home empty-handed. Eventually, in the nineties, he got fed up. "I said 'What is it going to take?'" Larian recalled. "He said, 'Bring me something that competes with Barbie, and I would buy it.'"

"Frankly speaking," Larian told the court, "I thought at the time he was being a little bit sarcastic." But the idea stuck with him. He wanted a hip fashion doll, so a few years later, when Marlow put MGA in touch with Bryant, he was interested. On September 1, 2000, Larian met with Bryant in his office. Larian remembered it was after lunch, as he'd had to sweep loose rice off his desk. His daughter, Jasmin, then eleven or twelve, was there too, hanging around the headquarters on her summer break. Bryant had brought a pitch book, a poster board, and what you could call a prototype—a "dummy doll," Frankensteined from parts he had at home (a Barbie body, Ken boots) and a spare head he found in Mattel's trash. He'd asked some of his coworkers, as a favor, to help make it look less like scrap—one drew a Bratz logo, with a halo over the "R." This prototype would later become a subject of great interest at Mattel, having been made by some of Barbie's employees, with some of Barbie's parts. But Larian dismissed the doll as irrelevant. "It was like a robot," he said. "To me it was very ugly, like an alien."

Larian was more focused on the drawings, he said, though he didn't love those either: "They looked weird," he said. "They had these big heads." But Jasmin liked them. She thought they were cool. And they were—much cooler than Barbie, though by then, that was not an especially high bar. With their Spice Girl makeup and hip-hugger jeans, the figures Bryant had sketched seemed to mimic a youth culture more confident, more modern, and certainly more diverse than Barbie's. Barbie had dutifully tacked on other races and ethnicities decades too late, but Bratz made a point of being multiracial from the start. In Bryant's pitch, there was a Hispanic doll, an Asian doll, a black doll, a white doll—none of which was an obvious protagonist, the way the white Barbie seemed to be. The focus was the "pack." Bryant's vision of a pluralistic doll society was about as nuanced as one might expect from a white guy in nineties Missouri. He frequently referred to the dolls' "urban" look. One of the doll's bios said her favorite food was "nothing." ("She's skinny?" a lawyer later asked. "Yeah," Bryant said.) But there was something appealing about their edge. Where Barbie had careers, the Bratz had interests. The Hallidae doll, Bryant wrote, "plays drums and spins the turntable, studies French, acting, political science."

"We were probably taking the biggest financial risk in the history of the company," Larian said. It would take millions to get the brand off the ground. But he was a gambler; he kept a shelf of framed dollar bills from the many bets he'd won. He decided to move ahead. The timeline here would later become essential: On September 18, 2000, while Bryant was still working for Mattel, Larian's lawyer drew up a contract. The executive first offered a full-time job, but Bryant wanted a Jack Ryan kind of deal—an independent contractor arrangement that would pay him in royalties. On October 4, Bryant signed the contract giving him an advance of $5,500 a month for six months, and 3 percent of Bratz's future profits. That same day, he gave his two weeks' notice, without telling his boss he planned to work for a rival. So he left the building, with little fanfare, on October 19. Larian would later claim that he had no idea Bryant continued to work on Barbie for those two weeks that autumn. Certainly, his emails suggested as much. "Carter, this is your big break in business life," Larian wrote on October 5. "You need to put in 16 hours a day, starting now on this and nothing else."

Bryant began meeting with the MGA team, trying to turn his two-dimensional drawings into three-dimensional dolls. He worked with Veronica Marlow, on their fashions, and ex-Mattel face painter Anna Rhee, on their makeup. He met with sculptor Margaret Leahy to construct some preliminary molds. The initial versions were too "va-va-voom," Bryant's new boss, Paula Garcia said. Garcia, who was Greek, liked that the dolls represented a range of ethnicities, but she was "cautious not to over stereotype," as she felt Carter's initial drawings had. At Hong Kong's Toy Fair in January of 2001, when MGA previewed four Bratz prototypes, held together by safety pins and Scotch tape, they had undergone several changes—their hips were slimmer, their chests were more subdued, and their ethnicities were more ambiguous. Now their names were Cloe, Jade, Sasha, and, in a nod to Larian's daughter, Jasmin.

The Bratz debuted that summer in Spain, but their sales, as Barbie's had been, were initially slow—slow enough for Toys "R" Us to cancel a $6 million order in October. Larian borrowed against his own house to double down on advertising. By December, it seemed to have worked. In just six months, Bratz made $23 million.

As newspapers covered Bratz's rise, Larian began to put a Ruth Handler–like twist on the doll's origin story. He told *Businessweek* he'd come up with the Bratz idea himself, inspired by his daughter. Later, he told *The Wall Street Journal*, he'd challenged his staff to a "fashion doll contest," and Bratz had been the winner. For the first two years of Bratz's existence, Carter Bryant's name never appeared in the press. That was not necessarily suspicious. Larian always kept his employees' names out of the papers, he said, to keep them from being headhunted. But it was hard to take Larian's word for it when, internally, he had sent directives like: "There must be no mention about Mattel or any of their properties, Carter, or any MGA Bratz parts, et cetera."

He also had a habit of denying past statements not put in writing. In one email, with the subject line "My Alzheimer's Disease," he joked: "Please note that I have been diagnosed with having Alzheimer's, and I don't remember anything anymore. So, if it is not in writing, I DID NOT approve it. I did not say it. Whatever."

In September of 2001, Mattel was in crisis. The nation was in crisis too—entering a period marked by intense paranoia, cartoonish nationalism, and crescendoing cries for war. Internally, Mattel was already there. The deadliest domestic attack since Pearl Harbor briefly boosted sales of military Barbies.[*] But the doll franchise as a whole was in "critical" condition, an internal report warned. "As a brand, Barbie did not appear to have evolved with the times or the consumer." Her demographic was shrinking and her sales were dropping. For once, Barbie's blankness seemed like a weakness. "The Barbie brand lacks personality depth," another report concluded, "because she is all things to all people."

Bratz, whose personality was the point, had exploited that weakness.

---

[*] Mattel had more trouble with another product called Heli-jet, a "missile-launching helicopter," which F.A.O. Schwartz pulled from its shelves because its packaging described a "diabolical villain . . . blasting urban buildings to pieces" from the roof of the World Trade Center.

Mattel tried to claw back the attention in 2002 with "MyScene," a Barbie flanker brand modeled on the Bratz—three dolls, Madison, Chelsea, and Barbie, with similarly oversized heads and feet. ("Encouraging," Mattel noted internally, "Bratz clearly lost share once MyScene was available.") But MyScene was merely a stopgap measure before the real rebuttal: "Flavas," a line of six "hip-hop themed" dolls, whose accessories included stick-on tattoos, a boom box, and a cardboard wall covered in graffiti. Mattel called them "the first reality-based fashion doll brand," but everyone could see they were at best, the second, and at worst, pretty racist—though Larian didn't distinguish himself on that front. "This is like 'gangster' Barbie," he told *The Wall Street Journal*. "The only thing that's missing is a cocaine vial."

The Flavas backlash was so fast and forceful that the dolls were pulled off the market almost immediately, as Barbie's guardians began to hyperventilate. "Barbie has become irrelevant," one senior vice president reported to Eckert, the CEO, in January 2004. "Girls are embarrassed to be seen playing with Barbie. Licensees are dropping Barbie right and left.... Flavas, a Bratz knockoff, can now be found in discount bins nationwide."

But the anonymous letter had opened the door for a new way Mattel could compete. Not long after its arrival, Mattel was contacted by a Hong Kong company called Cityworld, which produced a Bratz knockoff named "Funky Tweenz." MGA, of course, had sued Cityworld (along with its sister entity "Toys & Trends"), and in the course of those proceedings, the "Funky Tweenz" makers had learned about Carter Bryant. Cityworld's lawyers understood what news of Bryant's involvement might mean for Mattel. Bryant had signed agreements ceding ownership of all "inventions" he "conceived" at "any time during [his] employment" to Mattel. Like many workers in creative fields, toy designers faced a trade-off between the security of a staff job, which assigned the company any of their IP, and the independence of freelancing, which, though unstable, could become infinitely more lucrative. The wording of the Mattel agreements was less straightforward. Did "inventions" include any idea, an offhand doodle, a design for a doll Mattel would never make? Did "during [his] employment" mean while he was in the office, weekdays from nine to five, or did it include nights and weekends and lunch breaks? To Mattel, the answer was yes. If the company could prove that Bryant had "conceived" of his dolls while bound by that contract, Barbie's lawyers could argue that it was Mattel, not MGA, who owned the Bratz brand.

Eckert's Funky Tweenz tipsters had an obvious incentive in making that argument: if MGA did not own Bratz, the company could not sue Cityworld. Mattel arranged a secret "document-sharing agreement," and in November of 2003, the company's lawyers flew to Hong Kong to swap evidence about Bryant's work on Bratz. It was an unusual alignment of interests: an intellectual property titan and an accused counterfeiter.

If Larian and MGA had been cagey about Bryant's work on Bratz, Mattel and Eckert proved cagier still about this arrangement—what they knew and when they knew it. Eckert would insist, for years, that the company had not known that Carter Bryant had made Bratz until the Hong Kong trip in November 2003, a date notably within the statute of limitations for their legal claims. MGA tried to prove otherwise, though Eckert had a habit of "double-deleting" all his emails—first from his inbox, then from the trash. But Carter's relationship with Bratz had been flagged on a fan website in early 2002; Mattel's attorneys knew the site— they'd sent a cease-and-desist about it that same month. And evidence would emerge that five months *before* the anonymous letter, Mattel had begun investigating Bryant and gathering sensitive intel on Larian—his Social Security number, his wife's Social Security number, his property records, data on his neighbors, data on his temple, data on his kids. The company had, on several occasions, staked out MGA's headquarters.

But when Mattel finally sued Carter Bryant on April 27, 2004, the complaint didn't even mention Bratz. Mattel executives would insist for months that they had no interest in making a claim on Bratz, but were merely seeking a few thousand dollars over Bryant's breach of contract. But that seemed dubious. Just two weeks before filing suit, the head of Mattel's Girls Division had given a presentation on the "House on Fire" memo, declaring "war" on Bratz.

"Sides must be taken," the memo had warned, and they were. In November, Bryant filed his own suit, calling Mattel's contract litigation a ruse to "obtain control over the rights to 'Bratz.'" Soon, MGA joined in, intervening in Bryant's case, then filing a third suit the following spring, over what it described as Mattel's "unfair tactics of competition-by-intimidation" and "serial copycatting." The battle branched out into a maze of claims and counterclaims, amassing a docket of nearly eleven thousand filings, with over ten million pages of discovery—an archive of legal paper so extensive that, at one point, the court's box for filing physical copies snapped under the weight.

Over the next decade, the saga of Barbie versus Bratz would become "one of the largest and most aggressively litigated cases ever tried" at the nation's largest court of appeals. More than one reporter would compare it to *Jarndyce v. Jarndyce*, the interminable lawsuit in Charles Dickens's *Bleak House* that lasts for so long few can recall what it was originally about. In the fictitious Dickens case, though, the proceedings had gone on for so many years that the heat of feeling had leeched from them. This one was pitched like a battle. Mattel's lawyer would call Bryant "a double agent of the highest order." Larian would accuse Mattel of killing his father. Bryant would wind up in the ER. The barbs became so ugly, and borderline violent, that it seemed apt when, years into the case, the court appointed a mediator: Pierre-Richard Prosper, a former ambassador-at-large under George W. Bush, specializing in war crimes.

Even the dolls' world outside the courtroom seemed to come back to the case. A year before the first trial, MGA released *Bratz Kidz: Sleep-Over Adventure*, an inordinately bleak film despite being an animated movie set at a slumber party. Late at night, the Bratz decide to tell each other scary stories. One is set at a haunted house, where the Sasha doll finds herself alone at an empty fairground, wandering a hall of mirrors. She checks herself out in the mirrors, but her reflections stop mimicking her movements. These mirror images begin to cackle, taunting and teasing her. These other Sashas are not reflections at all, she realizes, but her doppelgängers. One of them leaps out, pushing Sasha into the mirror, trapping the real girl in the reflection's old place. "I was your reflection, and now I'm *you*," the evil twin gloats. "Enjoy! I know I'm going to." She walks out, leaving the group, leaving the real Sasha screaming, held hostage by her likeness.

CHAPTER 22

TWO BIG KAHUNAS

A few weeks after Carter Bryant met with Isaac Larian in the autumn of 2000, five hundred businesses in the Bay Area received what appeared to be hand grenades in the mail. The grenades were black, hard plastic, heavy as a paperweight, and such realistic imitations that two of the recipients' offices were evacuated by bomb squads. Anyone canny or stupid enough to examine them closely would have found a brief message. Businesses needed to "arm" themselves, it read, because there was a new weapon in town. The detonator pins, still attached, were embossed with a name: Quinn Emanuel.

The grenade stunt, it turned out, was an advertisement for the eponymous law offices of notorious litigator John Quinn. The Los Angeles firm was opening up a branch in San Francisco, and wanted an "edgy" campaign to attract the young Silicon Valley crowd. Quinn fired the agency, but it was an on-brand gesture for a firm that saw itself as a "special forces" operation. ("What would you like people to have in mind when they face you in litigation?" another Quinn ad later asked. "May we suggest dread?") In an industry dominated by century-old firms named for long-dead men, Quinn Emanuel, founded in 1986, had made its relative youth a calling card—swapping the austere wood paneling of white-shoe firms for frat-chic flat screens tuned to ESPN. Its associates, partners, and paralegals milled around in flip-flops, Hawaiian prints, jeans. A partner once greeted a journalist in a T-shirt "silk-screened with Charles Manson's face."

The casual dress code had always been a bit of a misdirect. Though Quinn Emanuel never attended to lawyerly convention, its loosened-tie look always belied a culture of extreme intensity—a place where associates often worked through holidays, weekends, vacations; where failure to bill at least two hundred hours each month could land you on a "low hours list"; where the unspoken rule on *pro bono* cases was: *take them on at your own risk*. Every summer, the firm led its associates on an "extreme" outdoor hike, a "death march" up Yosemite's Half Dome or Washington's Mount St. Helens. Once, after a ten-mile trek in Wyoming, the team arrived at a glacial lake nearly two Denvers above sea level. Quinn joked that he would hire whoever swam across. One intern peeled off his gear, breast-stroked across the hypothermic water, and got the job. No one embodied the firm's sink-or-swim severity more than its namesake partner, John Quinn. The penultimate child in a Mormon family of eight, an army brat, and an Ironman triathlete, he had once traveled to Pamplona and run with the bulls. One partner called him "the most competitive person I know." Another said, in one of those denials that seems to affirm its inverse: "I don't think he's an authoritarian."

Quinn Emanuel's selling point was that its attorneys were pure litigators—they did not spend time on merger deals or tax filings. They took cases to trial, and they usually won. For years, their logo was the fin of a shark. The firm's aggression did not make its lawyers many friends. "They're miserable sons of bitches," one defense attorney told me. "The minute you hear they're on the other side, it's an *oh shit* moment—not *oh shit* because you're scared, but because they don't play by the same rules of professional courtesy or ethics." And maybe that's what endeared them to early clients like Lockheed Martin—and Mattel.

When Quinn Emanuel took on Mattel's case in 2002, the firm deployed a small army of at least nine attorneys to investigate Barbie's claim on Bratz. As MGA told it, the lawyers lived up to their firm's reputation for making things hard—quibbling over deposition schedules, sending documents late at night, asserting "boilerplate objections" to discovery requests, before flooding their opponents with documents, and burying the salient information among boxes of "useless phone records and copies of Carter Bryant's own artwork." Bryant's lawyer called it "the most concerted effort to avoid discovery that I have ever been witness to in my career." Of course, navigating the rules of procedure to ensure juries see only the most persuasive evidence is part of how any good litigator wins a case, and Quinn's team was not alone in attempting it. Bryant "is misusing the discovery process to annoy Mattel and cause Mattel undue burden and expense," one Quinn attorney wrote. Each side nursed an antipathy for the other so strong it transformed the frequently dry prose of legal memos into bitchy jeremiads worthy of Livia Soprano.

The inter-law firm feuding became a news story in its own right when, weeks before the first trial, Quinn Emanuel's attorneys tried to book rooms at the Mission Inn, the nicest hotel in Riverside, California, only to find themselves effectively barred from the premises. MGA's law firm, Skadden Arps, had already taken over some dozen rooms and invoked an exclusivity clause to prevent the opposition from staying there, for "security purposes." ("Coke stays at one hotel," MGA's counsel explained. "Pepsi stays at the other.") But rather than opt for a less swanky Marriott, Mattel's lawyers asked the judge to intervene. "Wow," the judge said. "I really don't know if I have jurisdiction over the Mission Inn's reservation policy." In the end, the hotel's own lawyer came to court to broker a deal.

But if neither side was above hostile legal games, Quinn Emanuel played them better. The presiding judge was a George W. Bush appointee named Stephen Larson who sided with Mattel on several evidentiary motions. In the days before trial, Larson ruled that the "Inventions Agreement" Bryant had signed with Mattel—despite no such explicit mention in the text—had assigned not just work product, but all of the artist's "ideas" to Mattel while he was on its payroll, leaving the jury to decide only which specific ideas Mattel thus owned. Larson also allowed Mattel to bring up the fact that Bryant had downloaded a software called "Evidence Eliminator" shortly before handing over his laptop for inspection. Bryant eventually admitted he'd used the tool to make sure his porn habits didn't become a matter of public record, and his lawyers argued the name alone would taint the jury. But Judge Larson allowed it. Above all, the judge strictly limited any mention of Mattel's motivation in bringing the suit—that Barbie had been failing.

"I've said this numerous times," Larson told the court. "I don't believe Barbie is relevant to this at all."

A week before the trial was scheduled to start, Judge Larson made an announcement. Practically "on the courthouse steps," Carter Bryant had signed a confidential settlement with Mattel, the terms of which would not become public for several years. Bryant would remain one of the trial's most important characters, but his sudden departure clarified the suit's true stakes. This wasn't some employment dispute centered on a single guy. It was a brawl between what Bryant's lawyer called the "two big kahunas," two billion-dollar conglomerates battling over who ruled the fashion doll market.

When the trial began, John Quinn went to work describing a sprawling conspiracy to effectively bribe Bryant to betray his employer and create a hit doll while on the inside. As he told it, Mattel had not been a stagnant bureaucracy, weakened by bad deals and petrified of any change that could affect Barbie's market share. It was a font of originality matched only by maybe Willy Wonka. This was a place, one witness told the jury, that had developed a "radical" program called "Project Platypus"—an innovation bootcamp where twelve staffers from across Mattel would spend three months in an air hangar decked out "like a playground" and concoct a new toy line through a range of elaborate exercises: an improv comedy class, a "rapid-fire storytelling session," and a Japanese tea ceremony. Would a corporation desperate for originality have brought in such guest speakers as a clown, a brain wave researcher, a Jungian psychoanalyst, and a "professor of laughter"? (The implied answer was no.)

By contrast, Quinn said, MGA was a small, flailing company that owed its meager success not to original ideas, but to licensing others'. Larian's company was known for "producing *inexpensive*, shall we say, electronic toys," he said, "in the Far East." (They'd coveted Mattel's staff for years, Quinn would later add, claiming MGA had systematically hired Mattel's top talent, and rewarded those who stole information on their way out.) How could a middling toy maker "suddenly, overnight, become one of the most innovative toy companies in the world?" Quinn asked. "Simple: They took the design, they took the drawings, from a Mattel designer," and then "they covered it up."

It was improbable, Quinn argued, that Bryant had thought up Bratz in Missouri, over that autumn of 1998. He showed the jury a map of Bryant's route home from his job at Old Navy, pointing out that Kickapoo High School, his supposed inspiration, was far afield from his regular drive. Even if he *had* chanced by, Quinn said, Kickapoo students were not exactly at the cutting edge of youth culture, certainly no exemplar of diversity, being majority white. As Quinn told it, none of the witnesses who said they'd seen the drawings in 1998 could be trusted: Bryant's boyfriend, his mother, her friend—they all loved him. The truth, he argued, was that these cool dolls could not have come from some small town in Flyover, USA. They had been born, like so much American iconography, in Los Angeles, a year later, when Bryant was back at Mattel. He had actually been inspired by Lily Martinez, a fellow designer who had been working on a never-released line called Toon Teens—dolls with big heads and little bodies, inspired by a drawing she'd done for Barbie. Martinez remembered showing Bryant the mock-ups.

The secret project to develop Bryant's drawings, Quinn said, had also started much earlier than MGA claimed. He pulled up an invoice, filed four months before Bryant quit, for a project called "Angel," which he claimed was a code name for the nascent Bratz. He cast MGA's staff and Larian as veteran liars,[*] reeling off the CEO's interviews in the press, taking credit for Bratz's invention, while highlighting how internally Larian barred all talk of Carter Bryant. At one point, the MGA CEO had instructed a subordinate to Wite-Out the fax header on Bryant's contract, which showed he'd sent the document from Mattel's Barbie Collectibles department.

When MGA's attorney got up, he seemed like some sad vaudeville act forced to play after the Beatles. The attorney, a veteran litigator named Tom Nolan, told the jury that he would present the "rest of the story," an alternate account that would undermine Quinn's argument and reorient their understanding of what happened. But many of the details that could have helped reframe the narrative—from Barbie's crisis to Mattel's long

---

[*] As Mattel would later tell it, Larian had lied to even his own brother, buying him out of the company in 2000 without factoring Bratz into the value of his share. It's true that Larian bought his brother's 45 percent stake in MGA for $9 million on December 4, 2000, exactly two months after Bryant signed his contract. Farhad had sued three years later, claiming that Bratz had been underway as early as 1999, and accusing his brother of fraud. But the brothers had been negotiating well before Bryant left Mattel, and the California Court of Appeals determined there was "no evidence" of fraud. Farhad was ordered to pay $1 million in attorney fees and later testified he had been mistaken about the timing of Bratz.

history of lawsuits—had been excluded by the judge. The story Nolan was able to tell was muddled, sidetracked by digressions into the particulars of contract and copyright law, and hemmed in by the imposed limitations. No, "Angel" was not a code name, but a reference to another doll line, "Prayer Angels." Yes, Larian had taken credit for Bratz, but he'd been talking about the *dolls*, not Bryant's original drawings. And sure, Bryant had certain contractual obligations to Mattel. But Nolan argued he had never broken them. Bryant had agreed to give Mattel eight hours of work each day, Nolan said, "but he didn't give them his ideas and he didn't give them his soul."

When Larian took the stand, he seemed to misunderstand that the art of witness-questioning requires a delicate two-step. The attorney must extract a persuasive narrative, while navigating the rules of evidence, which—with their arcane specifications and requisite objections—prevent the witness from telling the story as they might to a friend. Larian seemed to view each question, not as a highly choreographed dance around the many obstacles of judicial procedure, but as an invitation to freestyle, to launch into his own spontaneous routine and explain to the jury exactly what had happened and why he was right. At various points, the judge instructed his lawyers to control their witness, but Larian was not someone who did well with constraint. After two months of testimony, the jury sided with Mattel on almost every count—finding that Bryant's drawings and the Bratz name belonged to Mattel, that the Bratz dolls had infringed upon those drawings, and that MGA and Isaac Larian had abetted Bryant in breaching his fiduciary duty.

As the trial began calculating damages, it seemed MGA didn't have much more to lose, and yet they managed to lose more. A week after the verdict, it came out that one of the jurors, a woman identified as Juror No. 8, had made racist comments about Iranians during deliberations. She believed Iranians to be "stubborn, rude, stingy," the court wrote. Her husband's Iranian clients were "thieves," she said, who had "stolen other person's [sic] ideas." Larian's lawyers immediately filed for a mistrial. This wasn't the first racist incident, they reminded the court. When Larian's rabbi sat in for jury selection, one of the jurors had called for him to remove his yarmulke on the grounds that it was "inappropriate." Instead, the rabbi left.

But though Larson found the juror's comments "outrageous," he did not find that they had impacted the verdict. Larson rejected MGA's bid for a mistrial. He not only upheld the original decision, he made it, from the Bratz side at least, even worse. He barred MGA from "producing or marketing virtually every Bratz female fashion doll," then or in the future. And he placed a "constructive trust" over all trademarks using the word "Bratz," effectively handing the entire Bratz portfolio—from the spin-off "Bratz Petz" to the video game *Bratz: Rock Angelz* to accessories like "Bratz Babyz Ponyz Buggy Blitz"—over to Mattel. "In effect," one filing summarized, "Barbie captured the Bratz." It seemed like a subplot out of MGA's own movie, *Bratz: Kidz Sleep-Over Adventure*—though if the ruling held, that was Mattel's now too.

Maybe it would have, had Larian not appealed to the Ninth Circuit, where the case wound up before a man Mattel had met before: *Barbie Girl* judge Alex Kozinski.

When I spoke with Judge Kozinski, he had just gotten a new webcam. It had a sharper resolution, an automatic focus, and something of a will of its own. The image was crisp enough, looking out onto a custom desk I'd heard a podcast host describe, accurately, as "absolutely enormous." But the automatic focus seemed to automatically focus on any source of movement—the slightest gesture sent it lurching from a wide panorama to a closeup on the judge's hairline. "I can't really control what it does," Kozinski's forehead explained. "It does what it does, but there it is."

Several things had changed since he'd told Mattel to chill. The man who had once written a *Forbes* guide on building his own computer now preferred a lower-tech life of landline phones and untamed lenses. Also, he was no longer a judge. Kozinski retired from the Ninth Circuit in 2017, after more than a dozen women accused him of making sexual comments in the workplace, including showing several of his clerks porn. One woman claimed he'd kissed her at a law function in 2008; another alleged he'd groped her during a car ride in the 1980s.

Kozinski had briefly considered rebutting the charges in court; in fact, he'd hired Quinn Emanuel to do it. But then he changed his mind. He had, in 1991, joined an opinion setting the "reasonable woman standard" for sexual harassment cases, holding that courts should "focus on the perspective of the victim," given that men may view some transgressions as "harmless social interactions." Ultimately, Kozinski decided to step down. "I've always had a broad sense of humor and a candid way of speaking to both male and female law clerks alike. In doing so, I may not have been mindful enough of the special challenges and pressures that women face in the workplace," he wrote in his resignation letter. "For this, I sincerely apologize."

A reasonable woman would not have been wrong to deduce that Kozinski had never observed strong distinctions between his private and professional life. As the lore went, he'd spent his school years "chasing girls," appearing not once, but twice on the game show *The Dating Game*. In 1968, he beat out soon-to-be sitcom star David Lander, who'd play Andrew "Squiggy" Squiggman on *Laverne & Shirley*, and won a date to the "Guadalajara Bowling Tournament." (His date stood him up; he found out, decades later, that she thought he'd acted like "such a jerk.") During his confirmation hearings in 1985, the inspector general investigated a more literal kind of professional-private transgression: how furniture Kozinski bought with state funds "wound up in his home."

As a judge, Kozinski was a perfectionist—sometimes demanding forty or fifty drafts, which he'd mark up "in several colors of ink," with supportive comments like: "This is an absolutely awful way to start the argument." But on the page, he sounded less like an authoritarian editor than a breezy nightclub emcee, lacing his opinions with pop culture allusions and sly pranks. In perhaps his most famous decision, about a monopolistic movie theater owner in Las Vegas, he covertly inserted the titles of over 200 films into the text; the opinion became so popular one law review published a "Rosetta Stone" to all the references. In the law, he reliably defended the right to ridicule authority, and off the clock, he made himself a frequent target. When the judicial blog *Underneath Their Robes* failed to include Kozinski among its contenders for "Male Superhottie of the Federal Judiciary," he submitted his own nomination, citing his "uncanny resemblance to Moses." He linked to several "sexy pictures of me jumping," adding: "I have it on very good authority that discerning females and gay men find graying, pudgy, middle-aged men with an accent close to Gov. Schwarzenegger's almost totally irresistible." He won. Later, when he became chief justice of the Ninth Circuit, a role largely allotted by seniority, he amended the press release to read: "Judge Kozinski also believes that looks count, though he can provide no support for that proposition."

During the first Bratz trial, Kozinski had been waylaid by another scandal. Perhaps unsurprisingly, the judge was prone to feuds, and after a prolonged public battle with a Beverly Hills lawyer over an internecine question of proper legal citations, the lawyer leaked a story to the *Los Angeles Times*. Kozinski had long maintained a personal website for his writing, but as the tipster revealed, anyone who used the site's search tool could turn up a trove of the judge's other files, stored on a computer server he shared with his family. Much of what one found there was anodyne—a cache of Weird Al videos, a program that built a virtual snowman, a picture of a bungee jumper shitting his pants midair. But Kozinski's curation of screenshots skewed a bit too 4chan for what the public expected for the federal judiciary: a forty-slide PowerPoint on trans porn stars; a picture of a teen boy, shall we say, succeeding where Marilyn Manson mythically required rib surgery; and at least two pictures of naked women painted, with remarkable precision, as cows. Headlines ranged from the staid "Explicit Website Images Mar Reputation" to the less euphemistic: "Meet the Cow Porn Judge!"

Kozinski's wife, attorney Marcy Tiffany, rose to his defense, arguing in an open letter that the coverage had misconstrued much of the server's contents. Of Kozinski's thousands of files, Tiffany wrote, "the vast majority was cute, amusing, and not in the least bit sexual in nature." As she saw it, the media had seized on a half dozen examples and taken them entirely out of context. Many articles had referred to a "bestiality" video, which one outlet described as a clip "of a half-dressed man cavorting with a sexually aroused farm animal." In reality, she pointed out, "it is a widely available video of a man trying to relieve himself [in] a field when he is attacked by a donkey he fights off with one hand while trying to hold up his pants with the other."

But in an unfortunate coincidence, Kozinski was at that exact time overseeing an obscenity case against a man accused of distributing bestiality videos. The judge declared a mistrial, recused himself, and called for an investigation into his own conduct. The inquiry culminated in Kozinski testifying for three hours before the Third Circuit. Kozinski apologized for embarrassing the court. His greatest regret, he told the judges, was that "whatever shame was cast on me personally, it reflected on my colleagues and our system of justice as well." The panel closed the case, concluding that Kozinski had already addressed the problem by taking the server offline and promising to password protect his personal files. These days, a visit to Alex.Kozinski.com yields the message:

> yeah ok
> nothing to see here

When I could see Kozinski, he was dragging from a long black vape. Between puffs, he brought up Ayn Rand. A longtime fan, he has "probably read every word she's ever written." He saw her speak live at the Ford Hall Forum in the seventies.* "Ayn Rand, of course, was a big believer in literary rights. "She was a total control freak," he said. "She was always claiming that people were stealing from her, that other people who were libertarian thinkers had all sort of stolen her ideas."

Libertarians were somewhat split on intellectual property rights, he said. Some, like him, saw them as limited, as rights that made room for others to borrow or even steal. But Rand understood them as more contiguous with tangible property. She saw the patent or copyright as a way to plant a flag, not on the particular expression of a concept, but on the idea itself. "What the patent or copyright protects is not the physical object as such," she wrote, "but the *idea* which it embodies."

This is, of course, wrong, legally speaking. "Not being a lawyer or

---

*It wasn't hard to see why he might have been drawn to her: a Jewish expat who'd fled a communist country and embraced Western capitalism with near-religious fervor; whose prolific and idiosyncratic writing had, for better or worse, attracted a cult following; whose reputation had been marred by a workplace sex scandal; whose most famous novel centered on a group of persecuted geniuses who withdraw their talents from the world, rather than justify themselves to society. As a student, Rand kept a meticulous movie diary, rating everything she watched on a scale of one to five. The judge, who for years hosted a courthouse movie night called "Kozinski's Favorite Flicks," has rated more than two thousand films on IMDb, under his moniker "E-Z Rider" (*Juror #2*—eight stars).

being a legal scholar, I don't think she appreciated how hard it is to define what an idea is," Kozinski said. "I mean, you can define claims; you can define specifications; you can define, to some extent, whether something is novel.... But defining what an idea is—it's very difficult.... It's just hard to say 'Boy, this is just a completely new idea. Nobody thought of this.'"

When the Bratz appeal came before Kozinski's appellate panel over the summer of 2010, it was the slipperiness of ideas that struck him—specifically that word's absence from Bryant's contract. The "Inventions Agreement" had ceded all of Bryant's "inventions" to Mattel, a category which it defined as "discoveries, improvements, processes, developments, designs, know-how, data computer programs and formulae." But contracts are made or broken by their phrasing, and this one had not used the word "idea." Quinn Emmanuel argued that the definitions were meant to be "illustrative, rather than exclusive," though, as MGA's attorneys would later observe, earlier versions of Mattel's standard contract *had* included the word "idea." It had been edited out, five years before Bryant was hired.

Moreover, Kozinski's panel reasoned, ideas were "markedly different" from the given examples. "Designs, processes, computer programs and formulae are concrete," the judges wrote, "unlike ideas, which are ephemeral and often reflect bursts of inspiration that exist only in the mind." Terms like "know-how" and "discoveries," they conceded, were less tangible, and left room for debate—but debate was precisely what the district court had not permitted. "The agreement could be interpreted to cover ideas, but the text doesn't compel that reading," the panel determined. The district court had "erred" in holding that it did. Nor was it the case, they wrote, that the phrase "at any time during my employment" necessarily included Bryant's nights and weekends. Perhaps "at any time" meant simply at any time during work hours—like lunchtime or coffee breaks. The panel agreed that Bryant's initial drawings fell under the scope of "inventions," but if he had worked on them on a Saturday night, did that make them Mattel's?

The Ninth Circuit ruled that Bryant's employment contract had been much more ambiguous than Larson had allowed. But even if Larson's interpretation *had* been airtight, his verdict had been far too broad, in the panel's opinion. By then, the Ninth Circuit used two primary tests for determining copyright infringement. For an idea with a wide range of expression, where the creator has many options at their disposal—a bildungsroman, or a zombie invasion movie—an infringing work need only show "substantial similarity" to the original. But for those ideas with a narrow range of expression, concepts that can only be articulated so many ways, the standard for infringement was much higher: the two works needed to be "virtually identical." (There are "only so many ways to paint a red bouncy ball on blank canvas," Kozinski wrote.) Larson had ruled that Bryant's preliminary sculpt fell in the first category. As he saw it, there were many ways to depict a fashion doll with exaggerated features. Thus, though the main Bratz sculpts were by no means identical to Bryant's original dummy, they were similar enough to be deemed copies.

Kozinski disagreed. When it came to Bryant's prototype, the Ninth Circuit concluded that its depiction of women with oversized heads and feet was both "unoriginal" and "unprotectable." Betty Boop, anime characters, Steve Madden models—they had beaten Bryant to it. And though, in theory, there may be many ways to realize an exaggerated doll physique, there was a reason so many of these predecessors shared similar proportions: they were "highly constrained" by social expectations of the female body. "One could make a fashion doll with a large nose instead of a small one, or a potbelly instead of a narrow waist," Kozinski wrote. "But there's not a big market for fashion dolls that look like Patty and Selma Bouvier."

> Little girls buy fashion dolls with idealized proportions—which means slightly larger heads, eyes and lips; slightly smaller noses and waists; and slightly longer limbs than those that appear routinely in nature. But these features can be exaggerated only so much: Make the head too large or the waist too small and the doll becomes freakish, not idealized.

Unlike the body, Kozinski agreed that the rest of the doll—the features based on Bryant's drawings—had a greater range of expression. There were infinite ways to *dress* the Bratz, or adjust their makeup, or style their hair. In 2007, he noted, the maker of a farting doll called "Pull My Finger Fred," had sued another toy company over their similar-looking products: "Fartboy" and "Fartman." The infringing doll maker, that court had found, could have easily designed "another plush doll of a middle-aged farting man that would seem nothing like Fred." Just as Fartboy could have a "blond mullet and wear flannel" or sport "shorts rather than blue pants," the Bratz dolls could have been styled in some new way that did not borrow from Bryant's original sketches.

But here too, Kozinski argued, Larson had been too broad. To establish "substantial similarity," a judge must filter out any of the work's "unprotectable elements"—the basic features obligated by a given form, like, say, the happy ending of a romcom. The judge's ruling must be based solely on the creative components subject to protection. But Larson, in his list of protectable elements, had included the Bratz's "distinct look or attitude," as well as their "aggressive" and "youthful" outfits. In a sense, he had fallen for the same fallacy as Ayn Rand. "Mattel can't claim a monopoly over fashion dolls with a bratty look or attitude, or dolls sporting trendy clothing," Kozinski wrote. "These are all unprotectable ideas."

Mattel's rights extend to only the "particular expression of the bratty-doll idea, not the idea itself," he continued. "Degas can't prohibit other artists from painting ballerinas, and Charlaine Harris can't stop Stephenie Meyer from publishing *Twilight* just because Sookie came first. Similarly, Mattel was free to look at Bryant's sketches and say, 'Good idea! We want to create bratty dolls too.'"

Because of the district court's errors, the panel concluded, "the entire case will probably need to be retried."

CHAPTER 23

THE BRATZ BRIEF

The same month Kozinski ordered a retrial, MGA's attorneys flew to Chicago to depose a new witness. For years, they had been aware of a document called "The Bratz Brief," an in-depth investigation into Bratz's impact on Barbie, which Mattel had seemingly commissioned sometime in 2003. It described, the lawyers wrote, "a Barbie brand on the decline long before Bratz ever entered the market," while conceding that Bratz's success had little to do with Carter Bryant's drawings. The legal team had received a copy in early 2008, but they had not brought it up at the first trial. None of the Mattel executives they deposed, including Eckert, seemed able to identify it. And besides, as Quinn Emanuel contested, Barbie's supposed decline had been irrelevant to the proceedings.

But in Chicago, that July of 2010, MGA deposed Sujata Luther, a woman who had worked in Mattel's research and strategy departments for nineteen years, beginning in 1984. She was well versed in Mattel's research methods; she had written much of the guidebook explaining them all. And Luther knew the Bratz Brief well. As it turned out, she had written much of that too.

Under oath, Luther told MGA that Eckert had in fact requested the report himself and had edited an early draft. Luther even recalled Eckert's complaints about a stray Britishism in the text—changing her anglicized "learnt" to "learned." But that was not Luther's only revelation. She also described, as MGA later recounted to the judge, how Mattel conducted global consumer research on a "near-daily basis," and archived it all in a centralized library. That library, MGA would allege, contained a range of relevant documents that had not been produced in the first trial, including a Bratz "cannibalization study" from January 2002, and, even more mysteriously, an internal report from New York's 2001 Toy Fair detailing confidential information on Bratz—months before the dolls had even debuted.

Just four days later, MGA interviewed another incendiary witness, a man named Sal Villaseñor. He had written the confidential early report on Bratz, and during his deposition, he explained how he did it. Beginning in the mid-nineties, until at least 2005, Villaseñor had worked in, and eventually ran, what became known as the Market Intelligence Department, a Mattel division that several executives, including Eckert, maintained did not really exist. In 2001, Villaseñor had flown to New York and snuck into MGA's private showroom under a fake identity. This was not a one-off endeavor. The Market Intelligence Department was tasked with sneaking into toy fairs around the world to gather information on rivals—a feat they accomplished using phony business cards for stores like "The Toy Shop," a name so generic no one could prove it did not exist. As part of the pose, they drafted fake invoices, fake ads, fake catalogs, and fake tax certificates. (The spies were regulars at the local Kinko's.)

This practice, Villaseñor claimed, dated back to before he joined the company in 1992. He'd received a training document, later known as the "How to Steal Manual," breaking down best practices for getting into toy fairs without detection. It instructed the toy spies on everything from how to dress (business casual, "comfortable shoes," either a "shoulder bag or briefcase with wheels"), to what to bring (driver's license, business cards, "proof of your business"), to how to devise the most persuasive cover story. At larger fairs, it was best to pose as a buyer. "Think about the size of your store," one passage read. "Try to keep it reasonably small. What type of toys you sell. How many employees. Where exactly your store is located. How many stores you have."

At one of the smaller fairs, the manual said, vendors were more likely to want press coverage; Mattel's agents were told to impersonate media. Villaseñor once claimed to be the editor of "the *Daily 49er* newspaper at Cal State Long Beach."

Mattel would try to write Villaseñor off as a rogue agent who acted on his own, but he regularly received promotions and performance bonuses, and expense reports showed that Mattel signed off on his purchases, such as more than $1,000 in camera equipment. At New York's Toy Fair, they put him up at the Waldorf Astoria. Each year, he gave presentations on his reports for huge crowds at Mattel's presentation theater. Villaseñor liked to give each of his reports playful themes. In 2002, it was "The Toy Olympics"—the paper was decorated with Olympic rings and had headings like "Girlie-Girl Event." Anyone who missed a show could read the reports in the ninth-floor Market Intelligence Department library if they had clearance. "This is great," one vice president told Villaseñor over email. "You just saved Mattel close to 1 million."

The new evidence, at first glance, could seem somewhat far afield from Carter Bryant and the question of who owned Bratz. But Mattel's case against MGA had ballooned out from Bryant and Larian to include, as Judge Larson summarized, "five more defendants and nine new legal claims, [and] a wide range of commercial disputes between the rival doll makers that spans three countries." In 2007, the company had amended their complaint to tell a new narrative: that MGA had operated a "widespread criminal enterprise," involving "numerous acts of mail and wire fraud," a series of predicate acts that ran afoul of RICO, the mob statute that took down Michael Milken.

As part of this alleged conspiracy, Mattel claimed, MGA had "cherry-picked" designers like Bryant, as well as a series of "high-ranking Mattel executives in foreign markets," who stole trade secrets before they quit. In the course of the case, Mattel had gotten in touch with the FBI, and had three MGA employees arrested in Mexico, where corporations could pursue criminal charges for trade secret theft. At trial, Mattel had accused MGA of systematically stealing its secrets. But now it appeared they'd spent at least fourteen years doing the same thing.

The late revelations upended MGA's case, but the company was, at first, poorly positioned to do much about it. The mercurial Isaac Larian had run through lawyers at a furious pace, leaving behind a "carnage" in his wake, as one told me. During the Mattel battle, firms O'Melveny & Myers, Skadden Arps, and Orrick Herrington had all come on and exited—or at least tried to. When Orrick attempted to quit in December 2010, Judge

Carter wouldn't allow it. With the trial about to start, there wasn't enough time to get a new team up to speed. Instead, they reached a compromise. The Orrick lawyers would stay on, but they would have a new partner: a criminal defense attorney named Jennifer Keller.

Keller officially joined the team on January 4, 2011, nine days before jury selection. "This is career suicide," a friend told her. The case looked like a clear loser, and Keller would be an easy scapegoat, the unprepared incompetent who'd come in too late. But she'd come up as a public defender, for whom having thirty minutes to prep a case was standard. Nine days sounded like a luxury. She also had a thing about being told what to do. "I was, among other things, expelled from the Catholic girls' high school I went to," Keller told me. "When they forced me to take Latin instead of Spanish, for example, I just didn't do the work." That this was so obviously a bad idea only made it sound more appealing to her. She was, as one outlet put it, California's "go-to trial attorney for difficult cases."

Keller was not the only newcomer. After just three years on the bench, Judge Larson had resigned, calling the salary inadequate for the job. The case had been transferred to Judge David O. Carter, a Clinton appointee in Orange County known for an idiosyncratic approach. In the nineties, he was known for duct-taping the mouths of defendants who swore or spit in the courtroom. He also called on plastic surgeons to remove parolees' gang tattoos pro bono. When he took on cases about Los Angeles's homelessness epidemic, he held a hearing on Skid Row, to ensure city officials had to face the constituents impacted by their policies.

Judge Carter had a reputation for working long days. He was sensitive about jurors' time—all working people whose hours in court, unlike the lawyers', were not necessarily billable. So he squeezed in hearings whenever he could, calling in the attorneys at the crack of dawn, keeping them until late at night, and frequently asking them to work weekends. When the courthouse refused to send a marshal to open the doors on a Saturday or Sunday, Carter would show up early to unlock them himself. "I lost twenty-seven pounds during the trial," Keller said, "because of not having time to eat." In keeping with Kozinski's ruling, and his own taste for economy, Carter had overhauled the proceedings. He put every dispute between MGA and Mattel on the table at once, from Bryant's contract all the way up to Barbie herself. Neither side would mention evidence spoilation—be it Bryant's software or Eckert's emails. Judge Carter was aware that there had been "a significant number of discovery abuses," and he warned both sides that he would bring it to an end.

When Keller stood up for opening statements January 18, 2011, she was less hindered than previous attorneys had been, free to narrate her defense more or less as she saw it. "This case is about how the world's biggest toy company tried to crush a small but successful competitor after it could not beat it in the marketplace," she told the jury.

She spoke in plain English, taking time to set the scene and reframing Larian as a passionate, funny guy whose inconsistencies were not malicious, but the by-product of his storytelling instincts and casual charisma. This was a guy who "was a waiter at the LAX restaurant," she emphasized. Unlike Mattel's executives, who had been hired into an already-baked behemoth, Larian had built his empire from the bottom up. She promised to show that Mattel, for all its "massive creative genius," had been out-flanked by Bratz, had failed to successfully knock them off, and had resorted to anti-competitive methods—punishing retailers who partnered with Bratz, pressuring stores to shelve Bratz in the back, and sending spies to surveil MGA employees and steal confidential information. When none of that worked, Mattel had finally sued to claim that it had "owned Bratz all along," Keller argued. "That's what really happened."

As the plaintiff, Mattel's team had given the first opening argument, then got come back up to rebut Keller's. But now *they* seemed like the sad second act, scrambling to redirect the narrative. In the first trial, Quinn Emanuel had presented Mattel as a font of wholesome creativity, skirting over Barbie's bad sales. But under the new rules, that would be a harder case to make. "It's true that people at Mattel became self-critical, started to wonder, you know, *How come this other product has become so successful?*" Quinn conceded. The jury was sure to see "memos with colorful names like 'House on Fire' and 'This is War.'" But that didn't mean that the company had lost its way. The authors of those memos had no idea, he said, that "they were losing market share to another Mattel design."

Nor was it as easy to present Eckert and his staff as honest brokers, unfairly maligned by MGA people, who were "dishonest and untruthful and lied." The new evidence suggested that, at the very least, there were liars on both sides. "It is, I acknowledge, an unfortunate regrettable fact," Quinn said, "that apparently a number of employees did use phony IDs at certain toy fairs, phony business cards to gain access to showrooms."

―❧―

The key to winning a trial, as Keller saw it, was picking the right jury. She'd learned as much during her defender days in Orange County, when it was even more conservative, and even less diverse. Addressing an O.C. jury usually meant "looking at twelves sets of crossed arms." The ability to read body language and establish some rapport could make the difference between a five-year sentence and six months' probation. The process was more art than science, but in Keller's opinion, she was pretty good at it. In general, she went for intelligent jurors, people who could follow the action closely and read between the lines. She also looked for subtle hints of their sympathies, if they would identify with a plaintiff, or see themselves in the defendant—signs which were not always straightforward. Larian thought she was crazy when she chose a Barbie collector from the conservative enclave of Coto de Caza. But Keller saw that the woman was a *New York Times* subscriber who watched Rachel Maddow. She thought: *She'll be open to our David and Goliath theme.*

The lawyers were eyeing the jury a few days into the trial, when Carter Bryant took the stand. Bryant had never been an energetic court witness; he'd always been nervous, uneasy. But now he looked as buoyant as a slashed tire. He was wan and gaunt. His skin had a gray pallor. In his deposition videos, Bryant had seemed sturdy and nourished. In court, it "looked like he had lost a hundred pounds."

Bryant had been brought to the stand by a Quinn Emanuel attorney named William Price, an accomplished litigator respected by even those who resented his employer. A federal judge once likened his examination style to a "symphony" and a "bloodletting." And from the minute he began asking questions, it was clear which one Price was going for. "Isn't it correct, sir," Price asked, "that you will testify falsely under penalty of perjury about a date concerning Bratz so that MGA gets intellectual property rights to Bratz?"

Bryant said no, but his other answers were less certain. He struggled to recall specific dates, or his own story, or much of anything at all. "Is it your feeling that you answered 'I don't remember, I don't recall' to dozens and dozens of questions since you took the stand?" Price asked. It was, Bryant agreed. He forgot so much that the judge sidebarred with MGA's attorneys, recalling that with a forgetful witness, the court would decide "whether the failure of recollection was innocent or not." But as the interrogation wore on, Bryant seemed to fold in on himself. He looked willing to say anything.

When he'd recruited unknowing Mattel colleagues to help with his secret project, Price asked, hadn't he "betrayed their trust"?

"Yes," Bryant conceded.

Price got even more adamant, pulling up quotes from Bryant's deposition, his first testimony, pouncing on any inconsistencies, implying that the designer had been coached by his lawyers. By the second day, the grilling had become so intense that the judge warned Price during a recess not to just "go down a litany of all the lies that you perceived Mr. Bryant might have stated at the first trial." Price's rationale, he explained, was to pin Bryant's caginess on Larian and his legal team. "MGA is going to get up here and not embrace him," Price said, "but attack him as a lying person who deceived Isaac Larian."

Keller thought Price was mistaken. She had been watching the jurors. "Bill had cross-examined Carter into the ground. I mean, day after day, after day, after day," she recalled. "He was getting the little sound bites, but he was losing the jury." When Keller took over, she began by asking Bryant about his bad memory. Price had implied that he was "faking it," or lying, she said, "but your memory problems are real, aren't they?" They were, Bryant said. Since this lawsuit was filed in 2004, had he "suffered from depression?" He had. Did he take medication for that? He did. Hadn't he been physically ill for years? Unable to sleep? That was true too. "I basically had to start relying on sleeping medications—Ambien, Lunesta," he said. Revisiting the case was rough, he admitted. It brought back bad memories. He'd tried to move past all this. "Now, are you trying as hard as you can to remember what you can?" Keller asked. Yes, Bryant said. He really was.

The portrait that emerged of Bryant was of a young designer who, for a moment, had floated to the top of his field, who had designed the toy market's hottest doll, had been desired by every toy company in the country. After the lawsuit, all of that had gone away. He felt "radioactive." His contracts had dried up. His money had disappeared. Bryant's on-again, off-again boyfriend had always juggled several businesses (among them: "Dark Ops," his brand of "tactical fighting knives") and he'd invested much of Bryant's earnings into long shot land development deals. One of them, an MGA lawyer told me, was a "luxury trailer park" in Arkansas. But 2007 had not been a good year for real estate investments, and when the market crashed, so had Bryant's assets. The designer had made more than $35 million in royalties off Bratz alone, but by the time he'd settled with Mattel, he had $40,000 in his bank account. He'd agreed to pay $2 million—though he hadn't yet paid anything, as that dwarfed his net worth. "I basically have no income right now," he explained.

Bryant began to cry and the jury seemed to soften. At least one of them teared up too. For all the damaging sound bites he'd given Price, the Bryant who answered Keller's questions did not come across like some Machiavellian liar. He seemed "beaten to pieces." In a way, he was. After leaving the courthouse, Bryant collapsed at the airport. He boarded his flight, then felt a pain in his neck, and some kind of dizziness. He couldn't walk. He left the tarmac in an ambulance.

The story of the trial had become much bigger than Bryant. It was, in Keller's view, a parable about a big fish trying to swallow a little one. In Quinn's, it was a heist, a caper about grizzled con artists stealing from the inside. Neither was quite right. But if the trial was, at its core, a face-off between two companies, it was also one between CEOs. Isaac Larian seemed to understand this. He made a point of appearing in court almost every day. Sometimes his wife was there. Sometimes his children. He bonded with the court marshals, posing for photos in the hall. "Your friendly neighborhood billionaire," one joked. Of course, Larian was not nice to everyone. Once, he muttered at Price: "I will never settle with you, you son of a bitch."

But when Eckert took the stand, the jury hadn't seen much of him. He'd appeared at opening arguments, but he hadn't really spoken. If

Larian seemed perhaps too invested, Eckert seemed absent and aloof. When John Quinn opened the examination, he tried to account for that. "Did you understand there's a court order," he asked, saying that "witnesses are not supposed to be in the audience and attend the Court until after they testify?"

"That's correct," Eckert said.

Technically, it wasn't. Mattel could have appointed Eckert as its "corporate representative," allowing him to attend trial daily. The attorneys had instead chosen Lily Martinez, the designer behind Toon Teens. It was an understandable decision. The one-time *Project Runway* guest judge was a visual reminder that, if Mattel's account was true, Bryant had not only betrayed some millionaire executives, but his colleagues and friends. (Keller suggested another reason; she was also "very, very attractive," the attorney said. "I mean truly *va-va-voom*.")

And yet Eckert's absence left him vulnerable to attack. "You know that when Mr. Larian is sitting here every single day and you are not, it looks bad to the jury, right?" Keller asked. The disparity was obvious enough that the judge eventually ordered Eckert to appear in court to avoid the possibility of bias. Afterward, the executive met with his lawyers in their conference room. One attorney claimed you could hear him yelling through the walls.

Larian did some yelling too. As in the first trial, Larian was prone to outbursts and unrelated digressions. When faced with unflattering evidence, he hedged or denied having seen it. He didn't read long emails, he'd say. He had ADD. Sometimes he contradicted his own statements. (Q: "You said it was some kind of fashion doll contest?" A: "I never said there was a fashion doll contest.") After a former MGA staffer claimed she'd seen Bryant months before he left Mattel, Larian dismissed her as untrustworthy. She'd tried to "extort" him by suing for pregnancy discrimination. ("Ladies and gentlemen of the jury," he said, she "was lying as you saw her lying today.") It was hard to predict what he might blurt out—that the case gave Bryant a stroke (it hadn't), that Mattel had killed his father, who had died (of natural causes) before the first trial. Once Price referred to Larian's "wives," then seemed to chuckle. He meant to say *wife's*, he corrected. But it wasn't the first time Larian felt he'd been accused of adultery in court, or received a bigoted slight.

LARIAN: Your partner said before [that] I have girlfriends in front of my wife, and now you said *wives* . . . You made this racial remarks in the last trial, and I do not appreciate it . . . I know you thought it's funny. I don't think it's funny.
PRICE: . . . I apologize, but I never made a racist remark, sir, and you know it.
LARIAN: I don't want to go to that, but you did make a racist remark in the last trial. It's on the record.
PRICE: No. That's disgusting.
LARIAN: You are disgusting.

Larian's inability to self-censor could be humanizing or funny. When Price cited Larian's quote in an article, he seemed to laugh it off. "Journalists write a lot of things," the executive said. "I read a newspaper article that says that your tie is worth what every jury spends on the weekend taking their families out for Sunday night dinner." For better or worse, Larian seemed incapable of uttering anything other than whatever came to mind. It made him seem unpredictable, unpolished, sometimes juvenile or petty. It also made him sound less like a CEO.

The same could not be said for Robert Eckert, a guy who seemed destined to have his picture framed in a row of men who looked like him. Eckert had been in the hot seat before. Around the time of the first trial, Mattel had been at the center of an international scandal, when it recalled nearly two million toys contaminated with lead paint. Over the summer of 2007, the company had been forced to make three recalls, then a fourth for a separate issue involving magnets that could choke children. Mattel blamed a subcontractor in China for one of the recalls; soon after, the manager of that subcontractor took his own life. Mattel had drawn scrutiny not just for the extent of the problem, but for its delay in sounding the alarm. Though the company had become aware of the lead in June of 2007, they hadn't reported it within twenty-four hours, as the Consumer Product Safety Commission required. They had waited almost two months. The company paid a civil fine of $2.3 million—then the third-highest in CPSC history. Eckert had been questioned before Congress, then appeared on TV, morning and night, one observer reported, "staring directly into the camera and apologizing for Mattel's failure."

Perhaps that was why, in court, Eckert struggled to speak in anything but corporate euphemism, as when he referred to mass layoffs as a "headcount reduction." When Keller took over questioning, she seized on his phrasing. "When you said you *reduced the headcount*," she asked, "that meant you laid off more than 500 employees the first year, right?"

ECKERT: I believe that's the case, yes . . .
KELLER: And you laid off another 980 the next year, 2001, right?
ECKERT: I don't know that to be the case.
KELLER: You closed your plant in Kentucky?
ECKERT: We did close the plant in Kentucky. I don't know what year it was.
KELLER: And that involved 980 jobs, all gone, right?
ECKERT: Gone from Kentucky, yes.
KELLER: . . . Well, the way you have made your company profitable is cutting people's jobs, right?
ECKERT: Um.
KELLER: Or reducing the headcount, as you like to say?

She pointed out that Mattel had sent off some of its top executives with severance packages worth tens of millions. By contrast, when Eckert learned that MGA had contracted with three Mattel seamstresses—middle-aged Hispanic mothers, one of whom had spent eighteen years at Mattel on a salary of $40,000—they'd been fired without a cent. "Do you care about them?" Keller asked. "To the extent I care about people," Eckert said, "yes."

Larian, of course, had laid off his share of workers too. But the trial was about drawing contrasts. Later, Keller asked Larian about Little Tikes, a toy company he'd acquired in Ohio. "My plan was to move Little Tikes to Mexico," he said. It would have saved him a lot in labor costs. But he didn't go through with it. "I went to Ohio and I met with the employees," he said. Some had "worked there over thirty and forty years, and it was their whole life, and I just couldn't. My heart wouldn't do it."

CHAPTER 24

THE MIDNIGHT RIDE

By the time Sal Villaseñor, the alleged "Market Intelligence" head, approached the witness stand, the jury had heard a half dozen Mattel executives wash their hands of him under oath. They had no idea he had gone to such lengths or used such suspect means. They had never even heard of a department called Market Intelligence. "You know," said Tim Kilpin, then the executive vice president of boys and girls brands, "I'm not remembering one." Nor had Alan Kaye, head of Human Resources: "That name, 'market intelligence,' I've never seen at Mattel."

General Counsel Robert Normile hadn't heard of it either. In fact, even as sat there, on the stand, that very day, he was still "questioning whether there was really a department" at all. During the trial, MGA had introduced internal Mattel emails and forms labeled "Market Intelligence Department." But at most, Normile said, it sounded like the work of one or two people. "That is not a department," he explained. Even Neil Friedman, the outgoing president of Mattel Brands, seemed oblivious to the goings-on of his subordinates. He certainly hadn't known that Sal Villaseñor was "manufacturing essentially fake identities."

> **KELLER:** Now, you have met with Sal Villaseñor yourself to discuss marketing intelligence?
> **FRIEDMAN:** I am not sure I did.
> **KELLER:** . . . Looking at page fifteen of your calendar, we see on Monday, October 31, 2005 . . . it says "Marketing Intelligence Update With Sal Villaseñor"?
> **FRIEDMAN:** That's correct.

KELLER: This is your own calendar, right?
FRIEDMAN: That's correct.

The day Villaseñor arrived, Keller questioned a former Mattel executive named Matt Turetzky, who, as a vice president of consumer research, had at one point been Villaseñor's boss. He had worked closely with two of the other spies; their fake business cards listed his home address. Turetzky had known about the fake identities, he said. But the whole thing had made him "uncomfortable." It seemed "unethical," a little "gray." He must have known right from wrong, Keller affirmed without irony—he had gone to Harvard Business School.

As Turetzky told it, Mattel had changed its code of conduct sometime in late 2002, barring the business card practice. After that, Villaseñor had been acting on his own. In pursuit of the straight and narrow, Mattel had hired an outside contractor, a journalist, to dig up information using honest means—though the journalist in question, Keller pointed out, was a former Mattel employee who had never written a single article. "So in order to not violate the code of conduct, you hired an outsider to do the same thing?" Keller asked. "No," Turetzsky said.

But when Villaseñor took the stand later that day, he insisted that Turetzky was not the only vice president apprised of his methods, and that he had not acted alone: at least eight Mattel researchers had gone to toy fairs undercover. His conduct had not been discouraged by his supervisors, he said, but actively egged on, well after the code of conduct changed in 2003. He had filed expense reports from Hong Kong in 2003, New York in 2004, Nuremberg in 2005. Certainly, Villaseñor didn't seem like someone who had decided, brazenly, to overrule his bosses and go it alone. The man who spoke to the jury seemed as beaten down as Bryant. Villaseñor, now in middle-age with few employment prospects, broke down on the stand. He was a good liar, he told the jury, he had gotten into toy fairs around the world. But he didn't like doing it. He didn't think of himself that way. He'd felt trapped. He knew if he stopped, he could lose his job.

The pressure had gotten worse in 2005, when a new boss told him to stop using the fake credentials. But though his methods had to change, the boss had said, the expectations would not. Villaseñor would still need to find confidential information. He just needed to do it by the book. It seemed like he was being asked to do something impossible, or worse, position himself to take the fall. It sounded like his boss was saying: Get it anyway, just don't tell me how.

Shortly before that Christmas, Villaseñor had decided to put the whole thing to an end. He'd written an email to Mattel's general counsel. The growing pressure "forced me to evaluate my role in the company," it read. His work conditions had become "intolerable," and he could no longer gather intelligence "through unlawful means." "My conscience does not allow me to continue in this role," he'd concluded, "and I do not feel I can take the pressure to engage in misrepresentations any longer." He'd known that there was pending litigation against Mattel, specifically involving Bratz. He'd been worried that these "undercover assignments" would expose him to "personal criminal liability."

Villaseñor had taken a mental health leave. He'd also hired a lawyer. He'd suspected that Mattel would not receive his letter with gratitude and understanding. He was right. As soon as they read the letter, Mattel's in-house attorneys had opened an investigation. At least one of them understood that Villaseñor's letter "might concern the MGA litigation." He'd sent it to Quinn Emanuel right away. Then Mattel had hired two more law firms—one to investigate Villaseñor, another to handle any lawsuits. To Mattel, this letter seemed like a "stickup"—a guy and his "opportunistic lawyer," who had "a little bit of dirt that they were trying to stretch to a lot of money." During negotiations, Villaseñor's lawyer conspicuously mentioned several executive severance packages—including the multimillions they'd paid Jill Barad.

But the company was in something of a conundrum, one attorney admitted at trial. If they fired Villaseñor while he was on medical leave, he could file a lawsuit. And if he filed a lawsuit, it would become a public document. And if, in that lawsuit, he described how he had been directed to doctor phony invoices and create false identities, well, that would be public too. Instead, they settled with Villaseñor for about $160,000. As part of the settlement, Villaseñor had agreed not to discuss "any allegations of wrongful conduct" during his employment. Specifically, he had agreed not to disclose them to any lawyers bringing a case against Mattel.

Eckert returned to the stand one week later, on April Fool's Day. The trial had been going on for three months. And in that time, the evidence of Mattel's espionage operation had become hard to refute. The day before, the jury had watched surveillance tape of Mattel's security team spying on a former Mattel employee who'd been leaving for MGA. The team had followed the staffer during his last two weeks, recording hours of video not just of him, but of his family. In front of the jury, this man had watched the footage of himself for the first time. "That's the back of our house," he'd said. "That's me and my daughter."

But Eckert seemed more ignorant than anyone. He hadn't known about the surveillance; he certainly hadn't signed off on it. "Until yesterday, I didn't even know somebody did videotape [his] family," Eckert said, though *The Wall Street Journal* had reported the allegation three years earlier. He had not heard of the Market Intelligence Department, either. He first learned of it when he was deposed for trial. The whole fake identity thing, that was new to him. He was as upset as everyone else. "Unfortunately, I think we have seen instances in this trial where people either did the wrong thing, or knew of someone who did the wrong thing," he said, "and those people didn't do the right thing and take the appropriate action."

But to him, it did seem like some things were being blown a bit out of proportion. Several witnesses had mentioned the "ninth floor library"—the supposedly centralized repository for Mattel's consumer research, the same one Sujata Luther and Villaseñor had mentioned in their depositions the previous summer. Eckert, first of all, had also never heard of that. "I didn't know one existed," he said, "a so-called 'library,' that is." Second of all, the "so-called library," was on the eighth floor, not the ninth. He knew that because, after all this fuss, he had taken it upon himself to seek it out. On the stand, Quinn asked him about what he'd found. As it turned out, Eckert attested, it wasn't much of a library at all. "It's a storage closet," he said, barely bigger than his own toy closet on the fifteenth floor. "It is largely what you would call brown legal file folders with catalogs, sheets."

Eckert was again out of the loop. As the trial trudged on, the mountains of legal paper its two parties produced only grew larger. The two legal teams continued to depose new witnesses, turn over new evidence, well into the proceeding's final weeks. After the jury left each evening, the courtroom devolved into furious squabbling and finger-pointing. Quinn had found evidence that, on a half dozen occasions, MGA staff had illicitly spied on Mattel toy fairs too, though the judge later ruled that they had only recovered public information. MGA too uncovered emails, confirming their hunch that Mattel had paid retailers not to do business with Bratz. In one instance, Mattel had gotten Kohls to drop MGA as a client for two full years. In closed hearings without the jury, each side accused the other of hiding evidence or abusing the court's rules. After Judge Carter ordered Quinn Emanuel to hand over notes from a Mattel investigation, they'd submitted the files so heavily redacted that several pages could have passed for fuzzy prints of Kazimir Malevich's painting *Black Square*. "The record should reflect I have handed Mr. Quinn a largely blank page," Keller complained to the judge. "There is nothing left on it."

But the most dramatic revelation had just come to the court's attention the week of Eckert's testimony. During a last-minute deposition, a Mattel attorney revealed that the ninth-floor library had been effectively dismantled, that after Villaseñor resigned, the legal team had packed up his files and brought them to the offices of Paul Hastings, the law firm handling his investigation. These files, which MGA's legal team claimed they'd never seen were not just meaningless tchotchkes from Villaseñor's cubicle, but thirty-five boxes of material, at least a quarter of which seemed to contain consumer research reports, stolen catalogs, video footage from his annual presentations, and memos Villaseñor had sent to the upper ranks of Mattel's leadership.

When Judge Carter heard about the new evidence, he couldn't hide his displeasure. He ordered an investigation, summoning both parties at 9 p.m. to the offices of Robert O'Brien, the case's Discovery Master, a meticulous attorney and a hawkish neocon who would later go on to replace John Bolton as Donald Trump's national security advisor in 2019. O'Brien had tasked several lawyers with examining the material, under penalty of "severe consequences" for any funny business. The investigation went on all night. "We had a midnight ride," one lawyer recalled, "the midnight ride of Paul Revere."

John Quinn was angry. He did not believe these boxes were relevant. The implication that Mattel or Quinn had buried evidence was "simply wrong," he said. None of these documents had been compelled by the court. Quinn was right. Technically, the judge had denied an MGA request that would have mandated these boxes. "I want them to stop going through our friggin' files," Quinn said.

But the judge eventually lost his patience. "Listen to me very carefully," he said. "My system only works with complete transparency. It only works with a modicum of honesty." Judge Carter was "extraordinarily concerned" that all this was coming in during the last week of trial. He felt that it went against "the spirit of the discovery rules," if not the letter of them. "I thought that the rules of discovery meant something to both parties," he said. "And I've become extraordinarily cautious now, as a Court."

So when Eckert took the stand, just days after the "midnight ride," and told the jury that the library was basically a broom closet, he had, perhaps unknowingly, set himself up. Judge Carter called a lunch recess. "The testimony for Mr. Eckert is that he recently went to investigate the whereabouts of Market Intelligence or the library," he said, after the jury left the room. "Mr. Eckert, I don't know if you're even aware—and I say this with all due respect—but that apparently is over at Paul Hastings."

Judge Carter didn't know if Eckert or Larian had been aware of their lawyers' hijinks, if they had been shielded or not, but it didn't matter. They were the CEOs. And they were responsible. And when trial resumed, Keller held Eckert to that:

> **KELLER:** You know, don't you, that the entire Market Intelligence library was actually carted off in boxes to an outside law firm and has been there since the material was turned over to them in 2006? You know that, right?
> **ECKERT:** No, I don't.
> **KELLER:** You don't know that your outside counsel, at the direction of the Law Department at Mattel, came in and carted off 35 boxes full of competitor information?
> **ECKERT:** No, I don't.
> **KELLER:** . . . Did you just visit the eighth-floor storage closet on your own, or were you directed to do so?

ECKERT: Um, I went with another gentleman . . . And with an attorney.

KELLER: So, you were directed to go look at the storage closet so you could come in here and say the Market Intelligence library was just a storage closet, basically, right?

✑

The Quinn Emanuel team had already been petitioning the judge to declare a mistrial, and after Keller's interrogation, they redoubled the effort, outlining, in motion after motion, the various offenses made by MGA's lawyers. Keller had baselessly implied, they wrote, that Mattel's toy recalls had "killed babies." Her co-counsel, Annette Hurst, had accused Mattel's forensic ink expert of being involved in "chemical warfare."* And now, Quinn argued, Keller had poisoned the jury by suggesting that Mattel had buried evidence, and that Quinn Emanuel had helped them do it. "She said 'outside counsel in this case.' She might as well have said Quinn Emanuel," John Quinn said at one point. "That's cheating."

Judge Carter did not declare a mistrial. But four days after Eckert left the stand for the last time, when Mattel's lawyers came up for closing arguments, cheating was still on their mind. This case was really about rigging the creative process, said William Price, the Quinn lawyer who'd grilled Bryant. "You're not supposed to compete with another company with its own information," he told the jury. "It's wrong." He pulled up the sound bites he'd extracted from Bryant and Larian, conceding their missteps and betrayals. They were the real villains, he said. All these

---

*The scientist, a Russian expat named Valery Aginsky, had gotten his degree at the "Military Academy of Chemical Defense" in Moscow. He had also worked at the Ministry of Internal Affairs alongside officers in the Soviet Secret Police—at a time when, one MGA lawyer told the judge, "the organization had its worst bribery and corruption scandal in its history," which included "murdering an agent of the KGB to cover it up." Judge Carter had ruled that MGA could ask about the expert's background but could not go into any "unfounded accusations." And yet Quinn argued that MGA had done so anyway. Was Aginsky's alma mater "involved in chemical warfare"? Hurst had asked. "Yes," he'd said. "Partially, yes."

stories about Mattel's misconduct—the baby killing, the chemical warfare, the missing boxes—they were merely distractions to hide "the fact that this may have been one of the biggest intellectual property heists that's ever occurred."

Perhaps with another toy company, known for another doll, this might have proved convincing. But it was Mattel, a corporation that had spent decades policing Barbie's reputation, ensuring its billion-dollar doll stayed squeaky clean, associated only with the wholesome, the upright, the chic. "Barbie stands for good. All others stand for evil," the "House on Fire" memo had said, but the Barbie of the trial had seemed significantly more gray. "What we have seen throughout Mattel's conduct is bullying, plain and simple," Keller said in her final pitch. The executives had bullied Bryant into depression, baited Larian into paranoia. They had bullied their own employees, firing devoted seamstresses, surveilling former executives. They had preached about fighting fair, while sending teams of spies to steal rival information. And once they'd been caught, they had bullied their own spies. It's "like the old *Mission: Impossible*," Keller said. "All of a sudden no one even knows Market Intelligence exists."

There was an old saying among trial lawyers, Keller told the crowd. *If you don't have the facts, you pound on the law. If you don't have the law, you pound on the facts. And if you don't have either one, you pound on the table.* For the past three months, she said, "we have heard a lot of pounding on the table from Mattel." Maybe John Quinn hadn't heard her. Because when he stood up for Mattel's last rebuttal, he punctuated his speech with periodic slaps on the podium—which, as it happened, was hooked up to a microphone. Some of the last sounds the jury heard at trial were the amplified echoes of an apparent confession: Barbie seemed to lack the law and the facts.

The jury deliberated for nearly two weeks. When they filed back into the courtroom on April 21, 2011, the audience was packed. Eckert sat by his lawyers, his face waxy and unmoving. Larian sat with his wife, daughter, and two sons. The unanimous verdict was the opposite of the original: Mattel did not own Bryant's Bratz drawings. Mattel did not own the subsequent Bratz dolls. Mattel had no claim on the Bratz trademark. Mattel had not only failed to prove that MGA had misappropriated its trade secrets; the jury found that it had stolen MGA's. "I don't think anyone should be able to bully someone and own everything," one juror later explained.

As the jury announced their decision, the Quinn lawyers blinked back surprise. Eckert massaged his forehead. Larian began openly bawling. "The American dream lives," he sobbed. At first, Judge Carter ruled that Mattel would have to pay $85 million in damages—about $3.4 million for each act of trade secret misappropriation.(Larian personally earned a bit more; it would later emerge that he had been shorting Mattel stock since at least 2005, turning a profit of some $28 million even though Mattel's stock had halved in that same period). But a later court struck down the award on a procedural issue. Like Hausser before him, Larian had waited too long to sue. The espionage claims were barred by the federal statute of limitations. In the end, Mattel would cover MGA's legal fees. But both parties would leave empty-handed.

Eckert had started the decade with legal bills and a stale doll. By the end of it, he still had both. Mattel's failure to settle would go down as a "tremendously bad decision," one stock analyst said. "They wasted $400 million or so of shareholder money to get zero return." But the case yielded more than bad line item on a balance sheet, it offered context, backstory, that thing Barbie was never supposed to have. The trial brought the jurors, and the media, as far into the fort at El Segundo as any outsider had ventured before, and the Mattel they saw was not, as Ernest Dichter once wrote, a company "delightfully and charmingly absorbed in the sheer fun of making toys." Had it ever been? The jury had evidently come to see Eckert's company as Keller did—as a "creepy" place, a corporation with "the most elaborate and sophisticated and intrusive investigation apparatus of just about any company you are going to ever see," a company where theft was so habitual someone wrote a manual on how to do it right. "They own your voice mails. Cameras are on you all the time," Keller had said. "They own you."

After the verdict, Larian went out to celebrate. The Mattel staff returned to El Segundo, an apt homebase for the doll, long hailed as the first, who had now come in second.

EPILOGUE

THE LAST RESORT

In 2006, about halfway through the Bratz case, three researchers at the University of Bath published a report on children's grasp of brand symbolism titled, quite Britishly, "*The Simpsons* Are Cool but Barbie's a Minger." Fifty years had passed since Mattel first sponsored *The Mickey Mouse Club*. The children of the aughts were now constantly exposed to what lead author Agnes Nairn called "commercially sponsored media." Kids consumed hours of television by the day; they were inundated with trademarks and logos in every aspect of their lives; entire advertising industries had emerged to target and micro-target their interests in the hopes of capturing some of the billions spent on children each year. And yet, the authors argued, few had undertaken to understand how children internalized these symbols, how they differentiated them from one another, and came to associate them with meaning.

As it turned out, many of these kids weren't differentiating much at all. "The younger children were not able to recall a lot of specific brand names," the researchers wrote. In a brainstorm about popular brands, the children did not just summon the names of games and toys, but those of athletes, pop stars, and TV actors—people they saw as products. "The children seemed to inhabit a seamless branded world," the study reported, "where celebrities, toys, TV shows and electronics were almost indistinguishable."

And yet, one product was more distinguishable from the rest.

Interviewer: OK, we'll go onto the next one. Barbie!
First Boy: Yuck!

(*Two boys get up and hide behind their chairs making gagging noises*)
Second Boy: I'm going to puke!
Interviewer: OK, come back, sit down. OK, come back, sit, sit, sit, sit. Great, OK, so you don't like it.
Second Boy: It makes me feel sick.
(*One boy continues to hide his eyes and the other keeps his back to the interviewer whilst talking*)

The girls' reactions were only slightly less slapstick:

Interviewer: OK, so we'll go onto the next one, Barbie.
First Girl: Urgh, no, please turn the page, no, please!!!
Second Girl: That is so not cool!!! Ugggh!!
Third Girl: Turn the next page, so not cool at all!!
First Girl: No!

The children—across genders, ages, private school and public—seemed to agree that Barbie was what one boy termed "a really bad classic." In a word, passé. The doll was a "last resort option," save for one particular form of play. "The one thing I like about Barbie," a participant said, "is that they're quite good at destroying."

First Girl: I still have loads of them so I can torture them . . . I'll torture them and pull their heads off. Coz they're not particularly cool unless . . .
Interviewer: They're not particularly cool unless you what?
First Girl: Torture them.

Though the study was small, its findings described a phenomenon many American parents could confirm in their home: kids were killing their Barbies. Not just breaking them, but mutilating them, cutting their hair, snapping off their legs, melting their skin, parachuting them off houses, and putting them in microwaves. "I kept having to squish their heads off," said one child. Said another: "I did like putting soap over them and burning them."

This was, on the one hand, a revelation on par with *dog bites man*. Children have surely been destroying dolls since the first desperate parent tied some twigs together into an approximation of human form. It was "the overriding desire of most little brats," Charles Baudelaire wrote in his 1853 essay "The Philosophy of Toys." "He twists and turns the toy, scratches it, shakes it, bangs it against the wall, hurls it on the ground," prying at its innards like "the populace besieging the Tuileries." This impulse toward disembowelment was, to Baudelaire, the child's "first metaphysical stirring"—an attempt to "get at and *see the soul* of their toys."

And yet when the professors published their research in 2006, it became an international news story. Barbie seemed to demand flesh wounds—inordinate in number and brutal in intensity. Why? The children certainly agreed the doll was unfashionable. Her uncoolness seemed at once tautological (*it's Barbie*) and to spring forth from myriad sources, none of which could singularly explain the vitriol she provoked. "Plastic is wasting the world's resources," one child explained. But many toys were plastic, including Action Man, whom the kids had already judged as cool. "Yeah," a girl reasoned, "but he's Action Man."

Their perceptions of Barbie were, of course, gendered. The doll was dismissed by boys as "for girls," and by girls, as for "girly girls." But there were likewise many girls' toys that seemed to have kept their appendages, including Bratz ("they're quite cool"). Barbie's effeminacy was tangled up, even among the girls, with another rationale, that she was "babyish." Many girls now saw the doll as a representation, not of the adults they would grow into, as Ruth had imagined, but as a relic of their younger selves, a toddler's idea of what a woman was supposed to be. "To disavow Barbie was to perform a rite of passage and to reject the past," the researchers wrote. And yet while other toys of younger childhood conjured feelings of warmth and nostalgia, these sentiments "were totally absent from the discussions of Barbie."

The professors offered another theory:

> The children never talked of one, single, special Barbie. She was always referred to in the plural... Most children not only had more

than one Barbie, they had a box of Barbies: and not just a box, a very large box.

To talk of Barbies was to talk of having "too many," of an implied "excess." Here, the doll was not a *she*, but a *them* composed of disposable *its*. How, in the end, could they see Barbie as anything else, this doll that had always been blank, that had dozens of personas, but no one personality, that had never been singular, but existed always as a second copied from a first? To mutilate any one member of the group was not, Nairn concluded, an expression of cruelty, as it might have seemed were Barbie understood as an individual. "From the child's point of view," she wrote, "they were simply being imaginative in disposing of an excessive commodity." They snapped and burned her as one might "pass papers through the shredder."

Though maybe there was a touch more emotion than the researchers let on. The dismemberment of any doll, Baudelaire argued, inevitably brought the "beginnings of stupor and melancholy." The tiny figure could seem so perfect an imitation of a person, but the child's search for its soul would always end empty-handed. With Barbie, one must imagine this experience multiplied. While she "masquerades as a person," Nairn wrote, "she actually exists in multiple selves."

By the time of the Bratz verdict, Mattel appeared to have done the kids' work for them. The company had made many desperate pleas for relevance to little avail—at one point, holding a press conference to announce that Barbie had broken up with Ken, before confirming, two years later, that the lovebirds had rekindled. They had produced a series of animated movies, toured a live Barbie musical, and paid for product placement on a popular TV show called *The Apprentice*. Barbie had joined YouTube, then Facebook; she had gotten tattoos and a (quickly discontinued) "Sugar Daddy Ken." For a time, Mattel had opened a $30 million Barbie-branded flagship store in Shanghai, complete with a cocktail bar, a restaurant, a Vera Wang–branded bridal section, and a full spa; it shuttered two years later in what *Forbes* called a "historical disaster." The company had even considered what many saw as a last resort, a live-action movie.

When Elliot Handler died over the summer of 2011, at the age of ninety-five, it seemed the final bookend to the era of unquestioned Barbie dominance. The the doll slid into one of its most devastating sales slumps in a quarter century. In 2012, Barbie sales dropped globally by three percent, then by six percent the year after, and by sixteen percent the year after that. *Frozen*'s Elsa dethroned Barbie as the most popular girl's toy that Christmas of 2014—the same year, Hasbro beat out Mattel for the Disney Princess license, a blow both symbolic and financial, which analysts estimated could cost the company some $500 million a year. All the while, China Labor Watch issued harrowing reports detailing "unceasing abuse" in the factories of Mattel's suppliers, from wage theft to toxic waste exposure to employee dorms that sleep twelve to a room. ("Many of the allegations are unfounded," Mattel said of one report.) Robert Eckert left the company to be replaced by a parade of similar suits—first by a Mattel vet who'd once run a company called "Basic Vegetable Products," then by the ex-chairman of Pepsi, the national shorthand for second-favorite. When the latter took over in 2015, Barbie sales had declined by a third in four years. "R.I.P. Barbie," went a *Huffington Post* headline, "America's Most Iconic Blonde Is Fading Out into History."

But betting against Barbie is generally a bad wager. And in 2016, history faded Barbie back in. The company had rehired an executive named Richard Dickson, who sought to modernize Barbie to appeal to millennial parents. The children who hated Barbie were beginning to have kids of their own, and they saw the doll as, per Dickson, "vapid, one dimensional, and worse, literally uninspiring." The company hired advertising firm BBDO to design campaigns that would "associate the doll more with empowerment." And Dickson did what Shackelford had done thirty years before: developed new segments, only these were aimed at making the doll more inclusive. That January, the company unveiled a collection they had been developing under the codename "Project Dawn"—a revamped Barbie with three new bodies: curvy, tall, and petite. Over the next few years, the collection would grow to include more than 175 dolls, with nine different body types, ninety-seven hairstyles, and thirty-five skin tones. Mattel would unveil Barbie with prosthetic limbs and hearing aids. They would introduce a blind Barbie with a walking stick, a sister with scoliosis, a Barbie with Down syndrome and a line of Barbie-like gender-neutral dolls called Creatable World, which children could customize as they saw fit.

It was in some ways the opposite of the lesson from the study. Mattel had not toned down Barbie's excess, they had made the doll literally more multiple than ever before. But in flooding the market with so many possible Barbies, they had likewise created the suggestion of the particular, targeting dolls at segments so specialized they could almost approximate the self. If a child wanted a brown-haired Barbie with an olive complexion, gray eyes, and a prosthetic leg, they could have it. If another wanted a Ken doll with narrow shoulders or vitiligo, or a "neon green buzzcut" and "orange platform shoes," they could have that too. They could have a bald Barbie, and one with albinism and a white afro, and one with thigh-length rainbow hair. Many kinds of jobs became many kinds of people—a trend which took a literal turn when Mattel began releasing several lines of dolls based on specific public figures, including Frida Kahlo, Amelia Earhart, Misty Copeland, Ava DuVernay, and Rosa Parks. The line would grow to include more than one hundred role models, some so niche one wonders if any child has ever heard of them (see: Anne Wojcicki, co-founder of 23&Me).

These new dolls generated plenty of positive news coverage; which perhaps helps explain why Mattel had a habit of announcing them before an earnings call where the company declared a loss. And as ever, Mattel rhymed with the times. The year the new bodies launched, the woman who once sported President Barbie's gold scarf lost the election to an eighties financier promising to bring back an America that had existed only in Barbieland. At just the right moment, Barbie appeared to turn a page, though not far enough that she could never turn it back.

"The thing was paradoxical," the writer Saul Bellow says in *Zelig*, Woody Allen's 1983 mockumentary about an enigmatic "human chameleon," whose ability to shapeshift and mirror his surroundings makes him one of the most beloved and reviled figures of the twentieth century. In the film, Zelig's condition allows him to instantly assume any weight, hair tint, eye color, or, with a Mattel-ish indelicacy, race, while posing as any number of professions, from pilot to doctor to Nazi. "What enabled him to perform this astounding feat was his ability to transform himself," Bellow goes on. "Therefore, his sickness was also at the root of his salvation. I think it's interesting to view the thing that way, that it was his very disorder that made a hero of him."

Eventually, the movie came out. The idea had been in the works since at least 2009 (not long, coincidentally, after Hasbro's *Transformers* proved that live action toy adaptations could be quite profitable). But like Mattel itself, the production had become a kind of Theseus's ship—constantly replacing its crew with new writers (*Sex and the City*'s Jenny Bicks, *Juno*'s Diablo Cody, *Ocean's 8*'s Olivia Milch), new actors (Amy Schumer, Anne Hathaway, Margot Robbie), and new production studios (Universal, Sony, Warner Bros.)—that it seemed it might never find its final form. The project seemed stalled out by 2018, when Mattel took on its fifth CEO in seven years.

The newcomer, a former IDF soldier and windsurfing instructor named Ynon Kreiz, seemed to understand the Mattel ethos right away. He took a pay package of $18.7 million—3,408 times that of his median employee, giving Mattel the second-highest CEO-to-worker pay ratio of any company then on the S&P 500. Among his first actions in charge: laying off 2,200 people. Despite Barbie's recovery, the company remained in bad shape—bloated inventory, a $3 billion debt load twenty-five times its earnings, and a brewing financial scandal involving still more "accounting errors." But Kreiz had not come to the company from a career in cheese or vegetables or soda. He had come up in television. Like the Handlers before him, he understood that the screen was the medium on which Barbie's future would be made. He planned, as he told staff in a one-page memo, to "transform Mattel in an IP-driven" toy company.

Of course, Mattel had always been an IP-driven company. And the movie rollout, with its flood of Barbie brand partnerships, was quintessentially Ruth. "The name Barbie is magic," she'd said in the sixties. Now the name was on Starbucks cups and Reebok sneakers and on Heinz "Barbiecue" sauce. Kreiz insisted that the production was "not about selling toys." But who needed to sell toys, when they could sell Barbie-branded candles, Barbie-branded furniture, eco-friendly Barbie bikinis, and a Barbie-branded "body butter" designed to disguise cellulite? The movie was the apotheosis of Barbie's ability to have things both ways. Here was a doll both plural and particular; a story populated by Barbies, which only paid attention to one. It was, like Barbie, a template the company could deploy for any other toy. Mattel announced plans to adapt more than a dozen of its properties into auteur-led prestige films—from Hot Wheels and He-Man, to Magic 8 Ball and UNO, to a gritty "A-24-type" adaptation of Barney.

But if Mattel had always been an IP-driven company, it was, in one respect, driving another way. This was not the company that had litigated its critics to death, that was only interested, as a vice president once put it, in "having fun without making fun." Here, the executives let Mattel be the butt of the joke—an outdated corporate giant obsessed with profit and run by bumbling men. The soundtrack featured a remix of "Barbie Girl," the song over which Barbie's makers once sued. Toward the end of the film, a Mattel executive got shot.

"They finally figured out that it's okay to make a little fun," Judge Kozinski told me. "I thought that showed an awareness that I did not see in the cases that I heard." And perhaps Mattel had evolved. But the company's suffocating approach to satire had likewise exhausted its use. They'd learned that lawsuits could no longer stifle their strongest critics. They merely cost money and generated bad press. The movie, however, did coincide with a new legal trend. Some trademark owners, the *Journal of Intellectual Property Law* noted, had begun "licensing their IP rights to effectively engage in self-parody of their own brand." Maybe the company had learned to live with criticism. Or maybe they'd decided to see it as another accessory they could sell.

꩜

While I was writing this epilogue, almost two years after the movie premiered, Barbie came back into the news. The presidential election had brought Donald Trump back to the White House, with something he hadn't had the first time: a modest popular mandate. He had campaigned on a seething rejection of both the social progress Barbie sought to capture and the economic realities Mattel had helped shape. He promised to balance the budget like a corporate executive, firing federal workers by the thousands, and to bring back the manufacturing multinationals had long-ago moved offshore.

Mattel soon found itself in the crosshairs. The company had already been sued by a Trump-aligned activist group, alleging its "diversity, equity, and inclusion" initiatives ran afoul of Title VII, the employment law Ruth's committee had written about some fifty years before. (Mattel's diverse doll lines, the group wrote, appeared to be "promoting a radical transgender agenda.") The next quarter, Mattel quietly struck any mention of DEI from its public filings and removed similar references from its corporate website. A spokesperson insisted the edits only reflected a "reporting change," not a shift in its guiding principles. Certainly, Mattel had not changed its position on low-paid labor. After Trump announced a 145 percent tariff on Chinese imports, Mattel told shareholders they planned to raise prices. Barbie had never been made in the United States, and she had no plans to immigrate now. Responding to Trump's plan to revitalize American manufacturing, Kreiz told CNBC: "We don't see that happening."

Here was Mattel as it had always been. Kreiz was as unwavering as Barad had been at the Clinton Economic Conference some thirty years before. But Trump seemed to take it as a personal slight, peppering his speeches all spring with odd digressions about dolls. Maybe children "will have two dolls instead of thirty," he told a televised Cabinet meeting in April. "I don't think a beautiful baby girl that's eleven years old needs to have thirty dolls," he continued in May. "I think they can have three dolls or four dolls." He never mentioned Barbie by name, but he didn't need to. The suggestion that girls buy fewer dolls was a basic rejection of Barbie's whole brand.

By mid-May, the president had declared an all-out "war on Barbie," as one headline put it, threatening to impose a 100 percent tariff on all Mattel's toys. Kreiz "won't sell one toy in the U.S.," the president promised. But in reality, the war proved harder to wage. Even as the new administration dismembered federal agencies through brute force, Trump's trade battle with China was marked by stops-and-starts, waffling between overt aggression and calls for a truce. By late spring, Trump had backed off the steepest tariffs, and stopped bringing up dolls. Maybe he understood that he was fighting something bigger than a single company. In one of his rants, at least, he'd made a small slip. He'd called Mattel a "country."

ACKNOWLEDGMENTS

I am immensely grateful to my editor, Nicholas Ciani, for emailing me sometime in 2019 and unknowingly, to me at least, setting off the chain of events that culminated in this book. Without his encouragement, edits, and significant patience, these pages would not exist. Thank you to my brilliant agent, Alice Whitwham, whose support over the past few years so far exceeded the mandate of agent that an accurate title would require an inelegant number of hyphens. Thank you especially to Carrie Frye, a genius, for divining a structure I often struggled to see.

This book was painstakingly fact-checked by Jordan Cutler-Tietjen and Sujay Kumar, wounding several fine-tooth combs in the process. If any errors remain in the text, and I hope none do, the failure is mine alone. Thanks to them and to all the researchers and archivists who lent me their time: Rachel P. Mervis, Mathias Boone, Hayley Byrnes, Emmett Fuchs, Lars Broder-Keil, Marina Nicoli, the Schlesinger Library, the New York Public Library, the National Archives and Records Administration, and especially Andrew Hayt at NARA Riverside, the National Barbie Doll Collectors Convention, the Strong Museum, and the great photographer Lara Young. I'm grateful for all the editors I've had the good luck to learn from: Chuck Strouse, Curtis Morgan, Molly Eichel, Marlow Stern, Tracy Connor, Leah Finnegan, Brandy Jensen, David O'Neill, and all my colleagues at *The Drift*.

This project would not have been possible without the many people who answered a cold call or email from a stranger and were kind enough to share their insights about dolls, both on the record and off. Thanks to all of you, you know who you are. I'm likewise indebted to several decades of Barbie collectors, historians, and journalists, whose research and reporting formed the foundation of this project—M. G. Lord, Orly Lobel, Jill Lepore, Siva Vaidhyanathan, Rusty Kern, and Rob

Goldberg, in particular, directed my research or shaped my thinking, and usually both.

Thank you to Jessica Helfand, font of design expertise. Thank you to Rebecca Panovka, Julian Waddell, Claire Benoit, Eloise Lynton, and Krithika Varagur, for surgical edits and a level of in-depth feedback they improbably gave out for free. Thank you to the many people who read versions of this manuscript, weighed in on the ideas therein, let me crash on their couch, or were otherwise kind: Signe Swanson, Hillary Buckholtz, Sophie Haigney, Keyian Vafai, Charlie Dulik, Kiara Barrow, Brandon Wardell, Jonah Max, Gabe Appel, Alessandra Hogan, Owen Prum, Story Ponvert, Fiona Drenttel, Isabelle Appleton, Marella Gayla, Luke Atkins, Elena Saavedra Buckley, Sophia O'Brien-Udry, Fence, Tommy, Mr. P, Marcus Mamourian, and everyone on the ex-Gawker Slack, who made writing for a reboot the most fun I've ever been paid to have. Thanks above all to Yonce Hitt and my parents, Jack and Lisa, the originals I've been ripping off for years, and Malcolm Drenttel, my first reader since 2011. Thank you again to everyone who spoke to me for this project, and everyone who did not ask how it was going.

NOTES

PART I: INTRO

3 *like water pollution*: "Oil's Unchecked Outfalls: Water Pollution from Refineries and EPA's Failure to Enforce the Clean Water Act," Environmental Integrity Project, January 26, 2023.

3 *pharmaceuticals in space*: Margaux MacColl, "Rockets, God and Peter Thiel: 36 Hours in the Gundo, Tech's Latest Startup Haven," The Information, April 5, 2024.

4 *"Please note we aren't"*: Email exchange with Carmyn Cosey, January 10, 2023.

5 *"on something Mattel did"*: William L. Hamilton, "Toymakers Study Troops and Vice Versa," New York Times, March 30, 2003.

5 *fourteen years*: Mattel v. MGA, Case No. 2:04-cv-09049-DOC-RNB, Dkt. 10323, Transcript, March 28, 2011.

5 *"corporate espionage"*: Carter Bryant v. Mattel, Case No. 2:04-cv-09049-DOC-RNB .Dkt: 10449, April 8, 2011.

6 *"not having a sense of humor"*: "Judge Says No to Mattel's Effort to Stop Artist's Photographic Critiques of Barbie," ACLU of Southern California, September 25, 2000.

CHAPTER 1

7 *quit quitting*: Ruth Handler papers, Schlesinger Library, Box 3, Folder 8.

8 *canned cream of mushroom soup*: Ruth Handler, Dream Doll, Longmeadow Press, 1994, 45.

8 *"I hated dolls"*: Ruth Handler papers, Box 32, Folder 13.

8 *"like fat, ugly, six-year-olds"*: Ruth Handler papers, Box 32, Folder 13.

9 *not quite true ... new nickname*: Ruth Handler papers, Box 33, Folder 2.

9 *"gamblers, rowdies"*: "Franconi's Hippodrome," Miriam and Ira D. Wallach Division, New York Public Library Digital Collections.

9 *"dancing horse named Johnston"*: "Franconi's Hippodrome Opens," Old New York Tours, May 2, 2015.

9 *Ruth's father ... four more children*: Ruth Handler papers, Box 9, Folder 15.

10 *"opposite ends of the wrong side of the tracks"*: Ruth Handler papers, Box 12, Folder 10.

10 *"starve to death in some garret"*: Ruth Handler papers, Box 32, Folder 13.

10 *She hitched a ride ... "terrible exciting"*: Ruth Handler, Dream Doll, 27–29.

10 *rented tux*: Ruth Handler papers, Box 1, Folder 5.

10 *"appalled at the waste of money" ... Thanks for the Memory*: Ruth Handler, Dream Doll, 30–31.

11 *"embarrassed to place an order"*: Ruth Handler papers, Box 32, Folder 13.

11 *"stupid guy"*: Ruth Handler papers, Box 32, Folder 14.

11 *DC-3 planes ... "not even from plastic scrap"*: Ruth Handler, Dream Doll, 40–59.

NOTES

12 *available to the public . . . cutting-edge toilets*: Matthew Haag, "The Hotel Guest Who Wouldn't Leave," *New York Times*, March 24, 2024.
12 *"brunettes two to one"*: Robin Gerber, *Barbie and Ruth*, Harper Business, 2010, 5.
13 *sixty thousand dolls*: Ruth Handler papers, Box 33, Folder 2. There are competing accounts about the quantity here. Robin Gerber cites a different number—twenty thousand dolls per week for six months. I've opted for the number Ruth remembered.
13 *"last year's caution"*: Edward McGuire, "Toy Fair Sales Upturn Bright Year for Kids," North American Newspaper Alliance, via *Selma Times-Journal*, March 19, 1959.
13 *subsurface missile launcher*: See Gay Pauley, "Toy Fair in New York Puts Accent on Science," *Ottawa Journal*, March 12, 1959; "Toy Makers Are Helping Uncle Sam in Science Race with Reds," Associated Press via *Plain Speaker*, March 10, 1959.
13 *"model of the Crucifixion"*: Elmer Roessner, "Toy Makers Capitalize on Birth Rate," *Johnson City Press-Chronicle*, March 13, 1959.
13 *"the doll was hated"*: Robin Gerber, *Barbie and Ruth*, 18.
13 *"fashion dolls are passé"*: Ruth Handler papers, Box 33, Folder 1.
13 *"will never accept this doll"*: Ruth Handler papers, Box 33, Folder 1.
13 *"Mr. God of the toy industry"*: Ruth Handler papers, Box 34, Folder 2.
13 *take a sample . . . roundups*: Robin Gerber, *Barbie and Ruth*, 18; William Robertson, "Atom Reactors, Peanuts Game, Cowboys Help Put Toy Fair Sales, Prices Over '58," *Wall Street Journal*, March 13, 1959; George Auerbach, "American, Foreign Toy Makers Display Wares Here This Week," *New York Times*, March 8, 1959.
13 *"but she cried"*: Robin Gerber, *Barbie and Ruth*, 19.

CHAPTER 2

15 *"that was Louis Marx and Company"*: Sarah Monks, *Toy Town*, PP Co. Ltd, 2011, 23.
15 *"Henry Ford of the toy industry"*: "The Little King," *Time*, December 12, 1955.
15 *Ghengis Khan*: "Final Days to Tour the Historic Marx Museum," Gypsy Road Trip, June 30, 2016.
15 *"you know, vibrations"*: Rusty Kern, *Marx Toy Kings Vol. I: 1919–1954*, Atomic, 2010, 97.
15 *spoke with an accent*: Rusty Kern, *Marx Toy Kings Vol I: 1919–1954*, 16, 19.
15 *"America's Toy King"*: "The Little King."
15 *Family of five*: "Builder Buys Marx Estate in Scarsdale," *New York Times*, April 3, 1982.
16 *"mink-lined foxhole"*: Westbrook Pegler, "Marx a Friend of U.S. Generals," *New York Daily News*, September 29, 1957.
16 *"ice-skating, and shoplifting" . . . "old toys with new twists"*: "The Little King."
16 *epicenter of global toy production*: "German Toys—A Cloud with a Silver Lining," *Printer's Ink*, September 15, 1921; Helmut Schwartz, "History of Nuremberg Toy Trade and Industry," Spielzeugmseum of Nuremberg.
17 *"Toys constitute" . . . "not exported"*: "The Toy Industry of Germany," *Scientific American* 91, No. 24 (December 10, 1904).
17 *"late to the party"*: Christopher Byrne, *They Came to Play: 100 Years of the Toy Industry Association*, Toph Welch Graphic Design, 2016.
17 *"gift" for the Native tribes*: Wadsworth Likely, "Toys Reflect Man's Culture," *Science News-Letter*, December 17, 1949; White, John, active 1585–1593, *Indian woman and young girl*, 1585, NC242.W53 H8, East Carolina University Digital Collections; "John White," *Encyclopedia Britannica*, January 31, 2025.

NOTES 283

17 *"compete with the Germans"*: Constance Eileen King, *The Collector's History of Dolls*, Bonanza Books, 1977, 139.
17 *A poem ran... "Toy M'F'RS USA"*: Christopher Byrne, *They Came to Play*.
17 *"does not mean 'made in Germany'"*: "A Brief History of Toy Fair," The Toy Guy.
18 *first American toy outpost in Japan*: Sarah Monks, *Toy Town*, PP Co. Ltd., 2011, 22, 23. See also: "The Little King."
18 *initials*: "Expansion of H.K.'s Toy Industry," *South China Morning Post*, August 23, 1958.
18 *"Excellent Louis Marx"*: Sarah Monks, *Toy Town*, 64.
18 *"two patent attorneys"*: Sarah Monks, *Toy Town*, 32.
18 *"a hunt-and-peck typist"*: William A. Henry III, "The Man with the Barefoot Voice," *Time*, March 28, 1983.
18 *"Huck Finn of radio"*: Albin Krebs, "Arthur Godfrey, Television and Radio Star, Dies at 79," *New York Times*, March 17, 1983.
19 *"an exact copy of ours"*: Ruth Handler, *Dream Doll*, 68.
19 *"beat Knickerbocker down"*: Ruth Handler papers, Box 34, Folder 2.
19 *four important lessons for aspiring toy makers*: Jack Searles, "Mattel—Growing Up in the World of the Young," *California Business*, August 31, 1970, clipped in Ruth Handler papers, Box 1, Folder 6.
19 *"real fears of espionage"*: Art Seidenbaum, "This Is a House That Jack Built," *Los Angeles Times*, December 15, 1963.
19 *"got to the ground floor"*: Sarah Monks, *Toy Town*, 32.
19 *"staff of the Soviet Army"*: "Bar Small Fry from Toy Fair," *Edinburg Daily Courier*, March 11, 1959.
19 *"defense work"*: Ruth Handler papers, Box 34, Folder 2.
19 *"DEFENSE. TOYS"... "strategic locations"*: Ruth Handler papers, Box 22, Folder 2.
19 *"unplayful competitor is not listening"*: Art Seidenbaum, "This Is a House That Jack Built."
20 *"We were literally locked up"*: Jerry Oppenheimer, *Toy Monster: The Big Bad World of Mattel*, Wiley, 2010, 45.
20 *$312 on ads*: "The Little King."
20 *"He didn't believe in"*: Rusty Kern, *Marx Toy Kings Vol I*, 16.
20 *10 percent were his*: "The Little King."
20 *smiley-face*: Kenneth Roman, "How the Advertising West Was Won," Medium, August 25, 2019.
20 *"ABC promised"*: Cy Schneider, *Children's Television: The Art, The Business, and How It Works*, NTC Business Books, 1987.
20 *The expense was gargantuan... "reach children as well"*: Cy Schneider, *Children's Television*, 15–19.
20 *Mr. Potato Head*: Cy Schneider, *Children's Television*. See also: "About Mr. Potato Head," Hasbro.com via Wayback Machine, cached September 25, 2008.
21 *"badly bent"... "rapidly fire fifty shots"*: Ruth Handler, *Dream Doll*, 81–83.
21 *plastic Kalashnikov*: Cy Schneider, *Children's Television*, 19–21.
21 *"named David Eisenhower"*: Ruth Handler, *Dream Doll*, 84.
21 *"biggest thing ever done on TV"*: Rusty Kern, *Marx Toy Kings Vol. II: 1955–1982*, Atomic, 2014, 96.

NOTES

21 *"King of Toys"*: Ruth Handler papers, Box 12, Folder 18.
21 *"Magic Marxie"*: Rusty Kern, *Marx Toy Kings Vol. II*, 96.
21 *The toyman liked to collect... Eisenhower*: Gen. Henry Arnold, from "The Little King"; Dwight Eisenhower, from Rusty Kern, *Marx Toy Kings Vol. I*, 91.
21 *"all his friends were great Generals"*: Rusty Kern, *Marx Toy Kings Vol. II*, 89.
22 *He went fishing... pen*: CIA Director Walter Bedell Smith, from Jimmy Powers, "The Powerhouse," *New York Daily News*, January 9, 1946; J. Edgar Hoover, from Rusty Kern, *Marx Toy Kings Vol. I*, 91; George C. Marshall, from Jimmy Powers, "The Powerhouse," *New York Daily News*, June 20, 1941; Eisenhower as godfather, from Wolfgang Saxon, "Louis Marx Sr. Is Dead at 85," *New York Times*, February 6, 1982; Pen, from Thomas R. Churdy, Letter to Francis Turner, May 10, 2019.
22 *Daniel Ellsberg*: Tom Wells, *Wild Man: The Life and Times of Daniel Ellsberg*, Palgrave Macmillan, 2001, 451–52; Beverly Gage, *G-Man: J. Edgar Hoover and the Making of the American Century*, Viking, 2022, 706; Timothy Naftali, "Daniel Ellsberg Interview Transcription," Nixon Library, May 20, 2008.
22 *"Edgar Hoover refused to investigate"*: Nixon White House tapes, May 9, 1973.
22 *Five-week tour*: Rusty Kern, *Marx Toy Kings Vol. I*, 77.
22 *"consultant to the Allies"*: Sarah Monks, *Toy Town*, 24.
22 *"his own purposes, of course"*: Rusty Kern, *Marx Toy Kings Vol. I*, 77.

CHAPTER 3

23 *"franchise fatigue"... "diminishing returns"*: "The 2023 Predictionary," Day One Agency, February 1, 2023.
23 *"Year of Reboots"*: Dara Drapkin-Grossi, "Explained: Was 2022 the Year of Movie Reboots?" Movieweb, December 28, 2022; Jeanine Poggi, "2017: The Year of the Reboot," *Ad Age*, December 2017.
23 *"most anticipated"... "four spin-offs"*: Molly Barth, "How Brands—and Capitalism—Killed Nostalgia," The Drum, December 19, 2023.
24 *Errol Flynn*: undated photograph, *Bild Zeitung*, Axel Springer archives; Interview with Lars Broder Keil, March 6, 2023.
25 *"No other man in Germany"*: Michael Sontheimer, "Kollegen und Konkurrenten," *Der Spiegel*, June 14, 2009.
25 *"This is the king himself speaking"*: Michael Jürgs, *Der Fall Axel Springer: eine deustche Biographie*, List, 1995, 20.
25 *"symbol of the radical transformation"*: "New Axel Springer Building Opens in Berlin," AxelSpringer.com, October 6, 2020.
26 *"a Nazi-uniformed buffer"... "loved so much"*: Ulrike Posche, "Aus dem Leben Eines Taugewas," *Stern*, February 29, 2008. Original German: *"Man machte mir den Vorschlag, mich für die Familie zum NS-uniformierten Prellbock herzugeben in einer Organisation, die keine großen weltanschaulichen Bekenntnisansprüche stellte, und die Politik mit dem von mir so geliebten Autosport vereinen ließ."*
26 *"inner willingness to fight"... "National Socialist ideology"*: Franz W. Seidler, "Das Nationalsozialistische Kraftfahrkorps Und Die Organisation Todt Im Zweiten Weltkrieg. Die Entwicklung Des NSKK Bis 1939," *Vierteljahrshefte Für Zeitgeschichte* 32, No. 4 (1984): 625–36. Original German: *"... innere Bereitschaft zu kämferischem*

Einsatz. *"Früher als andere Parteiführer erkannte er den Wert mobiler Verbreitung des nationalsozialistischen Gedankenguts und für die Wahlpropaganda."*

26 *Springer's family . . . German nationalism*: Father's paper, from: Volker R. Berghahn, *Journalists Between Hitler and Adenauer: From Inner Emigration to the Moral Reconstruction of West Germany*, 187; Springer's politics, from: Paul Hockenos, "The Scandalous History of America's Newest Media Baron," *Foreign Policy*, January 6, 2022; James Kirchick, "The Good Murdoch," *Tablet*, May 8, 2013.

26 *"It was clear to me since the end"*: Joachim Stave, "Zur Grammatik einer Zeitungssprache. 'Bild' sagt, wie es ist," *Sonntagsblatt*, May 7, 1959. Original German: *"Ich war mir seit Kriegsende darüber klar, daß der deutsche Leser eines auf keinen Fall wollte, nämlich nachdenken. Und darauf habe ich meine Zeitungen eingestellt."*

27 *sent the top editor to jail*: "Former London Editor Eilvester Bolam of *Daily Mirror* Was Jailed in Contempt Case," *New York Times*, April 28, 1953.

27 *"simple people"*: Michael Jürgs, *Der Fall Axel Springer*, 20.

27 *"One admiral told me"*: Richard Goldstein. "Christabel Leighton-Porter, a Comic Stripper, Dies at 87," *New York Times*, December 17, 2000.

28 *"tripe, trash, tits"*: "Sex, Smut and Shock: Bild Zeitung Rules Germany," *Der Spiegel*, April 26, 2004.

28 *"dog on a chain"*: Thomas Meaney, "Bild, Merkel and the Culture Wars: The Inside Story of Germany's Biggest Tabloid," *Guardian*, July 16, 2020.

28 *"secretly funneled"*: Murray Waas, "Covert Charge," *The Nation*, June 19, 1982. (Mr. Waas did not return a request for comment.)

28 *"emphatically"*: "Letters: Springer Denies Charge," *The Nation*, July 3, 1982.

28 *"completely penniless" . . . Marshall Plan*: Gudrun Kruip, *Das "Weld"-"Bild" des Axel Springer Verlag: Journalismus zwischen westlichen Werten und deutschen Denktraditionen*, R. Oldenbourg Verlag München 1999. 88–92. See also: William Blum, *Killing Hope: US Military and CIA Interventions Since World War II*, Zed Books London, 104; "The Americanization of Mr. Springer," *Ramparts*, Vol. 6 No. 11, June 15, 1968.

28 *"strong supporter of the United States"*: Charles Z. Wick, Letter to William J. Casey, May 12, 1981. CIA Reading Room.

28 *Springer's astrologer*: Claus Jacobi, "Eine Astrologin errechnete, wann Bild starten soll," *Bild*, June 19, 2002, Axel Springer archives.

28 *glued together the mockup himself*: Michael Jürgs, *Der Fall Axel Springer*, 169.

28 *Morse code . . . cigarillos*: Hans Bluhm, "Zur Geschichte der BILD-Lilli. Anmerkungen für Annette Wilken," July 22, 1996, Axel Springer archives.

29 *"I need something" . . . "continued to rage"*: Marie-Françoise Hanquez-Maincent, *Barbie: Poupée totem*, Autrement, 1998, 19–28. These quotes are Rolf Hausser's recollection of how Beuthien told the story, relayed to Hanquez-Maincent during her research and confirmed in an interview with the author. Original French: *Lilli, «sa fille» comme Beuthien aimait l'appeler . . .*

29 *"woman-child fantasy"*: Orly Lobel, *You Don't Own Me: How Mattel v. MGA Entertainment Exposed Barbie's Dark Side*, W. W. Norton & Company, 2017, 61.

29 *"Readers look for 'What Lilli said today"*: Marie-Françoise Hanquez-Maincent, *Barbie: Poupée totem*, 19–28; "Schwabinchen feiert den 1000. Geburtstag: AZ-Zeichner

286 NOTES

Reihard Beuthien holt seine Anregungen mitten in Schwabin," December 3, 1965, Axel Springer archives.

29 *"Five narrow letters"*: Hans Bluhm, "Zur Geschichte der BILD-Lilli."

29 *postcards... twenty-five years*: Silke Knaak, *German Fashion Dolls of the Fifties and Sixties*, BoD—Books on Demand, 2019, 41, 44; Axel Springer archives.

30 *"daughter"* ... *"double meaning"*: Marie-Françoise Hanquez-Maincent, *Barbie: Poupée totem*, 19–28; Schwabinchen feiert den 1000. Geburtstag: AZ-Zeichner Reihard Beuthien holt seine Anregungen mitten in Schwabin," December 3, 1965, Axel Springer archives.

30 *"U.S. Zone, Germany"*: King Features Syndicate, "The Best Years for Tin Toys Are 1945 to 1975," *Chicago Tribune*, August 11, 2021.

30 *"Americans to Zouaves"* ... *"personality figures"*: Reggie Polaine, *The War Toys: The Story of Hausser-Elastolin*, 86, 181.

31 *When Hitler* ... *slave labor*: Anne Barrowclough, "Blonde Hair, Blue Eyes, Athletic Build... Is Barbie Really an Aryan Fantasy?," *Australian*, March 8, 2014.

31 *"I had to take the greatest"* ... *"they weren't killed"*: Anne Barrowclough, "Blonde Hair, Blue Eyes."

31 *even comics*: Caitline McCabe, "'Smut and Trash': A Brief History of Comics Censorship in Germany," Comic Book Legal Defense Fund, September 9, 2016.

31 *"a loss of sales"* ... *"modern history"*: Reggie Polaine, *The War Toys: The Story of Hausser-Elastolin*, New Cavendish Books, 1991, 5.

32 *"You are the first"* ... *"found everywhere"*: Marie-Françoise Hanquez-Maincent. *Barbie: Poupée totem*, 19–28.

32 *"PYRM"*: Dieter Warnecke, "Bild-Lilli—Teil 2: Patente und Outfits," *Trödler*, No. 181, December 1994.

32 *two sizes*: Silke Knaak, *German Fashion Dolls of the Fifties and Sixties*, 13.

32 *"She was an irresistible gag"*: BillyBoy*, "Bild Lilli and the Queens of Outer Space," Fondation Tanagra.

32 *"escort"* ... *"sex doll"*: escort, from: MessyNessy, "Meet Lilli, the High-End German Call Girl Who Became Barbie," MessyNessyChic, December 19, 2022; call girl, from Jennifer Latson, "The Barbie Doll's Not-for-Kids Origins," *Time*, March 9, 2015; Fictional prostitute, from John Walsh, "Barbie was based on a cartoon prostitute who'd do anything for money," *Independent*, January 13, 2009; sex doll, from Ariel Levy, *Female Chauvinist Pigs: Women and the Rise of Raunch Culture*, Free Press, 2006, 187.

32 *"The prudery of the Nazi"*: Hans Bluhm, "Zur Geschichte der BILD-Lilli," Axel Springer archives.

32 *"Lilli was a sex ingredient"*: Anne Barrowclough, "Rolf Hausser, the Creator of the Bild Lilli Doll," Fondation Tanagra.

33 *"not intended for men more than for women"*: Marie-Françoise Hanquez-Maincent. *Barbie: Poupée totem*, 19–28.

33 *"Lilli keeps her legs together"*: untitled advertisement, *Spielzeug Export*, February 1956, 79.

33 *"Product for all"*: Silke Knaak, *German Fashion Dolls of the Fifties and Sixties*, 13.

33 *"pleasant to look at"*: Marie-Françoise Hanquez-Maincent, *Barbie: Poupée totem*, 19–28.

33 *"propagandistic activity"*: Memo dated March 13, 1954, Axel Springer archives. Original German: "Darüber hinaus ist es für Sonderaktionen zur Vorbereitung für Propagandisten-Tätigkeit in einzelnen Stäten der Bundesrepublik vorgesehen."

35 *"Unfortunately"... "we do not have any detailed"*: Email exchange with Margaret Galaske, Stadtarchiv Ludwigsburg, Sept. 5, 2023. Original German: *"Leider verfügen wir nicht über detaillierte Unterlagen zur Spielwarenfabrik Hausser."*
35 *"I absolutely didn't want to believe"*: Interview with Marina Nicoli, June 12, 2024.

CHAPTER 4

36 *Bertolt Brecht*: Alex Ross, "The Haunted California Idyll of German Writers in Exile," *New Yorker*, March 2, 2020.
36 *Adorno*: Upton Dell, "Theodor Adorno House Exterior," SAHARA Public Collection, via JSTOR, 1939..
36 *Thomas Mann*: "#MannsLA," podcast Villa Aurora & Thomas Mann House, May 25, 2020.
36 *Heinrich Mann*: "Heinrich Mann (1871–1950)," USC Library Research Guides.
36 *"hideous features"*: Walter Benjamin, "Toys and Play," *Walter Benjamin, Selected Writings Vol. 2, Part 1:1927–1930*, The Belknap Press of Harvard University Press, 1999, 119.
36 *Rainer Maria Rilke*: Rainer Maria Rilke, "Dolls: On the Wax Dolls of Lotte Pritzel," *On Dolls*, ed. Kenneth Gross, Notting Hill Editions, 2018, 51.
36 *"The more Romantic the writer"*: Evelyn Juers, *House of Exile: The Life and Times of Heinrich Mann and Nelly Kroeger-Mann*, Farrar, Straus & Giroux, 2011, 12.
36 *"pretty doll"... "lifeless doll"*: E. T. A. Hoffmann, "The Sandman," 1816, translated by John Oxenford, Virginia Commonwealth University, 1994.
37 *shot his lover, then himself*: Kleist wrote "On the Marionette Theater" in 1810 (*On Dolls*, ed. Kenneth Gross, 1.). He killed himself and his girlfriend as part of a suicide pact, on November 21, 1811. (Sadie Stein, "Final Chapter," *Paris Review*, October 16, 2014.)
37 *"Barbie's own debut"*: David. C. Smith, "How They Sell: Feel for Kids' Tastes, Massive TV Use Help Mattel Lead Toy Field," *Wall Street Journal*, November 24, 1964.
37 *Over the summer... Nuremberg*: Ruth Handler papers, Box 18, Folder 12.
38 *"absolutely transfixed"*: Ruth Handler, *Dream Doll*.
38 *"I didn't then know who Lilli was"* M. G. Lord, *Forever Barbie: The Unauthorized Biography of a Real Doll*, Walker Books, 1994, 26.
38 *"as early as 1946"*: Greiner & Hausser v. Mattel, "German Defense Statement," Docket No. 4HK O 4300/01, Nuremberg-Fürth District Court, April 4, 2002.
38 *"In 1957, she noticed"*: Ruth Handler papers, Box 12, Folder 10.
38 *a handwritten list of nightclubs to visit*: Ruth Handler papers, Box 18, Folder 11.
38 *some hundred ensembles*: Silke Knaak, *German Fashion Dolls of the Fifties and Sixties*, 12.
39 *biggest buyer*: "Germany Toy Companies Expect 1956 Exports to Set New High," *New York Times*, February 28, 1956.
39 *display carousel*: "Bild Lili Dolls and Mechanical Toys at the Nürnberg Toy Fair 1956," YouTube, February 24, 2021. Note: Mascha Eckert, archivist at Museen der Stadt Nürnberg, confirmed that the doll was "definitely" present at the 1956 fair. Mattel did not become an official vendor at Nuremberg until 1962, according to Eckert's records, but it is plausible, even likely, that an affiliate might have attended in earlier years. See also: Silke Knaak, *German Fashion Dolls of the Fifties and Sixties*.
39 *"From my personal opinion"*: Interview with Silke Knaak, April 4, 2023.
39 *In February, five months*: Louis Marx Co. & Greiner & Hausser v. Mattel, "Plaintiffs

NOTES

Further Answers to Defendant's Interrogatories," Case No. 341-61Y, Central District of California, January 3, 1962.
39 *at least two days*: Ruth Handler papers, Box 12, Folder 15.
39 *"I have yet to see"* ... *"in Beverly Hills"*: Cy Schneider, *Children's Television*, 26–28.
40 *"debatable"*: Billyboy*, *Barbie: Her Life and Times*, Crown Publishers, 1987, 19–22.
40 *"Tiffany's of toy stores"* ... *inlaid marble*: "Golden Shield Nominee Research Narrative and Plaque: Uncle Bernie's," Beverly Hills municipal report, April 2022.
40 *"more celebrities than at a premiere"*: Aline Mosby, "Share of Hollywood Fabulous Yule Loot Goes to Small Fry," *Brownwood Bulletin*, December 23, 1955.
40 *"best known toy store on the West Coast"*: Isidore Barmash, "FAO Schwarz Seeks Coast Unit: To Buy Uncle Bernie's Toy Menagerie, Beverly Hills," *New York Times*, April 24, 1965.
41 *"@ Mattel; the story on Bloomberg"*: Philippe Guggenheim, Reply to Mattel, LinkedIn, July 7, 2023.
41 *"This guy displayed the dolls in the window"* ... *"Blah blah blah"*: Interview with Philippe Guggenheim, June 27, 2024.
41 *"came regularly"* ... *years later, himself*: Roland Süssman, "Paul S. Guggenheim: le père d'une poupée <<Rich and Famous>>," *Israelitisches Wochenblatt*, March 27, 1987. Original French: Parmi la clientèle se trouvait la Présidente Directrice générale de Mattel, Mme Handler, qui venait régulièrement dans ce magasin pour voir les nouveautés importées d'Europe ... Lorsque Mattel a sorti Barie, quelqu'un l'a immédiatement copiée et commercialisé la copie. Il y a donc eu un procès où j'ai témoigné pour Mattel en expliquant notamment l'origine de l'affaire avec Lilly [sic]. Mattel a gagné le procès et m'a offert de racheter ma société ... inclus moi-même.
41 *five more orders ... in Munich*: Ruth Handler papers, Box 18, Folder 12.
42 *"Just as I was leaving"*: Ella King Torrey interview with Jack Ryan, December 1979, via M. G. Lord, *Forever Barbie*.
42 *"approximate size"*: Ruth Handler, *Dream Doll*, 6.
42 *"The Japanese are adept imitators"*: "Uncle Sam Is World Leader as Toy Maker," *Buffalo News*, December 22, 1926.
42 *"Japanese manufacturers are noted"* ... *"patronizing home labor!"*: "Mickey Mouse Makes Money—But It Goes to Japanese Toy Experts," *Columbia Missourian*, December 19, 1935.
42 *The stories, which trickled out*: Notably, this myth would follow the town of Usa, Japan, for years. When the area was officially incorporated as a city in 1967, rumors circulated that Japan had renamed the town explicitly to knock off American goods. This rumor lasted long enough that in 2000, Snopes published an explainer to debunk it. See: David Mikkelson, "Was a Town in Japan Renamed 'Usa' So Its Products Could Be Labeled 'Made in Usa'?," Snopes, September 25, 2000.
43 *"We were hearing that Japanese imports"*: C. Robert Jennings, "In the Toy Business, the Christmas Rush Is On," *New York Times Magazine*, May 19, 1968.
43 *"We couldn't make it in the United States"*: Jerry Oppenheimer, *Toy Monster*, 30.
43 *"Labor costs were high"*: Ruth Handler papers, Box 32, Folder 13.
43 *"in essence, the stuff of alchemy"*: Roland Barthes, *Mythologies*, Farrar, Straus & Giroux, 1972, 49.
43 *"Satan's resin"*: Elizabeth Royte, *Garbage Land*, Little, Brown & Company, 2005, 176.

43 *"Louis Marx is hated here"*: Ruth Handler papers, Box 3, Folder 14.
44 *"A lot fell through in translation"*: Interview with Carol Spencer, April 19, 2023.
44 *"very obedient"*: M. G. Lord, *Forever Barbie*, 33.
44 *"ideally suited"* ... *"nimble fingers"*: Ruth Handler, *Dream Doll*, 10.
44 *"blank"* ... *"fantasies into the doll"*: BillyBoy*, "Bild Lilli and the Queens of Outer Space."
44 *"had Oriental eyes!"*: Ruth Handler, *Dream Doll*, 10.

CHAPTER 5

45 three months: Ernest Dichter, "Proposal for a Motivational Research Study and Pre-Testing of Sales Appeals in the Field of Toys," December 1958, Hagley Museum Archives, Ernest Dichter papers, Box 51.
45 *"hottest intellectual vogues"* ... *"sex appeal"*: Daniel P. Kamienski, "Prescribing the American Dream: Psychoanalysts, Mass Media, and the Construction of Social and Political Norms in the 1950's," Graduate Dissertation, University of Montana, 2016.
46 *"look-a-like, act-a-like"*: Lawrence R. Samuel, *Freud on Madison Avenue: Motivation Research and Subliminal Advertising in America*, University of Pennsylvania Press, 2013, 14.
46 *"exuberant, balding"*: Vance Packard, *The Hidden Persuaders*, Ig Publishing, Reissue Edition, 2007, 33.
46 *"masculine perfume"*: Ernest Dichter, *Getting Motivated: The Secret Behind Individual Motivations by the Man Who Was Not Afraid to Ask "Why?"*, Pergamon Press, 1979, 49.
46 *"used Freudian and sexual references"*: Daniel Horowitz, "The Birth of a Salesman: Ernest Dichter and the Objects of Desire," 1986, Hagley Museum.
46 *"to turn the American mind"*: "Books: The Hidden Persuaders," *New Yorker*, May 18, 1957, 167–68.
46 forty-six weeks: "Bestseller List," *New York Times*, April 13, 1958.
47 *"unsuccessful salesman"*: Ernest Dichter, *Getting Motivated*, 49. Unless indicated otherwise, the quotes in the section come from Ernest Dichter's memoir, *Getting Motivated*.
47 *"sexual root of kleptomania"*: Wilhelm Stekel, "Sexual Root of Kleptomania," *Journal of Criminal Law and Criminology* 2, Issue 1, 1911.
49 *"the most prominent retailer"* ... *"high priest"*: Daniel Horowitz, "The Birth of a Salesman."
50 *"allowed to caress himself"*: Lynn Ames, "The View from Peekskill; Tending the Flame of a Motivator," *New York Times*, August 2, 1998.
50 *"frustrates a deep-seated desire"* ... *"sexual union"*: Ernest Dichter, *The Strategy of Desire*, Doubleday and Company, 1960, xi, 8.
50 *"gigantic world breast"*: Ernest Dichter, *Getting Motivated*, 42.
50 *"very gutsy"*: Ruth Handler papers, Box 32, Folder 13.
50 *"Motivational Theater"* ... *hidden cameras*: Lynn Ames, "The View from Peekskill."
51 *"Put the Libido Back in Advertising"*: Daniel Horowitz, "The Birth of a Salesman."
51 took the Mattel case: M. G. Lord, *Forever Barbie*, 38.
51 $300 million ... *"an unsatisfied need of youngsters"*: Vance Packard, *The Hidden Persuaders*, 138–39.
51 *"unsatisfied needs"*: All quotes from the Mattel study are from Ernest Dichter, "A Motivational Research Study in the Field of Toys for Mattel Toys Inc.," June 1959, Ernest Dichter papers, Hagley Museum.
51 *"Long legs, big breasts, glamorous"*: Lynn Ames, "The View From Peekskill."

NOTES

51 *"a painted doll who shouldn't"*: Sylvia Plath, ed. Karen V. Kukil, *The Unabridged Journals of Sylvia Plath*, Vintage, 2000.
51 *"as much as we could get"*: Ruth Handler papers, Box 33, Folder 2.
51 Pigtails to Ponytails: David C. Smith, "How They Sell."
51 *"I guess that you mean the sexy look"*: Ruth Handler papers, Box 16, Folder 12.
51 *"maturing earlier"* ... *"sensory apparatus"*: Saul Braun, "Life-Styles: The Micro-bopper," *Esquire*, March 1968.
51 *"Although our testing"* ... *"more specific"*: Ruth Handler papers, Box 16, Folder 12. Emphasis added.
51 *"brand image"* ... *"the 'Ideal' Toy Company"*: Ernest Dichter, "Draft Proposal for Brand Image Study," September 1, 1959, Ernest Dichter papers, Hagley Museum.

CHAPTER 6

56 *"festering swamp"*: Helen DeWitt, *Lightning Rods*, New Directions, 2012, 7.
56 *"dam the golden flood"* ... *"fires of hell"*: King Camp Gillette, *The Human Drift*, New Era Publishing Co., 1894, 9, 80.
57 *"It was almost as if Karl Marx"*: Russell B. Adams, *King C. Gillette, the Man and His Wonderful Shaving Device*, Little, Brown & Company, 1978, 13.
57 *possibly apocryphal*: Randal C. Picker, "The Razors-and-Blades Myth," Chicago Unbound, 2011.
57 *Christmas in July*: Christopher Byrne, *They Came to Play*.
58 *"to use network television 52 weeks"*: Ruth Handler papers, Box 22, Folders 11–19.
58 *"many imitators"* ... *"last quarter"*: Ruth Handler papers, Box 12, Folder 10. See also: Box 22, Folders 11–19.
58 *"'collection' type sequence"*: Ernest Dichter, "A Motivational Research Study in the Field of Toys for Mattel Toys Inc.," June 1959, Ernest Dichter papers, Hagley Museum.
58 *"Our Lady of Perpetual Income"*: Ross Anderson, "For the Love of Barbie," *Spy*, September/October 1994.
58 *"several hundred thousand"* ... *"Bubble Cut"*: Dieter Warnecke, *Barbie im Wandel der Jahrzehnte*, Wilhelm Heyne Verlag München, 1995, 56–64.
59 *"Mattel Creates Ken"*: Ruth Handler papers, Box 12, Folder 10.
59 *"action figure"*: Don Richard Cox, "Barbie and Her Playmates," *Journal of Popular Culture* 11, Issue 2, Fall 1977.
59 *As Barbie's social scene grew*: Dieter Warnecke, *Barbie im Wandel der Jahrzehnte*.
59 *The first iteration*: Shannon Carlin, "The History Behind Barbie's Ken," *Time*, July 20, 2023.
60 *"mid-century wood grains"*: Julie Lasky, "A Six Decade Tour of Barbie's Dreamhouses," *New York Times*, December 14, 2022.
60 *"She was a merchandiser's dream"*: John Riley, "Class in Our Time," *Esquire*, January 1970.
60 *"The name Barbie is magic"*: Ruth Handler papers, Box 16, Folder 12.
60 *"quickly spoken for"*: "Mattel, Inc., Block of 300,000 Shares Offered at $10 Each," *Wall Street Journal*, June 15, 1960.
60 *$50 million in annual sales*: "Mattel Sees Fiscal '63 Net, Sales Increasing to Records," *Wall Street Journal*, October 17, 1962.
60 *"well ahead of"*: "Many Toys Stay on Shelves as Sales Drop; Less Enthusiastic Store Promotion Noted," *Wall Street Journal*, December 19, 1962.

NOTES 291

60 *"Oh boy, what a big gala"*: Ruth Handler papers, Box 32, Folder 13.
60 *"Our stock went up to the sky"*: Ruth Handler papers, Box 33, Folder 1.
60 *In 1964 . . . Hawthorne, California*: "Mattel and Remco, Big Toy Makers, Indicate Pre-Christmas Sales Trailed Expectations," *Wall Street Journal*, December 28, 1964. For Geneva, see: Ruth Handler papers, Box 18, Folder 8.
60 *"Business is not only good"*: "Mattel Orders Ahead of Year Ago," *Wall Street Journal*, July 18, 1963.
60 *"We were gutsy people"*: Ruth Handler papers, Box 32, Folder 13.
60 *"once a toy craze"*: David C. Smith, "How They Sell." *Wall Street Journal*, November 24, 1964.
61 *"the biggest increase" . . . $100 million*: "Mattel Expects Fiscal '66 Net Above Prior Year," *Wall Street Journal*, August 27, 1965.
61 Mattelzapoppin': David C. Smith, "How They Sell."
61 *"clobbering each other"*: James Carberry, "Valley of the Dolls: How Mattel Inc. Went from Thriving Concern to Not-So-Thriving One," *Wall Street Journal*, June 20, 1973.
61 *"Mattel is energetic"*: David C. Smith, "How They Sell."

CHAPTER 7

62 *"He was the big bully"*: Jerry Oppenheimer, *Toy Monster*, 32.
62 *"He made very few friends"*: Sarah Monks, *Toy Town*, 32.
62 *"We were on our way up" . . . "no wrong"*: Ruth Handler papers, Box 32, Folder 13.
62 *He told colleagues . . . "a pretty girl doll"*: Rusty Kern, *Marx Toy Kings Vol. II*, 69.
63 *they'd applied for a U.S. patent*: Bild Lilli came out on August 12, 1955. The Haussers filed for an American patent on September 24, 1956. U.S. patent, No. 2,925,684.
63 *nearly $1.5 million*: Marx and Greiner & Hausser vs. Mattel Inc., Defendant's Answers to Plaintiff's Interrogatories, Case No. 341-61-Y, Southern District of California, May 14, 1962.
63 *not yet heard of Barbie . . . Louis Marx*: The Haussers claimed that they first heard about Barbie from Louis Marx and reached out sometime after. Mattel responded to the Haussers' first letter on May 18, 1960. The Haussers contacted Mattel again on June 3, 1960, and July 4, 1960, but Mattel's lawyers did not respond until March 23 1961. The contents of Mattel's first letter is unknown. In legal documents, Mattel claims it expressed interest in acquiring a license. The Haussers claimed, on the other hand, that Mattel had never made such an offer. Dan Miller, "In the Beginning, there was Lilli . . . ," *Miller's*, Winter 1997/1998, 79; Marx & Greiner & Hausser v. Mattel, "Defendant's Answers to Plaintiff's Interrogatories," Case No. 341-61-Y, Southern District of California, May 14, 1962.
63 *"simulating human walking movements"*: U.S. patent, No. 2,925,684.
63 *already being made in Hong Kong*: Sarah Monks, *Toy Town*, 67–69. Some have claimed that Marx first heard about Bild Lilli in Hong Kong. Monks tells the story of Marx seeing a clone of the doll in Hong Kong, becoming envious, and sending the manufacturer a fake cease-and-desist claiming to own the doll's worldwide rights. Monks's source, the Hong Kong toy maker Lam Leung-tim, claims he knew Marx was lying and called his bluff. As Lam tells it, he accompanied the toy king to the patent office and looked up the patent holder in person, where they learned the Lilli rights were in fact held by the Haussers. But the cease-and-desist Marx sent Lam, which Monks published, is dated

NOTES

June 17, 1960, roughly a week after Marx began negotiating with the Haussers (though before he had finalized the contract). Lam was right that Marx was dissembling, in other words, but not that he was lying outright. More to the point: Marx had heard about *Bild* Lilli before that interaction.

63 *That June . . . on July 4*: *Marx & Greiner & Hausser v. Mattel*, "Defendant's Answers to Plaintiff's Interrogatories," Case No. 341-61-Y, Southern District of California, May 14, 1962.

64 *"now conducting a campaign"*: *Marx & Greiner Hausser v. Mattel*, "Amended Answer to Complaint and Counterclaim," Case No. 341-61-WB, April 25, 1961. See also: *Mattel v. Greiner & Hausser*, Case No. 02-00322 NM (JWJx), 2001, Box 1, Folder 2.

64 *"I would guess" . . . "is not respected"*: *Mattel v. Greiner & Hausser*, Case No. 02-00322 NM (JWJx), 2001, Box 2, Folder 1.

64 *"Bonnie" was a Lilli clone*: "Bild Lilli Doll Clones, Competitors, and Look a Likes, 1960s," Doll Reference; "Louis Marx Dolls 1919–1979 USA," Doll Reference; Barbie Doll Clones, Competitors, and Look a Likes, 1960s," Doll Reference.

65 *"If Barbie was tawdry" . . . "fight fair"*: M. G. Lord, *Forever Barbie*, 57.

66 *"direct take-off" . . . "hoax upon the public"*: *Marx & Greiner & Hausser v. Mattel*, Case No. 341-61-Y, Southern District of California, "Plaintiff's Reply to Defendant's Counterclaims," September 15, 1961.

66 *"not already in the public domain"*: *Marx & Greiner & Hausser v. Mattel*, Case No. 341-61-Y, Southern District of California, "Defendant's Second Amended Answer and Counterclaim," August 11, 1961.

66 *nineteenth-century Vermont*: *Marx & Greiner & Hausser v. Mattel*, Case No. 341-61-Y, Southern District of California, "Defendant's Notice Under Title 35, Section 282," March 7, 1962.

66 *"conspired" . . . "confusingly similar appearance"*: *Marx & Greiner & Hausser v. Mattel*, Case No. 341-61-Y. Southern District of California, "Defendant's Second Amended Answer and Counterclaim," August 11, 1961.

67 *"This was legal jargon"*: M.G. Lord, *Forever Barbie*, 59.

67 *out-of-court settlement*: *Marx & Greiner & Hausser v. Mattel*, Case No. 341-61-Y. Southern District of California, "License Agreement," October 19, 1962.

67 *TV advertising*: *Marx & Greiner & Hausser v. Mattel*, "Defendant's Answers to Plaintiff's Interrogatories," Case No. 341-61-Y, Southern District of California, May 14, 1962.

67 *"the Barbie doll is testimony"*: Cy Schneider, *Children's Television*, 24.

67 *The following winter . . . in the States*: *Mattel v. Greiner & Hausser*, Case No. 02-00322 NM (JWJx), 2001, Box 2, Folder 1.

67 *In February of 1964 . . . Lockheed Aircraft*: *Mattel v. Greiner & Hausser*, Case No. 02-00322 NM (JWJx), 2001, Box 2, Folder 2.

68 *$21,600*: The Haussers were paid four lump-sum payments totaling 100,000 marks, 15,000 of which went to Axel Springer, and another 15,000 of which didn't arrive until Marx's license expired in 1970. *Mattel v. Greiner & Hausser*, Case No. 02-00322 NM (JWJx), 2001, Box 2, Folder 3.

68 *$85 million*: "Mattel Profits Reach a Record," *New York Times*, January 7, 1964.

68 *loose grasp of Mattel's profitability*: *Mattel v. Greiner & Hausser*, Case No. 02-00322 NM (JWJx), 2001, Box 2, Folder 4.

69 *"We have been successful"*: Letter to Silke Knaak from Collector Books, April 8, 2003.

NOTES 293

69 *"I spoke with Mattel's legal"*: Letter to Silke Knaak from Collector Books, February 28, 2003.
69 *"Talk from the Marx camp"*: Ruth Handler papers, Box 19, Folder 6.

PART II: INTRO

73 *One morning... Ken's penis*: Cy Schneider, *Children's Television*, 29–30.
73 *her very own address*: Cy Schneider, *Children's Television*, 30–31.
73 *handle the doll's mail*: Ruth Handler, *Dream Doll*, 88; Ruth Handler papers, Box 32, Folder 13.
73 *"enormous"*: Cy Schneider, *Children's Television*, 30.
73 *"We formed a Barbie"*: Ruth Handler papers, Box 32, Folder 13.
74 *Girl Scouts*: Cy Schneider, *Children's Television*, 30.
74 *"a boy doll"*: Ruth Handler papers, Box 32, Folder 13.
74 *"We were scared to death"*: Ruth Handler, *Dream Doll*, 89.
74 *"Our consumers pushed us"*: Ruth Handler papers, Box 33, Folder 2.
74 *"male organs"... "nothing outstanding"*: Ruth Handler papers, Box 32, Folder 13.
74 *"penis showing"... "bump"*: M. G. Lord, *Forever Barbie*, 49. All quotes from Charlotte Johnson are from this page.
74 *bulge*: Ruth Handler, *Dream Doll*, 90.
75 *"guys who made the decisions"*: Ruth Handler papers, Box 32, Folder 13.
75 *"Interest in detail is high"*: Ernest Dichter, "A Motivational Research Study in the Field of Toys for Mattel Toys Inc.," June 1959, Ernest Dichter papers, Hagley Museum.
75 *"permanent set of jockey shorts"... "arbitrarily eliminated both"*: Cy Schneider, *Children's Television*, 30.
76 *"down to the smallest detail"*: Ken advertisement, *Playthings*, March 1961.
76 *"almost no bulge"*: Ruth Handler papers, Box 32, Folder 13.

CHAPTER 8

77 *The horse trailer*: The anecdote in this first section comes from Gwen Florea and Glenda Phinney's memoir, *Barbie Talks!: An Unauthorized Exposé of the First Talking Barbie Doll*, iUniverse, 2001, 203, 214–220.
77 *thousand patents*: Associated Press, "Jack Ryan Dies at 65; Designer of the Barbie Doll," August 21, 1991.
77 *"fortune-tellers, jugglers"*: Zsa Zsa Gabor with Wendy Leigh, *One Lifetime Is Not Enough*, Delacorte Press, 1991, 230.
79 *150 parties*: John Riley, "Class in Our Time."
79 *For every patent*: Jerry Oppenheimer, *Toy Monster*, 92.
79 *"operative pumps and a stereo tape deck"*: John Riley, "Class in Our Time."
79 *"Fashion Queen Barbie"*: U.S. Patent No. 3,225,489; Dieter Warnecke, *Barbie im Wandel der Jahrzehnte*, Wilhelm Heyne Verlag München, 1995, 71. *"Miss Barbie"*: U.S. Patent No. 3,277,601; Warnecke, 74. *"Color 'n Curl Hair Set"*: U.S. Patent No. 3,382,607; Warnecke, 85. *"Twist 'n Turn Barbie"*: U.S. Patent No. 3,234,689; Warnecke, 91.
79 *Barbie's house... with clothes*: Kitturah Westenhouser, *The Story of Barbie Doll*, Collector Books, Second Edition, 1999, 120–34.
80 *Katharine Hepburn to the Hearsts*: Jerry Oppenheimer, *Toy Monster*, 19.

NOTES

80   *secret passageways*: Art Seidenhaum, "Home as a Theme Park," *Los Angeles Times*, April 20, 1977.

80   *elective lobotomy*: "Warner Baxter, 59, Film Star, Is Dead," *New York Times*, May 8, 1951.

80   *secret stairwell . . . "family" area*: *Dream House: The Real Story of Jack Ryan*, Season 1, Episodes 1 and 3. See also: John Riley, "Class in Our Time."

80   *at least one pony*: *Dream House*, Season 1, Episode 4.

80   *animatronic alligators*: Marvene Jones, "The Social Butterfly," *Los Angeles Evening Citizen News*, June 10, 1970.

80   *"real Italian royal crest" . . . uninstalled*: Art Seidenbaum, "Home as a Theme Park."

81   *"Everything around the house" . . . playing with it*: *Dream House*, Season 1, Episode 6.

81   *"Ryan's boys" . . . It's a Party*: Art Seidenbaum, "This Is a House That Jack Built," *Los Angeles Times*, December 15, 1962; Maggie Savoy, "Plenty of Jack in This Ivory Tower," *Los Angeles Times*, October 9, 1968; John Riley, "Class in Our Time"; C. Robert Jennings, "In the Toy Business, the Christmas Rush Is On," *New York Times Magazine*, May 19, 1968.

81   *"baggy, cold, saucer-like"*: John Riley, "Class in Our Time."

81   *Peter Lorre*: Ruth Handler papers, Box 8, Folders 1–3.

81   *"I had to marry Zsa Zsa"*: Zsa Zsa Gabor, *One Lifetime Is Not Enough*, 232–36.

81   *"That marriage cost me $400,000 a bang"*: Jerry Oppenheimer, *Toy Monster*, 88.

81   *"full-blown seventies-style swinger" . . . "lived there with him"*: Zsa Zsa Gabor, *One Lifetime Is Not Enough*, 232–36.

82   *"stopped eating altogether"*: Jerry Oppenheimer, *Toy Monster*, 57.

82   *"weren't good enough to play with him"*: Jerry Oppenheimer, *Toy Monster*, 20.

82   *"always empty"*: *Dream House*, Season 1, Episode 1.

82   *"scientific study of loneliness" . . . "serve them"*: Maggie Savoy, "Plenty of Jack in This Ivory Tower"; John Riley, "Class in Our Time."

82   *"to be accepted, liked, respected"*: John Riley, "Class in Our Time."

82   *"very controlled" . . . "disability"*: Interview with Carol Spencer, April 19, 2023.

83   *"He was a magician"*: *Dream House*, Season 1, Episode 1.

83   *"Any article about Jack"*: Jerry Oppenheimer, *Toy Monster*, 61.

83   *$400,000 . . . "We are very simple people"*: C. Robert Jennings, "In the Toy Business, the Christmas Rush Is On."

83   *only three people*: Ruth Handler papers, Box 26, Folder 6.

84   *nearly every Mattel patent*: Sydney Ladensohn Stern and Ted Schoenhaus, *Toyland: The High Stakes Game of the Toy Industry*, Contemporary Books, 1999, 66.

84   *"reluctant to credit"*: C. Robert Jennings, "In the Toy Business, the Christmas Rush Is On."

84   *"Plagiarize, plagiarize"*: Jerry Oppenheimer, *Toy Monster*, 63.

84   *He'd been reminded*: *Dream House*, Season 1, Episodes 4 and 6.

84   *his first wife, Barbara . . . sexual poses*: Jerry Oppenheimer, *Toy Monster*, 28, 53.

84   *"couldn't think of anything original"*: Ruth Handler papers, Box 32, Folder 13.

84   *"earlier publicity" . . . "yet to be bridged"*: C. Robert Jennings, "In the Toy Business, the Christmas Rush Is On."

85   *"Somebody slept in the guest room"*: John Riley, "Class in Our Time."

85   *Jerry Brown . . . invite list*: Jerry Oppenheimer, *Toy Monster*, 66.

NOTES

85 *Initially opposed to Richard Nixon*: Ruth Handler, *Dream Doll*, 136–37.
85 *"royalty checks"* ... *"shortchanging him"*: *Dream House*, Season 1, Episodes 1, 2, and 6.
85 *"falsely computed"* ... *"talking about"*: Ruth Handler papers, Box 26, Folder 6.
85 *"for as long as possible"*: *Dream House*, Season 1, Episode 6.
85 *tied up in lawsuits*: Art Seidenhaum, "Home as a Theme Park," *Los Angeles Times*, April 20, 1977.
86 *erase him from Barbie history*: Jerry Oppenheimer, *Toy Monster*, 9.
86 *partially paralyzed*: Associated Press, "Jack Ryan Dies at 65."
86 *"Little by little"*: *Dream House*, Season 1, Episodes 1 and 2.
86 *112-word entry*: "Billion Dollar Barbie," *New York Times*, March 27, 1994.
86n *"very buxom redhead"* ... *"a clothing-optional lifestyle"*: *Dream House*, Season 1, Episode 6.
86n *"where out of loneliness"* ... *"plays for the cows"*: "Hollywood's New Sex Symbol," *Spokesman Review*, July 6, 1974.
86 *"Your Sunday feature"*: Ruth Handler, Letter to Editor, *New York Times*, May 22, 1994.

CHAPTER 9

87 *"most pernicious threat"*: "Advertising: Officials Redraw Battle Lines," *New York Times*, October 28, 1964.
87 *"was nuts"*: Ruth Handler papers, Box 33, Folder 2.
87 *"live vagina-core"*: "Yeastie Girlz," Bandcamp.
87 *"thought 'girl talk' was stupid"*: Ruth Handler papers, Box 33, Folder 2.
87 *female friends*: Ruth Handler papers, Box 32, Folder 14.
87 *birth control*: "U.S. Approves Pill for Birth Control," *New York Times*, May 10, 1960. See also: "This Day in History: 1960 FDA approves 'the pill,'" History.com.
88 *"burst like a boil"*: Betty Friedan, *The Feminine Mystique*, Dell Publishing Co, Reprint, Second Edition, 1979, 17.
88 *One Harper's dispatch*: Marion K. Sanders, "A Proposition for Women," *Harper's Magazine*, September 1960.
88 *It was also in 1960* ... *"commercial consideration"*: "Playboy Interview: Helen Gurley Brown," *Playboy*, April 1963.
88 *eighteen secretarial jobs* ... *strictures of class*: Laurie Ouillette, "Inventing the Cosmo Girl: Class Identity and Girl-Style American Dreams," *Media Culture & Society* 21, 1999, 359.
88 *"I'm a materialist"*: "Big Sister," *Time*, February 9, 1968, 60.
88 *"marvelous product"*: Marsha Bryant, "Plath, Domesticity, and the Art of Advertising," *College Literature* 29, No. 17–34.
89 *"the problem"* ... *"trying to conform"*: Betty Friedan, *The Feminine Mystique*, 9–11.
89 *"that bitch"*: Daniel Horowitz, *Betty Friedan and the Making of "The Feminine Mystique,"* University of Massachusetts Press, 1998, 200.
89 *"pretty picture of femininity"*: Betty Friedan, *The Feminine Mystique*, 22.
89 *"the manipulator"* ... *"grow up to be women"*: Betty Friedan, *The Feminine Mystique*, 201–21.
89n *"always leave the housewife something to do"*: Vance Packard, *The Hidden Persuaders*, 78.
89n *"use the time saved to be an astronomer"* ... *"too far from the kitchen"*: Betty Friedan, *The Feminine Mystique*, 217–18.
90 *"We dared not give Barbie"*: Brock Milton, "Case of the Teen-Age Doll," *New York*

NOTES

Times, April 21, 1963. For timing of release, see: "Merdel Will Show Games at Toy Fair," *Ludington Daily News*, March 1, 1963.
90 *"Frankly, with me"*: Ruth Handler papers, Box 16, Folder 12.
90 *"They just don't want success"*: "The President Is a Lady: But Mattel chief doesn't think most women belong in business," *California Business*, March 3, 1970.
90 *"post-Lolita figure"*: Lisa Hobbs, "Barbie—The Hex Symbol of Modern Woman," *San Francisco Examiner*, January 23, 1965.
91 *"we will protest"*: "The National Organization for Women's 1966 Statement of Purpose," National Organization for Women, October 29, 1966.
91 *"greatest wrath"*: "Toy Fair Goes Sophisticate: Rag doll bows to science, women's lib, ecology kick," *Tampa Times*, March 31, 1972.
91 *"almost pathological hatred"* ... *"that bitch"*: "Hello Dolly!", R. R. Walker, *Nation*, May 15, 1965.
91 *"lascivious"* ... *"wrong with American culture"*: David. C. Smith, "How They Sell."
91 *"Just what is the character"* ... *"shaping the next generation"*: Donovan Bess, "Barbie and Her Friends," *Ramparts*, April 1965.
92 *"too controversial"* ... *"'horrify' adults"*: Random House records, Columbia University Library.
92 *"from your thinking"*: M. G. Lord, *Forever Barbie*, 148.
92 *"The toy industry has spoken"*: "Toy Fair Goes Sophisticate."
92 *"huge Freedom Trash Can"* ... *"female torture"*: "No More Miss America!," Redstockings press release, August 22, 1968.
93 *"A word to ardent feminists"*: Patricia Perrone, "Christmas Toyland: Better Than Ever," *Bangor Daily News*, December 18, 1969.
93 *"No Liberation for Barbie"*: "No Liberation for Barbie," *Kankakee Daily Journal*, June 23, 1980.
93 *"There were no women"* ... *"Because of You"*: Ruth Handler papers, Box 33, Folder 2.
93 *"It was concrete"*: Robin Gerber, *Barbie and Ruth*, 117.
94 *one of only eleven*: "Not Many Top Paid Women Execs," *Philadelphia Daily News*, April 27, 1973.
94 *"freak"* ... *"that bitch"*: Ruth Handler papers, Box 16, Folder 17; Box 32, Folder 16.
94n *"Over his phone speaker"* ... *"give me another one"*: Ruth Handler papers, Box 32, Folder 16.
94 *"not at all what I expected"* ... *"side of your mouth"*: "Life After White Collar Crime," *Savvy*, May 1980.
95 *Equal Opportunity Act*: Richard R. Rivers, "In America, What You Do Is What You Are: The Equal Employment Opportunity Act of 1972," *Catholic University Law Review*, Vol. 22, Issue, 2, Winter 1973; James C. McBrearty, "The 1972 EEOC Revised Guidelines Pertaining to Sex Discrimination," *Journal of Small Business Management*, Vol. 11, January, 1973; Erin Kelly and Frank Dobbin, "Civil Rights Law at Work: Sex Discrimination and the Rise of Maternity Leave Policies," *American Journal of Sociology* 105, No. 2. September 1999.
94 *"the same as any other temporary disability"* ... *"deserves more discussion"*: Ruth Handler papers, Box 6, Folders 1–2.
96 *"the better facets"*: "No Liberation for Barbie."

CHAPTER 10

97 *Eight days after*: "Imitation of Life," AFI Catalog.
97 *"lady's pictures"*: "A Movie Director Discusses Acting," *St. Louis Post-Dispatch*, May 11, 1958.
97 *"Barbie-doll child"*: Emanuel Levy, "Imitation of Life (1959): Sirk's Glorious, Oscar Nominated Melodrama Starring Lana Turner, Sandra Dee, and Juanita Moore," *Cinema 24/7*, August 15, 2009.
97 *"imitated life"*: Rob Nelson, "Passing Time," *City Pages*, June 11, 1997.
97 *Her thesis*: Mamie and Kenneth Clark. "The Development of Consciousness of Self and the Emergence of Racial Identification in Negro Preschool Children," *Journal of Social Psychology, S.P.S.S.I. Bulletin* 10: 591–99. See also: Leila McNeill, "How a Psychologist's Work on Race Identity Helped Overturn School Segregation in 1950s America," *Smithsonian*, October 26, 2017.
97 *"I didn't have any self-hatred"*: Reminiscences of Mamie Clark, Session 1, May 25, 1976, 26–30, Columbia University Oral History Archive.
98 *"something of a heckler in class"*: "Student Catches Prof's Eye, Hand," *Pittsburgh Courier*, November 7, 1953.
98 *"never wanted to imitate anyone"*: Robert Guthrie interview with Kenneth Clark, Cummings Center for the History of Psychology.
98 *four dolls*: Richard Kluger, *Simple Justice*, Vintage Books, Reprint, 2004, 315.
98 *"nice color" . . . "bad"*: Mamie and Kenneth Clark, "Racial identification and preference in Negro children," 1947, *Readings in Social Psychology*. Ed. Theodore M. Newcomb and Eugene L. Hartley for Society for the Psychological Study of Social Issues. Henry Holt and Co., 1947, 169–78.
98 *White House*: Richard Kluger, *Simple Justice*, 318–19.
99 *Later studies*: Gwen Bergner, "Black Children, White Preference: Brown v. Board, the Doll Tests, and the Politics of Self-Esteem," *American Quarterly* 61, No. 2, June 2009: Richard Kluger, *Simple Justice*, 354–56.
99 *"overwhelming majority"*: "Toy Fair Goes Sophisticate."
99 *"most laborious toy"*: "Negro Dolls for Christmas," *People Today*, December 5, 1950.
99 *"ultimately sabotaged"*: Gordon Patterson, "Color Matters: The Creation of the Sara Lee Doll," *Florida Historical Quarterly*, October 1994. See also: Virginia Lynn Moylan, "Sara Creech and Her Beautiful Doll," *Zora Neale Hurston's Final Decade*, University Press of Florida, 2012; Rob Golberg, *Radical Play: Revolutionizing Children's Toys in 1960s and 1970s America*, Duke University Press, 2023, 88–93.
99 *"Colored Chatty Cathy"*: "Vaughan-Weil: Layaway Toy Sale," *Birmingham News*, June 7, 1962, 53. See also: Rob Golberg, *Radical Play*, 90–91.
100 *"suburban apartheid"*: Mike Davis, "The Year 1960," *New Left Review* 108, November/December 2017.
100 *larger than Manhattan . . . four thousand arrested*: Gerald Horne, *Fire This Time: The Watts Uprising and the 1960s*, University Press of Virginia, 1995, 3.
100 *"mad dogs"*: Paul Jacobs, *Prelude to a Riot: A View of Urban America from the Bottom*, Random House, 1967, 5.
100 *"most beautiful suburban town" . . . "and WELCOME"*: Hadley Meares, "Hawthorne's Deceptively Sunny History," Curbed Los Angeles, January 30, 2008.

298 NOTES

100 *"N***er, Don't"*: All references to this sign cite James W. Loewen's book, *Sundown Towns: A Hidden Dimension of American Racism*, The New Press, 2005, but the detail appears there without a footnote or source. Loewen's Sundown Town database, maintained by Tougaloo College, cites an unattributed quote: "My dad told me that Hawthorne had a sign at the City Limits in the 30's that said, 'N***er, don't let the sun set on YOU in Hawthorne.'" See also: Laura Wexler, "Darkness on the Edge of Town, *Washington Post*, October 23, 2005.

100 *"rainbow coalition"*: Ruth Handler papers, Box 34, Folder 2.

100 *"United Nations"*: Robin Gerber, *Barbie and Ruth*, 86.

101 *"imaginative and constructive"*: *Business and the Development of Ghetto Enterprise*, The Conference Board, 1970, 7.

101 *Aerojet General*: The rocket manufacturer Aerojet General set up a black-managed subsidiary so quickly that it had soon hired staff and acquired a plant before its chairman had decided what, precisely, the factory would make—in the end, hospital tents for the army. *Business and the Development of Ghetto Enterprise*, 7, 94.

101 *"Mom and Dad"*: "It's a Wonderful Life: Thirty Years of Barbie and America," *Barbie Magazine*, Thirtieth Anniversary Issue, Winter 1990.

101 *"less endowed"*: Ruth Handler papers, Box 33, Folder 2.

101 *"lifelike bendable legs"*: "Mattel's Francie, Barbie's Modern Cousin with Lifelike Bendable Legs," *Lebanon Daily News*, November 24, 1966.

101 *"Gad Abouts"*: "'Francie Dolls,'" *Independent*, February 27, 1966.

101 *"virtually abandoned"*: Tom W. Smith, "Changing Racial Labels: From 'Colored' to 'Negro' to 'Black' to 'African American,'" *Public Opinion Quarterly* 56, No. 2 Winter 1992.

101 *"outmoded, even racist"*: Ann DuCille, "Dyes and Dolls: Multicultural Barbie and the Merchandising of Difference," *Black Studies Reader*, Routledge, 2004, 269.

102 *Mattel itself said*: "Business Bulletin: A Special Background Report on Trends in Industry and Finance," *Wall Street Journal*, November 16, 1967.

102 *"unite the community"*: Kitturah Westenhouser, *The Story of Barbie*, Collector Books, 1994, 176.

102 *"Mattel saw a marketing opportunity" . . . miscegenation*: Ann DuCille, *Skin Trade*, Harvard University Press, 1996, 33.

102 *"'small but vocal minority'"*: "Business Bulletin: A Special Background Report on Trends in Industry and Finance," *Wall Street Journal*, November 16, 1967.

102 *"preferred to act entirely on its own"*: *Business and the Development of Ghetto Enterprise*, 53.

CHAPTER 11

103 *Matt Drudge*: Philip Weiss, "Watching Matt Drudge," *New York* magazine, August 24, 2007.

103 *Reagan himself*: William Russell Ellis Jr., "Operation Bootstrap: A Case Study in Ideology and the Institutionalization of Protest," University of California, Los Angeles, Doctoral dissertation, 1969, 111.

103 *"Even the ultra-right-wing"*: Rob Goldberg, *Radical Play*, 127.

103 *out-of-work salesman . . . "communist infiltration"*: William Russell Ellis Jr., "Operation Bootstrap," 81, 95.

104 *"University of Watts"*: Rob Goldberg, *Radical Play*, 125.

104 *bureaucrats who "seek to control"*: Charles E. Brown, "How Negroes Fight Poverty in Watts: Operation Bootstrap Prepares," *Jet*, December 21, 1967.
104 *"We do not solicit"*: William Russell Ellis Jr., "Operation Bootstrap," 111.
104 *"have to be a greedy"... "private capital"*: "Shindana Discovers the Together Dolls," *Black Enterprise*, December 1970.
104 *The school offered*: "Social, Race Concerns Head Meeting Agenda," *Los Angeles Times*, April 20, 1968; "Black Dolls Are Now Big Business," *Ebony*, December 1969; Rob Goldberg, *Radical Play*; "'Bootstrap' to Train Service Station Men," *Los Angeles Times*, June 10, 1967; "Bootstrap Players to Perform," *Los Angeles Times*, October 8, 1967; Jack Jones, "Rites Pending for Louis Smith, 47," *Los Angeles Times*, January 7, 1976.
104 *some 400 students*: Charles E. Brown. "Operation Bootstrap Prepares Negros for Jobs in Ghetto," *Jet*. December 12, 1967.
104 *"It was frightening"*: Charlayne Hunter, "Black Doll Is 'Natural' Success," *New York Times*, February 20, 1971; David Crittendon et al., "The Legacy of Shindana Toys: Black Play and Black Power," *American Journal of Play* 13, Nos. 2–3 (Winter–Spring 2021.
105 *about $150,000 up front*: Historical accounts differ on the exact size of Mattel's contribution. In 1968, Mattel executive Vic Rado told the *Los Angeles Times* that the company invested "$150,000 initially," while *Ebony* reported in 1969 that "Mattel invested $475,000 in cash and $175,000 in equipment" over a nine-month period. Mattel vice president Art Spear put the donation at $200,000 in 1970, which is also the number a Shindana executive told *The New York Times* in 1976. I've opted for Rado's account, being the earliest and theoretically closest to the "upfront" cost, but my sense is the total contribution grew over time through equipment and other costs. Jack Jones, "Toy Firm Turns Over L.A. Doll Factory to Operation Bootstrap," *Los Angeles Times*, October 12, 1968; "Black Dolls Are Now Big Business"; "Shindana Discovers the Together Dolls"; "Maker of Black Dolls Finding Profits in Attitude Changes," *New York Times*, December 24, 1976.
105 *marketing seminar*: M. G. Lord, *Forever Barbie*, 169.
105 *"It is the first instance"*: Jack Jones, "Toy Firm Turns Over L.A. Doll Factory."
105 *"dipped in chocolate"*: "Black Dolls Are Now Big Business."
105 *"a doll with our features"*: "Give Black Children Toys," *Atlanta Journal*, October 22, 1974.
105 *"How does black look?"* Ann DuCille, *Skin Trade*, 16.
105 *Shindana's answer*: David Crittendon et al. "The Legacy of Shindana Toys."
106 *"stick it into the oven"*: M. G. Lord, *Forever Barbie*, 168.
106 *Quarter-million-dollar profit*: "Operation Bootstrap Retires Debt, Shows Healthy Profit," *Los Angeles Times*, December 16, 1971.
106 *the catalog grew*: "Maker of Black Dolls Finding Profits"; "A History of Shindana Toys: Dolls and Games with a Difference," Strong Museum of Play, Google Arts & Culture; Shindana catalog, 1976.
106 *"million-dollar hit"... daycare*: M. G. Lord, *Forever Barbie*, 160; "Smith Selling Black Dolls to Foster Spirit of Love," *Burlington Free Press*, December 24, 1975; Nadra Nittle, "Operation Bootstrap: Empowering the African American Community Through Entrepreneurship," PBS SoCal, November 19, 2019.
106 *"Nobody took them on"*: M. G. Lord, *Forever Barbie*, 170.

300 NOTES

106 *"Volunteer teachers"*: Jack Jones, "Rites Pending for Louis Smith."
107 *"A good motive for change is the profit motive"*: Chase Manhattan Bank advertisement, *Ebony*, September 1971, 103.
107 *"There is a conflict"*: "Shindana Discovers the Together Dolls."
107 *"ninety percent community people"*: "Smith Selling Black Dolls to Foster Spirit of Love."
107 *no work*: Russell Ellis, "Operation Bootstrap: Beginnings," *People Making Places: Episodes in Participation 1964–1984*. Institute for the Study of Social Change, University of California, Berkeley. 1987.
107 *"dried up to practically nothing"*: "Operation Bootstrap Retires Debt."
107 *White Buffalo ... "bashful about its consulting role"*: "Toy Makers Battle 'Bum Raps,'" *Chicago Daily News*, February 29, 1972. Clipped in Ruth Handler papers, Box 23, Folder 9.
107 *"Shindana is the company"*: Ruth Handler papers, Box 15, Folder 10.
107 *"I once suggested"*: Ruth Handler papers, Box 32, Folder 16.
107 *"the more they peel"*: "Black Dolls Are Now Big Business."
108 *"were directly impacted"*: Aria S. Halliday, *Buy Black: How Black Women Transformed US Pop Culture*, University of Illinois Press, 2022, 60.
108 *"Today, Smith says"*: "Operation Bootstrap Retires Debt."
108 *"I won't be happy"*: "Toy Makers Battle 'Bum Raps.'"
108 *"They claim that someday"*: Ruth Handler papers, Box 17, Folder 15.
109 *"If you would do that" ... "on their own"*: Ruth Handler papers, Box 15, Folder 7.
109 *"decreasing every day"*: Ruth Handler papers, Box 16, Folder 16.

CHAPTER 12

110 *Things had been going well*: Ruth Handler, *Dream Doll*, 128; "Mattel Building Toronto Plant," *Wall Street Journal*, July 25, 1963; Ernest A. Schonberger, "Assembly Lines Straddle the Border," *Los Angeles Times*, November 19, 1967; "Hit & Run: U.S. Runaway Shops on the Mexican Border," *NACLA's Latin America & Empire Report* Vol. IX, No. 5 (July–August 1975).
110 *"top-selling toy"*: James Carberry, "Valley of the Dolls."
110 *wholesalers discounts*: Ruth Handler papers, Box 25, Folder 10, "Mattel Inc. Reports of the Special Counsel and Special Auditor," 26–27.
110 *"revolutionary merchandising concept"*: Ruth Handler papers, Box 16, Folder 14.
111 *"more humanoid than ever" ... "increasingly temporary"*: Alvin Toffler, *Future Shock*, Bantam Books, 1970, 53.
111 *"there were more Barbie"* Ruth Handler papers, Box 16, Folder 13; "Mattel Inc. Says Net and Sales Increased in Year Ended Jan. 31," *Wall Street Journal*, March 9 1967.
111 *"regain a favorable corporate image"*: Ruth Handler papers, Box 25, Folder 10, "Mattel Inc. Reports of the Special Counsel and Special Auditor," 30.
111 *a low of $7*: Ruth Handler papers, Box 1, Folder 6.
111 *"'money man'"*: James Carberry, "Valley of the Dolls."
112 *"passion for secrecy"*: Noah Dietrich and Bob Thomas, *Howard, The Amazing Mr. Hughes*, Fawcett Books, 1972, 190.
112 *"close to a hundred" ... "no sign of peaking"*: "Litton Industry, Proving Poverty Pays," *Ramparts*, December 24, 1968.
112 *"synergy" ... "technology company"*: "Litton Industries Inc.," International Directory of Company Histories, Encyclopedia.com.

NOTES 301

112   *"considerable mental agility"* ... *"truly awesome"*: "Litton Industry, Proving Poverty Pays."
112   *"at least 100"*: Jack Searles, "Mattel—Growing Up in the World of the Young."
113   *"innovation in corporate finance"*: Arelo Sederberg, "New Preference Stock Working Well for Litton," *Los Angeles Times*, March 7, 1966.
113   *Wall Street whisperer*: Ruth Handler papers, Box 26, Folder 6; Box 25, Folder 10, "Mattel Inc. Reports of the Special Counsel and Special Auditor," 31; "Abreast of the Market," *Wall Street Journal*, September 26, 1967.
113   *struck Ruth as odd*: Jack Searles, "Mattel—Growing up in the World of the Young"; Ruth Handler papers, Box 25, Folder 9.
113   *"I never liked that man"*: Ruth Handler papers, Box 32, Folder 16.
113   *"You won't do"* ... *"things around here"*: Ruth Handler papers, Box 25, Folder 9.
114   *"You're a woman"*: Ruth Handler, *Dream Doll*, 128. For changing story, see also: Ruth Handler papers, Box 1, Folder 7.
114   *"did not share the analysts' concern"*: Ruth Handler papers, Box 26, Folder 6.
114   *What Ruth perhaps did not know*: Robert E. Wideman, "Litton Crosses the River," Master's Thesis for the Naval Postgraduate School, September 1976; Wallace Turner, "Allegations Against the Ash Focus on Accounting for Hughs and Origin of Litton Industries," *New York Times*, January 28, 1973.
114   *the very next year*: "Promotions Announced by Litton Firm," *Van Nuys News and Valley Green Sheet*, August 21, 1960.
114   *"If he's done nothing else"*: Jack Searles, "Mattel—Growing up in the World of the Young."
114   *"I'm going to fire"* ... *"some disaster here"*: Ruth Handler, *Dream Doll*, 130.
115   *"capitalize upon Mattel's ability"*: Ruth Handler papers, Box 13, Folder 1, "Mattel, Incorporated: First Acquisition Strategy Meeting," November 20, 1967, 1–9.
115   *"We binged"*: Ruth Handler, *Dream Doll*, 132.
115   *The next summer*: "Mattel Acquires Producer of School Supplies, Luggage," *Wall Street Journal*, November 16, 1965; "Mattel Agrees to Acquire Monogram Models for Stock," *Wall Street Journal*, August 27, 1968; "Mattel Says It Plans to Acquire Metaframe in Exchange of Stock," *Wall Street Journal*, June 25, 1969; "Mattel Gets Playground Equipment Maker," *Fresno Bee*, December 24, 1969; "Mattel Buying Audio-Magnetic," *Miami Herald*, June 7, 1970; Ruth Handler papers, Box 13, Folder 3.
115   *Roy "The Judge" Hofheinz*: "The Greatest Showman on Earth and He's the First to Admit It," *Sports Illustrated*, April 21, 1969.
115   *they were greeted* ... *Dianne Feinstein*: Ruth Handler, *Dream Doll*, 142–43.
116   *"cheapest promoter imaginable"*: Dave McKenna, "The Music Died with Some Help from D.C.," *Washington City Paper*, February 3, 2009.
116   *"Jumbo"*: Ruth Handler papers, Box 17, Folder 10.
116   *"spectacular gains"*: John Quirt, "Putting Barbie Back Together Again," *Fortune*, September 8, 1980, clipped in Ruth Handler papers, Box 1, Folder 7.
116   *"monstrous growth"*: Ruth Handler, *Dream Doll*, 133–34.
117   *Spear*: John Quirt, "Putting Barbie Back Together Again," *Fortune*, September 8 1980, 87.
117   *young tigers*: Ruth Handler papers, Box 13, Folder 4.
117   *"but also with itself"*: Ruth Handler papers, Box 25, Folder 10, "Mattel Inc. Reports of the Special Counsel and Special Auditor," 34.

117 *"I'm Peter Pan"*: "Sandra Salmans, "A Grown-Up's Winning Touch in Toys (Usually)," *New York Times*, February 14, 1985.
117 *"girth of"* ... *"Grandaddy of Concepts"*: John Tanasychuk, "Peter Pan Doesn't Like to Keep Toys in the Attic," *Windsor Star*, August 22, 1985.
117 *"Man Who Invented"*: Patricia Sullivan, "Bernard Loomis; Merged Toy Marketing, Saturday Cartoons," *Washington Post*, June 4, 2006. See also: David Owen, "Where Toys Come From," *Atlantic*, October 1986.
117 *"Pre-Mattel"*: Robert Spector, *Category Killers: The Retail Revolution and Its Impact on Consumer Culture*, Harvard Business School Press, 2005, 24.
118 *"continuing concept"*: John Tanasychuk, "Peter Pan."
118 *"dull-colored"* ... *"racing"*: Ruth Handler papers, Box 12, Folder 10.
118 *"They had been"* Ruth Handler papers, Box 33, Folder 1.
118 *"would have ranked"*: James Carberry, "Valley of the Dolls."
118 *Jack Wheeler*: George W. Woolery, *Children's Television: The First Thirty-Five Years*, The Scarecrow Press Inc, 1983, 142–43.
118 *The company went on to sponsor*: "Mattel's Silver Year: Giant Steps," *Playthings*, September 1970.
119 *Radnitz*: Ali Sar, "Radnitz: Fighting Syrup, Sadism," *Van Nuys News*, May 30, 1969.
119 *Federal Communications Commission*: "'Hot Wheels' TV Show May Be in Hot Water with Federal Agencies," *Wall Street Journal*, December 8, 1969; "Mattel, Topper, Du Pont Charged with False Ads," *Wall Street Journal*, November 27, 1970; "Mattel Says It Got Justice Agency Queries on Acquisition Moves," *Wall Street Journal*, March 4, 1970.

CHAPTER 13

122 *"became very possessive"*: Ruth Handler papers, Box 25, Folder 9.
122 *"became bitter toward"*: Ruth Handler papers, Box 25, Folder 9. For Spear title: Box 13, Folder 4.
122 *Yasuo Yoshida*: Ruth Handler papers, Box 26, Folder 6; Box 25, Folder 9, "Crestwood Club Cops 'Y' Tourney," *News-Pilot*, February 1, 1964; "Bowling Is Fun—and Profitable for Crestwood," *News-Pilot*, July 23, 1964; "Palmer at BDCC For VIP Tourney," *Desert Sun*, November 18, 1971.
122n *"Yoshida, being Japanese"* ... *Ruth never even met the man*: Ruth Handler papers, Box 25, Folder 9; Box 26, Folder 6.
122 *"I was fighting with Loomis"*: Ruth Handler papers, Box 25, Folder 9.
123 *"I was going to have to face"*: All Ruth quotes in this section are from Ruth Handler, *Dream Doll*, 149–59.
124 *"frankly mutilating"*: Stefano Zurrida, et al., "The Changing Face of Mastectomy (from Mutilation to Aid to Breast Reconstruction)," *International Journal of Surgical Oncology*, 2011.
124 *"There's only one thing"*: Ruth Handler papers, Box 8, Folders 1–3.
125 *"It was a game of hyperbole"*: James Carberry, "Valley of the Dolls."
125 *Mattel's Mexican assembly plant*: "Pérdidas por más de $100 Millones en un Siniestro," *El Informador*, October 1, 1970; "Toys, Dolls, Models, and Games: Production and Maintenance Workers of Mattel Inc. at Hawthorne and City of Industry, California," Report to the President on Investigation Nos. TEA-W-66 and TEA-W-67, United

States Tariff Commission, March 1971, 239; "Hit & Run: U.S. Runaway Shops on the Mexican Border."
125 *Two workers were found dead*: "4 Are Lost in Toy Firm Fire," Associated Press via *Modesto Bee*, October 1, 1970.
125 *"completely destroyed"*: Ruth Handler papers, Box 24, Folder 7.
125 *Mexican authorities . . . layoffs*: Ruth Handler papers, Box 13, Folder 7.
126 *employee profit-sharing plan . . . Bernie Loomis*: Ruth Handler papers, Box 26, Folders 3, 6.
126 *"secrecy"*: Ruth Handler papers, Box 13, Folder 7. Quote is attributed to "RKM," or R. Kenton Musgrave. For name, see Box 13, Folder 4.
126 *Rosenberg's Wall Street contacts*: Ruth Handler papers, Box 32, Folder 11.
126 *parking lots . . . "Tiffany's of cleaning"*: Ruth Handler papers, Box 25, Folder 9; Connie Bruck, *Master of the Game: Steve Ross and the Creation of Time Warner*, Simon & Schuster, 1994, 35.
126 *As the Bureau noted in 1965*: Connie Bruck, *Master of the Game*, 30–32; William Poundstone, *Fortune's Formula: The Untold Story of the Scientific Betting System That Beat the Casinos and Wall Street*, Hill and Wang, 2006, 85; Bill Doyle, "Bootlegger Abner Zwillman Was Considered the 'Al Capone of NJ,'" NJ1015.com, July 27, 2020.
127 *It had managed to acquire*: Connie Bruck, *Master of the Game*, 48, 50, 66; Untitled news item, *National Post*, July 19, 1969, 18.
127 *"as a go-go concern"*: "Life After White Collar Crime," *Savvy*, May 1980, 49.
127 *"considerably more money" . . . "make a deal"*: Ruth Handler, *Dream Doll*, 163–66.
127 *at their annual meeting*: Earl C. Gottschalk Jr., "It's Fun and Games and Clowning Around at Mattel Meeting," *Wall Street Journal*, May 20, 1971.
128 *Caesar P. Kimmel*: "Kimmel Built Parking Lot into Kinney Corp. Complex," *Ashbury Park Press*, July 25, 1971.
128 *The big sticking point*: Meeting description from Ruth Handler, *Dream Doll*, 163–66.
129 *"subversive"*: Ruth Handler papers, Box 12, Folder 8.
130 *"Mattel is alive and kicking"*: Dan Dorfman, "Heard on the Street," *Wall Street Journal*, June 4, 1971.

CHAPTER 14
131 *"Should old acquaintance" . . . "used to be fun"*: Ruth Handler papers, Box 17, Folder 10.
131 *In the sixties . . . close the factory down*: "Joint Hearing Before the Subcommittee on Employment Opportunities and the Subcommittee on Labor-Management Relations of the Committee on Education and Labor, House of Representatives, Ninety-Sixth Congress, Second Session on H.R. 5040," January 18, 1980, 172, 241.
132 *at eight a.m. on July 1*: "Dockers Vote 96% for Strike," *Dispatcher*, July 2, 1971; "Strike of 1971: Negotiations Research," Pacific Maritime Association, May 5, 1972; Richard Boyden, "Why the 1971-1972 ILWU Strike Failed," *New Politics Magazine* X, No. 2, Fall 1972.
132 *"I don't think many"*: Dan Dorfman, "Heard on the Street," *Wall Street Journal*, September 16, 1971.
132 *"squeezed" . . . "ficticious"*: Ruth Handler papers, Box 26, Folder 3.
132 *"unacceptable" . . . "artificially reduced"*: Ruth Handler papers, Box 25, Folder 10, "Mattel Inc. Reports of the Special Counsel and Special Auditor," 134–36.

304 NOTES

133 *Darrell Peters*: Ruth Handler papers, Box 25, Folder 10, "Mattel Inc. Reports of the Special Counsel and Special Auditor," 38–39.
133 *year-long deficit*: "Mattel Posts Deficit, Its First, in Fiscal '72; Net Loss $29.9 Million," *Wall Street Journal*, March 30, 1972; Ruth Handler papers, Box 17, Folder 10; Box 25, Folder 10, "Mattel Inc. Reports of the Special Counsel and Special Auditor," 42.
133 *"REASONS FOR BAD YEAR EXPERIENCE"*: Ruth Handler papers, Box 17, Folder 13.
133 *exit package*: "Mattel to Pay $60,000 a Year Through 1993 to Former Executive," *Wall Street Journal*, June 14, 1973; Ruth Handler papers, Box 32, Folder 11.
133 *Ruth set about undoing*: Ruth Handler papers, Box 13, Folder 10; "Mattel, Inc.," *New York Times*, May 26, 1972; A. H. Weiler, "Have Daughter, Will Travel," *New York Times*, June 25, 1972.
134 *"The business came in late"*: Leonard Sloane, "Sales Spree in Toyland," *New York Times*, December 24, 1972.
134 *"definite turnaround"*: "Mattel Says It Had 'Definite Turnaround' in Fiscal '73 Operations," *Wall Street Journal*, February 5, 1973.
134 *frantic call*: Ruth Handler papers, Box 25, Folder 10, "Mattel Inc. Reports of the Special Counsel and Special Auditor," 150–54.
134 *"troubled toy maker"*: "Mattel Alters Estimate of Fiscal '73 Operations, Says It Incurred Deficit," *Wall Street Journal*, February 26, 1973.
134 *"a fraud and deceit"*: Ruth Handler papers, Box 13, Folder 10.
135 *Ruth to resign*: Ruth Handler papers, Box 32, Folder 11.
135 *$41 to $2*: "Putting Barbie Back Together Again," John Quirt, *Fortune*, September 8, 1980.
135 *"It seems that we are paying"*: "Mattel Inc. Expects Profit for Fiscal '74," *Wall Street Journal*, June 18, 1973.
135 *"cumulative effect"* . . . *"whatever the actual figures"*: Ruth Handler papers, Box 25, Folder 10, "Mattel Inc. Reports of the Special Counsel and Special Auditor," 61–62, 137–139.
136 *unedited records*: Ruth Handler papers, Box 25, Folder 10, "Mattel Inc. Reports of the Special Counsel and Special Auditor," Part 2, 18–19.
136 *"Mrs. Invisible"*: Ruth Handler, *Dream Doll*, 171.
136 *like her father*: Ruth Handler, *Dream Doll*, 198.
136 *"egg-shaped glob"*: Ruth Handler, *Dream Doll*, 156.
137 *mostly older women*: Ruth Handler papers, Box 32, Folder 11.
138 *"let the error slide"*: Ruth Handler papers, Box 25, Folder 10, "Mattel Inc. Reports of the Special Counsel and Special Auditor," Part 1, 121–22.
138 *tedium was the point*: Stephen J. Sansweet, "Mattel Ex-Aides Tried Cover-Up, Report Asserts," *Wall Street Journal*, November 4, 1975.
138n *settled its five shareholder lawsuits for $30 million*: "Judge Clears Mattel's $30 Million Settlement of Class Action Suits," *Wall Street Journal*, March 16, 1976; "Mattel Seeks to Sue Arthur Andersen & Co. Over Audit Standards," *Wall Street Journal*, January 9, 1976; Ruth Handler papers, Box 24, Folder 6.
138 *"impartial trier of fact"*: "Three Former Mattel Aides Seek to Block Use of Data Collected on Alleged Fraud," *Wall Street Journal*, January 7, 1977; "Former Mattel Officials Lose Bid to Prevent Use of Data in Fraud Case," *Wall Street Journal*, March 16, 1977; Ruth Handler papers, Box 25, Folder 11.

138 *in the first place*: Ruth Handler papers, Box 26, Folder 6.
138 *"lying son of a bitch"*: Ruth Handler papers, Box 32, Folder 16.
139 *ten counts*: "Co-founder of Toy Firm Is Indicted," UPI via *Venture County Star*, February 17, 1978.
139 *"overt acts"*: Roy J. Harris Jr., "Mattel Ex-Chief, Others Indicted on Fraud Counts," *Wall Street Journal*, February 17, 1978.
139 *$256 million*: "Mattel Founder Fined $57,000 by Judge," UPI via *Honolulu Advisor*, December 9, 1978.
139 *"'purge the file'"*: Ruth Handler papers, Box 26, Folder 3.
139 *Yoshida and two*: "Fines of $5,000 Ordered," UPI via *World*, December 12, 1978.
139 *"I turned the other cheek" . . . not admit guilt*: Ruth Handler papers, Box 25, Folder 11.
139 *"If the* nolo contendere*"*: Ruth Handler papers, Box 26, Folder 8.
140 *"exploitative, parasitic"*: "Mattel Founder Fined."
140 *"received less severe"*: "Fifteen Years of Guidelines Sentencing," U.S. Sentencing Commission, November 2004, Preface.
140 *"To fill the void"*: Ruth Handler papers, Box 26, Folder 7.
140 *"The very thing that I had worked so hard to do"*: Ruth Handler papers, Box 32, Folder 13.
140 *"reparations" . . . not, technically, legal*: Ruth Handler papers, Box 23, Folder 14.

PART III: INTRO
145 *$3 trillion*: Connie Bruck, *The Predators' Ball: The Inside Story of Drexel Burnham and the Rise of the Junk Bond Raiders*, Penguin Books, 1989, 13.
145 *Western White House*: "Of Legends and Icons," Fairmount Century Plaza.
145 *"Practically every raider"*: James B. Stewart, *Den of Thieves*, Touchstone, 1992, 261.
145 *"vampire's plasma"*: Steve Coll, "Ivan Boesky on Top of the Stockpile," *Washington Post*, December 2, 1985.
145 *"The King"*: Connie Bruck, *The Predators' Ball*, 10.
145 *every photograph*: L. J. Davis, "Hollywood's Most Secret Agent," *New York Times*, July 9, 1989.
146 *"rug you could fly"*: Jesse Kornbluth, "Judge Kimba Wood Grows Up," *Wall Street Journal*, September 2, 1992.
146 *amateur magician*: Connie Bruck, *The Predators' Ball*, 14.
146 *"gangbang"*: Connie Bruck, *The Predators' Ball*, 12.
146 *"Michael Jackson or God"*: Connie Bruck, *The Predators' Ball*, 16.
146 *almost 50 percent*: John Ganz, *When the Clock Broke: Con-Men, Conspiracists, and How America Cracked Up in the Early 1990s*, Farrar, Straus & Giroux, 2024, 6.
146 *"Decade of Greed"*: Bill Taylor, "Crime? Greed? Big Ideas? What Were the '80s About?," *Harvard Business Review*, January/February 1992.
147 *"highest-paid employee"*: Steve Swartz, "Why Mike Milken Stands to Qualify for Guinness Book," *Wall Street Journal*, March 31, 1989.
147 *"Everybody walked away from them"*: "Mattel's Successful Retreat," *Businessweek*, May 16, 1977.
147 *guar gum*: Todd Coupee, "Slime Monster Game from Mattel (1977)," *Toy Tales*, July 9, 2024.

306 NOTES

147 *"flattened by a truck"*: John Quirt, "Putting Barbie Back Together Again," *Fortune*, September 8, 1980.
147 *"diet computer"*: Laura Landro, "With Mattel's New $50 Gadget, Eating Is a Series of Calculations," *Wall Street Journal*, January 25, 1982.
147 *"Intellivision"*: Stephen J. Sansweet, "Mattel Tries to Lure Skeptical Consumers by Selling Computer as High-Priced Fun," *Wall Street Journal*, March 14, 1980.
148 *upturned the entire industry*: It was not just that the movie blew past box office expectations; the toys and comics and a range of spin-off merchandise did too. "Never in character merchandising history has there been anything quite like it," Cy Schneider wrote. *Star Wars* triggered such avid demand that the manufacturer, Mattel's rival Kenner, ran out of stock before the first year, instead offering—in lieu of action figures or light sabers—$15 IOUs, essentially symbolic coupons that customers could later exchange for the real toys. It remains one of the most lucrative product licenses in history. Cy Schneider, *Children's Television*, 117–19; Pamela G. Holllie, "Santa Brings I.O.U.'s for *Star Wars*," *New York Times*, December 15, 1977; John Quirt, "Putting Barbie Back Together Again," *Fortune*, September 8, 1980; Alex Ben Block, "The Real Force Behind *Star Wars*: How George Lucas Built an Empire," *Hollywood Reporter*, February 9, 2012.
148 *"unbelievably ripped"*: Brian C. Baer, *How He-Man Mastered the Universe: Toy to Television to the Big Screen*, McFarland and Company, 2017, 25.
148 *the video game market collapsed*: Gary Putka, "Pounding of Home Video Game Sellers Spreads to Suppliers, Others Amid Weak Holiday Sales," *Wall Street Journal*, December 10, 1982; Laura Landro and Susan Feeney, "Fierce Competition in Video Games Behind Dive in Warner Stock Price," *Wall Street Journal*, December 10, 1982.
148 *"the most vulnerable"*: Stephen J. Sansweet, "Troubles at Mattel Seen Extending Beyond Fallout in Electronics Line," *Wall Street Journal*, December 1, 1983.
149 *"I believed in Barbie"*: Jessica Berens, "The Barbie Army," *Daily Telegraph*, December 20, 1997.
149 *"We were concerned"*: Connie Bruck, *The Predator's Ball*, 292.
149 *"The investor group"*: Scot J. Paltrow, "Mattel Plans to Give 45% Voting Stake to Group That Will Invest $231 Million," *Wall Street Journal*, May 4, 1984.
149 *"It just took the ability"*: Robert Gillott, "Debt Swaps Could Easy Latin Crisis," Associated Press via *Daily Press*, July 29, 1987.
149 *"buxom models"*: James B. Stewart, *Den of Thieves*, 137.

CHAPTER 15

150 *"Those were the days"*: Jerry Oppenheimer, *Toy Monster*, 111.
150 *$10.1 million settlement*: Jerry Oppenheimer, *Toy Monster*, 94.
151 *grew on command. "Of course, we didn't"*: "For Christmas, Dolls That Grow and Dolls That Don't," *New York Times*, November 22, 1975.
151 *plastic scrotum*: Rob Goldberg, *Radical Play*, 198.
151 *death threats*: M. G. Lord, *Forever Barbie*, 101.
151 *$100 million*: "Mattel's Successful Retreat," *Businessweek*, May 16, 1977.
151 *115 million*: Sue Wahlgren, "You've Come a Long Way . . . Barbie!," *Sunday Herald-Leader*, March 16, 1980.
152 *"Because the costumes"*: M. G. Lord, *Forever Barbie*, 112.

NOTES   307

152 *Kitty Black Perkins*: Elise Preston, "Kitty Black Perkins, who designed the first Black Barbie, reflects on her legacy," CBS News, February 22, 2024; Stephanie Finnegan, "Groundbreaking Glamor: 40+ Years Ago, the First Black Barbie Debuted," *Dolls*, February 24, 2020.
152 *"creating whole worlds"*: M. G. Lord, *Forever Barbie*.
153 *Carl von Clausewitz*: Philip Kotler and Ravi Singh, "Marketing Warfare in the 1980s," *Journal of Business Strategy* 1, Issue 3, Winter 1981.
153 *"Marketing warfare was really the key"*: *The Toys That Made Us*, Season 1, Episode 2, Dir. Tom Stern, December 22, 2017.
153 *"psychological warfare"*: Philip Kotler and Ravi Singh, "Marketing Warfare in the 1980s."
153 *Huggies . . . Luvs*: Davis Dyer, Frederick Dalzell, and Rowena Olegario, *Rising Tide: Lessons from 165 Years of Brand Building at Procter & Gamble*, Harvard Business School Press, 2004, 229.
153 *"In marketing"*: *The Toys That Made Us*, Season 1, Episode 2.
153 *"He said : Juuuuudy"*: *The Toys That Made Us*, Season 1, Episode 2.
154 *Hasbro had spent decades*: G. Wayne Miller, *Toy Wars: The Epic Struggle Between G.I. Joe, Barbie, and the Companies That Make Them*, Crown Business, 1998, 73–74.
154 *"snatch the No. 1"*: Philip S. Gutis, "Trying to Run a Bigger Hasbro," *New York Times*, August 4, 1985.
154 *sixteen hours*: *The Toys That Made Us*, Season 1, Episode 2.
154 *"Jem"*: Wendy Fox, "A Jem of a Challenge to Barbie," *Boston Globe*, November 4, 1986; Robert Perkins, "Toy Fair: A Buying Binge to Fill Santa's Bag," *Morning Union*, February 16, 1986; Robin Schatz, "Look Out Barbie Fans, Here Comes Jem," *Newsday*, February 17, 1986.
155 *"Credible first year"*: Wendy Fox, "A Jem of a Challenge to Barbie," *Boston Globe*, November 4, 1986.
155 *"We had that thing"*: *The Toys That Made Us*, Season 1, Episode 2.
155 *"clearly meant to be"*: Robert Perkins. "Toy Fair."
155 *"Whereas Barbie is"*: Gini Zemo, "Has Barbie's Competition Debuted?," *Ashbury Park Press*, December 7, 1986.
156 *"Jem happens to have pink hair"*: Ken Tucker, "So, Barbie, you wanna be a rock 'n roll star?," *Republic*, December 17, 1986.
156 *"The result"*: G. Wayne Miller, *Toy Wars*, 74–75.
156 *make the list*: Bill Menezes, "High-Tech Toys Beckon Christmas Shoppers," Associated Press via *Daily Item*, December 1, 1986.
156 *after two years*: G. Wayne Miller, *Toy Wars*, 74–75.
156 *"damn great bosoms"*: "The Sindy Project," Our Sindy Museum.
156 *"Dawn"*: "Talk of the Town: Dawn," *New Yorker*, March 20, 1971.
156 *Brooke Shields doll*: "Brooke Shields," Celebrity Doll Museum.
157 *open-ended . . . "direct shot at Maxie"*: James Hirsch, "Wary Toy Makers Exploit the Tired and Profitable," *New York Times*, February 18, 1989.
157 *"We have a concept [Barbie]"*: Patricia Gallagher, "Kenner Challenges Barbie with Miss America Doll," *Cincinnati Enquirer*, February 12, 1991.
157 *"Barbie says Miss America ripped"*: Marjorie Williams, "Toy Store Catfight," *Washington Post* via *Press & Sun-Bulletin*, August 2, 1991.

308 NOTES

157 *"heavyweight coalition"* . . . *"depended on its launch"*: "Barbie Wins a Round in Battle of the Dolls," Associated Press via *Star-Ledger*, September 26, 1991.
158 *"army of imitators"*: Nancy Gibbs, "Living: What Do You Want from Santa?," *Time*, December 12, 1988.
158 *"just superficial"*: Lisa Bannon, "Barbie's Booster: Toying with the Doll's Outdated Image Shaped Barad's Fortunes at Mattel," *Wall Street Journal*, March 11, 1997.
158 *1981*: "Two Executives Promoted by Mattel," *New York Times*, July 24, 1992.
158 *"fancy clothes"*: Hannah Tulinski, "Barbie as Cultural Compass: Embodiment, Representation, and Resistance Surrounding the World's Most Iconized Doll," *Cross Works*, College of the Cross, 2017.
158 *"used her good looks"*: Nancy Rivera Brooks, "Barbie's Doting Sister," *Los Angeles Times*, December 10, 1990.
158 *"highest-ranking female executive in the world"*: Interview with Judy Shackelford, May 20, 2024.
159 *"beyond anyone's wildest dreams"*: Kathleen Morris, "The Rise of Jill Barad," *Bloomberg*, May 21, 1998.
159 *"Barad's team"* . . . *give interviews*: Lisa Bannon, "Barbie's Booster."
159 *"marketed herself"*: Gretchen Morgenson, "Barbs of Criticism Slung at Barad," *New York Times* via *Austin-American Statesman*, November 13, 1999.
159 *one successor, but three*: David J. Jefferson, "Mattel Slates a Restructuring of Management," *Wall Street Journal*, October 28, 1986.
159 *four thousand workers*: "Mattel to Close Its Operations in Philippines: Bitter Strike Blames, 4,000 Will Lose Jobs," *Los Angeles Times*, January 29, 1988.
160 *"She led me to believe"*: Lisa Bannon, "Barbie's Booster."
160 *taken over new role*: "On the Move," *News Pilot*, August 21, 1986.
160 *"Barbie's flame"*: Carla Steiger-Meister, "Of Dolls, Barbie Is Still Queen," *New York Times*, February 12, 1989.
160 *"deal with history"*: Carey Winfrey, "Noxious Bogs & Amorous Elephants," *Smithsonian*, November 2005.
160 *"unabashed victory"*: Francis Fukuyama, "The End of History," *National Interest*, Summer 1989.
160 *"a symbol of perestroika"*: Tatyana Volskaya, "When Barbie Conquered the Soviet Union," RadioFreeEurope, March 9, 2009.
160 *judge handed him ten years*: Kurt Eichenwald, "Milken Gets 10 Years for Wall St. Crimes," *New York Times*, November 22, 1990.
160 *full-page ads*: Gail Appleson, "Top Execs Support Milken in Rousing Newspaper Ads," Reuters via *San Francisco Examiner*, April 1, 1989; John M. Doyle, "Milken, Brother Plead Not Guilty to Charges," Associated Press via *Fresno Bee*, April 8, 1989.
161 *full-throated defense*: Thomas Kalinske, "Milken Deserves Much Praise," *Los Angeles Times*, April 23, 1989.
161 *"the symbol of the 1980s"*: David A. Vise and Steve Coll, "The Two Faces of Greed," *Washington Post*, September 28, 1991.

CHAPTER 16

163 *forty-second year*: Though the convention was founded in 1980, it did not become an annual event until 1982. There was no convention in 1981. Bob Young, *The History of*

NOTES

      Barbie Collecting and Other Barbie Intrigue: An Unauthorized Record, Bob Young and Richard Nations, 2024, 26.
163 *Barbie-related merchandise*: Mia Maquire, "Ruggable's Barbie Collection Will Turn Your Home into a Dreamhouse," *Daily Beast*, April 12, 2023; Kristen Ward, Xbox press release, June 26, 2023; Justine Sterling, "An Honest Review of the New Barbie x Swoon Pink Lemonade," *Sporked*, May 24, 2023; Sander Lutz, "Barbie and Boss Beauties Make Joint Effort to Bring More Women into Web3," *Decrypt*, May 10, 2023.
165 *"There is just a fascination"*: Bob Young, *The History of Barbie Collecting*, 2.
165 *"interpreters of fate"* . . . *"his own collection"* Walter Benjamin, "Unpacking My Library," *Illuminations: Essays and Reflections*, Schocken Books, 1969, 59–67.
165 *The first devotees* . . . *"Barbie Bible"*: Bob Young, *The History of Barbie Collecting*, 2–5.
166 *Soon there was*: Bob Young, *The History of Barbie Collecting*, 104–15. Note: *Miller's* went by several names, initially *Miller's Barbie Collector*, then just *Miller's*, and finally, *Miller's Fashion Doll*.
166 *Mattel kept apprised*: Bob Young, *The History of Barbie Collecting*, 25–26.
166 *several mysteries about*: John Axe, "Billy Boy and Barbie," *Doll Reader*, August/September 1986; "Billy Boy Just Bonkers over Barbie," *Chicago Tribune*, June 5, 1985; Donna Kato, "Forever Barbie: Doll Enchants Designer," *Kansas City Star*, November 8, 1987.
167 *"At the time"* . . . *"rare jewels"*: "À propos des fondateurs," Fondation Tanagra.
168 *"Théâtre de la Mode"*: Juliette Peers, *The Fashion Doll: From Bébé Jumeau to Barbie*, Berg, 2004, 92; BillyBoy*, *Barbie: Her Life and Times*, 136–82.
169 *"He'd rather have one"*: Lala J. P. Lestrade, "Please Draw Me a Barbie Doll," Fondation Tanagra.
169 *apocryphal*: "Gustave Flaubert," *Encyclopédie Larousse*.
169 *300 percent*: "Bye-Bye, Holiday Barbie," *Wall Street Journal* via *Tampa Bay Times*, June 8, 1999.
169 *"Mattel had no intent"*: Mattel employee handbook, ca. 1999.
170 *"You can always"* . . . *"clump of plastic"*: Molly McCarthy, "To Avid Collectors Gathering in Falls, Barbie Always Will Remain Real Doll," *Buffalo News*, July 25, 1992.
170 *"Somebody knew"*: Carol Masciola, "Goodbye, Dollies as Collector's Treasure Is Lost," *Los Angeles Times*, October 14, 1992.
171 *"America's Favorite"*: Ross Anderson, "For the Love of Barbie," *Spy*, September-October 1994, 40–47.
171 *As the investigation* . . . *scalp Offield's collection*: Ross Anderson, "For the Love of Barbie."
172 *"could not stand"* . . . *"too lavish to produce"*: Lala J. P. Lestrade, "Please Draw Me a Barbie Doll."
172 *basement storage*: Anne Bogart, "A Doll for the 90's: Beautiful but No Bimbo," *New York Times*, March 14, 1990.
172 *million dollars*: Hannah Moore, "Why Warhol Painted Barbie," BBC, October 1, 2015.
172 *"basically out of desire"*: Lala J. P. Lestrade, "Please Draw Me a Barbie Doll."
172 *Mdvanii*: Anne Bogart, "A Doll for the 90's."
172n *"came to me in a dream"*: BillyBoy*, *Frocking Life: Searching for Elsa Schiaparelli*, Rizzoli Ex Libris, 2016, 107.
173n *"two monkeys dressed in rich Oriental brocades"*: Neal Gabler, "How an Early Hollywood

Family Became the Original Kardashians," *Los Angeles Magazine*, November 29, 2016.
173 *"to refuse all interviews"*: "Les maîtres des poupées," *L'Hebdo*, November 9, 2006.
173 *"Mattel forbid"*: Lala J. P. Lestrade, "Please Draw Me a Barbie Doll."
173 *250,000 people*: Denise Gellene, "Fits of Pink," *Washington Post*, May 15, 1997.
173 *$35 million . . . $220 million*: "Bye-Bye, Holiday Barbie."
173 *"trimmed with a chainsaw"*: "Barbie-Hair Barbie? Collectors Boycott Mattel over Beloved Pop Culture Icon," Associated Press via *Pharos-Tribune*, May, 11, 1997.
174 *"If De Beers let loose" . . . "We want our hobby back"*: "Bye-Bye, Holiday Barbie."
174 *"Barbie Grants a Wish Weekend"*: Lisa Bannon, "Now, Barbie Favors Legal Suits, Angering Fans and Judges Alike," *Wall Street Journal*, January 6, 1998.
174 *Mattel barred him . . . wine-serving sets*: Carla Wheeler, "The Barbie Wars," *San Bernardino County Sun*, May, 8 1997.
174 *"with barbed product reviews"*: Denise Gellene, "Fits of Pink."
174 *"We want the Millers' house"*: Steve Silberman, "Mattel's Latest: Cease-and-Desist Barbie," *Wired*, October 28, 1997.
175 *"It's just like the sixties"*: "Collectors Boycott Mattel over Bad-Haired Barbies," Associated Press via *Independent*, May 11, 1997.
175 *"PINK ANGER" . . . "Pink Land"*: Denise Gellene, "Fits of Pink."
175 *"bad hair"*: "Barbie-Hair Barbie?"
175 *"This isn't about" . . . "developed the image of Barbie"*: Carla Wheeler, "The Barbie Wars."
175 *The executives eventually*: Beverly Beyette, "Barbie: Celebrating Her 40th Birthday," *Los Angeles Times*, February 9, 1999.
176 *"loves the collectors"*: Denise Gellene, "Fits of Pink."
176 *"This is about big business"*: Carla Wheeler, "The Barbie Wars."

CHAPTER 17

177 *"We should start a business"*: "Critics Question Barbie's Self-Esteem (or Lack Thereof)," *New York Times*, October 2, 1992.
177n *An incomplete list of code names . . . "farts, belches, hacks, vomit"*: Patient reports, 1993–1994, Barbie Liberation Organization records, Igor Vamos.
177 *"patient reports" . . . "you lose your pants"*: Barbie Liberation Organization records, Igor Vamos. Interview with Igor Vamos, August 17, 2023; "BLO First Year Review," Barbie Liberation Organization records, Igor Vamos.
178 *"I've got a very strong negative feeling"*: David Firestone, "While Barbie Talks Tough, G.I. Joe Goes Shopping," *New York Times*, December 31, 1993.
178 *Adrien Piper*: Adam Zucker, "Come On Barbie, Let's Get Arty," Artfully Learning, July 10, 2023; Emily Colucci, "Why Is Everyone Sleeping on Adrian Piper's Teenage Doll Paintings?," Filthy Dreams, May 10, 2018.
178 *Cindy Sherman*: Dan Glaister, "The Girl Can't Help It," *Guardian*, August 8, 1997; "Master of the feminine cliché," *Daily Telegraph*, January 28, 1991.
178 *"Everyone saw a fat nose"*: Marge Percy, "Barbie Doll," *The Decline of Civilization*, December 1994.
179 *"Barbie has been reimagined"*: Dan Hunter and Greg Lastowka, "BarbieTM," *Tulane Journal of Technology & Intellectual Property*, August 15, 2015, 133–60.
179 *Scott C. Schulman*: Scott C. Schulman, "Barbie in Hell," *Harper's*, July 1994.

NOTES 311

179 "*Buddenbrooks Cycle*": Alice Kahn, "A Onetime Bimbo Becomes a Muse," *New York Times*, September 29, 1991.
179 "*Every businessman*": Thomas Mann, Trans. H. T. Lowe-Porter, *Buddenbrooks*, Martin Secker Ltd, 1922, 316–19; *for "abscess," rather than "growth"*: Adam Kirsch, "The Brothers Mann—and Nelly," *New York Review of Books*, October 27, 2011.
179 "*Douglas Sirk's melodramas*" . . . *off-brand Michael Jackson*: Lucas Hilderbrand, *Inherent Vice: Bootleg Histories of Videotape and Copyright*, Duke University Press, 2000.
180 "*HAPPY BIRTHDAY BILL / LOVE SEAN*": "Superstar, the Karen Carpenter Story," Internet Archive, Identifer No: produce-1_202030928, Added: September 28, 2023.
180 "*utilize Barbie's costumes*" . . . "*identical to the doll as possible*": Robert L Bernstein, Letter to Manuel Siwek, October 30, 1963, Random House archives, Columbia University.
181 "*Barbie has no biography*" . . . "*Only glamour befell Barbie*": M. G. Lord, *Forever Barbie*, 149.
181 "*always based on a product of some kind*": Interview with Pegi Goodman, July 17, 2023.
181 "*de-grit*" . . . "*scare*": Erica Rand, *Barbie's Queer Accessories*, Duke University Press, 1995, 58, 201.
181 "*Barbie TV Magazine*": Brian Lowry, "Mattel Jilts Barbie for Captain Power," *Hollywood Reporter*, February 27, 1987.
182 "*a lecture and an escort to the door*": Rachel Burchfield, "Sharon Stone Tried to Make Barbie in the 1990s, but Was Thrown Out of the Studio," *Marie Claire*, March 25, 2024.
182 Toy Story: Sheila Muto, "A Disney Film Gives New Life to Old Toys," *New York Times*, December 1, 1995.
182 *Mattel began inundating*: Lucas Hilderbrand, *Inherent Vice*.
182 *showed up at Haynes's office*: Zac Ntim, "Christine Vachon on the Banned Barbie Movie She Made with Todd Haynes," Deadline, July 3, 2023.
182 *combined legal threats . . . destroy them*: Lucas Hilderbrand, *Inherent Vice*.
182 "*post-literate*" . . . "*telepathy*": Saul Braun, "Life-Styles: The Micro-Bopper," *Esquire*, March 1968.
183 "*the core challenge facing the toy industry*": Fern Shen, "'Toys? But I'm 10 Now!,'" *Washington Post*, February 16, 2002.
183 "*Barbie Style*": Pauline Yoshiashi, "Mattel Shapes a New Future for Barbie," *Wall Street Journal*, February 12, 1990.
183 *Barbie art projects*: Steve Silberman, "Mattel's Latest: Cease-and-Desist Barbie"; Mark Napier, "The Distorted Barbie," *Enterzone*, Issue 7; Vicki Haddock, "It's the Attack of the Anti-Barbies," *San Francisco Examiner*, March 1, 1997; Mark Napier, "Sites That Allegedly Violate Mattel's Copyright," Napier.Interport, November 5, 1997.
184 "*a wave of Barbie knockoffs*": "The Unbearable Lifelessness of Barbie," *Mother Jones*, March 5, 2001.
184 "*Barbie was the blank canvas*": Rebecca Leung, "Becoming Barbie: Living Dolls," CBS News, July 29, 2004.
184 *two undertakings*: Craig Yoe, *The Art of Barbie: Artists Celebrate the World's Favorite Doll*, Workman Publishing Co., 1994; Nathaniel Wise and Steven Daly, *Alt.Culture: An A-to-Z Guide to the '90s Underground, Online and Over-the-Counter*, HarperCollins, 1995.

184 *"Holiday Inn expressionist"*: Franz Linz, "LeRoy, You're a Real Piece of Work," *Sports Illustrated*, October 21, 1985.
184 *World Financial Center*: Michael Kimmelman, "Does It Really Matter Who Sponsors a Show?," *New York Times*, May 19, 1996.
184 *"were horrified"*: Elain Velie, "The Complicated Legacy of Barbie Art," Hyperallergic, July 21, 2023. Burson also posted about the photograph on her Instagram.
184 *"vapid collection of glittering junk"*: M. G. Lord, "The Question Is: What Would Ken Think?," *New York Times*, December 1, 1995.
185 *"Mattel's public relations"*: Steven C. Dubin, "Why Barbie's Show Lacks Substance," *New York Times*, December 11, 1995.

CHAPTER 18

186 *Russ Troll*: Linda Shrieves, "Well-known Faces Are Hitting the Campaign Trail," *Orlando Sentinel* via *Corpus Christi Caller-Times*, August 20, 1992.
186 *Adam McKay*: "Morris the Cat for President? Purr," Associated Press via *Elmira Star-Gazette*, July 23, 1992.
186 *"star-spangled inaugural gown"*: Michael Lollar, "President Barbie Banks on Youth Vote," *Commercial Appeal*, July 17, 1992.
186 *robust toy-store exit polling*: "White House or Doll House? Barbie Begins Political Career," *Tallahassee Democrat*, July 14, 1992.
187 *"abortion issue"*: "For Barbie, Her Time Has Come," *Daily News*, July 13, 1992.
187 *"an exclusive contract"*: Michael Lollar, "President Barbie Banks on Youth Vote."
187 *"Ken, Barbie's preppy pal"*: "White House or Doll House?"
187 *accelerated sales*: Joseph Pereira, "War-Toy Makers Mobilize as Sales Rise," *Wall Street Journal*, January 31, 1991.
187 *Harold Brown*: John Otis, "Harold Brown, Carter Defense Secretary Who Advocated Arms Buildup, Dies at 91," *Washington Post*, January 5, 2019; "United Medicorp's Chairman Is Assuming Duties of President," *Wall Street Journal*, August 15, 1991.
187 *"Totally Hair Barbie"*: Eben Shapiro, "'Totally Hot, Totally Cool,' Long-Haired Barbie Is a Hit," *New York Times*, June 22, 1992.
187 *became Mattel's president*: "Two Executives Promoted by Mattel," *New York Times*, July 24, 1992.
187 *"tinsely gold scarf"*: "Talk of the Town: Right and Fitting," *New Yorker*, February 1, 1993.
187 *"there was a sensation"*: Chuck Klosterman, *The Nineties: A Book*, Penguin Press, 2022, 34.
188 *"Big Mergers Get Bigger in the '90s"*: Tim Smart, "Big Mergers Get Bigger in the '90s," *Washington Post*, October 26, 1997.
188 *"The most powerful"*: Naomi Klein, *No Logo: Taking Aim at the Brand Bullies*, Picador, 2000, 178.
188 *"playing monopoly" . . . 60 percent*: Joseph Pereira, "Playing Monopoly: The Toy Industry, Too, Is Merging Like Crazy to Win Selling Power," *Wall Street Journal*, October 28, 1994.
188 *"The predominance of Toys"*: Sydney Ladensohn Stern and Ted Schoenhaus, *Toyland: The High-Stakes Game of the Toy Industry*, Contemporary Books, 1990, 275.
188 *"On a relative basis"*: Pauline Yoshihashi, "Mattel Inc. Looks Forward to Christmas with Visions of $$$ Dancing on Its Head," *Wall Street Journal*, October 15, 1990.

NOTES 313

188 *$5.2 billion*: Stephen J Sansweet, "Toy Story: Mattel Offers $5 Billion in Unsolicited Bid for Rival Hasbro," *Wall Street Journal*, January 25, 1996.

188 *"bear hug"*: Steven Lipin, "Bidders Shun Hostile Label for Talks," *Wall Street Journal*, February 2, 1996.

188 *"Barbie proposed"*: G. Wayne Miller, *Toy Wars*, 292.

188 *"It could be the apocalypse"*: Joseph Pereira, "Toy Retailers Fear Playing with 'Mat-Bro,'" *Wall Street Journal*, January 26, 1996.

188 *rallying an opposition*: G. Wayne Miller, *Toy Wars*. 294–295.

189 *"scorched earth"*: Andy Pasztor, Joseph Pereira, and Steven Lipin, "Hasbro Faces New Stuggles Post-Mattel," *Wall Street Journal*, February 5, 1996.

189 *"There is no question"*: Andy Pasztor, "Mattel Growth Strategy to Pursue Acquisitions, Overseas Expansion," *Wall Street Journal*, July 15, 1996.

189 *bought Tyco*: Lisa Bannon and Joseph Pereira, "No. 1 Toy Maker Mattel Agrees to Buy No. 3 Tyco in $755 Million Stock Deal," *Wall Street Journal*, November 19, 1996.

189 *"Clinton Economic Conference"*: "Jill E. Barad and Clinton Economic Conference," C-SPAN user clip, December 14,1992.

189 *"bring down more barriers"*: Bob Davis and Lawrence Ingrassia, "After Years of Talks, GATT Is At Last Ready to Sign Off on a Pact," *Wall Street Jounral*, December 15, 1993.

189 *"pre-empt the regulatory"*: Daphne Wysham, "Big Business Hijacks the GATT," *The Nation*, December 17, 1990.

189 *"coddling dictators"*: John M. Broder and Jim Mann, "Clinton Reverses His Policy, Renews China Trade Status," *Los Angeles Times*, May 27, 1994.

190 *crackdown*: "Indonesia: Labour activists under fire," Amnesty International, April 30, 1994.

190 *pressing Western values . . . "severely impair Mattel's competitiveness"*: Eyal Press, "Barbie's Betrayal: The Toy Industry's Broken Workers," *The Nation*, December 30, 1996.

190 *Barbie factory in Bekasi*: Urban C. Lehner, "Barbie and Ken in Indonesia," *Wall Street Journal*, January 8, 1992.

190 *December of 1993*: Bob Davis and Lawrence Ingrassia, "After Years of Talks."

190 *"Barbie is the big winner"*: "U.S. Businesses Like Trade Pact as Whole, but Not Some Parts," *Wall Street Journal*, December 16, 1993.

190 *NAFTA*: Michael Wilson, "The North American Free Trade Agreement: Ronald Reagan's Vision Realized," The Heritage Foundation, November 23, 1993; Martin Crutsinger, "Trade Pact Sanctions Get Mixed Reviews," Associated Press via *Kokomo Tribune*, May 16, 1993.

190 *NAFTA would really benefit*: Richard W. Stevenson, "Selling a Free-Trade Pact with Mexico," *New York Times*, November 11, 1990.

190 *Fermín Cuza*: "With Nafta, Analysts See Winners, Losers," *Los Angeles Times*, November 14, 1993; "North American Free Trade Agreement: Hearings Before the Committee on Ways and Means and Its Subcommittee on Trade," U.S. House of Representatives, One Hundred Second Congress, Second Session, September 9, 15, 17, and 22, 1992, U.S. Government Printing Office, 1993.

191 *"increased company imports"*: Eyal Press, "Barbie's Betrayal."

191 *"sixth consecutive year"*: Andy Pasztor and lIsa Bannon, "Former Executive Says Mattel Inflated Sales and Used Questionable Earnings," *Wall Street Journal*, April 3, 1996.

314 NOTES

191 *"poster children of NAFTA"*: Michelle Mittelstadt, "Study: NAFTA Fails to Create New Jobs," Associated Press via *Ukiah Daily Journal*, September 4, 1995.

191 *Public Citizen study*: Bob Herbert, "Job Losses Only Thing NAFTA Created," *New York Times* via *Spokesman Review*, September 14, 1995.

191 *$20 billion*: Andrew Glass, "Clinton Bails Out Mexico, Jan. 31, 1995," *Politico*, January 31, 2019.

191 *"Mexico's junk-bond financier"*: Allen R. Myerson, "Has the U.S. Got a Horse for You: Mexico," *New York Times*, January 22, 1995.

191 *Zigong . . . "his desperate face"*: "Testimony of Li Qiang, Executive Director of China Labor Watch," U.S. China Economic Security Review Commission, Hearing on China's State Control Mechanisms and Methods, April 14, 2005, Washington, D.C.

191 *three years . . . fake passport*: Ambreen Ali, "Who's Afraid of Li Qiang?," The Wire China, May 17, 2020.

192 *C-SPAN*: "Qiang Li—2000," C-SPAN user clip, May 22, 2000.

192 *stiletto . . . "one of the few public sources"*: Ambreen Ali, "Who's Afraid of Li Qiang?"

192 *"a personal feud"*: Interview with Li Qiang, August 28, 2023.

192 *Hu Nianzhen*: Li Qiang, "Urgent Appeal for Help: Mattel Supplier Factory Female Workers Committed Suicide," China Labor Watch press release, June 29, 2011; Li Quiang, "Response to Mattel's Letter," China Labor Watch, December 2, 2015; "Mattel Odpowiedzialny Za Samobójstwo Pracowniczki?," Fabryka Koumikacji Spoleczne release, November 14, 2011.

193 *"motel" . . . "sterilization"*: Barbara Ehrenreich and Annette Fuentes, *Women in the Global Factory*, South End Press, 1983, 21.

193 *minimum wage*: Erica Rand, *Barbie's Queer Accessories*, 71.

193 *Harper's published*: Jeffrey Balliner, "Nike: The New Free-Trade Heel," *Harper's*, August 1992.

193 *Kathie Lee Gifford*: Barry Bearak, "Kathie Lee and the Sweatshop Crusade," *Los Angeles Times*, June 14, 1996.

193 *girl in Guangdong*: Kathy Chen, "A Teenager's Journey Mirrors Inner Migration That's Changing China," *Wall Street Journal*, October 29, 1996.

193 *"off-guard"*: Prakesh Sethi, Emre Veral, Jack Shaprio, and Olga Emiliavanova, "Mattel Inc.: Global Manufacturing Principles—A Life-Cycle Analysis of a Company-Based Code of Conduct in the Toy Industry," *Journal of Business Ethics*, November 16, 2011.

193 *"Simply stated"*: "Mattel Bans Child Labor in Its Factories," Reuters via *Fort McMurray Today*, November 21, 1997; "Union Plan Vetoed by Shareholders," Associated Press via *Atlanta Journal*, May 8, 1998.

193 *"maze of warring codes" . . . "Communist Manifesto"*: Naomi Klein, *No Logo*, 433.

194 *"It was totally unprecedented" . . . "an unparalleled degree of oversight"*: Jonathan Dee, "A Toymaker's Conscience," *New York Times Magazine*, December 23, 2007.

194 *"considerable pressure"*: Prakesh Sethi, Emre Veral, Jack Shaprio, and Olga Emiliavanova, Mattel, Inc.: Global Manufacturing Principles (GMP)—A Life-Cycle Analysis of a Company-Based Code of Conduct in the Toy Industry, *Journal of Business Ethics*, 2011.

194 *"I brought Ruth back"*: Robin Gerber, *Barbie and Ruth*, 247.

194 *John Amerman*: Ruth Handler papers, Box 33, Folder 2.

194 *"Ambassador of Dreams"*: Ruth Handler papers, Box 15, Folder 18.

NOTES   315

194   *started to slow*: Kathleen Morris, "The Rise of Jill Barad," *Businessweek*, May 25, 1998; "Mattel Shares Sink on News That Results Will Trail Forecasts," *Wall Street Journal*, July 3, 1996.

195   *Michele Greenwald*: Andy Pasztor, "Mattel Methods of Accounting Are Scrutinized," *Wall Street Journal*, April 11, 1996; Reed Abelson, "Truth or Consequences? Hardly," *New York Times*, June 23, 1996; "Mattel Documents Raise More Questions About Accounting," *Wall Street Journal*, July 12, 1996; Andy Pasztor and Lisa Bannon, "Former Executive Says Mattel Inflated Sales and Used Questionable Accounting," *Wall Street Journal*, April 3, 1996; Reed Abelson, "Mattel Clear of Accusations of Accounting Regularities," *New York Times*, July 17, 1996; Lisa Bannon, "Mattel Wins Victory in Suit Against Former Executive," *Wall Street Journal*, December 6, 1996; Lisa Bannon and Andy Pasztor, "Mattel CEO Moves to Shed Some Units, as Fourth-Quarter Profit Comes in Flat," *Wall Street Journal*, February 6, 1997.

195   *price-fixing conspiracy*: Federal Trade Commission v. Toys R Us, Inc., FTC No. 091 0082, Case No. 111-cv-00635 (7th Cir).

195   *settled a related lawsuit*: Dana Canedy, "Toys 'R' Us Settles Federal Antitrust Case," *New York Times*, May 26, 1999.

195   *"Barbie could no longer grow"*: John W. Torget and Sydney Finkelstein, "Learning from Mattel," Case No. 1-0072, Tuck School of Business at Dartmouth, 2002.

196   *"Cutting guidance twice" . . . "are getting a lot worse"*: Interview with Sean McGowan, May 31, 2023.

CHAPTER 19

197   *"the 'plastic' world of Barbie"*: Mattel Inc. v. MCA Records Inc., Case No. 97-6791 WMB (RNBx), Dkt 25, November 3, 1997.

197   *reggae dance cover*: At the time, they were playing under the name "Joyspeed." See: "Joyspeed—Itzy Bitzy Spider," Discogs.

197   *"If there are such funny"*: Mattel Inc. v. MCA Records Inc., Case No. 97-6791 WMB (RNBx), Dkt 25, November 3, 1997.

197   *340,000 copies*: Mattel Inc. v. MCA Records Inc., Case No. 97-6791 WMB (RNBx), Dkt 25, November 3, 1997.

197   *"antisocial themes" . . . "her arm"*: Mattel Inc. v. MCA Records Inc., Case No. 97-6791 WMB (NRx), Dkt 94, February 18, 1998.

197   *destroyed*: Mattel Inc. v. MCA Records Inc., Case No. 97-6791 WMB (RNBx), Dkt 187, August 3, 1998.

198   *Reagan appointee*: "O'Scannlain, Diarmuid Fionntain," Federal Judicial Center.

198   *"vehicle to poke fun"*: Mattel Inc. v. MCA Records Inc., Case No. 97-6791 WMB (RNBx), Dkt 94, February 18, 1998.

198   *"to draw consumer attention"*: Mattel Inc. v. MCA Records Inc., Case No. 97-6791 WMB (RNBx), Dkt 25, November 3, 1997.

198   *"intellectual property bully"*: Dan Hunter and Greg Lastowka, "BarbieTM."

198   *"reflect the world around her"*: Ruth Handler papers, Box 32, Folder 13.

198   *"technology of control"*: Dan Hunter and Greg Lastowka, "BarbieTM."

199   *"a slow erosion"*: Liz Somerstein, "Who Is Really Protecting Barbie: Goliath or the Silver Knight? A Defense of Mattel's Aggressive International Attempts to Protect Its Barbie Copyright and Trademark," *University of Miami Inter-American Law Review* (2008).

NOTES

199 The Great Republic's Peanut Stand: Siva Vaidhyanatha, *Copyrights and Copywrongs: The Rise of Intellectual Property and How it Threatens Creativity*, NYU Press, 2001, 69–80; Margalit Fox, "The Rights of Writers as a Twain Obsession," *New York Times*, February 16, 1998.
199 *eighteen thousand parts*: "Paige Compositor," Asme.org.
199 *unsanctioned mural of Minnie Mouse*: Brooks Barnes, "Mickey's Copyright Adventure: Early Disney Creation Will Soon Be Public Property," *New York Times*, December 27, 2022.
199 *"copyright in the American tradition"*: Siva Vaidhyanatha, *Copyrights and Copywrongs*, 11.
200 *"If nature has made"* ... *"harassment by lawsuits"*: Thomas Jefferson, *The Basic Writings of Thomas Jefferson*, Wiley, 1944, 712–14.
200 *"limited"*: Article I, Section 8, Clause 8, U.S. Constitution.
200 *first state copyright statute*: Siva Vaidhyanatha, *Copyrights and Copywrongs*, 44.
200 *"Whatever First Amendment"*: Alex Kozinski, "Trademarks Unplugged," *Trademark Reporter* 84, No. 4 (July–August 1994): 441–59.
200 *first known use*: Mark A. Lemley, "Property, Intellectual Property, and Free Riding," *Texas Law Review* 83, 2005.
200 *"hostile to patent owners"* ... *"in favor of patent holders"*: Joseph B. White, "Patent Injustice? How a Detroit Inventor Battled Years to Prove Ford Stole His Ideas," *Wall Street Journal*, April 6, 1990. (For suspicion of monopolies, see: Siva Vaidhyanatha, *Copyrights and Copywrongs*, 24.)
201 *"distinctive quality"*: *Mattel Inc. v. MCA Records Inc.*, 296. F.3rd. 894 (9th Cir. 2002), July 24, 2002.
201 *"scents, sounds, and colors"*: Rochelle Cooper Dreyfuss, "Reconciling Trademark Rights and Expressive Values: How to Stop Worrying and Learn to Love Ambiguity," *Trademark Law And Theory: A Handbook of Contemporary Research*, Graeme B. Dinwoodie and Mark D. Janis, eds., Edward Elgar Press, 2007.
201 *"Actually"* ... *"Sonny wanted"*: "Sonny Bono Copyright Term Extension Act," Congressional Record—House, October 7, 1998.
201 *"as many as 100"*: Joan H. Murphy, "Mattel—Where Security Isn't Child's Play," *Security Management* 34, Issue 1, January 1990.
201 *Petra*: Linda Rapattoni, "Barbie's Mattel Wants to Stop Swedish Doll Ads," UPI, March 23, 1991.
201 *Rockette figurine*: *Mattel Inc. v. Radio City Entertainment*, 63 U.S.P.Q.2d 1479 (S.D.N.Y. 2002), June 12, 2002.
201 *Claudene Christian*: *Christian v. Mattel, Inc.*, 286 F.3d 1118, 62 U.S.P.Q.2d 1385 (9th Cir. 2002), April 15, 2002; *Mattel, Inc. v. Luce, Forward, Hamilton & Scripps*, No. B143260, 2001 BL 5968 (Cal. App. 2d Dist.) December 13, 2001.
202 *Sindy* ... *"unwanted twin sister"*: G. Wayne Miller, *Toy Wars*, 66, 75–78.
202 *headlines*: Elsa McAlonan, "It's the Big Battle of the Toy Blondes, *Daily Record*, January 30, 1991; Martin Phillips, "Barbie's Barbs Hit Sindy for Six," *Daily Record*, December 23, 1992.
202 *"suburban nothing"*: Paul Farhi, "Mattel Forces Rival to Surgically Alter Doll," *Washington Post* via *Record Searchlight*, December 26, 1992.
202 *"Until the mid-1980s"*: Orly Lobel, *You Don't Own Me*.

NOTES 317

202 idea-expression: Siva Vaidhyanatha, *Copyrights and Copywrongs*; Robert C. Osterberg and Eric C. Osterberg, *Substantial Similarity in Copyright Law*.

202 "*of necessity vague*" . . . "*substantial similarity*": *Ideal v. Fab-Lu*, 360 F.2d 1021, 149 U.S.P.Q. 800 (2d Cir. 1966), May 23, 1966. Note: in the case of the former quote—"of necessity vague"—the judge is citing an earlier opinion, *Peter Pan Fabrics, Inc. v. Martin Weiner Corp.*, 274 F.2d 487, 489 (2d Cir. 1960).

202 more utilitarian than artistic: *Durham Industries, Inc. v. Tomy Corporation*, 630 F.2d 905 (2d Cir. 1980).

202 "*To extend copywritability*": *L. Batlin & Son, Inc., Appellee, v. Jeffrey Snyder D/b/a J. S. N. Y. and Etna Products Co.*, Appellants, 536 F.2d 486 (2d Cir. 1976).

203 "*no other way to trademark*": Dan Hunter and Greg Lastowka, "BarbieTM."

203 "*eternal look of compliant joy*" . . . "*has an overbite*": Marjorie Williams, "Toy Store Cat Fight," *Washington Post* via *Press & Sun Bulletin*, August 2, 1991.

203 egg cartons: Keith Kupferschmid, "Barbie: An IP Girl in an IP World," Copyright Alliance, August 3, 2023.

203 "*main thing*" . . . "*without any clothes on*": G. Wayne Miller, *Toy Wars*, 76–78.

203 "*five distinct disembodied*" . . . "*distance from Barbie's features*": Jake Rosen, "Doll Wars: When Barbie Dragged Sindy to Court," Mental Floss, January 19, 2017.

204 "*virginal*" . . . "*may need Botox in not too long a time*": *Mattel Inc. v. Radio City Entertainment*, "Brief for Plaintiff-Appellant" (2d Cir. 2006), March 3, 2006.

204 "*central features*" . . . "*will suffice*": *Mattel, Inc. v. Goldberger Doll Mfg. Co.*, 365 F.3d 133, 70 U.S.P.Q.2d 1469 (2d Cir. 2004).

204 "*fervent capitalist*" . . . "*she didn't like*": Jeffrey Cole, "My Afternoon with Alex: An Interview with Judge Kozinski," Litigation 30, No. 4, Summer 2004: 6–20, 74–75.

204 "*a prominent defender*": Emily Bazelon, "The Big Kozinski," *Legal Affairs*, January/February 2004.

204 email list: Scott Glover, "Judge Emailed Jokes to 'Gag List,'" *Los Angeles Times*, December 8, 2008.

204 "*Gay Olympics*": *Intern. Olympic Comm. v. San Francisco Arts*, 789 F.2d 1319 (9th Cir. 1986).

204 New Kids on the Block: *New Kids on the Block v. News Am. Publ'g, Inc.*, 971 F.2d 302, 23 U.S.P.Q.2d 1534, 20 Med. L. Rptr. 1468 (9th Cir. 1992), July 24, 1992.

205 "*If this were a sci-fi melodrama*" . . . "*Party Girl*": *Mattel Inc. v. MCA Records Inc.*, 296. F.3rd. 894 (9th Cir. 2002), July 24, 2002.

205 "*Words and images do*": Alex Kozinski, "Trademarks Unplugged," *Trademark Reporter* 84, No. 4 (July–August 1994): 441–59.

205 "*The parties . . . are advised to chill*": *Mattel Inc. v. MCA Records Inc.*, 296. F.3rd. 894 (9th Cir. 2002), July 24, 2002.

205 "*My Daddy Swears*": Vicki Haddock, "It's the Attack of the Anti-Barbies."

205 $2,000 . . . $1.2 billion: "Judge Says No to Mattel's Effort to Stop Artist's Photographic Critiques of Barbie," ACLU press release, September 25, 2000.

206 Thomas Forsythe: *Mattel v. Walking Mountain Prod.*, Case No. 2:99-cv-08543-RSWL-RZ, Dkt 123, October 11, 2000; *Mattel v. Walking Mountain Prod.*, 353 F.3d 792 (9th Cir. 2003).

206 Barbie dealer in Ohio: Lisa Bannon, "Now, Barbie Favors Legal Suits."

318 NOTES

206 *"virtually unheard of"*: Dan Hunter and Greg Lastowka, "BarbieTM."
206 *Susan Pitt*: "'Bondage Barbie' Gets a Boost," CBS News, November 8, 2002; Rebecca Tushnet, "Make Me Walk, Make Me Talk, Do Whatever You Please: Barbie and Exceptions," *Georgetown Law Faculty Publications and Other Works*, 2013, 1228; *Mattel Inc. v. Pitt*, 229 F. Supp. 2d 315, 64 U.S.P.Q.2d 1950 (S.D.N.Y. 2002).
206 *"Look, ma'am" . . . "sense of humor"*: Lisa Bannon, "You Can Call Her Barbie-Sue," *Wall Street Journal* via *News and Observer*, January 12, 1998.
206 *Hansen settled*: *Montwillo v. Tull*, 632 F. Suppl.2d 917 (N.D.Cal 2008).
206 *Adios Barbie*: Christian Berthelsen, "Mattel Sues Publisher Over Barbie Essays," *New York Times*, December 6, 1999.
206 *"waging one of the corporate world's"*: Lisa Bannon, "Now, Barbie Favors Legal Suits."

CHAPTER 20

207 *Less than a third*: "Americans Going Online . . . Explosive Growth, Uncertain Destinations," Pew Research Center, October 16, 1995.
207 *25 million*: "Battle for the Soul of the Internet," *Time*, July 25, 1994.
207 *"Tell me about" . . . "without blinking"*: "barbie dolls," Usenet post on alt.folklore.computers, April 5 1994.
208 *went viral*: "[alt.folklore.computers] Re: barbie dolls," Usenet post on alt.humor-best-of-usenet, April 15 1994; "Helen Keller Jokes!," Usenet post on rec.humor, May 6, 1995.
208 *"keep Mattel from getting upset"*: "What's the Point?," *Hacker Barbe Dream Basement Apartment*, December 1995.
208 *fake press release*: "Hacker Barbe Is Hacked," *Hacker Barbe Dream Basement Apartment*, May 6, 1994.
208 *"the official source"*: Mary Rogers, *Barbie Culture*, Sage Publications, 1999, 97.
208 *"Mattel's first official foray"*: Laurie Flynn, "Mattel to Sell Its Own Brand of Software," *New York Times*, December 25, 1995.
208 *"The Net was built" . . . "ever existed"*: "Battle for the Soul of the Internet."
209 *Among their many targets*: Anna Holmes, "Throwaway Bags," *New York Times*, January 10, 1999; Lisa Bannon, "Now, Barbie Favors Legal Suits"; Margot Mifflin, "These Magazines Offer More Than Just Girl Talk," *New York Times*, November 12, 1995; Alexandra Pecharich, "Author of 'Barbieland' Poems Talks About the Blockbuster Movie and Her Conflicted Relationship with the Famous Doll," FIU News, August 10, 2023; Mark Napier, "Sites That Allegedly Violate Mattel's Copyright," Napier.interport, November 5, 1997; Arlyn Tobias Gajilan, "Another Battle Over Barbie," Salon, May 18 1997; "Hey Kids! It's the 'Klaus Barbie'!," ArtComic.com, August 7, 1997; Letter from Mattel to Benjamin Wade, January 27, 1997; "More from Mattel," Usenet post on bit.mailing-list.cni-copyright, December 6, 1997.
209 *"We will protect our trademark"*: Arlyn Tobias Gajilan, "Another Battle Over Barbie."
209 *"only when she produced"*: Rosemary Coombe and Andrew Herman, "Culture Wars on the Net: Trademarks, Consumer Politics and Corporate Accountability on the World Wide Web," *South Atlantic Quarterly* 100, special issue on "Culture and the Law," ed. Gaurav Desai: 919–47.
209 *Barbie-related websites*: *Mattel Inc. v. Adventure Apparel*, No. Civ. 4085 (RWS) (S.D.N.Y. September 6, 2001); Randy Maniloff, "Meet Lawsuit Barbie: She's Been Busy at

Barbie's Courthouse," *ABA Journal*, July 25, 2023; *Mattel v. Internet Dimensions*, No. 55 U.S.P.Q.2d 1620, 5 ILRD 682 (S.D.N.Y. July 13, 2000); *Mattel, Inc. v. Barbie-Club.com*, No. 310 F.3d 293 (2d Cir. 2002); 310F.3d293, November 7, 2002; *Mattel, Inc. v. Anderson*, No. 04 CIV. 5275RCC, 2005 WL 1690528 (S.D.N.Y. July 18, 2005); *Mattel, Inc. v. Procount Bus. Servs.*, No. 03 CIV. 7234 (RWS), 2004 WL 502190 (S.D.N.Y. March 10, 2004); *Mattel, Inc. v. Glob. China Networks, LLC*, No. 07 CIV. 7418 (SAS), 2007 WL 3332662 (S.D.N.Y. October 23, 2007); *Mattel, Inc. v. Securenet Info. Servs.*, No. 99 CIV. 11813 (JSM), 2001 WL 521816 (S.D.N.Y. May 16, 2001); *Mattel, Inc. v. Auuisa Store, Inc.*, No. 22-CV-561 (PKC), 2023 WL 3626183 (S.D.N.Y. May 24, 2023).

210 *"despite it being"*: Dan Hunter and Greg Lastowka, "BarbieTM."

210 *"one of the most vociferous"*: Rosemary Coombe and Andrew Herman, "Culture Wars on the Net."

210 *"AN ACTUAL LETTER"*: Mark Napier, "The Barbie Closet," PotatoLand.org.

211n *"Fossil Barbie"*: Barbara Mikkelson and David Mikkelson, "Smithsonian Barbie," Snopes, November 16, 1999; EN Ganin, "The True Story of Harvey Rowe—Author of the 'Smithsonian Barbie' Story," Emganin.tripod.com via Wayback Machine, May 5, 1998.

211 *When Mattel got... dilution*: Mark Napier, "Does The Distorted Barbie Violate Mattel's Copyright?," Napier.Interport, October 30, 1997.

212 *"What's Wrong with McDonald's"*: Paul Lewis and Rob Evans, "McLibel Leaflet Was Co-written by Uncover Police Officer Bob Lambert," *Guardian*, June 21, 2013.

212 *"EToys"*: Adam Wishwart, *Leaving Reality Behind: The Battle for the Soul of the Internet*, Fourth Estate, 2004, 263, 283.

212 *"a unique form of legitimation"... "its own alterity"*: Rosemary Coombe and Andrew Herman, "Culture Wars on the Net."

212 *comment section*: Christian Crumlish, "Comments on The Daily Barbie," Greenspun.com, November 14, 1997.

213 *digital "mirrors"*: Anonymous, "Fighting Corporate censorship with a meme," Enterzone, December 6, 1998.

214 *$1.8 billion*: Abigail Goldman, "Mattel Makes Play to Revive Declining Sales of Barbie," *Los Angeles Times*, February 8, 2002.

214 *"among the 10 worst U.S. acquisitions"*: John W. Torget and Sydney Finkelstein, "Learning from Mattel."

215 *"The short-sellers knew"*: Herb Greenberg, "Mattel Has Nobody to Blame but Itself for The Learning Co. Fiasco," The Street, October 4, 1999.

215 *accumulated deficit*: Bruce Livesey and Tim Kiladze, "Kevin O'Leary: He's Not a Billionaire, He Just Plays One on TV," *Globe and Mail*, September 28, 2012.

215 *"channel stuffing"*: *David Satterthwaite v. Jill E. Barad, et al and Mattel Inc.*, Case No. BC219022. "Derivative Complaint." Superior Court of California, October 25, 1999.

215 *Two executives... left*: Lisa Bannon, "Two Top Mattel Officials to Leave in Reshuffling," *Wall Street Journal*, March 4, 1999.

215 *"wise purchases that will pay off"*: Lauren Klein, "A Precocious Portfolio: Companies Kids Know, Stocks They Can Love," *New York Times*, September 4, 1999.

215 *"had incurred millions of dollars"*: *David Satterthwaite v. Jill E. Barad, et al and Mattel Inc.*,

320 NOTES

       Case No. BC219022. "Derivative Complaint." Superior Court of California. October 25, 1999.
215 *turn a $50 million profit*: Bruce Livesy and Tim Kiladze, "Kevin O'Leary."
216 *"fighting to hold on to her job"* ... *"the full extent of the problems"*: Lisa Bannon, "Mattel Still Doesn't Grasp Snafu at Learning Co.," *Wall Street Journal*, October 8, 1999.
216 *"gone into hiding"*: Gretchen Morgenson, "Barbie's Guru Stumbles; Critics Say Chief's Flaws Weigh Heavily on Mattel," *New York Times*, November 7, 1999.
216 *"The bad news for 1999"* ... *"had on our results"*: Letter to Shareholders, Mattel Annual Report, 1999.
216 *"an undisclosed percentage of future profits"*: David Satterthwaite v. Jill E. Barad, et al and Mattel Inc., Case No. BC219022. "Derivative Complaint." Superior Court of California. October 25, 1999.
216 *"mega-settlement"*: Abigail Goldman, "Mattel Settles Shareholder Lawsuit for $122 Million," *Los Angeles Times*, December 6, 2002.
216 *cushy landing pad*: Lisa Bannon, "Mattel Proxy Says Barad Received Severance Package Near $50 Million," *Wall Street Journal*, May 1, 2000; "Mattel's Ex-Chief Gets a Big Severance Package," Reuters via *New York Times*, May 1, 2000.

PART IV: INTRO

219 *Angels Camp*: Randy Lewis, "The Frog That Jump-Started Mark Twain's Career," *Los Angeles Times*, May 14, 2015.
219 *"queer yarn"* ... *"The papers are copying it"*: Ron Chernow, *Mark Twain*, Penguin Press, 2025, 101–103.
220 *"Even a criminal"*: Unless otherwise indicated, all quotes in this section come from Mark Twain, *The Jumping Frog: In English, Then in French, Then Clawed Back into a Civilized Language Once More By Patient, Unremunerated Toil*, 1903.
220 *In reality, this quote*: "Quote Origin: History Does Not Repeat Itself, But It Rhymes," Quote Investigator, January 12, 2014.

CHAPTER 21

222 *His brother died*: Anne Barrowclough, "Blonde Hair, Blue Eyes, Athletic Build . . . Is Barbie Really an Aryan Fantasy?," *Australian*, March 8, 2014.
222 *news to him*: Greiner & Hausser v Mattel Inc., Case No. 4HK O 4300/01, Landgericht, Nürnberg-Fürth 4. Kammer f. Handelssachen, 4th Division for Commercial Matters, 2002.
222 *"an exact replica of the Lilli doll"*: Mattel v. Greiner & Hausser, Case No. 02-00322 NM (JWJx), Central District of California, "Plaintiff Mattel Inc.'s Notice of Motion and Motion for Preliminary Injuction and Supporting Memorandum," March 1, 2000.
222 *"reporting requirements"* ... *"this deception"*: Greiner & Hausser v Mattel Inc., Case No. 4HK O 4300/01, Landgericht, Nürnberg-Fürth 4. Kammer f. Handelssachen, 4th Division for Commercial Matters, 2002.
223 *"a perpetual ownership interest"*: Mattel v. Greiner & Hausser, Case No. 02-00322 NM (JWJx), Central District of California, "Declaration of Adrian M. Pruetz, Exhibit E," July 1, 2002.

223 *Kraft cheese*: Mattel v. MGA, Case No. 2:04-cv-09049-DOC-RNB, Dkt. 10120, Transcript, March 1, 2011.
223n *"was readily available"*: Mattel v. Greiner & Hausser, Case No. 02-00322 NM (JWJx), Central District of California, "Affidavit of R. Kenton Musgrave," January 31, 2002.
223n *"I have no old documents"*: Mattel v. Greiner & Hausser, Case No. 02-00322 NM (JWJx), Central District of California, "Affidavit of Adrian M. Pruetz, Exhibit D," January 31, 2002.
223n *"Rolf told me that he never knew"*: Dan Miller, "In the Beginning, there was Lilli . . . ," *Miller's*, Winter 1997/1998, 79.
223n *Marx did get permission*: Marx and Hausser v. Mattel, Case No. 341-61 Y, Southern District of California, "Stipulation re: answers to interrogatories," October 2, 1961.
223n *"You never would have predicted"*: Jerry Oppenheimer, *Toy Monster*, 188–89.
224 *"leaner and meaner"*: MGA v. Mattel, Case No. 2:05-cv-02727-SGL-RNB, Dkt. 1, "Complaint," April 13, 2005.
224 *slashing expenses*: "Mattel to Lay Off 980 Workers and Close a Plant," Bloomberg News via *New York Times*, April 5, 2001.
224 *"The downside of this conservative approach"*: Unbylined, "Mattel's New Toy Story," *Bloomberg*, November 18, 2002.
224 *"The house is on fire"* . . . *"All others stand for evil"*: Mattel v. MGA, Case No. 2:04-cv-09049-DOC-RNB, Dkt 10126, Transcript, March 2, 2011.
225 *"Dear CEO"*: Mattel v. MGA, Case No. 2:04-cv-09049-DOC-RNB, Dkt 10182, Transcript, March 9, 2011.
225 *maybe a dozen*: Mattel v. MGA, Case No. 2:04-cv-09049-DOC-RNB, Dkt 10121, Transcript, March 3, 2011.
225 *"little jaundiced"*: Mattel v. MGA, Case No. 2:04-cv-09049-DOC-RNB, Dkt 10182, Transcript, March 9, 2011.
225 *Southern California . . . "Saudi Arabia"*: Mattel v. MGA, Case No. 2:04-cv-09049-DOC-RNB, Dkt 9794, Transcript, February 2, 2011; Mattel v. MGA, Case No. 2:04-cv-09049-DOC-RNB, Dkt. 4371-27, Transcript, July 1, 2008.
225 *interest in art*: Carter Bryant v. Mattel, Case No. CV04-9049-TJH-PJWx, Dkt. 1, "Complaint," November 2, 2004; Mattel v. MGA, Case No. 2:04-cv-09049-DOC-RNB, Dkt 9795, Transcript, February 2, 2011.
226 *"Talk Is Cheap"*: Mattel v. MGA, Case No. 2:04-cv-09049-DOC-RNB, Dkt 9733, Transcript, January 27, 2011.
226 *"one of those weird kids"* . . . *got the gig*: Mattel v. MGA, Case No. 2:04-cv-09049-DOC-RNB, Dkt 9794, Transcript, February 2, 2011.
226 *180,000-square-foot*: Mattel v. MGA, Case No. 2:04-cv-09049-DOC-RNB, Dkt. 4371-2, Transcript, May 27, 2008.
226 *"fit into a preconceived marketing concept"* . . . *"Meet the Bratz"*: Mattel v. MGA, Case No. 2:04-cv-09049-DOC-RNB, Dkt 9794, Transcript, February 2, 2011.
227 *Alaska Momma*: Mattel v. MGA, Case No. 2:04-cv-09049-DOC-RNB, Dkt 10102, Transcript, February 24, 2011.
228 *Kashan . . . not using dumbbells*: Saba Soomekh, "Los Angeles Toy District: Isaac Larian," *Iranian Jewish Life in Los Angeles: Past and Present*, Digital Exhibit, UCLA Center for Jewish Studies, 2015.

322 NOTES

228 *$750 and a yellow blanket*: Parilja Kqvilanz, "He left the slums of Iran as a teen. Now he runs one of America's biggest toy companies," CNN, November 21, 2018.
228 *bankruptcy*: *Mattel v. MGA*, Case No. 2:04-cv-09049-DOC-RNB, Dkt. 4371-18, Transcript, June 11, 2008.
228 *The most powerful man . . . "'buy it'"*: *Mattel v. MGA*, Case No. 2:04-cv-09049-DOC-RNB, Dkt. 4371-16, Transcript, June 10, 2008.
229 *"Frankly speaking"*: *Mattel v. MGA*, Case No. 2:04-cv-09049-DOC-RNB, Dkt. 4371-17, Transcript, June 10, 2008.
229 *loose rice*: *Mattel v. MGA*, Case No. 2:04-cv-09049-DOC-RNB, Dkt 9844, Transcript, February 8, 2011.
229 *"It was like a robot"*: *Mattel v. MGA*, Case No. 2:04-cv-09049-DOC-RNB, Dkt. 4371-18, Transcript, June 11, 2008.
229 *"like an alien"*: *Mattel v. MGA*, Case No. 2:04-cv-09049-DOC-RNB, Dkt. 4371-14, Transcript, June 6, 2008.
229 *"They looked weird"*: *Mattel v. MGA*, Case No. 2:04-cv-09049-DOC-RNB, Dkt. 4371-17, Transcript, June 10, 2008.
229 *"She's skinny?"*: *Mattel v. MGA*, Case No. 2:04-cv-09049-DOC-RNB, Dkt 9794, Transcript, February 2, 2011.
230 *"plays drums"*: *Mattel v. MGA*, Case No. 2:04-cv-09049-DOC-RNB, Dkt 9794, Transcript, February 2, 2011.
230 *"We were probably taking"*: *Mattel v. MGA*, Case No. 2:04-cv-09049-DOC-RNB, Dkt. 4371-17, Transcript, June 10, 2008.
230 *without telling his boss*: *Mattel v. MGA*, Case No. 2:04-cv-09049-DOC-RNB, Dkt. 4371-4, Transcript, May 28, 2008.
230 *"Carter, this is your big break"*: *Mattel v. MGA*, Case No. 2:04-cv-09049-DOC-RNB, Dkt. 4371-17, Transcript, June 10, 2008.
230 *"va-va-voom"*: *Mattel v. MGA*, Case No. 2:04-cv-09049-DOC-RNB, Dkt. 4371-7, Transcript, May 29, 2008.
230 *"cautious not to over stereotype"*: *Mattel v. MGA*, Case No. 2:04-cv-09049-DOC-RNB, Dkt. 4371-8, Transcript, May 30, 2008.
230 *Scotch tape*: *Mattel v. MGA*, Case No. 2:04-cv-09049-DOC-RNB, Dkt. 4371-17, Transcript, June 10, 2008.
230 *$6 million order . . . $23 million*: *Mattel v. MGA*, Case No. 2:04-cv-09049-DOC-RNB, Dkt. 9703, Transcript, January 18, 2011.
231 *He told* Businessweek *. . . "any MGA Bratz parts, et cetera"*: *Mattel v. MGA*, Case No. 2:04-cv-09049-DOC-RNB, Dkt. 4371-15, Transcript, June 6, 2008.
231 *"My Alzheimer's Disease"*: *Mattel v. MGA*, Case No. 2:04-cv-09049-DOC-RNB, Dkt. 9865, Transcript, February 9, 2011.
231 *boosted sales of military Barbies*: Michelle Slatalla, "Home Front? Combat? A Mission for Barbie," *New York Times*, October 18, 2001; Julian E. Barnes, "Heroic Rescue Figures May Top Holiday Wishlists," *New York Times*, September 26, 2001.
231n *"missile-launching helicopter" . . . "urban buildings to pieces"*: Julian E. Barnes, "A Nation Challenged: The Toys," *New York Times*, September 26, 2001.
231 *"critical" . . . "once MyScene was available"*: *Mattel v. MGA*, Case No. 2:04-cv-09049-DOC-RNB, Dkt. 10125, Transcript, March 2, 2011.
232 *"Flavas"*: "Mattel Asks Girls 'What's Your Flava?' in an All-New Line of Fashion Dolls,"

NOTES 323

Mattel press release, July 24, 2003; Ruth La Ferla, "Undressed and Hot: Dolls Moms Don't Love," *New York Times*, October 26, 2003; "Toys: Flavas of the Week," *Newsweek*, August 3, 2003.

232 *"This is like 'gangster' Barbie"*: Maureen Tkacik, "To Lure Older Girls, Mattel Brings in a HipHop Crowd," *Wall Street Journal*, July 18, 2003.

232 *"Barbie has become irrelevant"*: Mattel v. MGA, Case No. 2:04-cv-09049-DOC-RNB, Dkt. 10125, Transcript, March 2, 2011.

232 *"inventions" . . . "during [his] employment"*: Mattel v. MGA, 616 F.3d 904, 96 U.S.P.Q.2d 1012, 30 IER Cases 1812 (9th Cir. 2010).

233 *"document-sharing agreement"*: Carter Bryant v. Mattel, Case No. CV04-9049-TJH -PJWx, Dkt. 1, "Complaint," November 2, 2004.

233 *"double-deleting"*: Mattel v. MGA, Case No. 2:04-cv-09049-DOC-RNB, Dkt. 8840, "Report and Recommendation of Electronic Discovery Special Master," August 19, 2010.

233 *given a presentation . . . "war"*: Mattel v. MGA, Case No. 2:04-cv-09049-DOC-RNB, Dkt. 10126, March 2, 2011.

233 *"obtain control over"*: Carter Bryant v. Mattel, Case No. CV04-9049-TJH-PJWx, Dkt. 1, "Complaint," November 2, 2004.

233 *"unfair tactics of competition"*: MGA v. Mattel, Case No. 2:05-cv-02727-SGL-RNB, Dkt. 1, "Complaint," April, 13, 2005.

234 *ten million pages*: Mattel v. MGA, Case No. 2:04-cv-09049-DOC-RNB, Dkt. 4371-8, Transcript, May 20, 2008.

234 *snapped under the weight*: Mattel v. MGA, Case No. 2:04-cv-09049-DOC-RNB, Dkt. 10772, Transcript, January 7, 2008.

234 *"one of the largest and most aggressively litigated"*: Carter Bryant v. Mattel, Case No. CV04-9049-TJH-PJWx, Dkt. 1, "Complaint," November 2, 2004.

234 *Bratz: Kidz Sleep-Over Adventure*: *Bratz: Kidz Sleep-Over Adventure*, Dir. Mucci-Fassett, 2007.

CHAPTER 22

235 *hand grenades*: Matthew B. Stannard, "Marketing Firm's Mailing of Gag Grenade Bombs," SFGate, September 21, 2000; Gail Diane Cox, "Law Firm's Explosive Ad Campaign Draws Critics, Attention," Law.com, September 21, 2000.

235 *"special forces"*: Brenda Sandburg, "Quinn's Quest," *The Recorder*, May 19, 2003.

235 *"May we suggest dread?"*: Jamie Hamilton, "Quinn Mocked for Boasting That It Fills Opponents with 'Dread,'" RollonFriday.com, December 11, 2020.

235 *a culture of extreme intensity*: Susan Beck, "Quinn Stands Out in Am Law 200," *The Recorder*, June 2, 2006; "Quinn Emanuel Urquhart & Sullivan LLP," Top Law Schools, February 2011.

236 *"most competitive person"*: Susan Beck, "Quinn Stands Out in Am Law 200."

236 *"I don't think he's an authoritarian"*: Brenda Sandburg, "Quinn's Quest."

236 *fin of a shark*: Michael Goldhaber, "In Search of Bigger Prey," TAL 2008, January 1, 2010.

236 *"boilerplate objections"*: Letter to Michael Zeller from Keith Jacoby, dated July 4, 2004; Mattel v. Carter Bryant, Case No. BC31498, Case File Vol. 2: September 13, 2004 to September 24, 2004.

236 *"useless phone records"*: Letter to John Quinn from Robert F. Millman, dated August 13,

324 NOTES

2004, *Mattel v. Carter Bryant*, Case No. BC31498, Case File Vol. 2: September 13, 2004 to September 24, 2004.

236 *"most concerted effort"*: *Mattel v. Carter Bryant*, Los Angeles Superior Court, Case No. BC31498, "Plaintiff Mattel Inc.'s Notice of Motion and Motion to Stay . . . ," November 2, 2004.

237 *"misusing the discovery process"*: *Mattel v. Carter Bryant*, Los Angeles Superior Court, Case No. BC31498, "Plaintiff Mattel Inc.'s Notice of Motion and Motion to Stay . . . ," November 2, 2004.

237 rooms at the Mission Inn: *Mattel v. MGA*, Case No. 2:04-cv-09049-DOC-RNB, Dkt. 5689, Transcript, April 22, 2008, and Dkt. 5688, Transcript, April 14, 2008.

237 reading of Bryant's contract: *Mattel v. MGA*, 616 F.3d 904, 96 U.S.P.Q.2d 1012, 30 IER Cases 1812 (9th Cir. 2010).

237 *"I've said this numerous times"*: *Mattel v. MGA*, Case No. 2:04-cv-09049-DOC-RNB, Dkt. 4371-4, Transcript, May 28, 2008.

238 *"two big kahunas"*: *Mattel v. MGA*, Case No. 2:04-cv-09049-DOC-RNB, Dkt. 10756, Transcript, May 19, 2008.

238 *"Project Platypus"*: *Mattel v. MGA*, Case No. 2:04-cv-09049-DOC-RNB, Dkt. 9706, Transcript, January 19, 2011; "Project Platypus: Reinventing Product Development at Mattel," Bloomberg News, July 10, 2005.

238 *"producing inexpensive, shall we say"*: *Mattel v. MGA*, Case No. 2:04-cv-09049-DOC-RNB, Dkt. 4371-2, Transcript, May 27, 2008.

239 Martinez remembered: *Mattel v. MGA*, Case No. 2:04-cv-09049-DOC-RNB, Dkt. 4371-5, Transcript, May 28, 2008.

239n It's true that Larian . . . *"no evidence"*: *Larian v. Larian*, 123 Cal.App.4th 751, 19 Cal. Rptr.3d 916 (App. 2d Dist., 2004).

239n $1 million . . . the timing of Bratz: *Mattel v. MGA*, Case No. 2:04-cv-09049-DOC-RNB, Dkt. 4371-27, Transcript, October 20, 2008.

239 Wite-Out the fax header: *Mattel v. MGA*, Case No. 2:04-cv-09049-DOC-RNB, Dkt. 4371-2, Transcript, May 27, 2008.

239 *"It is hard for a baby sheep"*: *Mattel v. MGA*, Case No. 2:04-cv-09049-DOC-RNB, Dkt. 4371-3, Transcript, May 27, 2008.

240 *"control their witness"*: *Mattel v. MGA*, Case No. 2:04-cv-09049-DOC-RNB, Dkt. 4371-17, Transcript, June 6, 2008.

240 Juror No. 8: *Mattel v. MGA*, Case No. 2:04-cv-09049-DOC-RNB, Dkt. 4155, "Order Regarding Juror No. 8," July 25, 2008.

240 Larian's rabbi: *Mattel v. MGA*, Case No. 2:04-cv-09049-DOC-RNB, Dkt. 5786, Transcript, July 25, 2008.

240 *"outrageous"* . . . verdict: *Mattel v. MGA*, 616 F.3d 904, 96 U.S.P.Q.2d 1012, 30 IER Cases 1812 (9th Cir. 2010).

241 *"constructive trust"* . . . *"captured the Bratz"*: *Mattel v. MGA*, 616 F.3d 904, 96 U.S.P.Q.2d 1012, 30 IER Cases 1812 (9th Cir. 2010).

241 *"absolutely enormous"*: Law Is My Ass Podcast, Episode 32, August 5, 2017.

241 hired Quinn Emanuel: "Quinn Emanuel Defends Judge Alex Kozinski as Misconduct Claims Mount," *The Recorder*, December 15, 2017.

241 *"reasonable woman standard"*: *Ellison v. Brady*, 924 F.2d 872 (9th Cir. 1991).

NOTES 325

242 *"I've always had a broad sense"*: Alex Kozinski, "Kozinski's Full Statement Announcing His Immediate Retirement," *Washington Post*, December 18, 2017.

242 *"such a jerk"*: Jeffrey Cole, "My Afternoon with Alex: An Interview with Judge Kozinski," *Litigation* 30, No. 4, Summer 2004, 6–20, 74–75.

242 *"wound up in his home"*: "Opponents Blow Whistle on Court Nominee," UPI via *Ventura County Star*, September 7, 1985.

242 *"several colors of ink"*: Philip Hager, "Democrats Grill Appeals Court Nominee," *Los Angeles Times*, November 2, 1985.

242 *"absolutely awful way"*: Chris Chrystal, "Judge Confirmation Hits a Snag," UPI via *Daily Citizen*, October 30, 1985.

242 *200 films . . . "Rosetta Stone"*: U.S. v. Syufy Enterprises, 903 F.2d 659 (9th Cir. 1990); "The Syufy Rosetta Stone," *Brigham Young University Law Review* (1992); John Roehmer, "Just Being Kozinski," *Daily Journal*, April 2, 2008.

242 *"Male Superhottie of the Federal Judiciary"*: "Courthouse Forum: The Hot Alex Kozinski," Underneath Their Robes, June 28, 2004.

243 *press release*: Debra Cassens Weiss, "'Hottie' Judge Kozinski Continues Joke in Press Release," *ABA Journal*, November 28, 2007; David Madden, "Gavel Passing to Mark Changing of the Guard for Ninth Circuit Court of Appeals," Public Information Office, U.S. Court for the Ninth Circuit, November 23, 2007.

243 *question of proper legal citations*: "In Re: Complaint of Judicial Misconduct," J.C. No. 03-08-900-50, Judicial Council of the Third Circuit, June 5, 2009.

243 *Much of what was found there*: Marcy Tiffany, "Alex Kozinski's Wife Speaks Out," Patterico's Pontifications, June 16, 2008; "Exclusive: Kozinski's Porn—Images from Judge Kozinski's Web Site," Patterico's Pontifications, June 16, 2008; Sara K. Smith, "Meet the Cow Porn Judge!," Wonkette, June 12, 2008; Paul Ellias, "Explicit Website Images Mar Reputation," Associated Press via *St. Louis Post-Dispatch*, June 13, 2008.

243 *"bestiality"*: "MAN CHASED BY LOVESICK DONKEY!," Crazy 8 Videos, YouTube, November 19, 2014.

243 *obscenity case*: "Judge Under Scrutiny Declares Mistrial in LA Obscenity Case," Associated Press via *Los Angeles Daily News*, June 13, 2008; Amir Efrati, "Kozinski Calls for Investigation of Himself," *Wall Street Journal*, June 12, 2008.

244n *Two thousand films on IMDb*: "E-Z Rider's Ratings," IMDb.

244 *"What the patent or copyright protects"*: "Patents & Copyrights," Ayn Rand, *Capitalism: The Unknown Ideal*, Signet, 1986, 30.

245 *Kozinski's appellate panel*: Mattel v. MGA, 616 F.3d 904, 96 U.S.P.Q.2d 1012, 30 IER Cases 1812 (9th Cir. 2010).

246 *"Fartboy" and "Fartman"*: JCW Investments v. Novelty Inc., 222 F. Supp. 2d 1030 (N.D. Ill., 2002).

CHAPTER 23

248 *"a Barbie brand on the decline"*: Mattel v. MGA, Case No. 2:04-cv-09049-DOC-RNB, Dkt. 8258, "MGA Partie's ex parte application . . . ," July 14, 2010.

248 *received a copy in early 2008*: Mattel v. MGA, Case No. 2:04-cv-09049-DOC-RNB, Dkt. 8673, "Motion for New Trial," August 31, 2010.

326 NOTES

248 *Sujata Luther: Mattel v. MGA*, Case No. 2:04-cv-09049-DOC-RNB, Dkt. 8258, "MGA Partie's ex parte application...," July 14, 2010.
249 *Sal Villaseñor*... *"close to 1 million"*: *Mattel v. MGA*, Case No. 2:04-cv-09049-DOC-RNB, Dkt. 10260, Transcript, March 22, 2011; Dkt. 10258, Transcript, March 22, 2011; and Dkt. 10259, Transcript, March 22, 2011.
250 *"five more defendants"*: *Mattel v. MGA*, Case No. 2:04-cv-09049-DOC-RNB, Dkt. 4992, "Phase II Discovery Mattel Order No. 3...," March 10, 2009.
250 *"widespread criminal enterprise"*: *Carter Bryant v. Mattel*, Case No. CV-04-9049-SGL, Dkt. 142, "Order Regarding Mattel's Motion for Leave to Amend," January 11, 2007.
250 *gotten in touch with the FBI*: *Mattel v. MGA*, Case No. 2:04-cv-09049-DOC-RNB, Dkt. 9703, Transcript, January 18, 2011.
250 *Judge Carter wouldn't allow it*: *Mattel v. MGA*, Case No. 2:04-cv-09049-DOC-RNB, Dkt. 9532, "Further Hearing Re: Patricia Glaser," December 21, 2010.
251 *"go-to trial"*: Jennifer Keller," KellerAnderle.com.
251 *Larson had resigned*: "U.S. Federal Judge Quits; Cites Flat Pay," Reuters, September 17, 2009.
251 *"hands-on"* ... *tattoos pro bono*: Christopher Goffard, "Meet the Judge at the Center of O.C. Riverbed Homeless Case Who Is Known for His Unconventional, Hands-On Approach," *Los Angeles Times*, February 20, 2018.
251 *duct-taping*: Jeanne Wright, "Judge to Continue Use of Duct Tape," *Los Angeles Times*, July 31, 1990.
251 *Skid Row*: Benjamin Oreskes, "With Homeless People as an Audience, Federal Judge Brings L.A. Officials to Skid Row," *Los Angeles Times*, February 4, 2021.
251 *long days*: *Mattel v. MGA*, Case No. 2:04-cv-09049-DOC-RNB, Dkt. 9660, Transcript, January 13, 2011, 113; and Dkt. 9659, Transcript of jury selection, January 13, 2011, 102.
252 *evidence spoilation*: *Mattel v. MGA*, Case No. 2:04-cv-09049-DOC-RNB, Dkt. 10339, March 29, 2011.
252 *"discovery abuses"*: *Mattel v. MGA*, Case No. 2:04-cv-09049-DOC-RNB, Dkt. 9863, February 9, 2011.
252 *"This case is about"* ... *"what really happened"*: *Mattel v. MGA*, Case No. 2:04-cv-09049-DOC-RNB, Dkt. 9703, Transcript, January 18, 2011.
252 *"It's true that people at Mattel"*: *Mattel v. MGA*, Case No. 2:04-cv-09049-DOC-RNB, Dkt. 9702, Transcript, January 18, 2011.
252 *"dishonest and untruthful and lied"*: *Mattel v. MGA*, Case No. 2:04-cv-09049-DOC-RNB, Dkt. 5570, Transcript, June 10, 2008.
253 *"gain access at showrooms"*: *Mattel v. MGA*, Case No. 2:04-cv-09049-DOC-RNB, Dkt. 9702, Transcript, January 18, 2011.
253 *"looked like he had lost"*: Interview with Jennifer Keller, January 19, 2025.
253 *"symphony" and a "bloodletting"*: "William C. Price," QuinnEmanuel.com.
253 *"Isn't it correct, sir"* ... *"innocent or not"*: *Mattel v. MGA*, Case No. 2:04-cv-09049-DOC-RNB, Dkt. 9733, Transcript, January 27, 2011.
254 *"betrayed their trust"* ... *"deceived Isaac Larian"*: *Mattel v. MGA*, Case No. 2:04-cv-09049-DOC-RNB, Dkt. 9750, Transcript, January 28, 2011.
254 *"I basically had to start relying"* ... *"radioactive"*: *Mattel v. MGA*, Case No. 2:04-cv-09049-DOC-RNB, Dkt. 9772, Transcript, February 1, 2011.

254 "Dark Ops" ... "tactical fighting knives": Mattel v. MGA, Case No. 2:04-cv-09049-DOC-RNB, Dkt. 4371-32 Transcript, July 3, 2008.
254 "I basically have no income right now": Mattel v. MGA, Case No. 2:04-cv-09049-DOC-RNB, Dkt. 9772, Transcript, February 1, 2011.
254 collapsed at the airport: Mattel v. MGA, Case No. 2:04-cv-09049-DOC-RNB, Dkt. 9865, Transcript, February 9, 2011.
254 "I will never settle with you": Mattel v. MGA, Case No. 2:04-cv-09049-DOC-RNB, Dkt. 9871, Transcript, February 11, 2011.
256 "Did you understand there's a court order": Mattel v. MGA, Case No. 2:04-cv-09049-DOC-RNB, Dkt 10120, Transcript, March 1, 2011.
256 "You know that when Mr. Larian" ... ordered Eckert to appear: Mattel v. MGA, Case No. 2:04-cv-09049-DOC-RNB, Dkt 10121, Transcript, March 1, 2011.
256 "You said it was some": Mattel v. MGA, Case No. 2:04-cv-09049-DOC-RNB, Dkt 9845, Transcript, February 8, 2011.
256 "Ladies and gentlemen of the jury": Mattel v. MGA, Case No. 2:04-cv-09049-DOC-RNB, Dkt 9844, Transcript, February 8, 2011.
256 chuckle: Mattel v. MGA, Case No. 2:04-cv-09049-DOC-RNB, Dkt 9866, Transcript, February 10, 2011.
257 "Your partner" ... "You are disgusting": Mattel v. MGA, Case No. 2:04-cv-09049-DOC-RNB, Dkt 9865, Transcript, February 9, 2011.
257 "Journalists write a lot": Mattel v. MGA, Case No. 2:04-cv-09049-DOC-RNB, Dkt 9868, Transcript, February 10, 2011.
257 Kraft salad dressing: Mattel v. MGA, Case No. 2:04-cv-09049-DOC-RNB, Dkt 10120, Transcript, March 1, 2011.
257 three recalls: David Barboza, "Scandal and Suicide in China: A Dark Side of Toys," New York Times, August 23, 2007; "Mattel, Fisher Price to Pay $2.3 Million Civil Penalty...," CPSC press release, June 5, 2009; M. Eric Johnson, "Mattel Inc: The Lead Paint Recall," Tuck School of Business at Dartmouth, Case No. 6-0033, December 16, 2010.
258 "headcount reduction" ... "as you like to say": Mattel v. MGA, Case No. 2:04-cv-09049-DOC-RNB, Dkt 10121, Transcript, March 1, 2011.
258 "Do you care about them?": Mattel v. MGA, Case No. 2:04-cv-09049-DOC-RNB, Dkt 10373, Transcript, April 1, 2011.
258 "My plan" ... "wouldn't do it": Mattel v. MGA, Case No. 2:04-cv-09049-DOC-RNB, Dkt 10285, Transcript, March 24, 2011.

CHAPTER 24
259 Tim Kilpin: Mattel v. MGA, Case No. 2:04-cv-09049-DOC-RNB, Dkt 10246, Transcript, March 22, 2011.
259 Alan Kaye: Mattel v. MGA, Case No. 2:04-cv-09049-DOC-RNB, Dkt 10226, Transcript, March 16, 2011.
259 Robert Normile: Mattel v. MGA, Case No. 2:04-cv-09049-DOC-RNB, Dkt. 10338, Transcript, March 29, 2011.
259 Neil Friedman: Mattel v. MGA, Case No. 2:04-cv-09049-DOC-RNB, Dkt. 10193, Transcript, March 11, 2011.
259 "Now, you have met with" ... "That's correct": Mattel v. MGA, Case No. 2:04-cv-09049-DOC-RNB, Dkt. 10194, Transcript, March 11, 2011.

328 NOTES

260 *"uncomfortable"* ... *"do the same thing"*: Mattel v. MGA, Case No. 2:04-cv-09049-DOC-RNB, Dkt. 10258, Transcript, March 22, 2011.

260 *broke down on the stand*: Mattel v. MGA, Case No. 2:04-cv-09049-DOC-RNB, Dkt. 10260, Transcript, March 22, 2011.

260 *The pressure had gotten worse*: Mattel v. MGA, Case No. 2:04-cv-09049-DOC-RNB, Dkt. 10271, Transcript, March 23, 2011.

261 *written an email*: Mattel v. MGA, Case No. 2:04-cv-09049-DOC-RNB, Dkt. 10346, Transcript, March 31, 2011; Dkt. 10338, Transcript, March 29, 2011, 137; and Dkt. 10269, Transcript, March 23, 2011.

261 *"might concern the MGA litigation"* ... *"a lot of money"*: Mattel v. MGA, Case No. 2:04-cv-09049-DOC-RNB, Dkt. 10338, Transcript, March 29, 2011, 130.

261 *two more law firms ... public too*: Mattel v. MGA, Case No. 2:04-cv-09049-DOC-RNB, Dkt. 10346, Transcript, March 31, 2011.

261 *settlement*: Mattel v. MGA, Case No. 2:04-cv-09049-DOC-RNB, Dkt. 10346, Transcript, March 31, 2011; Dkt. 10269, Transcript, March 23, 2011; and Dkt. 10338, Transcript, March 29, 2011.

262 *"That's the back of our house"*: Mattel v. MGA, Case No. 2:04-cv-09049-DOC-RNB, Dkt. 10370, Transcript, March 31, 2011, 11.

262 *"Until yesterday"* ... *"catalogs, sheets"*: Mattel v. MGA, Case No. 2:04-cv-09049-DOC-RNB, Dkt 10373, Transcript, April 1, 2011.

263 *"The record should reflect"*: Mattel v. MGA, Case No. 2:04-cv-09049-DOC-RNB, Dkt. 10271, Transcript, March 23, 2011.

263 *thirty-five boxes*: Mattel v. MGA, Case No. 2:04-cv-09049-DOC-RNB, Dkt. 10323, Transcript, March 28, 2011.

263 *Robert O'Brien*: Mattel v. MGA, Case No. 2:04-cv-09049-DOC-RNB, Dkt. 4640, "Order Appointing Discovery Master," January 6, 2009.

264 *Quinn was angry*: Mattel v. MGA, Case No. 2:04-cv-09049-DOC-RNB, Dkt. 10339, Transcript, March 29, 2011; Dkt 10373, Transcript, April 1, 2011; and Dkt. 10323, Transcript, March 28, 2011.

264 *"Listen to me very carefully"*: Mattel v. MGA, Case No. 2:04-cv-09049-DOC-RNB, Dkt. 10323, Transcript, March 28, 2011.

264 *"I thought that the rules of discovery"*: Mattel v. MGA, Case No. 2:04-cv-09049-DOC-RNB, Dkt 10373, Transcript, April 1, 2011.

264 *"The testimony for Mr. Eckert"* ... *"Paul Hastings"* Mattel v. MGA, Case No. 2:04-cv-09049-DOC-RNB, Dkt 10373, Transcript, April 1, 2011.

265n *"unfounded accusations"*: Mattel v. MGA, Case No. 2:04-cv-09049-DOC-RNB, Dkt 10104, Transcript, February 25, 2011.

265 *"involved in chemical warfare"*: Mattel v. MGA, Case No. 2:04-cv-09049-DOC-RNB, Dkt 10189, "Reply in Support of Supplemental Brief re: Mattel's Motion for Mistrial," March 13, 2011.

265 *"She said 'outside counsel in this case'"* ... *"cheating"*: Mattel v. MGA, Case No. 2:04-cv-09049-DOC-RNB, Dkt 10270, Transcript, March 25, 2011.

266 *"biggest intellectual property hoists"*: Mattel v. MGA, Case No. 2:04-cv-09049-DOC-RNB, Dkt 10449, Transcript, April 8, 2011.

266 *"What we have seen throughout"* ... *"pounding on the table"*: Mattel v. MGA, Case No. 2:04-cv-09049-DOC-RNB, Dkt 10450, Transcript, April 8, 2011.

NOTES

266 *"I don't think anyone" . . . "the American dream lives"*: Andrea Chang, "Bratz Doll Maker MGA Wins Court Battle with Mattel," *Los Angeles Times*, April 22, 2011.

266 *damages*: Originally, the jury awarded damages of $88.5 million, but Carter found they had made a calculation error, lowering the award to $85 million. *Mattel, Inc. v. MGA*, Dkts. 10701–10704, August 4, 2011.

267 *$28 million*: Robert Faturechi and Ellis Simani, "Wealthy Executives Make Millions Trading Competitors' Stock With Remarkable Timing," ProPublica, March 16, 2023.

267 *"tremendously bad decision"*: Nichola Groom, "Mattel Loses Lawsuit with MGA Entertainment over Bratz Dolls," Reuters via *Huffington Post*, April 21, 2011.

267 *"creepy" . . . "They own you"*: *Mattel v. MGA*, Case No. 2:04-cv-09049-DOC-RNB, Dkt 10450, Transcript, April 8, 2011.

EPILOGUE

269 *"commercially sponsored media" . . . "burning them"*: Agnes Nairn, Christine Griffin, and Patricia Gaya Wicks, "*The Simpsons* Are Cool but Barbie's a Minger: The Role of Brands in the Everyday Lives of Junior School Children," University of Bath, January 2006.

271 *"the overriding desire of most little brats" . . . "soul of their toys"*: Charles Baudelaire, ed. Kenneth Gross, "The Philosophy of Toys" (1853), in *On Dolls*, Notting Hill Editions, 11–21.

272 *"historical disaster"*: Jim Osman, "Mattel's Time Is Running Out Amid Federal Securities Probe, And Not Even Barbie Can Save It." *Forbes*, October 22, 2019.

273 *"unceasing abuse"*: China Labor Watch, "Mattel's Unceasing Abuse of Chinese Workers: An Investigation of Six Mattel Supplier Factories," October 15, 2013.

273 *"many of the allegations"*: China Labor Watch, "Mattel Says China Labor Watch Report of Violations 'Unfounded,'" November 17, 2011.

273 *"R.I.P. Barbie"*: Jillian Berman, "R.I.P. Barbie: America's Most Iconic Blonde Is Fading Out into History," *Huffington Post*, February 13, 2014.

273 *"vapid, one dimensional"*: Dr. Shaheena Janjuha-Jivrak, "How Mattel Reinvented Barbie to Become a Global Icon," *Forbes*, July 24, 2023.

273 *"associate the doll more with empowerment"*: Katie Hicks, "How Mattel Gave the Barbie Brand a Makeover," Marketing Brew, October 18, 2023.

274 *"neon green buzzcut"*: Barbie BMR1959 Doll box.

274 *"The thing was paradoxical"*: *Zelig*, dir. Woody Allen, 1983.

275 *$18.7 million—3,408 times*: Sarah Anderson and Sam Pizzigati, "Executive Excess 2019: Making Corporations Pay for Big Pay Gaps," Institute for Policy Studies, 26th Annual Report, September 2019.

275 *debt load . . . "accounting errors"*: "Mattel Completes Internal Investigation of Whistleblower Letter and Announces Remedial Actions," Mattel Proxy Statement, October 29, 2019.

275 *"transform Mattel into an IP-driven"*: Tracey Bowles, "Playtime Is Serious Business for Boss Who Saved Mattel from the Junk Box," *Times of London*, July 8, 2022.

276 *"having fun without making fun"*: Marshall Heyman, "The Barbie Closet: A Tweenage Dream," *Wall Street Journal*, February 13, 2012.

276 *"licensing their IP rights"*: Allison Richards, "Navigating the Trademark Parody Paradigm: Assessing the Impact of the 'Bad Spaniels' Decision on IP Owners, Creatives,

and Self-Parody in the Post–Jack Daniel's Era," *Journal of Intellectual Property Law* 31, No. 2 (July 2024).

277 *"promoting a radical transgender agenda"*: "America First Legal Files Federal Civil Rights Complaints Against America's Largest Toy Companies for Illegal Racial Discrimination and Promoting a Radical LGBT+ Agenda," America First Legal press release, December 19, 2023.

277 *"we don't see that happening"*: Sarah Whitten, "Mattel CEO Says Toy Manufacturing Won't Come to America, but Price Hikes Will," CNBC, May 6, 2022.

277 *"war on Barbie"*: Noria Doyle, "A War on Barbie: Why American Women and Children are the Target of Trump's Tariffs," *Milwaukee Independent*, May 15, 2025.

277 *"won't sell one toy"*: Adrian Volenik, "'He Won't Sell One Toy in the United States,' Says Donald Trump Suggesting a 100% Tariff on Mattel Which He Seemed to Mistake for a Country," Yahoo Finance, May 16, 2025.

INDEX

A

advertising:
  of Bratz dolls, 231
  children's advertising on television, 20–22, 45, 58, 67, 95–96, 117–19
  Betty Friedan on, 89
  of Mattel, Inc., 20–22, 45, 108–9, 115, 117–18
  motivational research and, 45–46, 48
  sexism in, 95–96
Allen, Woody, 274–75
Amerman, John, 159, 178, 189–90, 194
Aqua, 197–99, 205, 205n, 209
"Art, Design, and Barbie" exhibition, 184–85
Arthur Andersen, 136, 138n, 215
The Art of Barbie, 184
Audio Magnetics, 115, 135
Axel-Springer-Straße, 25, 34–35

B

Barad, Jill:
  acquisitions and, 195–96, 214–16
  on Barbie as pop art, 169
  on Barbie collectors, 176
  Barbie copyright and, 203–4
  Barbie marketing and, 158–60
  Barbie production and, 174
  child labor and, 193, 193n
  Clinton Economic Conference and, 189
  on labor issues, 277
  The Learning Company and, 214–16
  as Mattel president, 187, 194–95, 223
  severance package of, 216, 261
  Teen Talk Barbie and, 178
Barbie:
  accessories for, 38, 43, 58, 117–18, 151
  biographical detail for, 6, 35, 84, 181
  blank expression of, 44, 96, 231, 272
  box including designers, 169, 225
  breasts of, 8, 9, 52, 74, 124, 156, 160, 203
  cars of, 59–60
  children's attitudes toward, 269–72
  as "continuing concept" within toy line, 118
  cultural dominance of, 24–25
  desexualization of, 83
  development of, 7–9, 12, 37–40, 64
  editions of, 58–59
  face design of, 8, 9, 203–4
  fan mail of, 59, 73–74
  feminism and, 90–91
  as first adult doll, 8, 24–25, 37, 53
  gaze of, 92, 93
  gender roles and, 91–92
  hair of, 9, 12–13, 58, 59, 76, 152
  high heels of, 13, 32
  Japanese prototype of, 8, 13, 43–44
  knockoffs of, 64–65, 67, 201
  licensed goods of, 183
  Lilli compared to, 37, 39–40, 64, 84, 92, 120
  marketing of, 45, 50–51, 53, 54–55, 58, 111, 150–53, 158–60, 169, 182
  modernization of, 273
  motherhood and, 90
  name copyright of, 9
  new items tied to, 61
  origin story of, 84–85, 221
  outfits/wardrobe of, 8, 12, 13, 52, 58–59, 80, 91, 149–50, 158, 164, 168, 173
  parental attitudes toward, 52–53, 91
  parodies of, 197–98
  patent for, 63, 64

331

INDEX

Barbie (*cont.*)
  penmanship of, 181
  physique changes and, 203
  popularity of, 73, 76
  professional occupations of, 59, 91
  sales of, 53, 58, 60, 63, 68, 91, 110,
    151–52, 160, 175, 186, 195, 214, 223,
    223n, 237, 252, 273
  segmentation strategy and, 152, 159
  sexual symbolism of, 51–54, 182
  "Togetherness" look, 91–92
  Toy Fair New York and, 7, 13–14, 23, 25,
    44, 53, 87, 97
  websites on, 209–10
  whiteness of, 96
Barbie and the Rockers, 154–56, 159
Barbie Bazaar, 68, 166, 170, 173, 174
The Barbie Bulletin, 166
Barbie Collectibles, 225, 227, 239
Barbie collectors:
  history of, 165–66
  internet fan sites of, 208
  Mattel and, 166, 167–69, 171, 172–75
  national conventions and, 162–64, 169–70
  "never removed from box" status and,
    163, 178
Barbie.com, 208, 209
Barbie Disinformation Organization, 183
Barbie Fan Club, 60, 74, 120
Barbie Fashion Designer software, 208
"Barbie Girl" (song), 197, 241, 276
Barbie Liberation Organization, 178, 183–84
Barbie magazine, 60, 101, 181
Barbie movie, 4, 23–24, 41, 120, 141,
  163–64, 275–76
Barbie-related art, 178–83, 197–98, 205,
  205n
Barbie's Dreamhouse, 60, 79–80, 82
Barbie Sings!, 180
Barbie the Babysitter, 90, 91
Barnum, P. T., 116
Baudelaire, Charles, 271–72
Bellow, Saul, 274–75
Benjamin, Walter, 36, 165
Bernstein, Robert L., 180–81
Beuthien, Reinhard, 28–32, 62

Bild Lilli. *See* Lilli
Bild Zeitung, 27–30, 32–33, 35, 39
Billyboy*, 40, 166–69, 172–74, 172n, 225,
  227n
Birdsall, John, 107, 138
Black Barbie, 152
black dolls, 59, 99, 229
Bluhm, Hans, 29, 32
Bowie, David, 154, 183
brand symbolism, 269–70
Bratz dolls:
  Carter Bryant as designer of, 225,
    227–33, 238–39, 240, 248
  children's attitudes toward, 271
  lawsuits involving, 232–34, 272
  MGA Entertainment and, 224, 225, 233,
    234, 239–40, 239n, 241, 248–49
  personalities of, 230, 231–32
  pluralism of, 229–30
Broder-Keil, Lars, 34–35
Brooks, Mel, 86n
Brown, Harold, 187
Brown, Helen Gurley, 88, 92
*Brown v. Board of Education of Topeka,
  Kansas* (1954), 99
Bryant, Carter:
  appeal of Mattel's MGA lawsuit and,
    253–55, 256, 260, 265, 266
  as Barbie designer, 169, 226, 229–30,
    232–33, 239
  as Bratz designer, 225, 227–33, 238–39,
    240, 248
  Isaac Larian and, 228, 229–30, 233, 235
  Mattel's breach of contract lawsuit
    against, 233, 234, 236–37, 245–47,
    248, 250, 251, 255
  Mattel's MGA lawsuit and, 237–39, 239n,
    250
  Mattel's settlement with, 237–38
Buddenbrooks Cycle, 179
Bush, George H. W., 186, 189, 190
Bush, George W., 234, 237

C

Campbell, W. Joseph, 207
Carpenter, Karen, 179–80, 182

INDEX   333

Carpenter, Richard, 182, 197
Carson/Roberts, 20–21, 39, 73
Carter, David O., 251–52, 263–67, 265n
Carter, Jimmy, 187
Casey, William, 28n
Chatty Cathy, 99
China, 189, 191–92, 277–78
China Labor Watch, 192–93, 273
Christie, 59, 108, 152
CIA, 22, 28, 28n
Cityworld, 232, 233
Clark, Kenneth, 98–99, 104
Clark, Mamie, 98–99, 104
Clinton, Bill, 186–87, 189–92, 201, 251
Clinton, Hillary, 187, 274
Clinton Economic Conference, 189, 277
The Collectors Encyclopedia of Barbie Dolls and Collectibles, 165
Colored Chatty Cathy, 99, 101
Color Magic Barbie, 59
Color 'n Curl Hair Set, 79
Congress of Racial Equality (CORE), 103
consumerism, 22, 40, 89, 198
Consumer Product Safety Commission, 257
Coombe, Rosemary, 212
copyright issues:
  Barbie as work of art and, 162
  Barbie fan magazines and, 174–75
  Barbie name and, 9
  BillyBoy*'s alt-Barbie and, 173
  Disney and, 199, 201
  idea-expression dichotomy, 202
  infringement determination tests and, 245–47
  Lilli doll and, 67–68
  Malibu Barbie's head and, 92
  Miss America dolls and, 157
  parody/satire distinction, 199
  terms of, 200–201, 200–201n
  tests of infringement, 201, 245–46
  Mark Twain on, 199
Creatable World, 274
Cronk, Ruth, 166, 170
Crumlish, Christian, 211–13
culture jacking, 164

Cuza, Fermín, 190–91
cybersquatting, 210

D

Daily Mirror, 27, 29, 33, 49
Day-to-Night Barbie, 158
defense industry, 3, 5, 19–20
DeWein, Sibyl, 165–66
Dichter, Ernest:
  on Barbie's outfits, 58
  on depth interviews, 82
  on focus groups, 50–51
  Betty Friedan and, 89, 89n
  on Ken's penis, 73, 75–76
  market research and, 47–49
  Mattel as client of, 46, 50–55, 267
  motivational research and, 47, 48–50, 84, 152
  on sexual symbolism, 49–50, 51, 76
Disney:
  copyright and, 199, 201
  factories of, 192
  Hasbro and, 223, 273
  Mattel's deferral of debt to, 195
  Mattel's preschool toys produced for, 159, 223
  The Mickey Mouse Club sponsorship and, 20–21, 39, 45, 58
Distorted Barbie, 210–14
dolls:
  baby dolls, 8, 24, 38
  children's destruction of, 271
  fashion dolls, 13
  in German literature, 36–37
  Miss America dolls, 157–58
  paper dolls, 8, 37, 84
  Raggedy Ann, 17, 45
  stereotypes of, 91
  as symbols of racial consciousness, 97–99
  toy industry and, 8, 17, 24
  See also Barbie; Bratz dolls
Dolls of the World collection, 152
Doll Tests, 98–99, 104–5
Drag Queen Barbie, 205
Drexel Burnham Lambert, 147, 149

334 INDEX

Drexel High Yield Bond Conference, 145, 149
Drudge, Matt, 103
duCille, Ann, 101–2, 105
Dunnegan, William, 211

E

Eckert, Robert:
  appeal of Mattel's lawsuit against MGA and, 252–53, 255–56, 257, 258, 262, 263–66, 267
  "The Bratz Brief" and, 248–49
  Carter Bryant's work on Bratz and, 233, 248
  on Market Intelligence Department, 249, 264–65
  as Mattel president, 223–25, 232
  resignation from Mattel, 273
Eegee, 65
Eisenhower, David, 21
Eisenhower, Dwight, 15, 21–22
Elastolin, 30
Elite Creations Inc., 65
Ellsberg, Daniel, 22n
Equal Employment Opportunity Commission (EEOC), 94–95
Erving, Julius Winfield II, 106
Esquire, 27, 48–49, 49n, 53–54, 60, 84, 85, 182

F

F.A.O. Schwartz, 231n
Fashion Queen Barbie, 79
FBI, 126–27, 250
Federal Communications Commission, 119
Federal Reserve, 93–94
Federal Trade Commission, 119, 195, 204
Federal Trademark Dilution Act of 1995, 201
Feelin' Groovy Barbie, 169
Feld, Irvin, 116, 127–28
femininity, 88, 92–93
feminism, 87–93, 96, 131
First Amendment, 197–98, 200
Fisher-Price, 188, 191, 194, 224
Florea, Gwen, 77–79

focus groups, 50–51, 90
Forsythe, Thomas, 206, 209
Fossil Barbie letter, 210–11, 211n
franchise fatigue, 23
Francie, 59, 101–2, 120, 152, 156, 173–75
Franz Carl Weber, 37–38
Freud, Sigmund, 45–50, 54, 153, 182
Friedan, Betty, 87, 89–91, 89n
Friedman, Neil, 259–60

G

Gabor, Zsa Zsa, 77, 81
gender politics, 91–92
Gene doll, 227, 227n
General Agreement on Tariffs and Trade (GATT), 189, 190, 193
Germany:
  adult toy doll in, 24–25
  dolls in German literature, 36–37
  toy production in, 16–17, 22, 30–31, 36, 37–38, 39, 42
  See also Lilli
Gerwig, Greta, 163
G.I. Joe action figures, 59, 153, 177–78, 188, 203
Gillette, King Camp, 56–57, 58, 164
Great Shape Barbie, 149
Greenpeace, 212
Greenwald, Michele, 195, 195n
Greiner & Hausser, 31–32
Growing Up Skipper, 151
Gruelle, Johnny, 17
Guggenheim, Paul, 40–42, 67, 223
Guggenheim, Philippe, 41

H

Hacker Barbe, 207–8, 209
Hall, Robert, 103–5, 107
Handler, Barbara, 7–9, 37–40, 84
Handler, Elliot:
  Carter Bryant and, 226
  death of, 273
  European trip of 1956, 37–38, 39, 62–63
  on government oversight, 102
  Ruth Handler's relationship with, 7, 9–12, 114–15, 124, 124n

Ruth Handler's stock analysts address and, 93
Roy Hofheinz and, 115–16
Hot Wheels and, 118
as industrial designer, 10–11
Ken's penis debate and, 73
Kinney Services and, 128, 129
in Los Angeles, 40
Louis Marx and Company as competition of, 15, 17, 43–44, 64
as Mattel, Inc. founder, 5
Mattel's brand image and, 55
on Mattel's success, 60
on Mattel's turnaround, 134, 135
New Yorker Hotel reception and, 12
Operation Bootstrap and, 104–5, 107, 108
painting of, 140
plastic designs of, 11–12, 18
Jack Ryan and, 81, 83, 84–86
Carol Spencer on, 120–21
on television advertising, 20–21, 58
on toy industry statistics, 109
"Uke-A-Doodle" design of, 18, 19
See also Mattel, Inc.
Handler, Kenneth, 7, 37, 39–40
Handler, Ruth Mosko:
archives of, 121
on Barbie as inspired by wooden doll book, 66
Barbie doll development and, 7–8, 86
Barbie marketing and, 45, 53, 54–55, 182, 276
on Barbie's backstory, 35, 38, 41, 231
on Barbie's motherhood, 90
biography of, 12
biopsies of, 123–24
cigarette smoking of, 7, 12, 124
civil responsibility gestures and, 102
death of, 223
Ernest Dichter and, 50–51, 54–55
on divisionalization of Mattel, 117, 122, 124–25
Dream Doll memoir of, 68, 107, 121, 124, 129
European trip of 1956, 37–38, 41, 62–63

family background of, 7, 9–10, 14, 136
fears of Mattel coup, 129, 134–35
Federal Reserve address and, 93–94
on feminism, 87, 90, 93
gambles taken by, 7, 14, 21
gambling habit of, 136
on government oversight, 102
grand jury charges against, 139–40, 151
Elliot Handler's relationship with, 7, 9–12, 114–15, 124, 124n
innocence maintained by, 140–41
insider trading accusations and, 134
integration of work force at Mattel, 100
international toy fair trip of 1970, 122–23
and Japanese toy industry, 42–43, 44
Ken's penis debate and, 73–76
Kinney Services and, 127, 128–30
Lilli doll and, 35, 37–42, 44, 64
Louis Marx and Company as competition of, 15, 17, 62, 64
mastectomies of, 124, 140
as Mattel board co-chairman, 135
as Mattel executive vice president, 94, 94n, 110
as Mattel founder, 5, 114
as Mattel president, 111, 121, 124–25, 135
on Mattel's growth, 60
on Mattel's losses, 132–33
as Mattel spokeswoman, 194
as mother, 7–8
New Yorker Hotel reception and, 12, 13, 44
prosthetic breast business of, 136–37, 140
"revolutionary merchandising concept" branding of, 110–11
Seymour Rosenberg and, 111, 113–17, 129–30, 137, 138
Jack Ryan and, 83, 84–86
Judy Shakelford as successor of, 150
on Shindana Toys, 107, 108
stereotypes of, 94
taking credit for ideas and, 158
on television advertising, 20–21, 58
"Uke-A-Doodle" theft and, 18–19
on unions, 131

336 INDEX

Handler, Ruth Mosko *(cont.)*
  wardrobe of, 124
  on "the World of Barbie," 58
  on Yasuo Yoshida, 122, 122n
  See also Mattel, Inc.
Hansen, Paul, 205–6, 212
Happy Holiday Barbies, 169
Hasbro:
  Disney license and, 223, 273
  dolls of, 153–56, 201–2
  earnings forecast of, 196
  G.I. Joe action figure and, 59, 153, 203
  Jem and the Holograms and, 154–55, 201
  Mattel's attempt to buy, 188–89, 194
  Sindy doll and, 203–4
  Transformers movie and, 275
Hastings, Paul, 263, 264
Hausser, Kurt, 30–31, 33–35, 39, 63–64, 66–69, 222–23
Hausser, Lilly, 222
Hausser, Max, 30–31, 33–35, 39, 63–64, 66–69, 222–23
Hausser, Otto, 30–31, 33–35, 39, 63–64, 66–69, 222–23
Hausser, Rolf, 30–35, 39, 62–64, 66–69, 222–24, 223n, 267
Haynes, Todd, 179–80, 179n, 182, 197
He-Man doll, 148, 155, 276
Henzel, Ian, 175
Herman, Andrew, 212
Hilton, Robyn, 86n
Hispanic Barbie, 152
Hitler, Adolph, 25–26, 28, 30–31
Hoffmann, E. T. A., 36–37
Hofheinz, Roy, 115–16, 135
Holder, Sandi, 175
Holiday Barbie, 174
Hong Kong, 63–65, 260
Hoover, J. Edgar, 22, 22n
Hot Wheels, 62, 118, 119, 122, 138, 276
Hu Nianzhen, 192–93
Hufstedler, Seth, 137–38
Hughes, Howard, 111–12, 114
Humphrey, Hubert, 101
Hunter, Dan, 198–99
Hurst, Annette, 265, 265n
Hurst, Fannie, 97, 99
Hurston, Zora Neale, 99

I

Ideal Toy Company, 65, 99
Imitation of Life (film), 97, 99
Indonesia, 190, 193
Institute for Motivational Research, 49, 50, 89
intellectual property:
  cybersquatting and, 210
  legal scope of, 200–201
  Mattel lawsuits and, 198–99, 204, 206
  Mattel's licensing and, 118, 148, 166
  Mattel's restrictions on, 4
  toy industry and, 43
  Mark Twain and, 199
Intellivision, 147–49, 148n
The International Barbie Doll Collectors Gazette, 166
Internet:
  Barbie collector fan sites on, 208, 209
  dot-com boom and, 214
  Mattel cease-and-desist cases and, 209–14

J

Jackson, Michael, 146, 180
Jacobs, Cliff, 94n
Jane's Journal (*Daily Mirror* comic strip), 27, 29, 33, 49, 84
Japan:
  Barbie prototype produced in, 8, 13, 43–44
  foreign goods copied in, 42–43
  Ken prototype produced in, 75–76
  Lilli doll knockoffs manufactured in, 65
  toy production in, 18, 30, 42–44, 131
Jefferson, Thomas, 200
John Birch Society, 103
Johnson, Charlotte, 8, 75, 83, 150, 170
Johnson, Lyndon, 22n, 102, 104

K

Kalinske, Tom, 160–61
Keller, Jennifer, 251–56, 258, 259–60, 263, 264–67

Ken, 59, 73–76, 80, 92, 120, 151
Kennedy, Jackie, 59
Kenner Products, 138, 157
KGOY (kids getting older younger), 182–83
Kimmel, Caesar P., 128
Kimmel, Emmanuel, 126–27, 127n, 128
Kinney Parking, 126, 127n
Kinney Services, 126–27, 128, 131, 147
Klein, Naomi, 188, 193–94
Kleist, Heinrich von, 37
Klosterman, Chuck, 187
Knaak, Silke, 35, 39, 69
Knickerbocker Plastics, 18–19
Kokusai Boeki Kaisha, 43
Kozinski, Alex, 204–5, 241–47, 244n, 248, 251, 276
Kreiz, Ynon, 275–77

L
Larami Corp., 65
Larian, Farhad, 228, 239n
Larian, Isaac:
    appeal of Mattel's lawsuit, 240–41, 252, 253, 254, 255–57, 258, 264, 265, 266–67
    Bratz dolls and, 229–31, 239n, 240
    Carter Bryant and, 228, 229–30, 233, 235
    on Mattel's Flavas line, 232
    Mattel's lawsuit against MGA and, 234, 239, 239n, 240, 250
    MGA Entertainment and, 228–29, 238, 239n
Larian, Jasmin, 229–30, 266
Larson, Stephen, 237–38, 240–41, 245–47, 250, 251
The Learning Company, 214–15, 223
Lestrade, Jean Pierre (Lala), 167–69, 172–73
Li Qiang, 191–94
Lilli:
    as adult doll, 32–33, 52, 74
    Barbie as patent infringement of, 64–67
    Barbie compared to, 37, 39–40, 64, 84, 92, 120
    Joe Blitman on, 174
    as comic strip character for *Bild Zeitung*, 29–30, 39
    as doll, 29, 31–33
    fan mail of, 59
    Ruth Handler and, 35, 37–42, 44, 64
    history of, 34–35, 41, 63
    injection molding and, 43
    licensing of, 63–64, 65, 69, 222
    as marketing for *Bild Zeitung*, 33, 35
    Louis Marx's selling of, 64–65
    merchandise related to, 163
    Dan Miller on, 222
    outfits of, 32, 38–39
    patent for, 63–69
    Jack Ryan on, 84
    sex as subtext of, 32, 52
    U.S. distribution of, 40, 41, 63
Litton Industries, 112–13, 114, 115, 116, 122n, 126
Loomis, Bernie, 117–18, 122, 126, 132–33, 138–39
Lord, M. G., 65, 67–68, 152, 181, 184–85
Los Angeles, California:
    Freedom City, 104, 105
    German expats in, 36
    South Central neighborhoods of, 100, 104, 105
    Watts riots of 1965, 100–101, 102, 103, 104, 106, 107
Louis Marx and Company:
    advertising and, 20, 21–22
    as America's Toy King, 15–16
    Barbie imitations sold by, 64–65
    Elm Tool and Machinery and, 18
    Lilli doll license of, 63–64, 65, 66, 67, 69, 222–23, 223n
    as Mattel competitor, 21–22, 62, 64, 65
    Mattel countersued by, 66, 222
    Mattel's out of court settlement with, 67
    Mattel suit of 1961 and, 65–67, 222, 223
Lucas, George, 148
Luther, Sujata, 248, 262

M
McGowan, Sean, 156, 196
McKendall, Lisa, 209

338 INDEX

Madden, Steve, 227, 246
Magic 8 Ball, 276
Maisner, Bernard, 181
Malaika, 106
Malevich, Kazimir, 263
Malibu Barbie, 92, 93
Manet, Edouard, 92, 179
Mann, Heinrich, 36
Mann, Thomas, 36, 179
market saturation, 56, 111
Marlow, Veronica, 227–28, 229, 230
Marshall, George C., 22
Marshall, Thurgood, 98–99
Martinez, Lily, 239, 256
Marx, Karl, 23, 48, 57
Marx, Louis:
    advertising and, 20, 21–22
    on Barbie doll, 62–63, 64, 84
    German toy industry and, 22
    on Ruth Handler, 69
    Japan and, 18, 43–44
    on Lilli doll, 35, 63–64
    military interests of, 21–22, 22n
    patents and, 200
    in toy industry, 15–18, 62
    See also Louis Marx and Company
Marx, Patricia, 22n
Masters of the Universe, 148, 161
Matchbox cars, 118, 188
Matson, Harold, 11, 19
Mattel, Inc.:
    accounting practices and, 133, 134, 135–36, 137, 138, 139, 195, 215, 275
    acquisitions of, 115, 119, 128, 133, 135, 188–89, 191, 195–96
    advertising of, 20–22, 45, 108–9, 115, 117–18
    annual sales of, 110, 134
    bankers forcing regime change and, 134–35
    Barbie collectors and, 166, 167–69, 171, 172–75
    Barbie doll as grown-up woman and, 7–8, 24–25
    Barbie name licenses and, 60
    on Barbie's backstory, 35, 38
    "bill and hold" strategy of, 126, 132, 137, 138, 139
    black dolls released by, 99
    brand image of, 55, 61
    "The Bratz Brief" document, 248–49
    Burp Gun of, 21, 66
    campus of, 3–4, 5
    code of conduct changes, 260
    Communication Department, 164
    "Concord Project" of, 115, 128
    crisis of 2001, 231–32, 238, 248
    demand for low-paid workers and, 189–90
    Design Center of, 121, 226
    Ernest Dichter and, 46, 50–55, 267
    divisionalization of, 117, 118, 122
    doll furniture of, 11–12
    Electronics Division, 149, 154
    EPS (earnings per share) and, 111, 123
    Esquire features and, 53–54, 60
    executive bonuses and, 191
    factories of, 60, 110, 159, 190, 273
    film production and, 119, 133
    former employees of, 120–21
    Global Manufacturing Principles of, 193
    growth of, 60–61, 62, 110, 159, 188, 195, 196, 214
    Ruth Handler's fears of coup, 129, 134–35
    Heli-jet of, 231n
    "House on Fire" memo of, 224, 233, 252, 266
    "How to Steal Manual," 249
    integrated work force of, 100, 102
    "inventory obsolescence" approach of, 138
    as IP-driven company, 275–76
    Japanese production and, 43–44
    Ken doll introduced by, 59
    Ken's penis debate and, 73–75
    Kinney Services and, 126–30
    labor abuses and, 192–94, 193n
    layoffs of, 126, 159, 224, 258, 275
    licensing intellectual property and, 118, 148, 166
    Lilli patent infringement and, 65, 66
    on Lilli stories, 35, 37

losses of, 132–33, 134, 215–16
Louis Marx and Company as competitor of, 21–22, 62, 64–66
Market Intelligence Department, 249, 250, 259–60, 262, 264–65, 266
market research of, 50–51, 54–55
Mexican assembly plants of, 110, 125–26, 131, 132, 137–38, 194, 224
The Mickey Mouse Club sponsorship and, 20–21, 39, 45, 58
Michael Milken's investment in, 149, 151, 154, 160, 160n, 161
National Barbie Doll Collectors Convention and, 164–65
"ninth floor library" of, 262, 263, 264
offshoring of, 8, 131
Operations, 122
originality and, 19, 20
origin story of, 37, 84
product website of, 208
profits of, 110, 111
"Project Platypus" and, 238
as public company, 58, 60, 73, 110, 132
push programs of, 195
quarterly profits and, 58, 132
Research and Development Department of, 19–20, 74, 77, 84, 86, 248–49
revenue shortfall of, 196
sales of, 194
sales quotas of, 125
seasonal sales and, 57–58, 115, 126
secrecy of, 4, 5, 6, 19–20, 126
shareholders of, 73, 110
Shindana Toys and, 105–9
special counsel investigation and report on, 136, 137–38
stock price of, 111, 113, 116, 127, 130, 132, 135, 139, 147, 216, 223, 267
sublicense of Lilli patent and, 67–68
talking toys of, 77
tariffs and, 277–78
television production and, 118–19
tensions within, 121–22, 133
"This is War" memo of, 224, 233, 252
toy recalls of, 257, 265
unions and, 131–33, 159, 193–94

Mattel Acoustics Lab, 77
Mattel All-Occasion Gift Center (MAOGC), 111
Mattel Brands, 259
Mattel Collections, 184
Mattel International, 41–42
Mattel lawsuits:
  against Arthur Andersen, 138n
  against Barbie infringers, 5, 6, 35, 42, 108, 157, 201–2, 205–6
  against Barbie-related works, 198, 205
  against Carter Bryant, 233, 234, 236–37, 245–47, 248, 250, 251, 255
  against MGA, 232–34, 238–41, 239n, 243, 250
  Barbie collectors and, 166, 173
  on Barbie origin date, 38
  Barbie-related art and, 182
  Carter Bryant's confidential settlement and, 237–38
  cease-and-desist cases and, 209–14
  class action lawsuits regarding Ringling, 135
  editorial control of Barbie content and, 198, 266
  ex-employee's whistleblower lawsuit, 195, 195n
  Ruth Handler's depositions and, 40
  Rolf Hausser's *Miller's* interview and, 68–69
  intellectual property law and, 198–99
  Lilli doll patent rights and, 63–69, 222
  Louis Marx and Company's 1961 suit and, 65–67, 222, 223
  MGA's appeal against, 240–41, 245–47, 248, 249, 250–53, 254, 255–57, 258, 259–67, 272
  Miller's magazine and, 174–76
  press coverage of, 202
  Jack Ryan and, 85–86
  SEC fraud lawsuit, 135, 139, 147
  shareholder lawsuits, 134, 135, 138n, 216
  special counsel report as evidence and, 138
  Superstar film and, 180
Mattelzapoppin' (musical), 61

MCA Records, 197, 200, 205
Mdivani, Isabelle "Roussy," 172–73, 172–73n
MGA Entertainment:
  acquisitions of, 258
  appeal of Mattel's lawsuit, 240–41, 245–47, 248, 249, 250–53, 254, 255–57, 258, 259–67, 272
  Bratz dolls and, 224, 225, 233, 234, 239–40, 239n, 241, 248–49
  lawsuit against Mattel, 233–34
  Mattel's lawsuit against, 232–34, 238–41, 239n, 243, 250
  products of, 228–29, 238
  Skadden Arps as law firm of, 237
Midge, 59, 91, 92, 120
Milken, Michael, 145–47, 149, 151, 154, 160–61, 160n, 191, 250
Miller, Barbara, 174–76
Miller, Dan, 174–76, 222, 223n
Miller, G. Wayne, 156, 202
Miller's magazine, 68–69, 166, 174–76, 222
Miss America Barbie, 93, 94
Miss America dolls, 157–58
Miss America pageant, 92
Miss Barbie, 59, 79
Mosko, Sarah, 10, 123
motivational research, 45–46, 47, 48–50, 84, 89, 152
Murdoch, Rupert, 26, 145
Musgrave, R. Kenton, 67
MyScene Barbie, 232

N

NAFTA (North American Free Trade Act), 190–91
Nairn, Agnes, 269, 272
Napier, Mark, 210–14
National Barbie Doll Collectors Convention, 162–64
National Guard, 100
National Organization for Women, 87, 91, 151
National Socialist Motor Corps, 26, 30
Nazis, 30–31, 48
Nearly Me, 136–37

New Kids on the Block, 204–5
New Yorker Hotel, 12, 13, 44
Nicoli, Marina, 35, 41
Nixon, Richard, 85, 94–95
Nolan, Tom, 239–40
Nuremberg, Germany, 30, 38, 39, 41, 62, 260

O

O&M Hausser, 22, 30–35, 39, 63–64, 65, 68, 222
Odom, Mel, 227n
Offield, Glen, 169–72
offshore manufacturing, 8, 18, 107, 131, 190–91, 277
Old, Anne Zielinski, 184
O'Leary, Kevin, 214–16
Operation Bootstrap, 102, 103–9
Optigan, 128, 135
Orrick Herrington, 250–51

P

Packard, Vance, 46, 51, 89n
Perkins, Kitty Black, 152, 169
Perot, Ross, 186, 190
Petty Girls, 27, 49, 53–54
Philippines, 159, 193
Pigtails to Ponytails (film), 53
Pink & Pretty Barbie, 148
Pitman, Melissa, 175–76
Plath, Sylvia, 52–53, 88–89
Plimpton, George, 148, 148n
Poodle Parade Barbie, 173, 175
President Barbie, 186–87
Price, William, 253–57, 265–66
Project Dawn collection, 273–74

Q

Quinn, John, 235–36, 238–39, 256, 262–66, 265n
Quinn Emanuel:
  appeal of Mattel's MGA lawsuit and, 252–53, 255, 256, 261–66, 265n, 267
  Alex Kozinski and, 241
  Mattel's Carter Bryant lawsuit and, 236–37, 245

Mattel's MGA lawsuit and, 238, 248
reputation of, 235–36

R

racial consciousness, 97–99
racial essentialism, 105
Radio City Music Hall, 201, 203–4
Radnitz, Robert, 119, 133
Rand, Ayn, 244–45, 244n, 247
Random House books, 60, 180
Rasted, Søren, 197
Reagan, Ronald, 100, 103, 145–47, 161, 187–88, 190, 204
Ringling Bros., 115–16, 127–28, 135
Robbie, Margot, 4, 141, 275
Rockette figurine, 201, 203–4
Rosenberg, Seymour:
  accounting practices of, 133, 137, 138
  credentials of, 111–13
  exit package of, 133, 135
  on federal investigations of Mattel, 119
  insider trading accusations and, 134
  Kinney Services and, 126–27, 128, 129–30
  as Mattel business manager, 111, 113, 114–17
  on Mattel's losses, 132–33
  Mattel special counsel report on, 137, 138
  nolo contendere plea of, 139–40
  Carol Spencer on, 121
  Yasuo Yoshida and, 122, 122n
Ross, Diana, 146, 152
Ross, Steve, 128–29
Rowe, Harvey, 211n
Ryan, Ann, 81, 85, 86n
Ryan, Barbara, 84
Ryan, Jack:
  Bel-Air home of, 80–81, 85–86
  death of, 86, 194
  departure settlement and, 150
  design of Barbie's appendages, 8, 63
  Ruth Handler and, 83, 84–86
  on Japanese production, 44
  loneliness and, 82, 86n
  marriages of, 77, 81–82, 86

as Mattel designer, 19, 42, 79–80, 82–83, 86
Mattel Research and Development Department and, 77, 84, 86
parties of, 77–79, 82, 83
patents authored by, 77, 79, 83–84, 85, 111
royalties of, 79, 83, 85, 126, 135, 138, 230
Carol Spencer on, 121

S

Samuel, Lawrence R., 45–46
Schlesinger Library, Cambridge, Massachusetts, 87–89, 121
Schneider, Cy, 39–41, 73, 76
Schwartz, Stephen, 155–56
Securities and Exchange Commission (SEC), 135–37, 139, 147, 195
Sert, Josep Maria, 172–73n
Sert, Misia, 172–73n
Sethi, Prakash, 194
Seuss, Dr., 198
sexism, 95–96
sexual symbolism, 49–50, 51, 76
Shackelford, Judy, 150–55, 156, 157, 158–60, 273
Shaft (film), 106
Shanghai, 272–73
Sherman, Cindy, 178
Shindana Toys, 105–9
shopgiving, 177–78, 178n
Simpson, O. J., 106, 198
The Simpsons (television show), 167, 179
Sindy doll, 156, 201–4
Singh, Ravi, 153
Sirk, Douglas, 97–98, 179, 179n
Skadden Arps, 237, 250
Skipper, 59, 151, 166, 181
Skooter, 59
Slade the Super-Agent, 106
Slime, 147
Sloggett, Bruce Scott, 171–72
Slovak, Frank, 122n
Smith, Lou, 103–5, 107–8
Smith, Marva, 107
Smithsonian, 170

Smithsonian, 210–11, 211n
Smyrner, Ann, 33–34
Spear, Arthur:
　executive committee appointments of, 159
　Ruth Handler's relationship with, 137, 138
　Tom Kalinske and, 161
　as Mattel president, 135, 147
　Mattel's hiring of, 117
　Mexican assembly plant fire and, 125–26
　Michael Milken and, 149
　on Operation Bootstrap, 107
　Operations at Mattel and, 122
　SEC and, 136, 137
Spencer, Carol, 44, 83–84, 85, 120–21, 169
Spielberg, Steven, 189
Springer, Axel, 25–29, 26–27n, 28n, 30, 33–34, 68
Star Wars (film), 148
Stein, Bruce, 150, 156–57, 188, 214–15
stock-parking agreements, 160n
Strong Museum, Rochester, New York, 121
Superstar (film), 179–82
SuperStar Barbie, 151, 156, 169, 203
Surprise Gift Wagon, 228
Sweet, Roger, 148

T

Takasugi, Robert, 140
Talking Barbie, 59, 77, 170
Talking Julia, 152
Talking Tamu, 106
tariffs, 277
Teen Talk Barbie, 177–78, 179
television:
　children's advertising and, 20–22, 45, 58, 67, 95–96, 117–19
　franchise fatigue and, 23
　toy-based TV franchises, 118
Title VII of Civil Rights Act, 94, 95, 277
Totally Hair Barbie, 187
Toy Center, New York, 9, 16, 19
Toy Fair New York:
　Barbie and, 7, 13–14, 23, 25, 44, 53, 87, 97
　Hasbro and, 154–55
　Mattel and, 6, 21, 39, 102, 111, 131, 232, 249–50, 260
　protests and, 91
　Shindana and, 105–6
　timing of, 18
toy industry:
　action figures and, 59, 74
　age compression in children and, 183
　Cold War and, 13
　consolidation of, 109, 196
　copyright law and, 202–3
　Federal Trade Commission and, 195
　in Germany, 16–17, 22, 30–31, 36, 37–38, 39, 42
　Gulf War and, 187
　intellectual property rights and, 43
　in Japan, 18, 30, 42–44, 131
　Louis Marx in, 15–18, 62
　racial consciousness and, 99
　seasonal sales and, 57–58, 110, 188
　secrecy of, 5, 155
　sexual symbolism and, 51–52
　theft in, 18–20
　toy electronics and, 147
　in U.S., 9, 17, 30
Toy Industry Hall of Fame, 17
Toy Manufacturers of the USA, 17, 43
Toys "R" Us, 187–88, 195–96, 214–15, 230
Toy Story (film), 182
trademark claims, 67–69, 174–75, 198, 200–201, 206, 209
Trailer Trash Barbie, 205, 212
Trump, Donald, 263, 274, 277–78
Trump, Ivanka, 192
Turco Manufacturing Co., 115, 135
Turetzky, Matt, 260
Turner, Lana, 40, 97
Twain, Mark, 9, 199, 201, 219–21
Twist n' Turn Barbie, 79, 111
Tyco, 188, 189, 195
Tzu, Sun, 153

U

Uncle Bernie's Toy Menagerie, Beverly Hills, 40, 41, 147
U.S.-China Relations Act, 192

U.S. Constitution, 200, 201
U.S. Copyright Office, 162, 200–201n
U.S. Customs, 157–58
U.S. Department of Justice, 112, 119, 138
U.S. Olympic Committee, 204
United States Sentencing Commission, 140
U.S. Supreme Court, 95, 99, 205
University of Bath, 269
UNO, 276
Usenet, 208

V

Vaidhyanathan, Siva, 199–201
Vamos, Igor, 177–78, 178n
video games, 147–49
Villaseñor, Sal, 249–50, 259–63
Voltskaya, Tatyana, 160

W

Waas, Murray, 28n
Wagner, Ray, 117
Walk Lively Barbie, 156
Wal-Mart, 195, 196, 228–29
Wanda Career Girl, 106
Warburg, Pincus, 149, 160n
Wardlow, Priscilla, 174
Warhol, Andy, 40, 167, 168–69, 172
Warnecke, Dieter, 35
Warner Bros., 127
Warner Communications, 147
Warren, Earl, 99
Weird Science (film), 179
Weissbrodt, Max, 31–32
Wick, Charles Z., 28n
Wong, Anna May, 172
World of the Young, 115, 119
World Trade Organization, 189
World War I, 17
World War II, 11, 30
Wright, Frank Lloyd, 17
Wright, John, 17

Y

Yorty, Sam, 105
Yoshida, Yasuo, 21, 122, 122n, 133, 139

Z

Zelig (film), 274–75
Zemby, Zachary, 11
Zwillman, Abner "Longie," 127n

ABOUT THE AUTHOR

Tarpley Hitt is a journalist in Brooklyn, New York, where she is an editor at and contributor to *The Drift* magazine. She has previously reported on culture and money for *The Daily Beast* and *Gawker*, and her work has also appeared in *The New Yorker, The Nation, The New York Times, Bookforum, The Paris Review, The Guardian, Air Mail, Deseret,* and *Miami New Times*.